Lecture Notes in Computer Science 14783

Founding Editors

Gerhard Goos
Juris Hartmanis

Editorial Board Members

Elisa Bertino, *Purdue University, West Lafayette, IN, USA*
Wen Gao, *Peking University, Beijing, China*
Bernhard Steffen, *TU Dortmund University, Dortmund, Germany*
Moti Yung, *Columbia University, New York, NY, USA*

The series Lecture Notes in Computer Science (LNCS), including its subseries Lecture Notes in Artificial Intelligence (LNAI) and Lecture Notes in Bioinformatics (LNBI), has established itself as a medium for the publication of new developments in computer science and information technology research, teaching, and education.

LNCS enjoys close cooperation with the computer science R & D community, the series counts many renowned academics among its volume editors and paper authors, and collaborates with prestigious societies. Its mission is to serve this international community by providing an invaluable service, mainly focused on the publication of conference and workshop proceedings and postproceedings. LNCS commenced publication in 1973.

Armando Castañeda · Constantin Enea ·
Nirupam Gupta
Editors

Networked Systems

12th International Conference, NETYS 2024
Rabat, Morocco, May 29–31, 2024
Proceedings

　Springer

Editors
Armando Castañeda
National Autonomous University of Mexico
Mexico City, Mexico

Constantin Enea
École Polytechnique
Palaiseau, France

Nirupam Gupta
École Polytechnique Fédérale de Lausanne
Lausanne, Switzerland

ISSN 0302-9743　　　　　　ISSN 1611-3349　(electronic)
Lecture Notes in Computer Science
ISBN 978-3-031-67320-7　　　ISBN 978-3-031-67321-4　(eBook)
https://doi.org/10.1007/978-3-031-67321-4

© The Editor(s) (if applicable) and The Author(s), under exclusive license to Springer Nature Switzerland AG 2024

This work is subject to copyright. All rights are solely and exclusively licensed by the Publisher, whether the whole or part of the material is concerned, specifically the rights of translation, reprinting, reuse of illustrations, recitation, broadcasting, reproduction on microfilms or in any other physical way, and transmission or information storage and retrieval, electronic adaptation, computer software, or by similar or dissimilar methodology now known or hereafter developed.
The use of general descriptive names, registered names, trademarks, service marks, etc. in this publication does not imply, even in the absence of a specific statement, that such names are exempt from the relevant protective laws and regulations and therefore free for general use.
The publisher, the authors and the editors are safe to assume that the advice and information in this book are believed to be true and accurate at the date of publication. Neither the publisher nor the authors or the editors give a warranty, expressed or implied, with respect to the material contained herein or for any errors or omissions that may have been made. The publisher remains neutral with regard to jurisdictional claims in published maps and institutional affiliations.

This Springer imprint is published by the registered company Springer Nature Switzerland AG
The registered company address is: Gewerbestrasse 11, 6330 Cham, Switzerland

If disposing of this product, please recycle the paper.

Preface

This volume contains the papers accepted at the 12th edition of the International Conference on Networked Systems (NETYS), which was held from May 29–31, 2024 in Rabat (Morocco). NETYS aims to bring together researchers and engineers from the theory and practice of distributed and networked systems. The scope of the conference covers all aspects related to the design and development of these systems. Additionally, this year NETYS also featured works on the emerging topic of distributed machine learning.

For this edition, we received 42 submissions. Each submission was reviewed by at least two, and on average by 2.9, members of the Program Committee, which consisted of 29 international experts spanning all relevant fields related to networked & distributed computing and distributed machine learning. Following a discussion by the Program Committee, 14 regular papers and 3 short papers were selected based on their originality and quality for publication in this volume. In addition to the presentation of these contributed papers, the conference program included keynotes by the following renowned researchers:

1. Roberto Baldoni (Sapienza University of Rome, Italy)
2. Robert Basmadjian (UM6P, Benguerir, Morocco)
3. Martijn de Vos (EPFL, Switzerland)
4. Azadeh Farzan (University of Toronto, Canada)
5. Edward Gorbunov (MBZUAI, UAE)
6. Rachid Guerraoui (EPFL, Switzerland)
7. Hicham Janati (Télécom Paris, France)
8. Gustavo Petri (Amazon Web Services, UK)
9. Achour Mostefaoui (University of Nantes, France)
10. Rafael Pires (EPFL, Switzerland)
11. Abdelfettah Sghiouar (Google, Sweden)

As program chairs of NETYS 2024, our deepest gratitude goes to everyone who contributed to the success of the conference. Foremost, we sincerely thank the authors for their high-quality contributions and the keynote speakers for their engaging and insightful presentations. We warmly thank the members of the Program Committee and the external reviewers for their constructive reviews and active participation in the discussions. Our special gratitude goes to all who contributed to the organization of NETYS 2024, in particular, the members of the Organizing Committee and the Web Master. Finally, we thank the general chairs Ahmed Bouajjani (Université de Paris, France), Mohammed Erradi (ENSIAS, Rabat, Morocco), and Rachid Guerraoui (EPFL, Lausanne, Switzerland) for their helpful guidance and invaluable feedback.

We are grateful to our partners & sponsors: University Mohammed V de Rabat, ENSIAS, Google, Amazon, Conseil Ingénierie et Developpement (CID), Henceforth, Mohammed VI Polytechnic University, King Abdullah University of Science and Technology (KAUST), Springer, Fondation Hassan II pour les Marocains Résidant à l'Etranger and AAGI.

Lastly, we would like to thank EasyChair, which helped us manage and organize the submission of papers, the review process and the preparation of the conference proceedings.

June 2024

Armando Castañeda
Constantin Enea
Nirupam Gupta

Organization

Program Committee

Vitaly Aksenov	ITMO University, Russia
Sonia Ben Mokhtar	CNRS Lyon, France
Ismail Berrada	UM6P, Morocco
Silvia Bonomi	Sapienza University of Rome, Italy
Armando Castaneda	UNAM, Mexico
Yu-Fang Chen	Academia Sinica, Taiwan
Martijn de Vos	École polytechnique fédérale de Lausanne, Switzerland
Mohamed El Kamili	Hassan II University of Casablanca, Morocco
Constantin Enea	École Polytechnique, France
Javier Esparza	Technical University of Munich, Germany
Panagiota Fatourou	University of Crete, Greece
Eduard Gorbunov	Mohamed bin Zayed University of Artificial Intelligence, United Arab Emirates
Nirupam Gupta	École polytechnique fédérale de Lausanne, Switzerland
Lukáš Holík	Brno University of Technology, Czech Republic
Mohamed Jmaiel	University of Sfax, Tunisia
Eric Koskinen	Stevens Institute of Technology, USA
Burcu Kulahcioglu Ozkan	Delft University of Technology, The Netherlands
Sandeep Kulkarni	Michigan State University, USA
Mikel Larrea	University of the Basque Country UPV/EHU, Spain
Matthieu Perrin	Nantes Université, France
Rafael Pinot	Sorbonne Université, France
Rafael Pires	École polytechnique fédérale de Lausanne, Switzerland
Srivatsan Ravi	University of Southern California, USA
Geovani Rizk	EPFL, Switzerland
Luis Rodrigues	Universidade de Lisboa, Portugal
Lili Su	Northeastern University, USA
Pierre Sutra	Télécom SudParis, France
Amitabh Trehan	Durham University, UK
Lewis Tseng	Clark University, USA

Additional Reviewers

Abid, Amal
Biswas, Sayan
Chen, Adam
Czerner, Philipp
Emmanuel, Fouotsa
Fersi, Ghofrane
Gulcan, Ege Berkay
Guttenberg, Roland
Hassan, Ahmed
Havlena, Vojtěch
Iaousse, M'Barek
Jindal, Anish

Kanellou, Eleni
Lakhlifi, Soufiane
Moses Jr., William K.
Neto, João
Nicola, Mihai
Petrescu, Diana
Reguieg, Hamza
Sharma, Rishi
Síč, Juraj
Trinca, Thibaud
Vujasinovic, Milos

Contents

Sharding in Permissionless Systems in Presence of an Adaptive Adversary 1
    Emmanuelle Anceaume, Davide Frey, and Arthur Rauch

Concurrent Wait-Free Graph Snapshots Using Multi-versioning 32
    Gaurav Bhardwaj, Ayaz Ahmed, and Sathya Peri

Challenger: Blockchain-based Massively Multiplayer Online Game
Architecture 50
    Boris Chan Yip Hon, Bilel Zaghdoudi, Maria Potop-Butucaru,
    Sébastien Tixeuil, and Serge Fdida

Agent-Driven BFS Tree in Anonymous Graphs with Applications 67
    Prabhat Kumar Chand, Manish Kumar, and Anisur Rahaman Molla

Some New Results With k-Set Agreement 83
    Carole Delporte-Gallet, Hugues Fauconnier, and Mouna Safir

A Domain Specific Language for Testing Distributed Protocol
Implementations 100
    Cezara Dragoi, Srinidhi Nagendra, and Mandayam Srivas

Tool Augmented LLMs for Big Data Analysis 118
    Mohammed Ali Essabri, Jamal Rebii, and Mohammed Erradi

Static Data Race Detection via Lazy Sequentialization 124
    Bernd Fischer, Giulio Garbi, Salvatore La Torre, Gennaro Parlato,
    and Peter Schrammel

Algebraic Computations in Anonymous VANET 142
    Dariusz R. Kowalski, Miguel A. Mosteiro, and Austin Powlette

Federated Learning for Enhanced Medical Image Analysis 157
    Sanaa Lakrouni, Slimane Bah, and Marouane Sebgui

Towards Stronger Blockchains: Security Against Front-Running Attacks 171
    Anshuman Misra and Ajay D. Kshemkalyani

Distributed Station Assignment Through Learning 188
    Lu Dong, Miguel A. Mosteiro, and Michelle Wang

Short Paper: An Efficient Framework for Supporting Nested Transaction in STMs 204
  Nischay Ranjan, Rohit Kapoor, and Sathya Peri

Enhancing Cost and Latency Efficiency Through Service Placement in Containerized Fog-Cloud Computing Environments 211
  Driss Riane, Widad Ettazi, and Ahmed Ettalbi

Towards Generating a Dataset for Failure Prediction in Microservices Applications 225
  Ilyass Tarhri, Driss Allaki, and Hamza Kamal Idrissi

Dynamic Resource Allocation for 5G Device-to-Device Communication Based on Expected SARSA 231
  Shashini Thamarasie Wanniarachchi and Volker Turau

BeRGeR: Byzantine-Robust Geometric Routing 247
  Brown Zaz, Mikhail Nesterenko, and Gokarna Sharma

Author Index 265

Sharding in Permissionless Systems in Presence of an Adaptive Adversary

Emmanuelle Anceaume, Davide Frey, and Arthur Rauch[✉]

IRISA/Université de Rennes/CNRS/Inria, Rennes, France
arthur.rauch@inria.fr

Abstract. We present SplitChain, a protocol intended to support the creation of scalable proof-of-stake and account-based blockchains without undermining decentralization and security. This is achieved by using sharding, i.e. by splitting the blockchain into several lighter chains managed by their own disjoint sets of validators called shards. These shards balance the load by processing disjoint sets of transactions in parallel. SplitChain distinguishes itself from other sharded blockchains by reducing the synchronization constraints among shards while maintaining security guarantees in an asynchronous setting. A dedicated routing protocol enables transactions to be redirected between shards with a low number of hops and messages. Finally, the protocol is designed to dynamically adapt the number of shards to the system load to avoid over-dimensioning issues encountered in static sharding-based solutions.

Keywords: Blockchain · Sharding · Distributed ledger · Scalability

1 Introduction

Blockchain technology is well known to provide a tamper-proof "append-only" distributed-ledger abstraction. The immutable nature of this ledger implies a constant growth of its storage requirements, with every block being retained for eternity. Not only does this impact storage, but it also increases the communication requirements for a new honest party to join the system as it needs to download the entire blockchain from the network in order to have a consistent view of the transaction history. Sharding is a scaling solution involving splitting the blockchain into several smaller blockchains, called "shards", each processed and stored by its respective set of validators. Allocating validators to separate shards better balances communication and storage loads, accommodating more efficient network growth to achieve near-linear throughput scalability as the number of shards increases. However, sharding poses several challenges.

Firstly, since the system is partitioned, a shard can be compromised using a smaller malicious proportion of the total number of validators compared to what is required for classic blockchains. In order to ensure shard safety, it is necessary to implement an unbiased and verifiable random allocation of validators to prevent the adversary from targeting a particular shard. It is also necessary to periodically relocate validators to prevent the adversary from amassing corrupted validators inside a shard. Secondly, it is necessary to ensure both the verification and atomicity of cross-shard transactions. A cross-shard transaction refers to a transaction made between users managed by different shards. As each shard only knows the state of the users stored in its blockchain, it is necessary to ensure that *(i)* an invalid transaction will not be accepted by any shard, and *(ii)* a valid transaction partially accepted by the involved shards can be aborted so that funds cannot be locked up indefinitely or duplicated. To solve both problems there must exist some minimal amount of synchronization among shards. Most sharded-based solutions, including Elastico [4], Omniledger [3], RapidChain [11] or Ethereum 2.0, achieve this using a global synchronization blockchain maintained by every validator in addition to their shard's blockchain. In addition, sharding solutions based on a fixed number of shards (static sharding) are penalized by an uneven distribution of transactions, as revealed by our experiments on Ethereum.

Contributions. We propose SplitChain, a fully decentralized state sharding solution such that,

- Shards progress at their own pace without requiring the maintenance of a synchronization blockchain or any heavy synchronization mechanisms;
- Shards keep a loosely synchronized view of each other's state to guarantee the processing of any cross-shard state updates in a bounded number of consensus executions;
- Shards are tolerant to a fast adaptive adversary controlling less than a third of all validators by relying on a novel distributed attribution mechanism;
- Shards self-adapt to the current payload of the system by self merging and splitting the set of accounts, while adapting to the presence of hot-spots;
- Shards efficiently forward transactions by leveraging the properties of hypercubic routing protocols.

The remainder of the paper is as follows: Sect. 2 presents the system model. Section 3 describes a chain's structure and block creation. Section 4 is dedicated to the management of transactions that span different chains and the assignment of validators to chains. Section 5 introduces the system's routing protocol. Section 6 investigates SplitChain's security properties. Finally, Sect. 7 compares SplitChain to previous state-of-the-art sharding solutions.

2 Model of the System

2.1 Accounts and Validators

Splitchain uses the account model to provide durable identities to its users and to enforce single-input single-output transactions for easier transaction management. Accounts are divided into two categories: user accounts and validator accounts. Users can send and receive transactions, while validators participate in SplitChain's protocol.

Definition 1 (Accounts). *Accounts are persistent balances identified by a public key hash.*

Definition 2 (Validators). *Validator accounts are special accounts created by users to participate in SplitChain's protocol. All validator accounts possess the same constant amount of currency called stake.*

Any user can create a validator by submitting the corresponding amount of stake through a transaction. Users may possess multiple validators concurrently. Stake serves as a limited resource to render the cost of Sybil attacks impractical. Users specify a (bounded) number of *"cue"* blocks (see Definition 6) for the existence of their validator, after which the validators expires and its stake is returned.

2.2 Network Model

We consider a peer-to-peer network of validators that self-divide into several chains. Both the number of chains and validators vary over time to withstand a dynamic and open environment. Communication delays are finite but not bounded, in particular there are no bounds on the time taken to deliver messages or any preservation of the order of those messages, conforming to the asynchronous communication model.

2.3 Threat Model

Definition 3 ((μ,δ)-adaptive adversary). *We consider a Byzantine adversary that never controls more than a fraction $0 \leq \mu < 1/3$ of validators.[1] Furthermore, the adversary is adaptive over a period $\delta \geq 3$, in the sense that if the adversary chooses to corrupt some newly attributed validator, this corruption will be effective after δ successive consensus executions.*

2.4 Cryptographic Functions

Beyond common cryptographic functions, i.e. a hash function and asymmetric signatures, validators use verifiable random functions(VRF) [5] to generate pseudo-random hashes. VRFs are computed privately using a validator's private key, however their result is publicly verifiable using the validator's public key. Validators also use Merkle trees to prove the inclusion of data in a dataset without knowing its content. Every leaf of the Merkle tree is labelled with the hash of a data item, and every node other than the leaves is labelled with the hash of the concatenation of the labels of its child nodes. The root of the tree serves as the commitment to the dataset, and the Merkle path of a data, i.e. the hashes of the sibling nodes of the nodes that connect a leaf to the root of the Merkle tree, serves as the proof of the inclusion of the data. The (μ,δ)-adversary's computational power is restricted to match standard cryptographic assumptions.

---

[1] Given that validators all hold the same amount of stake, this equates to controlling less than μ of the total validation stake.

3 Structure of the Blocks

There are two types of blocks in SplitChain: *chaining blocks* and *transaction blocks*. Each transaction block is paired with a chaining block: the two constitute the outcome of a single consensus execution. The index of a block refers to its position in the chain.

Definition 4 (Transaction blocks). *Transaction blocks contain all the transactions accepted by validators during a consensus execution.*

Definition 5 (Chaining blocks). *Chaining blocks store the hash of the previous chaining block of their chain and the Merkle root of the transaction block produced during the same consensus execution.*

Definition 6 (Cue block). *Let N_{cue} be some positive integer. $\forall k \geq 0$, every chaining block at position $k \times N_{cue}$ of a chain is called a cue block. A cue block points to both the previous chaining block and the previous cue block.*

Chaining blocks are akin to traditional block headers. A chaining block of a chain C contains a list of hashes. In particular, it provides the Merkle roots of the transaction block produced during their consensus execution, and of the accounts managed by the chain as well as the fingerprints needed for cross-chain transaction verification. It also contains the list of the latest known chaining block indices of the chains other than C, which we refer to as the fingerprint of the block. The interested reader may refer to Fig. 1 in the Appendix. For synchronization purposes, chaining blocks are disseminated to all chains using SplitChain's dedicated routing protocol described in Sect. 5. In contrast, transaction blocks of chain C are only stored by the validators participating in C's consensus executions.

4 Handling Multiple Chains

4.1 Assigning Validators to Chains

Each block of each chain is created via the local execution of a consensus algorithm. Consensus committees are periodically renewed (at each consensus execution) and their members are selected via two stages. The rationale of both stages is to prevent the (μ, δ)-adversary from predicting, and thus manipulating, members of consensus committees. Briefly, starting from their *initialization chains*, validators are uniformly distributed over their *reference chains* (first stage), and then uniformly distributed over their *consensus chains* (second stage). Validators stay forever in their initialization chain (that is as long as they want to actively participate in the creation of SplitChain's blocks), they stay for N_{cue} blocks (see Definition 6) in their reference chain, and finally they stay for no more than the duration of three consensus executions in their consensus chains. Hence, for any chain C_i, and for any validators v, v' and v'' of Splitchain, at time t, C_i can be the initialization chain of v, while it is the reference chain of v' and finally the consensus chain of v''.

Initialization Chain. Any user u wishing to actively participate in block creation must first register a *validator account*, with a given amount of stake. Validator accounts allow users to participate in different consensus executions. A single user can create multiple validator accounts if they own enough currency. Let $v = (sk_v, pk_v)$ be u's validator. User u submits a transaction to instantiate v's stake on what we call v's *initialization chain*. This chain, denoted by $C^{\text{init}(v)}$, is the chain whose label is the closest to $addr_v = H(pk_v)$ (by closest we mean the chain whose label minimizes the numerical value of the xor between $addr_v$ and the chain's label. The routing mechanism is described in Sect. 5). Initialization chains provide a stable anchor point for validators and allow them to prove the existence of their accounts. However, they do not contribute to SplitChain's security. Indeed, some malicious validator v' can iteratively invoke the cryptographic hash function to sit on some targeted chain $C^{\text{init}(v')}$. The current consensus committee of $C^{\text{init}(v)}$ updates the list L of new validators with v and inserts L's Merkle root into the chaining block under construction (see "Future Initialization Proof" in Fig. 1). When the next cue block of $C^{\text{init}(v)}$ is created (see Definition 6), the consensus committee in charge of that cue block will assign each new validator of L to their *reference chain* (see Algorithm 3 in Appendix B). Specifically, Algorithm 3 shuffles L (using the seed of the cue block), partitions L into N sub-lists of $\lfloor |L|/N \rfloor$ validators, where N is the current number of chains of SplitChain, and assigns each random sub-list to one of the N chains of SplitChain. The Merkle root of L and the proof of validator assignment to their reference chain is included in the cue block (see Algorithm 1 in Appendix B). The chain to which v will be assigned is called v's *reference chain* and is denoted by $C^{\text{ref}(v)}$. At every cue-block creation, Algorithm 1 is executed so that v is periodically re-assigned to a new reference chain.

Reference Chain. Each reference chain $C_1, \ldots, C_N$ of SplitChain assigns uniformly at random its V/N referenced validators to the N *consensus chains* of SplitChain, where V is the total number of referenced validators in SplitChain. It is important to note that to face a (μ, δ)-adaptive adversary, validator v can not be attributed to the consensus committee of $C^{\text{cons}(v)}$ more than $\delta - 1$ consecutive times. Hence to be assigned to its consensus chain $C^{\text{cons}(v)}$, validator $v = (sk_v, pk_v)$ generates its consensus credential as a new key pair $(sk_{\text{cons}(v)}, pk_{\text{cons}(v)})$ and sends a signed credential storage request to the current consensus committee of $C^{\text{ref}(v)}$. Validator v regenerates its credentials every δ attributions. This signed request contains $addr_v$, ref_v and $H(pk_{\text{cons}})$, proving the legitimacy of v's request. If the request is valid, v's consensus credential is added by the current consensus committee of $C^{\text{ref}(v)}$ to the list L of validators that will be used by Algorithm 3 to build N sub-lists of $\lfloor |L|/N \rfloor = V/N^2$ validators each. Such a sub-list is called a *reference set*, and each sub-list is assigned uniformly at random to one of the N chains os SplitChain. The chain to which v is assigned is called v's consensus chain and is denoted by $C^{\text{cons}(v)}$. The Merkle root "Credentials" (see Fig. 1) of this list is added to the chaining block. Merkle paths are sent to the referenced validators of $C^{\text{ref}(v)}$ to serve as credential proof.

The current consensus committee of $C^{\text{ref}(v)}$ sends to each consensus chain a transaction that contains the size of the reference set they have allocated to it. This allows validators to know the total amount of stake inside their consensus committee.

Consensus Chain. To join the consensus committee of $C^{\text{cons}(v)}$, v issues a "join" request to $C^{\text{cons}(v)}$ using SplitChain's dedicated routing protocol. Upon receipt of the request, the core validators of $C^{\text{cons}(v)}$ directly reply to v with the list of core validators (see Sect. 5.2) and a sub-list of the current consensus committee members chosen at random. We call these validators the bootstrapping validators of v. The number of bootstrapping validators is large enough so that, with high probability $1 - \varepsilon$, with $\varepsilon \in (0,1)$, at least one of them is honest. As chaining blocks cannot be forged by the (μ, δ)-adversary without taking over a chain's consensus, the proofs they contain are sufficient to verify the authenticity of the data provided by the bootstrapping validators. Thus, only one honest bootstrapping validator is sufficient for a successful bootstrap of v to $C^{\text{cons}(v)}$. Bootstrapping validators will provide v with $C^{\text{cons}(v)}$'s state. This state corresponds to the latest state of $C^{\text{cons}(v)}$'s user accounts, the proofs of attribution of the current consensus committee and the list of core validators. Note that the fingerprint of the latest chaining block b of $C^{\text{cons}(v)}$ contains the latest chaining-block index of each chain of SplitChain known to the consensus committee of $C^{\text{cons}(v)}$ when b was created. Therefore, the latest chaining block b contains the chaining block index of each reference chain used to create the current consensus committee of $C^{\text{cons}(v)}$. From this list, v establishes the list of attribution proofs of the committee, requesting the missing chaining blocks from its bootstrapping validators if necessary. Algorithm 4 in Appendix B presents the detailed pseudo-code of v's attribution to its consensus chain.

4.2 Creation of the Blocks of a Chain

As described above, each chain C_i of Splitchain plays the role of a consensus chain. By construction the consensus committee of C_i contains V/N validators. (Note that Sect. 4.3 presents a partial attribution policy that can replace the one presented in Sect. 4.1, when SplitChain is made of sufficiently many chains). For performance reasons, V/N validators cannot all be involved in each consensus execution. The solution we propose relies on a particular asynchronous consensus called the merge consensus algorithm [7]. This algorithm leverages the cryptographic sortition lottery introduced by Algorand [2] to elect, in a non-interactive and private way, a subset of the committee members. This subset has a bounded expected size that is large enough to handle adversarial behaviors, but independent of the size of the consensus committee. The consensus algorithm runs a series of asynchronous rounds, such that at each round, a new subset of validators is elected via cryptographic sortition. The algorithm ensures, with high probability (whp), that all the transactions proposed by honest validators at the beginning of a consensus execution are included in a block after a finite number of rounds.

4.3 Leveraging a Large Number of Chains

As explained in Sect. 4.1, all reference chains send their latest chaining block containing the Merkle root of their reference set to all the consensus chains. This allows the consensus committee of each chain to be updated with V/N^2 attributed validators. Once these sets have been received, consensus executions can be triggered (see Sect. 4.2). We call this policy the *total attribution policy*. It ensures that consensus committees cannot be compromised by a (μ, δ)-adversary with overwhelming probability (see Theorem 2). However, it introduces significant delays in the presence of a large number of chains.

When the number of chains is large enough (i.e., $N > 10$) the following *partial attribution* policy is more appropriate. A random subset of S reference chains is selected among the N chains of SplitChain. Each consensus committee contains $S(V/N^2)$ validators instead of $N(V/N^2)$. The S new reference sets of the next consensus committee are selected as follows: Let L be the list of chains included in the latest fingerprint of C_i. List L is randomly shuffled using the random seed of the latest chaining block of C_i. The first S chains in L become the reference chains providing the new reference sets of the next consensus of C_i.

For safety reasons, partial attribution cannot be used in the presence of only a few reference chains, as the (μ, δ)-adversary can concentrate its power to manipulate these few chains. Theorem 3 provides a lower bound S_{min} on S as a function of the total number of reference chains. Due to asynchrony and because the consensus committee of a chain C_i only waits for S reference sets to initiate the consensus, the chaining block of a chain C_j listed inside the fingerprint of the latest chaining block of C_i may be older than the actual latest chaining block of C_j. We call $\rho(N, S)$ the difference between the latest chaining block index of C_j and the latest chaining block index of C_j mentioned inside the fingerprint of C_i. To prevent the adversary from taking advantage of $\rho(N, S)$ to corrupt the new reference sets of C_i, we require its adaptivity to be reduced to $\delta + \rho(N, S)$ and the duration of a validator's membership to be reduced from $\delta - 1$ to $\delta - \rho(N, S)$. So, for the partial attribution policy, we consider a $(\mu, \delta + \rho(N, S))$-adaptive adversary. To bound the value of $\rho(N, S)$ with high probability, the consensus committee of C_i is required to wait for the delivery of any new block b appearing in the fingerprint of the chaining blocks of one of the S new reference committees. Similarly, any new chaining block inside b's fingerprint must be delivered by C_i's committee before initiating a new consensus execution. Theorem 4 provides an upper bound on $\rho(N, S)$.

4.4 Pruning and Verifying Transactions

It is important to limit the amount of data stored by validators to prevent bootstrapping costs from linearly increasing with the number of blocks in a chain. We propose a pruning method that guarantees near-constant bootstrapping costs. Specifically, each validator v of the consensus committee of $C_i^{\text{cons}(v)}$ stores only all the cue blocks of $C_i^{\text{cons}(v)}$ as checkpoints and only the latest k chaining and transaction blocks of $C_i^{\text{cons}(v)}$. This allows v to respond to users that wish to verify old transactions that were validated in the latest k blocks. Users wishing to prove the inclusion of old transactions (i.e., those belonging to transaction blocks $b_i, \ldots b_\ell$, that have been deleted) must locally store the chaining blocks between $b_i, \ldots b_\ell$ and the next cue block. Cryptographic links between consecutive chaining blocks are then enough to recursively prove the existence of a pruned chaining block. The inclusion of the transaction is proven as per usual by the user against the Merkle root of the transactions contained in the chaining block. Each validator also stores the latest cue block of all the other chains: this supports the validator attribution strategy described in Sect. 4.1, as cue blocks contain the initialization proofs of validators.

4.5 Cross-Chain Transactions

Splitchain's transactions take place between any two user accounts.

Definition 7 (Cross-chain transactions). *When both accounts of a transaction are not managed by the same chain, a transaction is said to be cross-chain.*

The chain in charge of handling a transaction is the one whose label prefixes the emitter account (denoted by C_{send} in the following). Cross-chain transactions are handled in two steps: the withdrawal operation and then the deposit operation. The withdrawal operation occurs when the transaction is inserted in a transaction block of C_{send}. During the creation of the new transaction and chaining blocks, the consensus committee members of C_{send} determine the list of cross-chain transactions inside the transaction block and generate the corresponding *relay transactions*, which they organize as a Merkle tree T. A relay transaction contains the user's initial transaction and the Merkle path of the relay transaction inside T. The Merkle root "relay TX" (see Fig. 1) of T is included into the new chaining block under construction. Consensus committee members of C_{send} then send the relay transaction to the receiver's account chain. As chaining blocks are propagated to all chains, the consensus committee members of the receiver's chain can verify the completion of the withdrawal operation and include the relay transaction in the next transaction block of their chain, which confirms the deposit operation, completing the cross-chain transaction. Note that transactions are always redirected to the chain whose label prefixes the identifier of the emitter account, whereas relay transactions are redirected to the chain of the receiver account.

4.6 Grouping User Accounts

Users exchanging on a frequent basis may want to avoid the latency introduced by cross-chain transactions. Thus, we introduce the notion of group accounts that allow users of the same group to always be part of the same chain. A group account is a collection of accounts sharing the same group identifier, i.e. a key hash. When a user u wishes to open an account inside a group gid, u only needs to submit a transaction to a non-existent account (gid, pk_u). Similarly, when a user wishes to withdraw from a group, they can simply submit a transaction to transfer all their account funds elsewhere.

5 Routing

5.1 Hypercube, Merging and Splitting Operations

SplitChain initially starts with a single chain C whose label is the empty chain of bits ε. If during N_{cue} consecutive blocks, the average number of transactions per block exceeds some threshold T_{split}, then C triggers a split. Splitting is an operation that allows a chain of label l to be replaced by two chains of labels $l|0$ and $l|1$, called siblings, each taking over half of the accounts of the original chain. If the original chain C is labeled ε, then both new chains will be labeled 0 and 1 respectively. Conversely, if during N_{cue} consecutive blocks the average number of transactions per block is lower than a threshold T_{merge}, the chain initiates a merge with its sibling chain. Both chains merge in a single one whose label corresponds to the maximal prefix of their previous labels. By design, each chain label is unique. Our topology is inspired by hypercubic networks [1]. A hypercube of dimension d contains 2^d vertices. Each vertex is assigned a d-bit label. Two vertices are neighbors if the numerical value of the xor of their labels is equal to a power of 2, i.e. if their labels differ by only one bit. For example, in Fig. 3, vertex 000 is a neighbor of vertices 001, 010 and 100. The number of hops between two vertices can be determined using the Hamming weight of the xor of their labels. The diameter of the hypercube, i.e. the maximum number of hops between the two most distant vertices, is d. We use the following approach to match each chain to one or more vertices of a hypercube: Let k be the number of bits of the longest chain label. Splitchain conforms to a subgraph of a hypercube of dimension k, where each chain whose label has exactly k bits is mapped to the vertex of the same label, and each chain whose label contains strictly less than k bits is mapped to all vertices whose labels are prefixed by the chain's label. Thus, in Fig. 3, chain 01 is mapped to vertices 010 and 011. As a result, when all chain labels are k bits long, the network corresponds to a hypercube of dimension k. A hypercube of dimension k can be constructed recursively by connecting two hypercubes of dimension $k-1$. This allows the dimension of the hypercube to be changed dynamically with k: if k increases, each vertex of label l of size $k-1$ is divided into two vertices of labels $l|0$ and $l|1$. Figure 3 shows the transition from a hypercube of dimension 2 to a hypercube of dimension 3 after chain 00 splits into (i.e., is replaced by) two chains 000 and 001. Similarly, if k decreases, vertices are merged in the same way as for chains. This ensures that no vertex represents two chains simultaneously.

5.2 Core Validators

To limit the number of messages transmitted by validators and hence to improve the usage of network resources, we introduce the notion of core validators. The number of core validators is chosen to ensure that at least one honest validator belongs to the core. Election of core validators is as follows. When validator v is attributed to the consensus committee of $C^{\text{cons}(v)}$, v triggers twice the cryptographic sortition lottery at round 0. Once for determining whether it will executes round 0 of the merge-consensus algorithm (see Sect. 4.2) and a second time to determine whether it will be part of $C^{\mathrm{cons}(v)}$'s core. Both invocations of the cryptographic sortition lottery use the same parameters except for parameter τ, which represents the expected number of successful winners, so that core validators represent a subset of the validators elected for round 0 of the merge consensus. If successful, v is part of the core of $C^{\mathrm{cons}(v)}$ until its consensus credentials expire, which corresponds to the duration that represents $\delta - 1$ consecutive consensus executions (v tries to be elected in the core of $C^{\mathrm{cons}(v)}$ only once during the lifespan of its credentials). Once elected, core validators send their proof of election along with their consensus messages, guaranteeing with any high probability that all committee members of $C^{\mathrm{cons}(v)}$ will agree on the list of core validators at the end of the merge consensus execution. The hash of the list of new core validators will be included in the chaining block decided as the outcome of the merge consensus (see Fig. 1). Core validators are in charge of executing the routing protocol. They maintain two routing tables: A core routing table containing the list of the core validators of neighboring chains for cross-chain communication, and a consensus table containing the list of their consensus committee members. By using their core routing table, core validators forward transactions to the core validators of the neighboring chain whose label is closest to the transaction's destination. On the other hand, the consensus table is used to broadcast messages within their consensus committee. Only core validators keep track of the list of committee members.

5.3 Core Routing Table

Definition 8 (Core routing table). *The core routing table of chain C_i, $1 \leq i \leq N$, contains the list of the core validators of C_i's neighbouring chains.*

Core routing tables, denoted by RT^{core}, are maintained by core validators and contain the lists of core validators of all of its neighboring chains in the hypercube. For any two neighboring chains C_i and C_j, $RT_i^{\mathrm{core}}[j]$ contains a linked list made of at most $\delta - 1$ elements. The k-th element of $RT_i^{\mathrm{core}}[j]$, $k \leq \delta - 1$, contains the k-th most recent core proof of C_j and points to the core validators it proves (see Fig. 2a). Upon receipt of a new chaining block b of C_j, core validators of C_i create and insert in block order a new element containing the core proof of b. Note that the core validators of C_j send separately the set of new core validators and chaining block b. Once received, it is verified using the core proof of b and then linked to the new element.

5.4 Consensus Table

Definition 9 (Consensus routing table). *The consensus routing table of a chain C_i contains the list of validators of the consensus committee of C_i.*

Core validators also keep track of the consensus committee members. All intra-chain communication are handled by core validators, reducing the number of messages within a chain. This also isolates intra-chain communications from the overall network, allowing chains to be added without overloading SplitChain. A consensus routing table, as shown in Fig. 2b, contains the list of consensus committee members sorted by reference chains and chronological order of attribution proof (the Merkle root called "Credentials"). The structure is composed of N linked lists of at most $\delta - 1$ elements, the i-th element of the j-th linked list containing the i-th most recent attribution proof of the validators referenced by the chain C_j. Each element points to the list of attributed validators. This list is updated upon receipt of validators "join" requests. When a core validator receives a new chaining block b from some chain C, it inserts in block order a new element containing b's attribution proof and removes the $\delta - 1$ element if needed. This allows the gradual replacement of validators with old credentials, to prevent the (μ, δ)-adversary from compromising consensus committees. In addition, organizing validators with the proof of attribution of the chaining blocks ensures that when a proof expires, all the validator credentials proven by the proof also expire, whether these validators ever participated to the merge consensus executions or not. This prevents the adversary from withholding credentials to build up enough consensus credentials to take over a chain.

6 Security Analysis

In this section we analyze the security of SplitChain. Specifically we first show that an adversary cannot tamper or predict randomness of block seeds, and then we evaluate the probability of corruption of a chain's consensus committee as well as the probability of corruption of a chain's routing core. For the purpose of SplitChain, we can assume that at any time the total number of validators is arbitrarily large. For space constraints, all the proofs are presented in Appendix B.

6.1 Randomness Creation

The security analysis of SplitChain relies on the assumption that for any chain C of SplitChain, and for any instantiation $k \geq 1$ of the merge consensus, the seeds of the chaining blocks preceding the k-th one of C have been generated in an unbiased and unpredictable way. Theorem 1 is essential to prevent the adaptive adversary from manipulating the outcome of the cryptographic sortition lotery.

Theorem 1. *Let $\epsilon \in (0, 1)$ be the security parameter of SplitChain. The seed of any chaining block cannot be tampered with or predicted in advance by the adversary with any high probability $1 - \epsilon$.*

6.2 Variation in Size of Reference Sets

Lemma 1 shows how fairly the attribution algorithm of SplitChain (i.e., Algorithm 3) distributes validators between the different consensus committees.

Lemma 1. *Let $E_1, E_2, ..., E_N$ be the reference sets produced by Algorithm 3. Then $\forall j, k \in \{1, ..., N\}, \mid |E_j| - |E_k| \mid \leq 1$.*

6.3 Safety of Consensus Committees

To ensure that the (μ, δ)-adversary cannot take over the consensus execution of any consensus chain C, the consensus committee of C must contain less than a third of corrupted validators. We examine the probability of corruption of the consensus committee of an arbitrary chain C for both the total attribution policy and the partial one. Recall that μ represents the proportion of malicious validators in SplitChain and N represents the current number of chains of SplitChain.

Total Attribution. As long as the proportion μ of corrupted validators in SplitChain is less than $1/3$, Lemma 2 shows that the (μ, δ)-adaptive adversary must distribute its corrupted validators evenly in the reference sets.

Lemma 2. *The probability of corruption of a consensus committee by the (μ, δ)-adaptive adversary is maximized when corrupted validators are equally distributed among all reference chains.*

Theorem 2 provides the probability p_c of corruption of a consensus committee when the total attribution policy is applied.

Theorem 2. *For any security parameter $\epsilon \in (0,1)$, for any proportion of corrupted validators $\mu < 1/3$, there exists a finite consensus committee size c_{min} such that $\forall c \geq c_{min}$, the probability p_c that a committee of c validators is corrupted satisfies $p_c < \epsilon$, where $p_c = 1 - \sum_{\ell=0}^{\lfloor c/3 \rfloor} \binom{c}{\ell} \mu^\ell (1-\mu)^{c-\ell}$.*

Figure 4a illustrates Theorem 2 for different values of μ and ϵ.

Partial Attribution. We prove that the partial attribution is secure in presence of a $(\mu, \delta + \rho)$-adversary. Let S represent the number of randomly selected reference chains among the N chains of SplitChain. Theorem 3 gives the probability of corruption p_S of a partially attributed consensus committee. It provides a lower bound S_{min} on the number of reference chains S such that a consensus committee built with the partial attribution policy using $S \geq S_{min}$ reference chains has probability less than ϵ to be corrupted.

Theorem 3. *For any safety parameter $\epsilon \in (0,1)$, for any proportion of corrupted validators $\mu < 1/3$, there exists a finite number of reference sets S_{min} such that $\forall S \geq S_{min}$, the probability p_S that a consensus committee composed of S reference sets is corrupted satisfies $p_S < \epsilon$, with $p_S = 1 - \sum_{k=0}^{\lfloor S/3 \rfloor} \binom{S}{k} \mu^k (1-\mu)^{S-k}$.*

Figure 5b displays the value of S_{min}/N for $\epsilon = 10^{-6}$ as a function of the adversary proportion μ in SplitChain and for different values of N. The value of S_{min} decreases when the number N of chains of the system increases. However, when the adversary proportion μ becomes very close to $1/3$, S_{min}/N tends to 1 and total attribution is needed. Our experiments run on Ethereum show that both policies can be safely applied on Ethereum (see Appendix D).

6.4 Resistance Against an Adaptive Adversary

The objective of this section is to analyze whether the adversary can benefit from the partial attribution policy to corrupt a targeted consensus committee via the manipulation of a given reference set S_{j*} of a chain C_{j*}. Specifically, let $\mathcal{C}(t)$ be the consensus committee of chain C at time t, and $\mathcal{B}(t) = \{S_1, \ldots, S_{j*}, \ldots, S_N\}$ be the set of the last reference sets sent by the N chains of SplitChain that have been received by $\mathcal{C}(t)$. From the partial attribution policy (see Sect. 4.3), $\mathcal{C}(t)$ randomly selects S sets from $\mathcal{B}(t)$ to determine the composition of the next consensus committee $\mathcal{C}(t+1)$ at time $t+1$. Consensus committee $\mathcal{C}(t+1)$ on its turn will randomly select S sets from $\mathcal{B}(t+1) = \{S_1^{(1)}, \ldots, S_{j*}, \ldots, S_N^{(1)}\}$, where $S_i^{(1)}$ represents the last reference set received by $\mathcal{C}(t+1)$ and sent by C_i. Note that, by the asynchrony of the system, all communications from the chains may be arbitrarily long, delaying accordingly the receipt of reference sets, and in particular the new reference set of C_{j*}. Thus $\mathcal{C}(t+1)$ may still consider the obsolete reference set S_{j*} as the latest reference set of C_{j*}. Let $\rho_{(N,S)}$ be the upper bound on the difference between the chaining block index of the obsolete reference set S_{j*} and the latest chaining block index of C_{j*}. Consensus committee $\mathcal{C}(t+\rho_{(N,S)})$ will randomly select S reference sets from $\mathcal{B}(t+\rho_{(N,S)}) = \{S_1^{(\rho_{(N,S)})}, \ldots, S_{j*}, \ldots, S_N^{(\rho_{(N,S)})}\}$. Suppose that reference set S_{j*} is never selected during the first $\rho_{(N,S)} - 1$ random selections. Recall that for the partial attribution policy (see Sect. 4.3), we assume a $(\mu, \delta + \rho_{(N,S)})$-adaptive adversary. Were reference set S_{j*} selected after $\rho_{(N,S)}$ validator attributions, the adversary could already have corrupted the validators of S_{j*}. Let $\chi_{\rho_{(N,S)}}$ be the probability that a consensus committee uses a reference set that has been obsolete for at least $\rho_{(N,S)}$ consecutive validator attributions. Theorem 4 shows that $\chi_{\rho_{(N,S)}}$ is less than the security parameter ϵ. Figure 5a illustrates that $\rho_{(100,24)} = 5$.

Theorem 4. $\forall N, \forall S \leq N, \exists \rho_{((N,S)} > 0$ such that $\chi_{\rho_{(N,S)}} < \epsilon$.

6.5 Safety of the Election of Core Validators

Validators of the core of a chain are crucial for intra- and cross-chain communications. There must always be at least one honest core validator to ensure the routing of messages in a chain. In the following, T represents the lifespan of consensus credentials, $\mu' = \mu(T)/(T-1)$ refers to the maximum proportion of corrupted validators eligible for the core and c is the number of validators of any consensus committee. We use $1 \leq r \leq T$ to designate the T last consensus of a chain and refer to the number of validators that joined the consensus committee during consensus r as c_r. Theorem 5 shows that there exists a finite core size above which the probability p_{core} that the core is corrupted is smaller than ϵ.

Theorem 5. For any safety parameter $\epsilon \in (0,1)$, for an adaptive adversary with $\delta \geq 3$, there exists a finite core size τ_{min} such that $\forall \tau \geq \tau_{min}$, the probability p_{core} that a core of τ validators is corrupted satisfies $p_{core} < \epsilon$, with $p_{core} = (1 - \tau/c)^{(1-\mu')(c-c_T)}$.

Figure 4b plots τ_{min} as a function of the consensus committee size c for different values of δ. As observed, τ_{min} quickly stabilizes as c increases. We also notice that τ_{min} decreases very rapidly when δ increases.

7 Related Work

While several sharded blockchains have been proposed in recent years, we focus on previous works that have introduced new concepts that have influenced the design of SplitChain.

Elastico [4] is the first sharded blockchain. Its validators are divided into shards, each one creating a block of transactions, which are then aggregated into a "global-block" to add to the system's unique blockchain. The shards are renewed after each global-block, ensuring strong safety against adaptive adversaries at the expense of synchronization and storage costs, i.e., validators store the entire system. As a safeguard against Sybil attacks, each validator must solve a PoW puzzle, whose solution also determines which shard it belongs to. Elastico cannot ensure atomicity in cross-shard transactions [3], leading to permanent fund locking. Its attribution protocol coupled with its small shard size (approx. 100 validators) yields a very high corruption probability of 2.76% [3] per shard per block. In comparison, SplitChain splits computation and storage between the different chains at the cost of a slower adaptive adversary. SplitChain implements a pruning mechanism for the blocks of the chains and gradually renews the validators of the chains, limiting the bootstrapping overhead of new validators. SplitChain supports cross-chain transactions natively and includes a routing protocol designed for chains to route transactions in a logarithmic number of hops in proportion to the total number of chains in the system. Finally, we do not rely on PoW, which requires a synchronous communication model and whose use is controversial because of its excessive energy consumption.

Omniledger [3] improves upon Elastico. It uses a more scalable consensus algorithm, increasing the size of its shards, thus reducing the probability of their corruption. It features shards with separate ledgers to better distribute storage costs and adapts classic distributed checkpointing principles to prune shard ledgers. It provides a synchronous lock/unlock client-driven mechanism to handle cross-shard transactions, although at the expense of lightweight-client compatibility and significant latency and safety issues [8]. The UTXO model is not adapted to sharding, as its cross-chain transactions can consume UTXOs stored in different chains, having a significant impact on throughput as the number of shards increases. Omniledger reduces the cost of shard reconfiguration by bounding the number of validators shuffled in each of its day-long epochs, however, Omniledger requires a global blockchain for validator allocation. In contrast, SplitChain shuffles a small number of validators of a chain after each block to withstand an adversary adaptive over a small, configurable number of consensus instances and does not require any global blockchain to manage validator identities. Validators can handle the management and routing of cross-chain transactions autonomously, preserving lightweight-client compatibility.

Zilliqa [9] is an account-based sharded blockchain that handles smart contracts. It inherits all the problems of Elastico except for its ability to handle validators on a separate chain. It does not shard transactions storage. Moreover, it cannot provide atomicity for cross-shard transactions.

RapidChain [11] is a UTXO-based sharded blockchain that distinguishes itself from Omniledger by featuring a transaction routing protocol inspired by Kademlia, enabling message routing in $\log n$ steps without any special client interaction. To reduce the size of its shards, RapidChain uses a synchronous consensus algorithm tolerating a proportion of $1/2$ Byzantine nodes. RapidChain thus inherits problems of Elastico and Omniledger, namely the use of PoW for validator enrollment (Elastico) and the use of the UTXO model (Omniledger). On the other hand, Splitchain is asynchronous, does not require PoW and routes transactions through a small subset of validators (the core) thereby significantly reducing message load.

Monoxide [10] is the first sharded blockchain to implement the use of PoW for shard consensus. It allows each miner to finalize and propose new transaction blocks to multiple shards simultaneously, amplifying and distributing their mining capabilities within the system. Its cross-shard transactions are handled in a lock-free manner. However, to guarantee the safety of Monoxide, the majority of miners are required to work for most if not all shards. This causes centralization problems and contradicts the load-distribution principle of sharding, requiring large throughput, storage and computation costs from miners. This behavior causes Monoxide to resemble more to a parallelization solution than to an actual sharded system like SplitChain.

8 Conclusion

We have presented SplitChain, a protocol supporting the creation of scalable account-based blockchains without undermining decentralization and security. SplitChain distinguishes itself from other sharded blockchains by minimizing the synchronization constraints among shards while maintaining security guarantees. Specifically, SplitChain is the first permissionless sharded blockchain that does not require a dedicated shard or a global blockchain to attribute validators to their consensus chain. This avoids the need for a global reconfiguration of the shards each time a new batch of validators is added to the system. A dedicated routing protocol enables transactions to be redirected between shards with a low number of hops and messages. Finally, SplitChain dynamically adapts the number of shards to the system load to avoid over-dimensioning issues encountered in static sharding-based solutions. Further research will investigate the practical performance of SplitChain through its implementation and the potential use of sharding to enhance user privacy.

A Figures

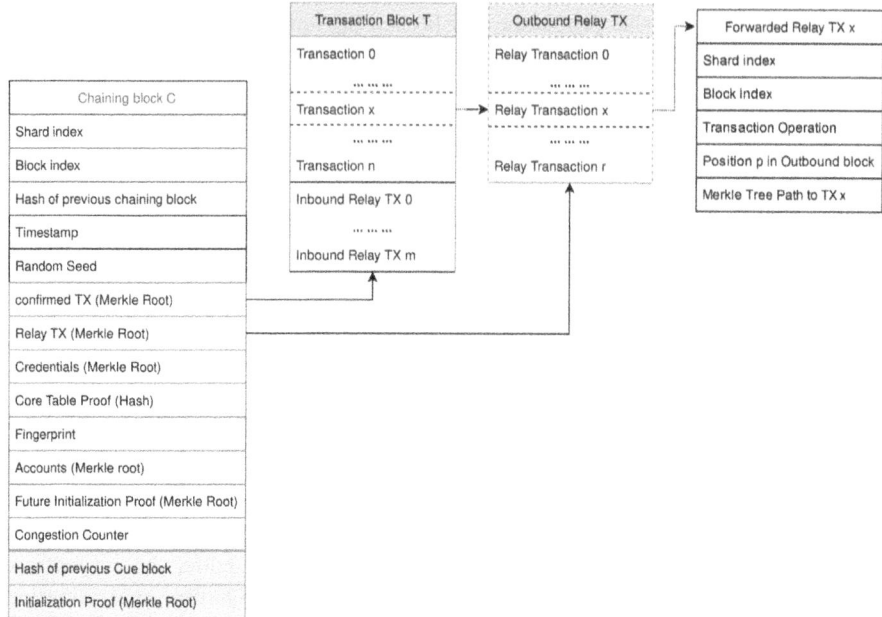

Fig. 1. Composition of a chaining block (bottom fields only belong to cue blocks.)

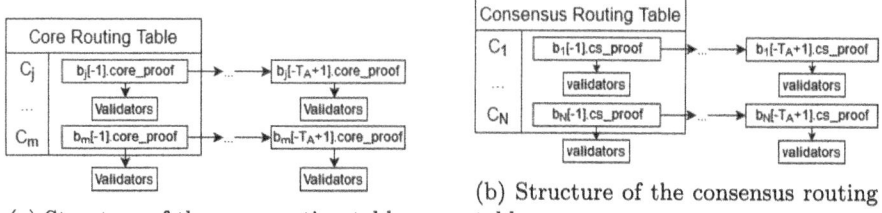

(a) Structure of the core routing table

(b) Structure of the consensus routing table

Fig. 2. Routing tables

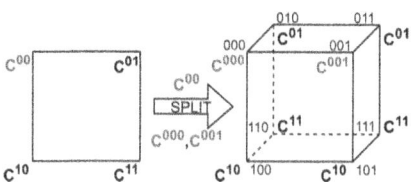

Fig. 3. Mapping of vertices and chain labels after a chain split causing an increase in hypercube dimension.

B   Algorithms

Algorithm 1: Initializing a validator account

input : The validator account registering transaction tx.
1 **function** initialize(tx, pk_{val})
2   send(tx).to_any()
3      $b \leftarrow$ wait_for_validation(tx)
4      $C_{\text{init}} \leftarrow b.chain$
5      $b_{\text{init}} \leftarrow$ wait_for_cue_block(C_{init})
6      $tx_{\text{init}} \leftarrow (\text{"}init\text{"}, pk_{val})$
7      $ack, \pi_{\text{init}} \leftarrow$ wait_for_ack(tx_{init})
8      $core\_table[C_{\text{init}}] \leftarrow ack.table$
9   **return** $\pi_{\text{init}}, b_{\text{init}}, C_{\text{init}}, core\_table$

output : The validator's initialization proof and cue block and its initialization chain's label and core table.

Algorithm 2: Referencing a validator

1 **function** reference($\pi_{\text{init}}, core\_init$)
2      $pk_{\text{cons}}, sk_{\text{cons}} \leftarrow$ generate_keys()
3      $tx \leftarrow (\text{"}credential\text{"}, \pi_{\text{init}}, pk_{\text{cons}})$
4   send(tx).to($core\_init$)
5      $b, \pi_{\text{ref}} \leftarrow$ wait_for_validation(tx)
6      $C_{\text{ref}} \leftarrow b.chain$
7   **return** $\pi_{\text{ref}}, pk_{\text{cons}}, sk_{\text{cons}}, C_{\text{ref}}$

output : The validator's referencing proof.

Algorithm 3: Attribution algorithm

input : The list of validators L to attribute to chains, the number N of chains, a random seed $seed$.
1 **function** attribution($L, N, seed$)
2      $L \leftarrow$ shuffle($L, seed$)
3      $sets \leftarrow []$
4      $\alpha \leftarrow \lfloor |L|/N \rfloor$
5      $r \leftarrow |L| - N \times \alpha$
6   **for** $i \leftarrow 0$ **to** $N - 1$ **do**
7         $sets.append([])$
8   **for** $j \leftarrow 0$ **to** $\alpha - 1$ **do**
9             $sets[i].append(L.pop())$
10   **if** $r > 0$ **then**
11            $sets[i].append(L.pop())$
12            $r \leftarrow r - 1$
13   **return** $sets$

Algorithm 4: Join a chain for consensus

input : The reference proof π_{ref}.
1 **function** join_consensus(π_{ref}, core_table)
2     $tx \leftarrow ("join", \pi_{\text{ref}})$
3   send(tx).to_core(C_{ref})
4     $ack \leftarrow$ wait_for_ack(tx)
5     $core\_table[C_{\text{cons}}] \leftarrow ack.table$
6   The validator bootstraps itself to the chain using the list of nodes provided in the ack message
7   **return** *core_table*

C Proofs

C.1 Randomness Creation

Theorem 1. *Let $\epsilon \in (0,1)$ be the security parameter of SplitChain. The seed of any chaining block b cannot be tampered with or predicted in advance by the adversary with any high probability $1 - \epsilon$.*

Proof. We assume the existence of a preceding chaining block $C[k-1]$ with a proper pseudorandom seed s_0. This block may be the genesis block of SplitChain if k is the first consensus of the system. Similarly, if the system consists of multiple chains, we suppose that the seeds of the preceding blocks of these chains are also pseudorandom and unpredictible.

The attribution of the new validators of the consensus committee of $C[k]$ is based on the last seeds of its reference chains. As these seeds are both pseudorandom and unpredictable, the result of the attribution of the new validators of

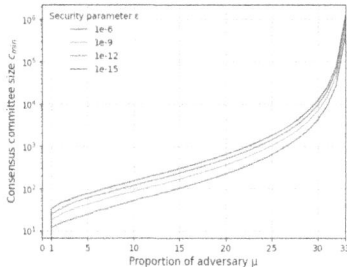
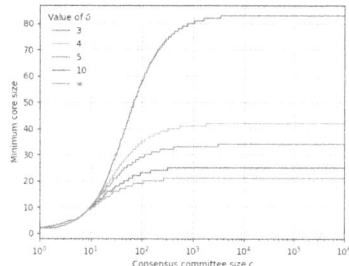

(a) Minimum number of validators c_{min} of a consensus committee as a function of μ for different safety probabilities $1 - \epsilon$.

(b) Minimum core size τ_{min} as a function of the consensus committee size c for different values of adversary adaptivity δ

Fig. 4. (a) Minimum number of validators c_{min} of a consensus committee as a function of μ for different safety probabilities $1 - \epsilon$. (b) Minimum core size τ_{min} as a function of the consensus committee size c for different values of adversary adaptivity δ

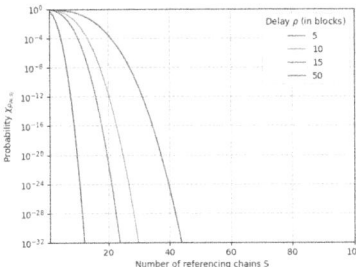
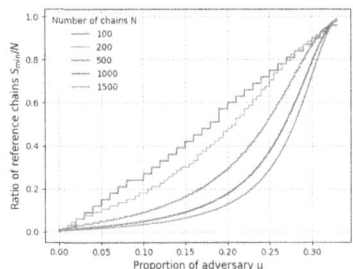

(a) Probability $\chi_{\rho(N,S)}$ as a function of the number of reference chains S and the delay in blocks ρ for $N = 100$ chains.

(b) Required proportion of reference chains to achieve partial attribution with probability $1 - 10^{-6}$ as a function of μ for different values of N.

Fig. 5. (a) Probability $\chi_{\rho(N,S)}$ as a function of the number of reference chains S and the delay in blocks ρ for $N = 100$ chains. (b) Required proportion of reference chains to achieve partial attribution with probability $1 - 10^{-6}$ as a function of μ for different values of N.

$C[k]$ using these seeds is also pseudorandom and unpredictable. As the adversary needs δ blocks of delay to corrupt validators, it is not possible for it to target the validators of the reference committees quickly enough to influence the randomness of the attribution. Furthermore, in the case of partial attribution, the adversary cannot predict which of the system's chains will serve as the reference chains of the consensus committee of $C[k]$, as they are also randomly chosen using the seed of $C[k-1]$. Thus, if the preceding seeds are unpredictable, the adversary cannot temper the randomness of the attribution of new validators for $C[k]$'s consensus committee.

Furthermore, the verifiable random function (VRF) used in the pseudorandom sortition algorithm (see Sect. 4.2) run by new validators of the consensus committee to determine if they are part of the core uses the seed of $C[k-1]$ and the private key of the validators. As the seed used by the sortition function is both pseudorandom and unpredictable, and the core contains at least one honest validator with high probability $1 - \epsilon$, the new seed of $C[k]$ obtained by hashing the concatenation of the core validator's public keys is both pseudorandom and unpredictable. Thus, the adversary cannot predict or manipulate the value of the new seed in advance. □

C.2 Fair Attribution of Reference Sets

Lemma 1. Let $E_1, E_2, ..., E_N$ be the reference sets produced by Algorithm 3. Then $\forall j, k \in \{1, ..., N\}$, $| |E_j| - |E_k| | \leq 1$.

Proof. Let N and L be respectively the number of reference sets to be produced and the set of validators to be attributed. The algorithm first assigns $\alpha = \lfloor |L|/N \rfloor$ validators to each set. This makes $r = |L| - \alpha N < N$ validators to be attributed. Then for the r remaining validators, the algorithm assigns each of them to a different set. This results in $0 \leq r < N$ sets of $\alpha + 1$ validators and $N - r$ sets of α validators. □

C.3 Consensus Committee Safety

Let $A = \mu V$ be the total number of corrupted validators in SplitChain. Let A_i be the number of corrupted validators in the reference set of C_i, $1 \leq i \leq N$. We have $A = \sum_{i=1}^{N} A_i$. Recall that the attribution of any validator lasts for $\delta - 1$ consecutive consensus. Let A_i^k be the random variable that represents the maximal number of malicious validators attributed by the $(\ell + k)$-th instance of Algorithm 3 executed in C_i, for any $\ell \geq 1$ and $k \in [1, \delta - 1]$. We have $A_i = \sum_{k=1}^{\delta-1} A_i^k$.

Each reference chain C_i, $1 \leq i \leq N$, sends a new reference set of validators to a chain C_j to update the consensus committee membership of C_j. Let $X_{i,j}$ be the random variable that represents the number of corrupted validators assigned by C_i to the consensus committee of C_j. We have $0 \leq X_{i,j} \leq A_i$. Specifically, the number of new corrupted validators $X_{i,j}^k$ attributed by C_i to the $(\ell' + k)$-th consensus committee of C_j, for any $\ell' \geq 1$ and $k \in [1, \delta - 1]$, is less than or equal to A_i^k and we have $X_{i,j} = \sum_{k=1}^{\delta-1} X_{i,j}^k$.

Let Y_j be the random variable that represents the number of corrupted validators in the consensus committee of a chain C_j. We have that Y_j is the sum of the corrupted validators of all the reference sets attributed to C_j by its reference chains.

Lemma C.1. $X_{i,j}^k$ *follows a hypergeometric distribution with parameters* $V/(N(\delta - 1))$, $V/((\delta - 1)N^2)$ *and* A_i^k.

Proof. The reference set attributed by the $(\ell + k)$-th instance of Algorithm 3 in C_i to the consensus committee of C_j, for any $\ell \geq 1$ and $k \in [1, \delta-1]$, is a dichotomous population of size $V/(N(\delta - 1))$ composed of A_i^k corrupted validators and $(V/(N(\delta-1))) - A_i^k$ honest validators. Each validator in this population can only be allocated to one consensus committee, hence the sampling is drawn without replacement. Finally, validators are evenly allocated between the N consensus chains, so each attribution subset contains $V/((\delta - 1)N^2)$ validators. Hence, $X_{i,j}^k \sim H(V/(N(\delta - 1)), V/((\delta - 1)N^2), A_i^k)$. □

C.4 Consensus Committee Safety with the Total Attribution Policy

Recall that in the total attribution policy, the consensus committee of any chain C_j of SplitChain is fed with the reference sets of each chain of SplitChain. Thus we have $Y_j = \sum_{i=1}^{N} X_{i,j} = \sum_{i=1}^{N} \sum_{k=1}^{(\delta-1)} X_{i,j}^k$.

Lemma 2. *The probability of corruption of a consensus committee by the (μ, δ)-adaptive adversary is maximized when corrupted validators are equally distributed among all reference chains, i.e., $\forall i, \forall k, A_i^k = A/(N(\delta - 1))$.*

Proof. By definition of Y_j and by applying Lemma C.1, we have

$$Y_j = \sum_{i=1}^{N} X_{i,j} = \sum_{i=1}^{N} \sum_{k=1}^{(\delta-1)} H\left(\frac{V}{N(\delta-1)}, \frac{V}{(\delta-1)N^2}, A_i^k\right), \qquad (1)$$

and the expectation of Y_j is given by

$$E(Y_j) = \sum_{i=1}^{N} \sum_{k=1}^{(\delta-1)} \left(\frac{V}{(\delta-1)N^2}\right)\left(\frac{(\delta-1)NA_i^k}{V}\right) = \sum_{i=1}^{N} \sum_{k=1}^{(\delta-1)} \frac{A_i^k}{N} = \frac{A}{N}. \qquad (2)$$

The average proportion of the (μ, δ)-adaptive adversary in a consensus committee is therefore $(A/N)/(V/N) = A/V = \mu$. Note that this value is independent from A_i^k. Therefore, the adversary can only maximize its chances of corrupting the consensus committee of C_j by increasing the variance of Y_j. The variables $X_{i,j}^k$ are drawn from disjoint populations, and are therefore independent. Thus, the variance of Y_j is given by summing the variances of random variables $X_{i,j}^k$:

$$\begin{aligned}
\mathrm{Var}(Y_j) &= \sum_{i=1}^{N} \sum_{k=1}^{(\delta-1)} \frac{V}{(\delta-1)N^2} \frac{(\delta-1)NA_i^k}{V} \left(1 - \frac{(\delta-1)NA_i^k}{V}\right) \frac{\frac{V}{N(\delta-1)} - \frac{V}{(\delta-1)N^2}}{\frac{V}{N(\delta-1)} - 1} \\
&= \sum_{i=1}^{N} \sum_{k=1}^{(\delta-1)} \frac{A_i^k}{N} \left(1 - \frac{(\delta-1)NA_i^k}{V}\right) \frac{\frac{V(N-1)}{(\delta-1)N^2}}{\frac{V}{N(\delta-1)} - 1} \\
&= \sum_{i=1}^{N} \sum_{k=1}^{(\delta-1)} \left(\frac{A_i^k}{N} - \frac{(\delta-1){A_i^k}^2}{V}\right) \frac{V(N-1)}{N(\delta-1)(V-N)} \\
&= \frac{V(N-1)}{N(\delta-1)(V-N)} \left(\frac{1}{N}\sum_{i=1}^{N}\sum_{k=1}^{(\delta-1)} A_i^k - \frac{(\delta-1)}{V}\sum_{i=1}^{N}\sum_{k=1}^{(\delta-1)} {A_i^k}^2\right) \\
&= \frac{V(N-1)}{N(\delta-1)(V-N)} \left(\frac{A}{N} - \frac{(\delta-1)}{V}\sum_{i=1}^{N}\sum_{k=1}^{(\delta-1)} {A_i^k}^2\right). \qquad (3)
\end{aligned}$$

To maximize $\mathrm{Var}(Y_j)$, the (μ, δ)-adversary must choose the A_i^k so that to minimize $\sum_{i=1}^{N} {A_i^k}^2$, with $0 \leq A_i^k \leq V/(N(\delta-1))$ and $\sum_{i=1}^{N}\sum_{k=1}^{(\delta-1)} A_i^k = A$. Intuitively, $\sum_{i=1}^{N}\sum_{k=1}^{(\delta-1)} {A_i^k}^2$ is minimal when $A_i^k = A/(N(\delta-1))$. We formulate this hypothesis by the following inequality, where v_i^k represents the deviation of A_i^k from $A/(N(\delta-1))$, such that $-A/(N(\delta-1)) \leq v_i^k \leq V/(N(\delta-1)) - A/(N(\delta-1))$ and $\sum_{i=1}^{N}\sum_{k=1}^{(\delta-1)} v_i^k = 0$. We have:

$$\sum_{i=1}^{N}\sum_{k=1}^{(\delta-1)}A_i^{k^2} \leq \sum_{i=1}^{N}\sum_{k=1}^{(\delta-1)}(\frac{A}{N(\delta-1)})^2$$

$$< \sum_{i=1}^{N}(\frac{A}{N(\delta-1)}+v_i^1)^2 + (\frac{A}{N(\delta-1)}+v_i^2)^2 + \ldots + (\frac{A}{N(\delta-1)}+v_i^{(\delta-1)})^2$$

$$N(\delta-1)(\frac{A}{N(\delta-1)})^2 < \sum_{i=1}^{N}(\delta-1)(\frac{A}{N(\delta-1)})^2 + \sum_{k=1}^{(\delta-1)}v_i^{k^2} + 2\frac{A}{N(\delta-1)}\sum_{k=1}^{(\delta-1)}v_i^k \quad (4)$$

$$\frac{A^2}{N(\delta-1)} < \frac{A^2}{N(\delta-1)} + \sum_{i=1}^{N}\sum_{k=1}^{(\delta-1)}v_i^{k^2}$$

$$0 < \sum_{i=1}^{N}\sum_{k=1}^{(\delta-1)}v_i^{k^2}$$

We notice that inequality 4 stands when any deviation v_i^k is different from 0, that is, any other distribution than $A_i^k = A/(N(\delta-1))$ results in a greater value of the sum and reduces the variance of Y_j. Therefore, to maximize the variance of Y_j, i.e., to maximize the corruption probability of the consensus committee of C_j, malicious validators must be evenly distributed across the k executions of Algorithm 3. □

Lemma C.2. *The probability p_c that a consensus committee of chain C_j is corrupted by the adversary is given by*

$$p_c = P\left(Y_j > \lfloor\frac{c}{3}\rfloor\right) = 1 - \sum_{l=0}^{\lfloor\frac{c}{3}\rfloor}\binom{c}{l}(\mu)^l(1-\mu)^{c-l} \quad (5)$$

Proof. A consensus committee is corrupted if the sum of the adversary's validators is greater than one third of the chain. By applying Lemma 2 to Eq. 1, we can express the probability of corruption p_c of a consensus committee as:

$$p_c = P\left(Y_j > \lfloor\frac{V}{3N}\rfloor\right)$$

$$= 1 - P\left(\sum_{i=1}^{N}\sum_{k=1}^{(\delta-1)}H\left(\frac{V}{N(\delta-1)},\frac{V}{(\delta-1)N^2},\frac{A}{N(\delta-1)}\right)\right)$$

$$\leq \lfloor\frac{V}{3N}\rfloor \quad (6)$$

The binomial distribution is a good approximation of the hypergeometric distribution when the population is sufficiently larger than the sample size, which is commonly accepted as a sampling fraction of 0.1 [6]. That is, $H(m,n,p) \approx B(n,p/m)$ when $n/m < 0.1$. In our case, $(V/((\delta-1)N^2))/(V/(N(\delta-1))) < 0.1$ imposes that $N > 10$. Thus, we assume that the number of chains N is always greater than 10. By applying this approximation to Eq. 6, we can simplify our equation:

$$P(Y_j \le \lfloor \frac{V}{3N} \rfloor) = \lim_{V \to \infty} P(\sum_{i=1}^{N} \sum_{k=1}^{(\delta-1)} H(\frac{V}{N(\delta-1)}, \frac{V}{(\delta-1)N^2}, \frac{A}{N(\delta-1)}) \le \lfloor \frac{V}{3N} \rfloor)$$

$$= P(\sum_{i=1}^{N} \sum_{k=1}^{(\delta-1)} B(\frac{V}{(\delta-1)N^2}, \frac{A}{V}) \le \lfloor \frac{V}{3N} \rfloor)$$

$$= P(B(\sum_{i=1}^{N} \sum_{k=1}^{(\delta-1)} \frac{V}{(\delta-1)N^2}, \mu) \le \lfloor \frac{V}{3N} \rfloor) \qquad (7)$$

$$= P(B(\frac{V}{N}, \mu) \le \lfloor \frac{V}{3N} \rfloor)$$

$$= \sum_{k=0}^{\lfloor \frac{V}{3N} \rfloor} \binom{\frac{V}{N}}{k} (\mu)^k (1-\mu)^{\frac{V}{N}-k}$$

Let c be the constant representing the minimal number of validators needed to ensure the proper and safe execution of a chain. By replacing V/N with c in Eq. 7, we can calculate the probability of corruption of a chain by the adversary:

$$P(Y_j > \lfloor \frac{c}{3} \rfloor) = 1 - \sum_{k=0}^{\lfloor \frac{c}{3} \rfloor} \binom{c}{k} (\mu)^k (1-\mu)^{c-k}$$

□

Theorem 2. For any security parameter $\epsilon \in (0,1)$, for any proportion of corrupted validators $\mu < 1/3$, there exists a finite consensus committee size c_{min} such that $\forall c \ge c_{min}$, the probability p_c that a committee of c validators is corrupted satisfies $p_c < \epsilon$, where $p_c = 1 - \sum_{\ell=0}^{\lfloor c/3 \rfloor} \binom{c}{\ell} \mu^\ell (1-\mu)^{c-\ell}$.

Proof. Probability p_c is given by Lemma C.2. Let $c = V/N$ be the number of validators inside a consensus committee, and $\mu = A/V$ the proportion of corrupted validators in SplitChain, with $\mu < 1/3$. We know from Eq. 2 that the average number $E(Y_j)$ of corrupted validators in a consensus committee is $A/N = \mu c$. We also know from Lemma C.2 that $p_c = 1 - P(Y_j \le \lfloor c/3 \rfloor)$, with $Y_j \sim BinomialDistribution(c, \mu)$.

Let $\mu = 1/3$. Then $E(Y_j) = c/3$. By definition of the statistical mean, we have $\lim_{c \to \infty} P(Y_j \le E(Y_j)) = 0.5$. Thus, when $\mu = 1/3$, $\lim_{c \to \infty} p_c = 0.5$. However, SplitChain strictly requires that $\mu < 1/3$. As $E(Y_j) < c/3$ when $\mu < 1/3$, $\lim_{c \to \infty} P(Y_j \le \lfloor c/3 \rfloor) = 1$ and $\lim_{c \to \infty} p_c = 0$. By definition, the cumulative distribution function is monotone increasing, so p_c is monotone decreasing. Thus, there exists a value c_{min}, such that for any $\epsilon < 1$ and $c \ge c_{min}$, $p_c < \epsilon$. □

C.5 Consensus Committee Safety with the Partial Attribution

Let S be the number of reference sets required for a chain C_j to update its $(\ell+k)$-th consensus committee before initiating a new consensus execution. Let

$R_a^k \geq N$ be the number of referencing sets corrupted by the adversary among the N reference sets proposed to C_j by the chains of SplitChain at some attribution execution $(\ell'+k)$. The number of corrupted reference attributed to the $(\ell+k)$-th consensus committee of C_j is the random variable $S_a^k \leq S$.

Lemma C.3. *The number of corrupted validators Y_j is maximized when the corrupted validators are equally distributed among the R_a reference chains, i.e. $\forall C_i \in R_a, A_i = \mu'V/N$, where μ' is the new proportion of corrupted validator inside the S_a corrupted reference chains, such that $\mu' \geq \mu$.*

Proof. This result is obtained by applying Lemma 2 with S referencing chains instead of N and μ' instead of μ. □

Lemma C.4. *S_a follows the hypergeometric distribution with parameters $H(N, R_a, S)$.*

Proof. The reference sets correspond to a dichotomous population of size N composed of R_a corrupted sets and $N - R_a$ honest sets. Each set in this population can only be allocated once to the same consensus committee, hence the sampling is drawn without replacement. Finally, only S sets are chosen at random, thus the number of randomly selected corrupted sets S_a follows the hypergeometric distribution $H(N, R_a, S)$. □

Lemma C.5. *The proportion of malicious validators inside a consensus committee $S_a \times (\mu'/S)$ is maximized when the reference chains targeted by the adversary are fully corrupted, i.e. when $\mu' = 1$.*

Proof. The average value of S_a is: $E(S_a) = S\frac{R_a}{N} = S\frac{(\mu/\mu')N}{N} = S\frac{\mu}{\mu'}$. This corresponds to an average adversary proportion of $E(S_a)\frac{\mu'}{S} = \mu$ corrupted reference validators. Note that this mean value doesn't depend on μ'.

The adversary proportion's variance is:

$$V_a(S_a\frac{\mu'}{S}) = \frac{\mu'^2}{S^2}S\frac{R_a}{N}\frac{N-R_a}{N}\frac{N-S}{N-1}$$
$$= \frac{\mu'^2}{S}\frac{\frac{\mu}{\mu'}N}{N}\frac{N-\frac{\mu}{\mu'}N}{N}\frac{N-S}{N-1}$$
$$= \frac{\mu'^2}{S}\frac{\mu}{\mu'}(1-\frac{\mu}{\mu'})\frac{N-S}{N-1}$$
$$= \frac{\mu}{S}(\mu'-\mu)\frac{N-S}{N-1}$$

The derivative function of the adversary proportion's variance is $\frac{\partial}{\partial \mu'}V_a(S_a\frac{\mu'}{S}) = \frac{\mu}{S}\frac{N-S}{N-1}$, whose roots are $N = S$ and $\mu = 0$. If $S = N$, then all the available reference validators are used and the proportion of corrupted reference validators is μ. For $\mu > 0$, $\mu' \leq 1$ and $0 < S < N$, the derivative is always positive. Hence, the adversary proportion's variance is ascending for $\mu \leq \mu' \leq 1$ and reaches its maximum when $\mu' = 1$. □

Lemma C.6. *(Probability of corruption of a partially attributed consensus committee).*

$$p_c = P(Y_j > \lfloor c/3 \rfloor) = P(S_a > \lfloor S/3 \rfloor) = 1 - \sum_{k=0}^{\lfloor S/3 \rfloor} \binom{S}{k}(\mu)^k(1-\mu)^{n-k} \qquad (8)$$

Proof. A consensus committee is corrupted if it contains more than one third of malicious validators. As the committee is composed of S reference sets, this corresponds to $S(V/3N^2)$ validators. By definition of Y_j and by applying Lemma C.3, we have:

$$p_c = P(\sum_{i=1}^{S_a} H(\frac{V}{N}, \frac{V}{N^2}, \frac{V}{N}\mu') > \lfloor S\frac{V}{3N^2} \rfloor) \qquad (9)$$

Let $\lim_{V,N\to\infty} \frac{V}{N^2} = c$, c being the fixed number of validators within an attribution subset.

$$\lim_{V,N\to\infty} P(Y_j > \lfloor S\frac{V}{3N^2} \rfloor) = \lim_{V,N\to\infty} P(\sum_{i=1}^{S_a} H(\frac{V}{N}, \frac{V}{N^2}, \frac{V}{N}\mu') > \lfloor S\frac{V}{3N^2} \rfloor)$$

$$= \lim_{V,N\to\infty} P(\sum_{i=1}^{S_a} H(\frac{V}{N}, c, \frac{V}{N}\mu') > \lfloor S\frac{c}{3} \rfloor)$$

$$= P(\sum_{i=1}^{S_a} B(c, \mu') > \lfloor S\frac{c}{3} \rfloor)$$

$$= P(B(S_a c, \mu') > \lfloor S\frac{c}{3} \rfloor)$$

We know from Lemma C.5 that this value is maximized when $\mu' = 1$, thus we obtain $p_c = P(S_a c > \lfloor S(c/3) \rfloor) = P(S_a > \lfloor S/3 \rfloor)$. As a reference set contains at least one validator, i.e. $c \geq 1$, the minimum number of consensus validators of a chain is S. From Lemma C.4, we know that $S_a \sim H(N, R_a, S)$. As $\mu' = 1$, $R_a = \mu N$. Thus:

$$p_c = \lim_{V,N\to\infty} P(S_a > \lfloor S/3 \rfloor)$$

$$= \lim_{N\to\infty} P(H(N, \mu N, S) > \lfloor S/3 \rfloor)$$

$$= P(B(S, \mu) > \lfloor S/3 \rfloor)$$

$$= 1 - \sum_{\lfloor S/3 \rfloor}^{k=0} \binom{S}{k}(\mu)^k(1-\mu)^{S-k}$$

$\square$

Theorem 3. For any security parameter $\epsilon \in (0,1)$, for any proportion of corrupted validators $\mu < 1/3$, there exists a finite number of reference sets S_{min} such that $\forall S \geq S_{min}$, the probability p_S that a consensus committee composed of S reference sets is corrupted satisfies $p_S < \epsilon$, with $p_S = 1 - \sum_{k=0}^{\lfloor S/3 \rfloor} \binom{S}{k} \mu^k (1-\mu)^{S-k}$.

Proof. We know from Lemma C.6 that the number of fully corrupted reference sets in a committee is $p_c = P(S_a > \lfloor S/3 \rfloor) = 1 - P(S_a \leq \lfloor S/3 \rfloor)$, with $S_a \sim B(S, \mu)$. The average number of fully corrupted reference sets in a consensus committee is $E(S_a) = S\mu$.

Let $\mu = 1/3$. Then $E(S_a) = S/3$. By definition of the statistical mean, we have $\lim_{S \to \infty} P(S_a \leq E(S_a)) = 0.5$. Thus, when $\mu = 1/3$, $\lim_{S \to \infty} p_c = 0.5$. However, SplitChain strictly requires that $\mu < 1/3$. As $E(S_a) < S/3$ when $\mu < 1/3$, $\lim_{S \to \infty} P(S_a \leq \lfloor S/3 \rfloor) = 1$ and $\lim_{S \to \infty} p_c = 0$. Because the cumulative distribution function is by definition monotone increasing, p_c is monotone decreasing. Thus, there exists a value S_{min} such that for any $\epsilon > 0$ and $S > S_{min}$, $pc < \epsilon$. □

C.6 Partial Attribution Policy: Probability to Corrupt a Given Consensus Set

Lemma C.1. *Let $\chi_{\rho_{(N,S)}}$ be the probability that a consensus committee uses a reference set that has been obsolete for at least $\rho_{(N,S)}$ consecutive validator attributions. Then $\chi_{\rho_{(N,S)}} \leq P(H(N,S,1) = 0)\Big(P(H(N,S,1) = 0)p_{2,S} + P(H(N,S,1) = 1)p_{2,S-1}\Big)$, where H is the hypergeometric distribution and*

$$p_{i,k} = \begin{cases} 1, & \text{if } i > \rho_{(N,S)} \\ 0, & \text{if } k \geq N \\ P(H(N,S,1) = 0) \sum_{j=0}^{min(S,k)} \Big(P(H(N,S,k) = j) \\ (P(H(N,S,1) = 0))^j p_{i+1,k+S-j} \Big) \end{cases}$$

Proof. We first assume that all chains are up to date, i.e. at time t, each chain knows the penultimate block $t-1$ of all other chains. Because of the asynchrony, we adopt the worst-case scenario and assume that the index of chain C_1 is only updated by a chain C_2 if C_1 is selected for the partial attribution of C_2, i.e. a new chaining block of C_1 is required to initiate the consensus of C_2.

Let χ_1 be the probability that C does not draw C'. Since all chains are up to date, none of the drawn chains contain block indices unknown to C, therefore $\chi_1 = P(H(N,S,1) = 0)$. Given that C can draw itself, the number of new chain block indices is equal to S with probability $P(H(N,S,1) = 0)$ or equal to $S-1$ with probability $P(H(N,S,1) = 1)$. If a chain whose block index is greater than $t - 1$ is selected, it may contain a new block index of C' or any other new chain block indices greater than $t - 1$. We approximate this probability by considering only the probability that the chain drew C' during its last draw, i.e.

$P(H(N, S, 1) = 0)$. Thus, we obtain:

$$\chi_2 \leq \chi_1 \bigg(P(H(N,S,1) = 0) \Big(\sum_{j=0}^{S} P(H(N,S,S) = j)(P(H(N,S,1) = 0))^j \Big)$$

$$+ P(H(N,S,1) = 1) \Big(\sum_{j=0}^{S-1} P(H(N,S,S-1) = j)(P(H(N,S,1) = 0))^j \Big) \bigg)$$

Let $p_{2,k} = P(H(N,S,1) = 0) \sum_{j=0}^{min(S,k)} P(H(N,S,k) = j)(P(H(N,S,1) = 0))^j$. Then $\chi_2 \leq \chi_1 \Big(P(H(N,S,1) = 0) p_{2,S} + P(H(N,S,1) = 1) p_{2,S-1} \Big)$. Taking into account the case where $k \geq N$, i.e. all chains have been drawn at least once (so the probability that C' has not been drawn is 0), we can apply the formula of $p_{i,k}$ iteratively until $i = \rho_{(N,S)}$. □

Theorem 4. $\forall N, \forall S \leq N, \exists \rho_{(N,S)} > 0$ such that $\chi_{\rho_{(N,S)}} < \epsilon$.

Proof. Direct from Lemma C.1 □

C.7 Safety of the Core

Definition C.10. *The core of a chain is composed of the new core validators of the last $\delta - 2$ consensus. Let $X = X^A + X^H$ be the number of validators in the core, where X^A is the number of malicious core validators and X^H the number of honest core validators. We respectively denote X_r^A and x_r^H the number of corrupt and honest new core validators at the r-th last consensus, with $X_r = X_r^A + X_r^H$.*

Lemma C.7. *The probability that the core of a chain is corrupted is given by*

$$p_{core} = (1 - \tau/c)^{(1-\mu')(c - c_{(\delta-1)})} \tag{10}$$

Proof. New core validators are elected by sortition during each consensus. A validator can only be elected as a core validator during its first consensus. Furthermore, the list of new core validators is only determined at the end of the consensus execution. Thus, core validators can only join the core for $\delta-2$ consensus executions. The probability of a validator u being elected as a core validator is $B(w_u, \tau/w)$ [7], where B is the binomial distribution, w is the total validation stake of the consensus committee and w_u is the stake of validator u. In SplitChain, all validators have the same validation stake, thus $w_u = 1$ and:

$$\begin{aligned} X &\sim \sum_{(\delta-2)}^{r=1} \sum_{c_r}^{i=1} B(1, \tau/c) \\ &\sim B(\sum_{(\delta-2)}^{r=1} c_r, \tau/c) \\ &\sim B(c - c_{(\delta-1)}, \tau/c) \end{aligned} \tag{11}$$

We consider the worst case where the adversary concentrates the corrupted validators of the consensus committee among the new validators of the last $\delta - 2$ consensus. Following the same logic as with Eq. 11, with a proportion of $\mu' = \mu(\delta - 1)/((\delta - 2))$ corrupted validators, we obtain $X^H \sim B((1 - \mu')(c - c_{(\delta-1)}), \tau/c)$. Thus, the probability of corruption p_{core} of the core is:

$$\begin{aligned}p_{core} &= P(B((1-\mu')(c - c_{(\delta-1)}), \tau/c) = 0) \\ &= \binom{(1-\mu')(c-c_{(\delta-1)})}{0}(\tau/c)^0(1-\tau/c)^{(1-\mu')(c-c_{(\delta-1)})-0} \\ &= (1-\tau/c)^{(1-\mu')(c-c_{(\delta-1)})}\end{aligned}$$

$\square$

Theorem 5. *For any security parameter $\epsilon \in (0,1)$, for an adaptive adversary with any delay $\delta \geq 3$, there exists a finite core size τ_{min} such that $\forall \tau \geq \tau_{min}$, the probability p_{core} that a core of τ validators is corrupted satisfies $p_{core} < \epsilon$, with $p_{core} = (1 - \tau/c)^{(1-\mu')(c-c_{(\delta-1)})}$.*

Proof. We know from Lemma C.7 that $X^H \sim B((1 - \mu')(c - c_{(\delta-1)}), \tau/c)$, with $\mu' = \mu((\delta - 1))/((\delta - 2))$. The expected proportion of honest core validators is $E(B((1-\mu')(c-c_{(\delta-1)}), \tau/c)) = \tau(1-\mu') + \tau(c_{(\delta-1)}/c)(\mu' - 1)$. As μ' decreases when δ increases, with $\lim_{\delta \to \infty} \mu' = \mu$, $\forall \delta \geq 3$, $\mu < 1/3 \Rightarrow \mu' < 2/3$. If $\mu = 1/3$ and $\delta = 3$, then we have $E(B((1-\mu')(c-c_{(\delta-1)}), \tau/c)) = \tau/6$. As p_{core} decreases with the value of δ and τ, $\exists \tau_{min}$ such that $\forall \delta \geq 3$ and $\forall \tau \geq \tau_{min} > 0$, we have $p_{core} \leq \epsilon$, where $\epsilon < 0.5$ is the security parameter. $\square$

D Experiments

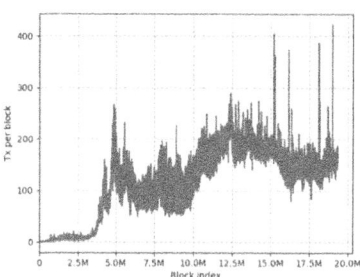

Fig. 6. Number of transactions per block (Ethereum)

To evaluate the efficiency of SplitChain's dynamic sharding compared to static sharding, we replay the entire transaction history of Ethereum from its launch in July 2015 to block $19,353,052$ in March 2024. This amounts to a total of more than 2.280 billion transactions. Blocks and transactions are extracted from a go-ethereum node using ethereum-etl, then stored and ordered in an SQLlite3 database. Our experiment is implemented in C++. Figure 6 displays the average number of transactions for each group of consecutive $1K$ blocks.

To assess the efficiency of transaction allocation for static sharding and SplitChain, we evaluate, for each $1K$ block segment, the minimum, average and maximum number of transactions processed by the chains in each of the two models. Figures 7a and 7b display the distribution of transactions for a static sharding solution of 32 and 256 chains. In both cases, the difference between the average and the maximum is very high: At block 12.5 billion, the maximum is 17 times higher than the average for 32 chains, and 131 times higher for 256 chains. In particular, we notice that the maximum load is almost identical in the two cases, indicating that although multiplying the number of chains by 8 reduces the average load on the chains, the distribution of transactions remains uneven.

Figure 7c shows the variation of the number of chains in SplitChain. We have opted for a split threshold of 20 transactions and a merge threshold of 5 transactions per block. Having a low split threshold reduces computation time and the volume of information transmitted between validators within a chain, resulting in faster consensus and lower transaction-confirmation latency. Chains

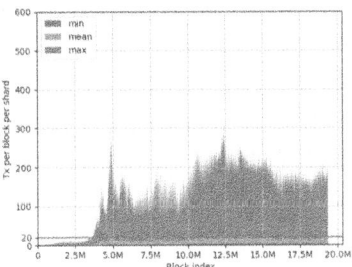

(a) Number of transactions per block per chain, 32-chains static sharding

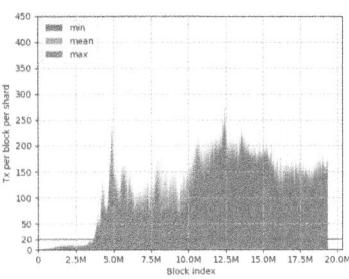

(b) Number of transactions per block per chain, 256-chains static sharding

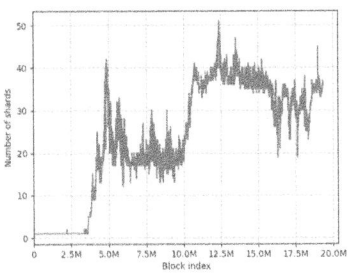

(c) Number of chains per 1K blocks segment, SplitChain

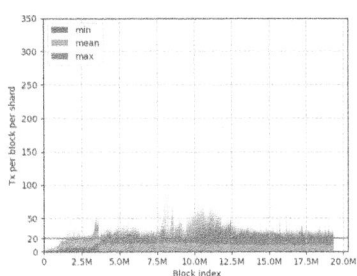

(d) Number of transactions per block per chain, SplitChain

Fig. 7. Efficiency of transaction distribution between chains.

decide whether to split or merge every $1K$ blocks. We observe a strong correlation between the number of chains and the number of transactions. The number of chains used by SplitChain is also low, reaching 51 at most. Finally, Fig. 7d shows the distribution of transactions in SplitChain. We notice that once a given total number of transactions has been reached (around 100 transactions per block), the average load quickly stabilizes at around 10 transactions per block, with a maximum load that is only 2.5 times higher at block 12.5 billion. Indeed, splitting chains efficiently spreads the load of the busiest chains, while creating far fewer chains than static sharding for the same label length. We conclude from this experiment that SplitChain's dynamic sharding better distributes transactions across different chains than static sharding.

Hotspot Addresses. Ethereum's history includes hotspot accounts, i.e. accounts producing a very large number of transactions during one or several 1,000-block segments. Given that a user account cannot be spread over multiple chains, a hotspot address causes repeated splits in the chain handling it, resulting in the creation of a multitude of unused chains that cannot be merged. The following method is used to detect hotspots and cancel a split operation.

Let m be our hotspot-address detection parameter. Let's divide the account space of a chain C into 2^m subsets. Each subset corresponds to the account space of a descendant chain of C after m divisions. We say that C contains a hotspot if the same subset of C contains enough transactions to initiate a split. In that case, C does not split. For our experiment, we chose $m = 10$, which corresponds to 1024 subsets.

References

1. Anceaume, E., Ludinard, R., Sericola, B.: Performance evaluation of large-scale dynamic systems. Sigmetrics Perform. Eval. Rev. SIGMETRICS **39** (2012)
2. Gilad, Y., Hemo, R., Micali, S., Vlachos, G., Zeldovich, N.: Algorand: scaling byzantine agreements for cryptocurrencies. In: Proceedings of the 26th Symposium on Operating Systems Principles, SOSP 2017, pp. 51–68. Association for Computing Machinery, New York (2017). https://doi.org/10.1145/3132747.3132757
3. Kokoris-Kogias, E., Jovanovic, P., Gasser, L., Gailly, N., Syta, E., Ford, B.: Omniledger: a secure, scale-out, decentralized ledger via sharding. In: 2018 IEEE Symposium on Security and Privacy (SP), pp. 583–598 (2018). https://doi.org/10.1109/SP.2018.000-5
4. Luu, L., Narayanan, V., Zheng, C., Baweja, K., Gilbert, S., Saxena, P.: A secure sharding protocol for open blockchains. In: Proceedings of the 2016 ACM SIGSAC Conference on Computer and Communications Security, CCS 2016, pp. 17–30. Association for Computing Machinery, New York (2016). https://doi.org/10.1145/2976749.2978389
5. Micali, S., Rabin, M., Vadhan, S.: Verifiable random functions. In: 40th Annual Symposium on Foundations of Computer Science (Cat. No. 99CB37039), pp. 120–130 (1999). https://doi.org/10.1109/SFFCS.1999.814584
6. Montgomery, D.C.: Introduction to Statistical Quality Control, 6th edn. Wiley, New York (2009)

7. Saunois, G., Robin, F., Anceaume, E., Sericola, B.: Permissionless consensus based on proof-of-eligibility. In: 2020 IEEE 19th International Symposium on Network Computing and Applications (NCA) (2020)
8. Sonnino, A., Bano, S., Al-Bassam, M., Danezis, G.: Replay attacks and defenses against cross-shard consensus in sharded distributed ledgers. In: 2020 IEEE European Symposium on Security and Privacy (EuroS&P), pp. 294–308 (2020). https://doi.org/10.1109/EuroSP48549.2020.00026
9. The ZILLIQA Team. The zilliqa technical whitepaper (2017). https://docs.zilliqa.com/whitepaper.pdf
10. Wang, J., Wang, H.: Monoxide: scale out blockchains with asynchronous consensus zones. In: 16th USENIX Symposium on Networked Systems Design and Implementation (NSDI 2019), Boston, MA, pp. 95–112. USENIX Association (2019). https://www.usenix.org/conference/nsdi19/presentation/wang-jiaping
11. Zamani, M., Movahedi, M., Raykova, M.: Rapidchain: scaling blockchain via full sharding. In: Proceedings of the 2018 ACM SIGSAC Conference on Computer and Communications Security, CCS 2018, pp. 931–948. Association for Computing Machinery, New York (2018). https://doi.org/10.1145/3243734.3243853

Concurrent Wait-Free Graph Snapshots Using Multi-versioning

Gaurav Bhardwaj[✉], Ayaz Ahmed, and Sathya Peri

Indian Institute of Technology Hyderabad, Hyderabad, India
cs19resch11003@iith.ac.in

Abstract. Graphs stand out as a paramount data structure for addressing real-world challenges. The binary relationships among entities or objects are vital in navigating intricate, real-time issues seen in areas like blockchain, social networks, scheduling, biological systems, and telecommunications. Unlike static graphs with immutable vertices and edges, dynamic graphs adapt to the ever-changing real-world scenarios by allowing modifications to both vertices and edges. In this context, we introduce a concurrent, lock-free dynamic graph that enables the addition, deletion, and retrieval of vertices and edges. Furthermore, we present the novel wait-free snapshot algorithm capable of both full and partial graph snapshots using multi-versioning. These snapshots pave the way for advanced graph analytics tasks, including SSSP, getpath, BFS, and more.

1 Introduction

The Graph Data Structure has emerged as a focal point of research interest within both academic and industrial circles, owing to its myriad real-life applications spanning blockchains, mapping systems, machine learning algorithms, biological networks, social networks, and more. Graphs adeptly delineate the intricate connections and structures among objects by delineating paired entity relations. Take, for instance, the use of graphs in social networks, where they serve as a visual representation of user relationships, streamlining tasks like recommendation generation, trend identification, and user behavior forecasting. Unlike traditional data structures such as linked lists, hash tables, and trees, graphs boast distinct advantages across a diverse array of application domains. Consequently, the resolution of graph-related challenges has assumed a prominent position in the realm of research across multiple disciplines.

The rise of multi-core processors has propelled parallel programming and concurrency to the forefront of research. Tailored to accommodate the escalating number of threads or tasks, concurrent data structures aim to enhance scalability, ensuring optimized performance in expansive systems or during system expansion. An array of concurrent data structures, such as Stacks [11], Queues [13,17,20], Linked-Lists [6,9,10,26,29], Hash-Tables [21,22], and others, have been developed to harness the benefits offered by multi-core processors.

Blocking mechanisms such as locks and barriers are commonly employed in concurrent applications but can introduce bottleneck issues like deadlocks.

© The Author(s), under exclusive license to Springer Nature Switzerland AG 2024
A. Castañeda et al. (Eds.): NETYS 2024, LNCS 14783, pp. 32–49, 2024.
https://doi.org/10.1007/978-3-031-67321-4_2

Consequently, researchers have explored non-blocking progress conditions to ensure both efficiency and correctness. In an *obstruction-free* setting, threads operate without acquiring locks, guaranteeing that at least one thread completes its task within a finite number of steps in the absence of obstructions. *Lock-free* execution [14] ensures that at least one thread can finish its operation within a finite number of steps [14]. *Wait-free* execution [12,14], provides the highest level of progress guarantee by ensuring that all processes can complete within a finite number of steps.

Dynamic graphs, however, present a unique challenge as they continuously evolve, with updates potentially arriving at a rapid pace, sometimes reaching tens or even hundreds of thousands of updates per second. Managing these updates concurrently in multicore environments can be particularly challenging, as synchronizing them to ensure consistent graph analytical operations becomes increasingly difficult. Real-life applications of graph analytics operations on dynamic graphs yield invaluable insights. For instance, analyzing user interactions in e-commerce or social network contexts can offer valuable insights into user behavior, potential fraud detection, and network security.

An essential criterion for concurrent data structures and algorithms is correctness. In this paper, we consider the correctness as *linearizability* [15]. A concurrent execution is linearizable if for every method in the execution, effects of the method are considered to occur instantaneously at some point denoted as *Linearization Point* (LP) between its invocation and response.

1.1 Related Work

Graph operations can be primarily categorized into two types: 1) Point Operations, which encompass adding, removing, and looking up operations, and 2) Set Operations, which involve partial or full snapshots. These snapshots can subsequently be used for more advanced operations such as BFS, getpath, SSSP, and more.

Significant advancements have recently emerged in the realm of optimizing graph data structures for multicore systems. Kallimanis et al. [16] pioneered a concurrent dynamic bounded graph, offering wait-free dynamic graph point operations and facilitating graph traversal. In a separate endeavor, Chatterjee et al. [5] introduced an unbounded concurrent linearizable graph model, supporting lock-free point operations and obstruction-free set operations. Their design leveraged a lock-free linked list to manage vertices and edges within the adjacency list. Subsequently, Chatterjee et al. [4] enhanced this structure by integrating a hash table for vertices and a linked list for edges.

Expanding upon Chatterjee et al.'s framework [5], Bhardwaj et al. [2] devised a method to create a wait-free snapshot of the graph. Their approach drew inspiration from the snapshot algorithm for iterators developed by Petrank and Timnat [24]. While this technique captures a comprehensive snapshot for executing advanced graph analytics functions, it lacks support for partial snapshots. This deficiency renders it resource-intensive for tasks such as SSSP, GetPath, BFS, and similar operations.

GraphOne [18] introduced a novel strategy for updates utilizing batch processing. They maintain versions of the adjacency list to facilitate graph analytics operations and execute deferred updates on edges and vertices in batch form. Feng et al. [8] proposed an incremental model focused on efficiently computing graph analytical operations like Breadth-First Search and Single Source Shortest Path. Their method involves maintaining data structures optimized for these operations, which are continually updated with each modification to the graph. However, it's important to note that their implementation lacks complete dynamism, as it does not support the addition or deletion of vertices.

Multiversion concurrency control has long been employed in various domains such as database systems [28], transactional memory [7,19], and shared memory data structures. This approach enables concurrent data updates while preserving multiple versions of the data in history, each associated with a timestamp. These distinct versions facilitate consistent data reads from different versions concurrently without interfering with ongoing update operations. Wei et al. [27] introduced a wait-free snapshot algorithm utilizing multiversioning. Similarly, Nelson et al. [23] proposed a similar approach, albeit utilizing locks for version updates. In recent years, significant research attention has been devoted to range queries and snapshot-based techniques built upon these foundational approaches.

In many contemporary applications, such as single-source shortest-path computations, reachability queries, and various approximation algorithms, there is a pressing demand for wait-free partial snapshots. These applications often require targeted access to specific portions of a graph rather than its entirety. Traditional snapshot methods, while effective for full graph access, fall short when precision and efficiency in partial graph access are paramount. Given this context, there is a clear gap in the current landscape of snapshot algorithms. To address this, we propose a wait-free snapshot(partial and full) algorithm to provide efficient, targeted access while ensuring concurrent operations remain unhindered. We have integrated the multi-version concurrency control concept from Wei et al. [27] into our graph implementation to achieve wait-free partial snapshots.

Our Contribution: This paper presents the design and implementation of a dynamic versioned graph data structure. Our graph data structure offers full dynamism, enabling concurrent lock-free point operations. It also incorporates the capability to perform wait-free graph set operations. The contributions of this work are summarized below:

- For a directed Graph $G = (V, E)$, we present an Abstract Data Type (ADT) in Sect. 3.1.
- The data structure component of our graph implementation is described in Sect. 3.2.
- Our implementation of the ADT operations is discussed in Sect. 4.
- A comparison of our implementation with its counterparts is provided in Sect. 5. The code is available at https://github.com/PDCRL/VersionConcGraph.git.

2 Preliminaries and Background

Our implementation adheres to a conventional shared memory model, where a finite set of processors is accessible by a defined number of threads operating asynchronously. These threads interact by executing operations on shared objects and obtaining corresponding responses. The system is equipped with support for atomic read, write, and compare-and-swap (CAS) instructions.

We have devised a versioned graph data structure modeled after Chatterjee et al. [4], where vertices and edges are organized in an adjacency list format. Vertices are stored within a concurrent lock-free hash table [21], while edges are managed using a concurrent lock-free linked list [9]. To ensure consistency in graph analytics operations, we have integrated the concept of versioning from Wei et al. [27]. In addition to supporting graph point operations as described in [4], our implementation extends its capabilities to encompass various wait-free graph set operations, using partial and full snapshots of the graph.

Pseudocode Convention: The pseudocode featuring the Algorithm is outlined in Algorithm 1.1, 1.2, 1.3, 1.4, 1.5, 1.6, 1.7, and 1.8. Throughout this paper, the pseudocode is crafted using a blend of C and JAVA-style programming languages. For accessing the member field x of a class object pointer P, we utilize the notation P.x. To convey multiple variables returned from an operation, we adopt the notation $\langle x_1, x_2, ..., x_n \rangle$.

3 Graph Data Structure

3.1 The Abstract Data Type (ADT)

We focus on implementing a simple directed weighted graph, denoted as $G = (V, E)$, where V denotes the set of vertices and E denotes the set of directed edges (ordered pairs of vertices). Each edge connects an ordered pair of vertices from V and is associated with a weight. Every vertex $v \in V$ is linked to an immutable and unique key $k \in K$, where K is a totally ordered set. A vertex $v \in V$ with key k is represented as $v(k)$. The notation $e(k, l, w)$ is used to indicate an edge from $v(k)$ to $v(l)$ in the set E with weight w.

ADT operation on G is defined below. The graph point operations are first described.

1. ADDVERTEX(k) adds a vertex $v(k)$ in V if $v(k) \notin V$ and returns "VERTEX ADDED" otherwise returns "VERTEX ALREADY PRESENT".
2. REMOVEVERTEX(k) removes the vertex $v(k)$ from V if $v(k) \in V$ and returns "VERTEX REMOVED" otherwise returns "VERTEX NOT PRESENT".
3. ADDEDGE(i,j,w) adds an edge $e(i, j, w)$ in E if $e(i, j, w) \notin E$ and returns "EDGE ADDED" otherwise returns "EDGE ALREADY PRESENT".
4. REMOVE(i, j) removes the edge $e(i, j)$ from E if $e(i, j) \in E$, and returns "EDGE REMOVED"; otherwise, it returns "EDGE NOT PRESENT".

5. CONTAINSVERTEX(k) returns "VERTEX PRESENT " if $v(k) \in V$ otherwise returns "VERTEX NOT PRESENT ".
6. CONTAINSEDGE(i,j) returns "EDGE PRESENT " if $e(i,j,w) \in E$ otherwise returns "EDGE NOT PRESENT ".

We now describe the set operations implemented by us.

7. BFS (v) returns sequence of vertices in the BFS order if $v \in V$ otherwise returns "VERTEX NOT PRESENT ";
8. SSSP (v) returns set of all the vertices along with the distance δ from v such that $\forall u \in V \wedge$ u is connected to v $\delta(u)$ is the minimum total weight of any directed path from v to u.
9. SNAPSHOT returns the consistent snapshot of the graph.

While we have only delved into a subset of graph set operations within our ADT, it's important to note that our implementation is equipped to handle a wide array of such operations. The approach for these operations is akin to those we have discussed, as they rely on the partial or dynamic snapshot of the graph. This versatility allows our implementation to adapt to various graph-related tasks beyond those explicitly mentioned seamlessly.

3.2 Graph Data Structure Components

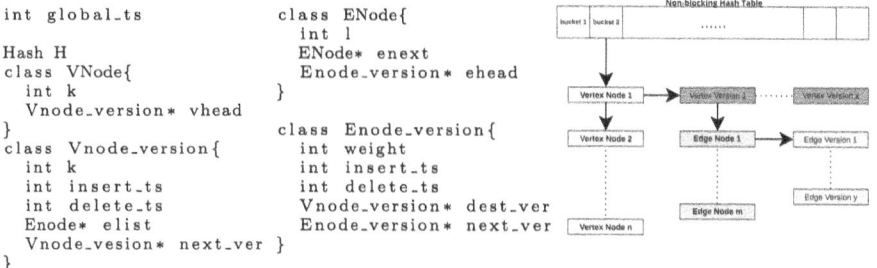

Fig. 1. Graph Datastructure Components.

In our implementation, we have maintained vertices, denoted as Vnode, within a concurrent resizable hash table H [21]. Each Vnode maintains a list of versions, documenting the history of a specific vertex through a pointer variable known as vhead. Every version of a vertex, referred to as Vnode_version, records the vertex's history by capturing both the insert and delete timestamp of that version. These timestamps facilitate the determination of the time span during which a particular vertex was active. Vnode_version node in the version lists are maintained in the descending order of their insert timestamp where pointer next_ver points to the next version available. These versions ensure that a new entry is not appended to the list unless the delete timestamp of the preceding version is established, thus preserving the sequential order.

Additionally, each `Vnode_version` maintains a list of all outgoing edges in the form of a linked list, with the individual edges represented as `Enode` nodes. Similar to `Vnode`, we adopt a versioning approach to track the history of edges. Each edge version list is comprised of `Enode_version` nodes, where each `Enode_version` captures both the insert timestamp and the delete timestamp of that specific version. Notably, each `Enode_version` also preserves a pointer to the corresponding destination vertex version node, simplifying graph traversal.

Additionally, we have a global shared counter $global\_ts$ to track the current timestamp of the data structure. Whenever a graph update occurs, $global\_ts$ is used to record the timestamp of the update. This enables us to pinpoint precisely when a particular data element was active within the data structure. Furthermore, each time a graph set operation commences, the system atomically fetches and increments this global timestamp. This mechanism allows us to examine all vertices and edges that existed during that specific timespan. For more details, please refer to Fig. 1.

4 Algorithm Description and Reasoning

This section will elaborate on the various ADT operations discussed in Sect. 3.1. As previously mentioned, our data structure utilizes an adjacency list where vertices are stored in a lock-free concurrent Hash Table. Each vertex is managed within a bucket in the Hash Table, and the outgoing edges are organized in the form of a lock-free linked list as shown in Fig. 1.

The initiation of any ADT operation involves a search for the vertex within the hash table. The hash table comprises buckets containing vertices arranged in an unsorted linked list. When searching for a vertex, it traverses the complete list of vertices within the relevant bucket. Adding a vertex not currently present in the vertex list of its bucket is achieved atomically by placing it at the head of the linked list. This ensures a streamlined and efficient addition process. Furthermore, our approach incorporates versioning when removing a vertex from the linked list. During removal, we set the delete_ts (delete timestamp) for the vertex, applying a version control concept for effective data structure management.

```
1:  AddVertex(i)
2:      curr_Vnode ← H.FindV(i)
3:      if (curr_Vnode = nullptr) then
4:          newVnode = new VNODE(i)
5:          if (H.INSERT (newVnode) ) then
6:              SETTS(newVnode)
7:              return VERTEX ADDED
8:          else
9:              return VERTEX ALREADY PRESENT
10:     else
11:         curr_ver ← READ(curr_Vnode.vhead)
12:         if (curr_ver.delete_ts = ∞) then
13:             return VERTEX ALREADY PRESENT
14:             SETTS(curr_ver)
15:             new_ver = new VNODE_VERSION(i)
16:             if (cas(curr_Vnode.vhead, curr_ver, new_ver))
                then
17:                 SETTS(new_vesion)
18:                 return VERTEX ADDED
19:         else VERTEX ALREADY PRESENT
```

Algorithm 1.1. ADDVERTEX Operation.

4.1 Lock-Free Vertex Operations

AddVertex operation is given in lines 1 to 19 in Algorithm 1.1. The `FindV` method, denoted at line 2, conducts a search for the vertex in the Hash Table and returns the corresponding *VNode* if the vertex is present; otherwise, it returns *nullptr*. If the vertex is not found in the Hash Table, a new *VNode* is created at line 4, and an attempt is made to insert it into the Hash Table at line 5.

In the case where the insert operation fails, it implies that another concurrent thread has successfully inserted the *VNode* into the Hash table, and it simply returns "VERTEX ALREADY PRESENT " at line 9. On the other hand, if the insertion of the *VNode* into the hash table is successful, the timestamp of the newly inserted *VNode* is set at line 6. Finally, the operation concludes by returning "VERTEX ADDED " at line 7.

```
20: RemoveVertex(i)                          28:         setTs(curr_ver)
21:    curr_Vnode ← H.FindV(i)               29:         return VERTEX REMOVED
22:    if (curr_Vnode = nullptr) then        30:     else
23:        return VERTEX NOT PRESENT         31:         setTs(curr_ver)
24:    else                                  32:         return VERTEX NOT PRESENT
25:        curr_ver ← read(curr_Vnode.vhead) 33:     else
26:        if (curr_ver.delete_ts = ∞) then  34:         setTs(curr_ver)
27:            if (cas(curr_ver.delete_ts,∞,−1)) 35:     return VERTEX NOT PRESENT
       then
```

Algorithm 1.2. RemoveVertex Operation.

```
36: ContainsVertex(i)                        42:     if (curr_ver.delete_ts = ∞) then
37:    curr_Vnode ← H.FindV(i)               43:         return VERTEX PRESENT
38:    if (curr_Vnode = nullptr) then        44:     else
39:        return VERTEX NOT PRESENT         45:         setTs(curr_ver)
40:    else                                  46:         return VERTEX NOT PRESENT
41:        curr_ver ← read(curr_Vnode.vhead)
```

Algorithm 1.3. ContainsVertex Operation.

If the vertex is already present in the Hash Table, the `FindV` method returns the corresponding *VNode*. It proceeds to read the current version from the version list of the *VNode* associated with the vertex, located at its *vhead*. If the *delete_ts* (delete timestamp) of the current version is set to ∞, it indicates that the vertex exists, and we can return "VERTEX ALREADY PRESENT " at line 13.

However, if the delete timestamp suggests that the vertex has been marked for deletion, we set the timestamp of the version at line 14 (if not already set) using method setTs (given in Algorithm 1.8) and initiate the creation of a new version. By trying to set the *delete_ts*, the AddVertex is helping the RemoveVertex method. Subsequently, an attempt is made to atomically add the newly created vertex version to the head of the version list using `CAS` at line 16. Upon a successful `CAS` operation, the timestamp (*insert_ts*) for the newly added vertex version is set to the current global timestamp, and the operation returns "VERTEX ADDED ". In the event of a `CAS` operation failure, signifying

Concurrent Wait-Free Graph Snapshots Using Multi-versioning 39

```
47: AddEdge(i, j, w)                              64:          return EDGE ALREADY PRESENT
48:   ⟨sv, dv⟩ ← H.FindVplus(i, j)               65:          n_Ever ← new Enode_
49:   if (sv ∨ dv) then                                       version(dv, w)
50:      return VERTEX NOT PRESENT               66:          if (cas(c_Enode.vhead, c_Ever,
51:   else                                                       n_Ever)) then
52:      c_ENode ← sv.FindE(j)                   67:             setTs(c_Enode)
53:      if (c_ENode = nullptr) then             68:          else goto Insert Version
54:         n_Enode ← new Enode(j, d_ver, w)     69:          if (sv.delete_ts ≠ ∞) then
55:         if (sv.insert(n_Enode)) then         70:             setTs(sv)
56:            setTs(n_Enode)                    71:             if (sv.delete_ts < n_Ever.
57:         else                                              insert_ts) then
58:            c_ENode ← sv.FindE(j)             72:                return VERTEX NOT PRESENT
59:            goto Insert Version               73:          if (dv.delete_ts ≠ ∞) then
60:      else                                    74:             setTs(dv)
61:         Insert Version:                      75:             if (dv.delete_ts < n_Ever.
62:         c_Ever ← READ](c_Enode.vhead)                     insert_ts) then
63:         if (c_Ever.delete_ts = ∞             76:                return VERTEX NOT PRESENT
             ∧ c_Ever.weight = w) then           77:          return EDGE ADDED
```

Algorithm 1.4. AddEdge Operation.

that another concurrent thread has successfully added the version, the operation concludes by returning "VERTEX ALREADY PRESENT "at line 19.

RemoveVertex operation is detailed from lines 20 to 35 in Algorithm 1.2. Utilizing a multi-versioning approach for consistent snapshots, this operation refrains from physically deleting a vertex. Instead, it marks the active version as deleted by setting the delete timestamp ($delete\_ts$). Following a similar pattern to AddVertex, this operation commences by locating the vertex in the hash table.

If the vertex is not present in the hash table, the operation promptly returns "VERTEX NOT PRESENT "at line 23. In the event that the vertex is found in the Hash Table, it examines the $curr\_ver$ (current version) on the version list of the corresponding $VNode$. If the $delete\_ts$ of the $curr\_ver$ is not set to ∞, indicating that the vertex exists. Setting the $delete\_ts$ undergoes a two-step process. Initially, it is atomically set to -1 using the CAS operation at line 27, signaling to other threads that this version is marked for deletion. Subsequently, the $delete\_ts$ is set to the current global timestamp at line 28, and the operation returns "VERTEX REMOVED "at line 29.

```
78: RemoveEdge(i, j)                             92:          cas(c_Ever.delete_ts, ∞, −1)
79:   ⟨sv, dv⟩ ← H.FindVplus(i, j)               93:          setTs(c_Ever)
80:   if (sv ∨ dv) then                          94:          if (sv.delete_ts ≠ ∞) then
81:      return VERTEX NOT PRESENT               95:             setTs(sv)
82:   else                                       96:             if (sv.delete_ts < c_Ever.delete_ts)
83:      c_ENode ← sv.FindE(j)                                then
84:      if (c_ENode = nullptr) then             97:                return VERTEX NOT PRESENT
85:         return EDGE NOT PRESENT              98:             if (dv.delete_ts ≠ ∞) then
86:      else                                    99:                setTs(dv)
87:         c_Ever ← READ(c_Enode.vhead)         100:               if (dv.delete_ts < c_Ever.delete_ts)
88:         if (c_Ever.delete_ts ≠ ∞) then                    then
89:            setTs(c_Enode)                    101:               return VERTEX NOT PRESENT
90:            return EDGE NOT PRESENT           102:         return EDGE REMOVED
91:         else
```

Algorithm 1.5. RemoveEdge Operation.

If the CAS operation fails, implying that another concurrent thread has set the $delete\_ts$ to -1, the operation proceeds to set the timestamp for the current version and returns "VERTEX NOT PRESENT" at line 32. Similarly, if the $delete\_ts$ of the current version is not ∞, indicating that it is already marked for deletion, the $delete\_ts$ is set to the current global timestamp, and the operation returns "VERTEX NOT PRESENT" at line 35.

ContainsVertex operation is given in line 36 to 46. Upon invocation, it yields "VERTEX PRESENT" if the vertex is indeed present; conversely, it yields "VERTEX NOT PRESENT" if the vertex is absent.

The algorithm first seeks the corresponding $Vnode$ for the vertex within the Hash table at line 37. Should the vertex not be found in the Hash Table, indicating its absence, the algorithm promptly returns "VERTEX NOT PRESENT" at line 39. Conversely, if the $Vnode$ is found within the Hash Table, the algorithm proceeds to check whether the deletion timestamp ($delete\_ts$) for the current version ($curr\_ver$) of the vertex is set. In the event that the timestamp is not set, denoting that the vertex has not been deleted, the algorithm concludes by returning "VERTEX PRESENT". Conversely, if the timestamp is set, implying the vertex has been deleted, the algorithm updates the timestamp at line 45 and then returns "VERTEX NOT PRESENT".

4.2 Lock-Free Edge Operations

AddEdge is described in Algorithm 1.4, facilitates the addition of an edge between vertices i and j with weight w. It begins by inspecting the vertices in the Hash Table at line 48 using the `FindVplus` method. This method retrieves the latest vertex version for both the source and destination vertices if their delete timestamps are not set. If either vertex is not present or their deletion timestamp is already set, indicating deletion, the operation returns `nullptr` and "VERTEX NOT PRESENT" is returned at line 50.

If both source and destination vertices exist in the Hash Table, the algorithm checks if the $ENode$ for the destination vertex exists in the edge lists of the source vertex. The `FindE` method returns the $ENode$ for an outgoing edge to the destination vertex at line 52; otherwise, it returns `nullptr`. If no $ENode$ exists for the destination vertex, a new $ENode$ is created and atomically inserted into the edge list at line 55. Upon successful insertion, the timestamp for the newly added edge is set at line 56. If the insertion fails due to concurrent modification by another thread, the algorithm attempts to find the $ENode$ for the destination vertex again in the edge list at line 58, and proceeds to add a new edge version node on the newly found $ENode$.

Once the $Enode$ for the destination vertex is found in the edge list, we find its latest edge version. If the delete timestamp of the latest edge version is not set and the weight is also equal to the current weight, we simply return "EDGE ALREADY PRESENT" at line 64. Otherwise, it creates a new edge version node at line 65 and atomically adds the new version on the vhead of $Enode$ using CAS. If CAS succeeds, then it sets the timestamp at line 67. If the CAS fails, then some other thread must have added a new version and we retry adding a new version from line 61.

```
103:  ContainsEdge(i, j)                        115:          return EDGE NOT PRESENT
104:      ⟨sv, dv⟩ ← H.FindVplus(i, j)          116:      if (sv.delete_ts ≠ ∞) then
105:      if (sv ∨ dv) then                     117:          setTs(sv)
106:          return VERTEX NOT PRESENT         118:          if (sv.delete_ts < c_Ever.insert_ts)
107:      else                                             then
108:          c_ENode ← sv.FindE(j)             119:              return VERTEX NOT PRESENT
109:          if (c_ENode = nullptr) then       120:      if (dv.delete_ts ≠ ∞) then
110:              return EDGE NOT PRESENT       121:          setTs(dv)
111:          else                              122:          if (dv.delete_ts < c_Ever.insert_ts)
112:              c_Ever ← read(c_Enode.vhead)           then
113:              if (c_Ever.delete_ts ≠ ∞) then 123:              return VERTEX NOT PRESENT
114:                  setTs(c_Ever)             124:      return EDGE PRESENT
```

Algorithm 1.6. ContainsEdge Operation.

Upon a successful CAS operation, it's possible that either the source or destination vertex has already been deleted prior to the insertion of the edge. In such scenarios, we verify whether the delete timestamp for the source and destination vertices is already set or not, as indicated in lines 69 and 73, respectively. If either the source or destination vertex is already deleted, we examine whether the delete timestamp of the vertex is less than the insertion timestamp of the edge. In this situation, we can infer that the edge was added after the deletion of a vertex, and therefore, we simply return "VERTEX NOT PRESENT "without altering the newly added edge.

If the delete timestamp of the vertex is the same as the edge insertion timestamp, we can linearize the edge's insertion just before the vertex's deletion. Conversely, if the delete timestamp of the vertex is greater than the insert timestamp of the edge, we can conclude that the vertex was deleted after the insertion of the edge, and thus, we return "EDGE ADDED ". In cases where the delete timestamp of the vertex is not set, indicating the vertex still exists, the addition of the edge is deemed successful.

RemoveEdge method, is described in Algorithm 1.5, serves to eliminate the edge connecting the source vertex and the destination vertex from the graph, should it exist. Analogous to the AddEdge operation, RemoveEdge begins by searching for the source and destination vertices, returning "VERTEX NOT PRESENT "if either vertex is absent. Subsequently, it locates the ENode corresponding to the destination vertex in the edge list of the source vertex. If the ENode is absent, it signifies that the edge does not exist. Conversely, if the ENode is present, RemoveEdge examines the delete timestamp of the latest version. If the delete timestamp is already set, indicating that the edge has been deleted, "EDGE NOT PRESENT "is returned. Otherwise, the delete timestamp is initially set to −1, followed by setting it to the current global timestamp.

Following the setting of the delete timestamp of the edge, RemoveEdge verifies whether the source or destination vertex has been deleted. If either vertex has been deleted, it checks whether the deletion occurred before the edge deletion. In such a scenario, "VERTEX NOT PRESENT "is returned; otherwise, "EDGE REMOVED "is returned.

ContainsEdge method, detailed in Algorithm 1.6, is designed to determine the presence of an edge and retrieve its weight if it exists. Similar to preceding edge-related methods, it begins by verifying the presence of both the source and destination vertices. If either vertex is not found, the method promptly returns "VERTEX NOT PRESENT ". Subsequently, it checks the presence of the edge itself. If the edge is not found, "EDGE NOT PRESENT "is returned.

In the event that the edge is indeed present, CONTAINSEDGE further ensures that neither the source vertex nor the destination vertex has been concurrently deleted before the edge was added, as indicated by checking the timestamp of the deleted vertex. If such deletion is detected, "VERTEX NOT PRESENT "is returned to indicate that the edge cannot be accessed due to the deletion of one of its vertices. Otherwise, the weight of the edge is returned as expected.

```
125: BFS(i)                                136:     top ← Q.POP()
126:   ts ← GETTS()                        137:     c_edge ← top.enext
127:   ⟨v_ver⟩ ← H.FindVplus(i, ts)        138:     while c_edge do
128:   if (v_ver = nullptr) then           139:       e_ver ← FINDEV(c_edge, ts)
129:     return VERTEX NOT PRESENT         140:       if (e_ver) then
130:   else                                141:         d_v ← e_ver.dest_ver
131:     queue⟨Vnode_version⟩ Q            142:         if (d_v.k ∉ bfs_l) then
132:     list bfs_l                        143:           bfs_l.INSERT(d_v.k)
133:     bfs_l.INSERT(v_ver.k)             144:           Q.PUSH(d_v)
134:     Q.INSERT(v_ver)                   145:       c_edge ← c_edge.enext
135:     while (!Q.EMPTY()) do             146:     return bfs_l
```

Algorithm 1.7. BFS Operation.

4.3 Wait-Free Graph Set Operation

All graph set operations, such as SSSP, BFS, SNAPSHOT, GETPATH, leverage the versioning mechanism previously discussed. Consequently, an atomic fetch and increment operation is performed on the global timestamp before initiating any graph set operation. Subsequently, the operation traverses through the vertices or edges that were active during the timestamp retrieved, ensuring a consistent snapshot. Due to space constraints, we focus solely on discussing the BFS operation in this paper, as the remaining graph set operations follow a similar approach.

```
147: setTs(Vnode_version v)                155: read(Vnode_version v)
148:   c_ver ← v.head                      156:   if (v.insert_ts = −1 ∨ v.delete_ts = −1)
149:   if (c_ver.insert_ts = −1) then             then
150:     ts ← global_ts                    157:     SETTS(v)
151:     cas(c_ver.insert_ts, −1, ts)      158:   return v
152:   if (c_ver.delete_ts = −1) then      159: getTS()
153:     ts ← global_ts                    160:   ts ← global_ts
154:     cas(c_ver.delete_ts, −1, ts)      161:   cas(global_ts, ts, ts + 1)
                                           162:   return ts
```

Algorithm 1.8. Pseudocode of SETTS, READ and GETTS Operation.

BFS. This method systematically explores a graph's vertices reachable from a specified source vertex in BFS (Breadth-First Search) order. Commencing with the GETTS operation at line 126, the algorithm initiates an atomic fetch and increment operation on the global timestamp. The retrieved timestamp, denoted as t, serves as the reference point for collecting all vertices and edges existing at that particular timestamp.

The FINDVPLUS method returns an active version of the source vertex (if it exists) based on the timestamp t. If no vertex version is identified, it gracefully returns nullptr, signaling a non-existent vertex version. The algorithm then proceeds to create a queue that encapsulates all the vertex version nodes requiring traversal, commencing from the source vertex node. Simultaneously, a list is instantiated to track the order in which vertices are traversed during the BFS exploration.

The algorithm strategically dequeues elements one by one, inspecting all edges present at timestamp t. It appends the destination vertices of these edges to the queue and to the BFS list if they have not been visited previously. This process continues until the queue is empty, indicating the completion of the BFS traversal. Subsequently, the algorithm returns the list of vertices traversed during the BFS exploration.

4.4 Memory Management

We have leveraged the concept of multi-version concurrency control [19] to execute consistent snapshots efficiently. As the number of update operations escalates, the count of version nodes in the graph increases as well. This often results in storing versions that far are too old to serve any useful purpose, thus leading to bloating of memory. To address this challenge, we have integrated **DEBRA** [3], a lock-free memory reclamation algorithm, into our solution. Our implementation meticulously tracks ongoing graph-set operations by threads along with their timestamps. This enables us to identify outdated versions within the graph's history and reclaim those versions accordingly, thereby ensuring optimal memory utilization.

5 Evaluations

Experimental Setup. Our experimentation took place on a system equipped with an AMD EPYC 7452 CPU housing 64 cores, featuring a clock speed spectrum ranging from 1.5 GHz to 2.3 GHz. Each core operates with two logical threads and possesses exclusive 32KB L1 data and instruction caches. Collaboratively, core pairs share a 512KB L2 cache and a substantial 16MB L3 cache. The system's robust configuration extends to 252GB of RAM and a 2TB hard disk. Running on Ubuntu 18.04.6 LTS. The code, compiled using g++ 11.1.0 with -std=c++17, is intricately linked with pthread and atomic libraries. Our methodology involves averaging results from multiple runs, with a strategic cache pre-warming during the initial iterations.[1]

---

[1] The code is available at https://github.com/PDCRL/VersionConcGraph.git.

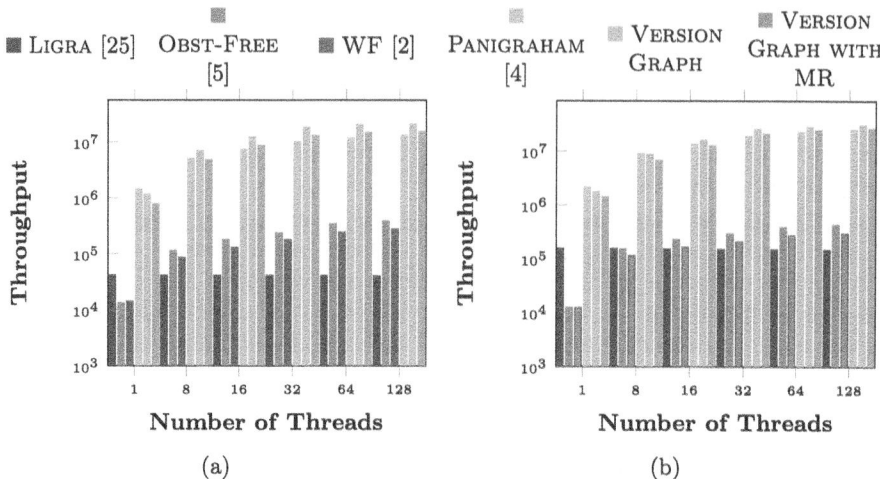

Fig. 2. Performance of our implementation compared to its counterparts for point operations. x-axis: Number of threads. y-axis: Throughput. a) Update Heavy Workload, b) Read Heavy Workload.

In each experiment, we initialize the data structure with input vertices and edges of wiki-vote [1] dataset. Subsequently, we generate a random permutation for ADT point operations and graph set operations. The distribution is over the following ordered set of operations: ADDVERTEX, REMOVEVERTEX, CONTAINSVERTEX, ADDEDGE, REMOVEEDGE, CONTAINSEDGE. Specifically:

1. Read Heavy Workload: 3%, 2%, 45%, 3%, 2%, 45%
2. Update Heavy Workload: 12%, 13%, 25%, 13%, 12%, 25%, 2%

For graph set operations, the distribution equally samples from all other point operations.

Algorithms: We have conducted a comparative analysis between our versioned graph algorithm and several state-of-the-art graph algorithms, including: (a) LIGRA [25] (b) Obstruction Free Graph Snapshot (OBST-FREE) [5], (c) Wait-free Graph Snapshot (WF) [2], (d) PANIGRAHAM [4]. We aimed to encompass all algorithms that are fully dynamic, allowing concurrent addition and removal of vertices and edges. We chose not to compare our results with GraphOne [18], as Panigraham [4] significantly outperforms it.

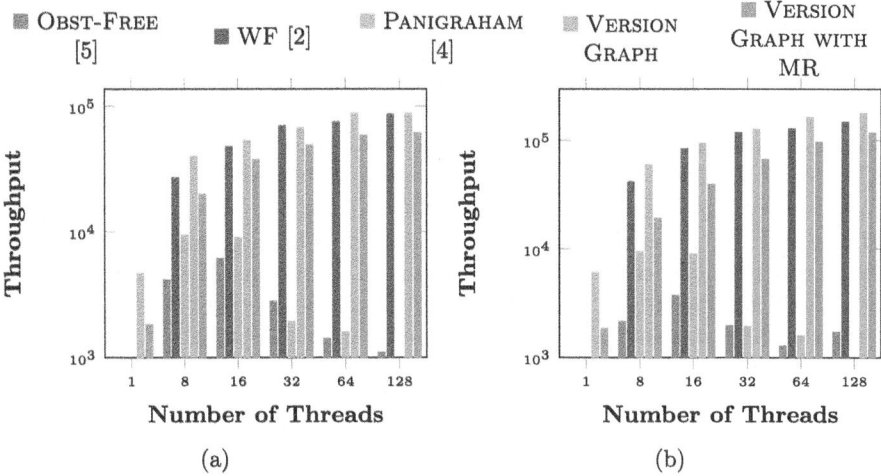

Fig. 3. Performance of our implementation compared to its counterparts for complete snapshot operation. x-axis: Number of threads. y-axis: Throughput. a) Update Heavy Workload with complete Snapshot, b) Read Heavy Workload with complete snapshot.

Memory Management imposes a substantial overhead on the performance of lock-free data structures. Interestingly, some of the algorithms we compared with did not incorporate any memory reclamation technique. Thus, in our results, we present findings for both scenarios: with and without memory reclamation.

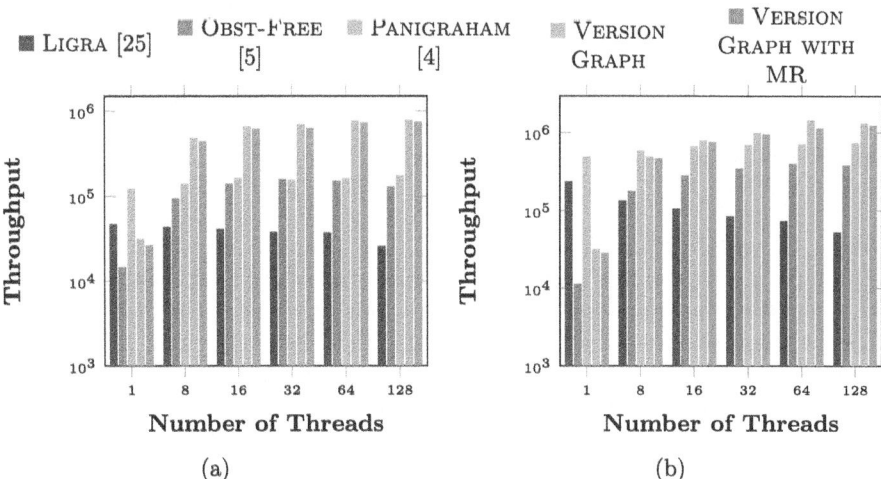

Fig. 4. Performance of our implementation compared to its counterparts for BFS operation. x-axis: Number of threads. y-axis: Throughput. a) Update Heavy Workload with BFS, b) Read Heavy Workload with BFS.

Graph Point Operation. In our comparative analysis, we assessed our implementation for point operations against state-of-the-art algorithms in Fig. 2. Despite the overhead of maintaining versions, our VERSION GRAPH algorithm demonstrated superior performance compared to its counterparts. It outperformed all other algorithms except PANIGRAHAM [4], by a large degree of magnitude. However, when compared to PANIGRAHAM [4], VERSION GRAPH showcased a noteworthy improvement, achieving a 20% higher throughput. Furthermore, our loss in throughput due to garbage collection remained minimal, especially considering the absence of concurrent graph-set operations. We conducted comparisons with and without memory reclamation, considering that many of our counterparts do not employ any memory reclamation techniques.

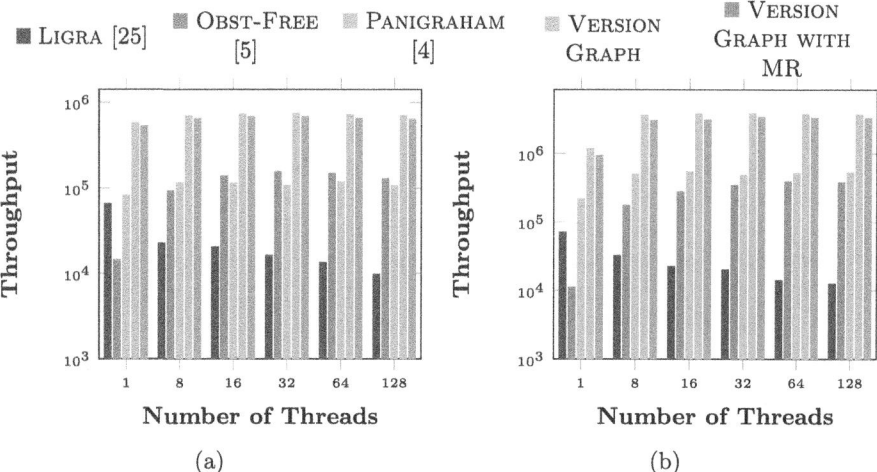

Fig. 5. Performance of our implementation compared to its counterparts for SSSP operation. x-axis: Number of threads. y-axis: Throughput. a) Update Heavy Workload with SSSP, b) Read Heavy Workload with SSSP.

Graph Complete Snapshot Operation. The complete snapshot operation of a graph plays a crucial role in concurrent graph processing, particularly for tasks like calculating Betweenness Centrality, All Pair Shortest Path, Diameter, etc. This operation enables efficient execution of such tasks by providing a consistent view of the graph. We have compared our implementation with its counterparts for a complete snapshot in Fig. 3. Our implementation of the complete snapshot operation showcased remarkable performance compared to its obstruction-free counterparts, exhibiting a superiority with a large degree of magnitude. Notably, without memory reclamation, our multi-version graph surpassed WF [2] by a significant margin of 20%, primarily attributable to the substantial overhead of graph construction. While we incurred some performance loss due to memory reclamation, it's important to note that we compared our implementation without memory reclamation against counterparts as all its counterparts lack memory reclamation mechanism.

Graph Set Operation with Partial Snapshot. In Figs. 4 and 5, we compared our implementation against counterparts in terms of graph set operations like BFS and SSSP. Leveraging the wait-free nature of our algorithm and others being obstruction-free, we managed to surpass them in performance with a significant degree of magnitude. Notably, with a single thread, the obstruction-free variants exhibited superior performance compared to the wait-free version, owing to the absence of obstructions. However, as the number of threads increased, the performance of the obstruction-free algorithm declined due to an escalation in obstructions.

6 Conclusion

In our implementation, we introduce a novel approach to concurrent graph processing, incorporating a wait-free mechanism for both partial and complete snapshots using multi-version concurrency control. Our algorithm ensures lock-free execution for all point operations and wait-free performance for graph analytics operations, surpassing its counterparts by a significant margin. Notably, our implementation marks the first instance of a wait-free partial snapshot operation in graph processing. However, the current implementation performs point operation lock-free, so making it wait-free is another future work.

Funding Information. The work is partially funded by SERB, GoI research project: CRG/2022/009391.

References

1. SNAP Stanford network analysis project: wiki-vote dataset. https://snap.stanford.edu/data/wiki-Vote.html. Accessed Mar 2024
2. Bhardwaj, G., Peri, S., Shetty, P.: Brief announcement: non-blocking dynamic unbounded graphs with wait-free snapshot. In: Dolev, S., Schieber, B. (eds.) International Symposium on Stabilizing, Safety, and Security of Distributed Systems, pp. 106–110. Springer, Cham (2023). https://doi.org/10.1007/978-3-031-44274-2_9
3. Brown, T.A.: Reclaiming memory for lock-free data structures: there has to be a better way. In: Proceedings of the 2015 ACM Symposium on Principles of Distributed Computing, pp. 261–270 (2015)
4. Chatterjee, B., Peri, S., Sa, M., Manogna, K.: Non-blocking dynamic unbounded graphs with worst-case amortized bounds. In: International Conference on Principles of Distributed Systems (2021)
5. Chatterjee, B., Peri, S., Sa, M., Singhal, N.: A simple and practical concurrent non-blocking unbounded graph with linearizable reachability queries. In: ICDCN 2019, Bangalore, India, January 04-07, 2019, pp. 168–177 (2019)
6. Chatterjee, B., Walulya, I., Tsigas, P.: Help-optimal and language-portable lock-free concurrent data structures. In: ICPP, pp. 360–369 (2016)

7. Chaudhary, V.P., Juyal, C., Kulkarni, S., Kumari, S., Peri, S.: Achieving starvation-freedom in multi-version transactional memory systems. In: Atig, M.F., Schwarzmann, A.A. (eds.) NETYS 2019. LNCS, vol. 11704, pp. 291–310. Springer, Cham (2019). https://doi.org/10.1007/978-3-030-31277-0_20
8. Feng, G., et al: Risgraph: a real-time streaming system for evolving graphs to support sub-millisecond per-update analysis at millions ops/s. In: Proceedings of the 2021 International Conference on Management of Data, pp. 513–527 (2021)
9. Harris, T.L.: A pragmatic implementation of non-blocking linked-lists. In: DISC, pp. 300–314 (2001)
10. Heller, S., Herlihy, M., Luchangco, V., Moir, M., Scherer III, W.N., Shavit, N.: A lazy concurrent list-based set algorithm. Parallel Process. Lett. **17**(4), 411–424 (2007)
11. Hendler, D., Shavit, N., Yerushalmi, L.: A scalable lock-free stack algorithm. J. Parallel Distrib. Comput. **70**(1), 1–12 (2010)
12. Herlihy, M.: Wait-free synchronization. ACM Trans. Program. Lang. Syst. **13**(1), 124–149 (1991)
13. Herlihy, M., Luchangco, V., Moir, M.: Obstruction-free synchronization: double-ended queues as an example. In: ICDCS, pp. 522–529 (2003)
14. Herlihy, M., Shavit, N.: On the nature of progress. In: OPODIS, pp. 313–328 (2011)
15. Herlihy, M.P., Wing, J.M.: Linearizability: a correctness condition for concurrent objects. ACM Trans. Program. Lang. Syst. (TOPLAS) **12**(3), 463–492 (1990)
16. Kallimanis, N.D., Kanellou, E.: Wait-free concurrent graph objects with dynamic traversals. In: OPODIS, pp. 1–27 (2015)
17. Kogan, A., Petrank, E.: Wait-free queues with multiple enqueuers and dequeuers. In: PPOPP, pp. 223–234 (2011)
18. Kumar, P., Huang, H.H.: Graphone: a data store for real-time analytics on evolving graphs. ACM Trans. Storage (TOS) **15**(4), 1–40 (2020)
19. Kumar, P., Peri, S., Vidyasankar, K.: A timestamp based multi-version STM algorithm. In: ICDCN, pp. 212–226 (2014)
20. Ladan-Mozes, E., Shavit, N.: An optimistic approach to lock-free FIFO queues. Distrib. Comput. **20**(5), 323–341 (2008)
21. Liu, Y., Zhang, K., Spear, M.: Dynamic-sized nonblocking hash tables. In: PODC, pp. 242–251 (2014)
22. Michael, M.M.: High performance dynamic lock-free hash tables and list-based sets. In: SPAA, pp. 73–82 (2002)
23. Nelson, J., Hassan, A., Palmieri, R.: Bundled references: an abstraction for highly-concurrent linearizable range queries. In: Proceedings of the 26th ACM SIGPLAN Symposium on Principles and Practice of Parallel Programming, pp. 448–450 (2021)
24. Petrank, E., Timnat, S.: Lock-free data-structure iterators. In: International Symposium on Distributed Computing (2013)
25. Shun, J., Blelloch, G.E.: Ligra: a lightweight graph processing framework for shared memory. SIGPLAN Not. **48**(8), 135–146 (2013). https://doi.org/10.1145/2517327.2442530
26. Timnat, S., Braginsky, A., Kogan, A., Petrank, E.: Wait-free linked-lists. In: OPODIS, pp. 330–344 (2012)
27. Wei, Y., Ben-David, N., Blelloch, G.E., Fatourou, P., Ruppert, E., Sun, Y.: Constant-time snapshots with applications to concurrent data structures. In: Proceedings of the 26th ACM SIGPLAN Symposium on Principles and Practice of Parallel Programming, pp. 31–46 (2021)

28. Weikum, G., Vossen, G.: Transactional Information Systems: Theory, Algorithms, and the Practice of Concurrency Control and Recovery. Morgan Kaufmann (2002)
29. Zhang, K., Zhao, Y., Yang, Y., Liu, Y., Spear, M.F.: Practical non-blocking unordered lists. In: DISC, pp. 239–253 (2013)

Challenger: Blockchain-based Massively Multiplayer Online Game Architecture

Boris Chan Yip Hon[✉], Bilel Zaghdoudi, Maria Potop-Butucaru, Sébastien Tixeuil, and Serge Fdida

Sorbonne Universite, CNRS, LIP6, 75005 Paris, France
{boris.hon,bilel.zaghdoudi,maria.potop-butucaru,sebastien.tixeuil, serge.fdida}@lip6.fr

Abstract. We propose Challenger a peer-to-peer blockchain-based middleware architecture for narrative games, and discuss its resilience to cheating attacks. Our architecture orchestrates nine services in a fully decentralized manner where nodes are not aware of the entire composition of the system nor its size. All these components are orchestrated together to obtain (strong) resilience to cheaters. The main contribution of the paper is to provide, for the first time, an architecture for narrative games agnostic of a particular blockchain that brings together several distinct research areas, namely distributed ledgers, peer-to-peer networks, multi-player-online games and resilience to attacks.

Keywords: multiplayer online games · peer-to-peer architecture · blockchain · cheating resilience

1 Introduction

A video game is an electronic game involving human-machine interaction and visual feedback. Multiplayer games feature players, either competing or collaborating in Player Versus Player or Player Versus Environment modes. Massively Multiplayer Online Games (e.g. World of Warcraft) support hundreds to thousands of players online, with or without direct interaction. Traditionally, these games were designed in a client-server mode. However, the scalability of this architecture becomes harder and harder to maintain because of the bottleneck points at the server level. To prevent this, game editors provision resources (e.g. bandwidth, hardware, replication facilities) to quickly absorb spikes in the number of players. To avoid the inherent cost of the provisioning peer-to-peer architectures have been recently explored. Their major advantage is the distribution of computational tasks across nodes, with each node serving as both server and client. Even though this design philosophy seemed to be the holy grail, P2P architectures became quickly the target of various attacks and cheating behaviours [16,23] at the game level, application level, or protocol level. For example, some attacks target the interruption of information dissemination having as a consequence confusing players about the game's current stage. Other attacks perform illegal game action hence allowing clients to unfairly manipulate the game state, bypassing its physical laws. Finally, unauthorized access to information yields to the exploitation of undisclosed information. Academic research struggled for decades to study and propose solutions for the cheating methods reviewed in [23]. Initial publications aim to enhance or devise algorithms for cheating detection, such as dead reckoning [22], area of interest in Emanuele et al. [3], and secure referee selection problem by Webb et al. [17]. Subsequent works [14,22] broaden the platforms including mobile devices. Additionally, advancements in signature protocols [8] and the introduction of new hybrid architectures (e.g. [11,12,22]) aim to address attack vectors through design improvements like trust between peers, information disclosure, and pair clustering. Recently, the resurgence of studies (e.g. [4,13]) on specific attack vectors has occurred through software utilization and artificial neural networks. Despite the prolific work on preventing cheating in multiplayer online games, cheating still prevails and evolves in online games. The recent advances in distributed ledgers opened a new direction of research interesting to be explored in the context of cheating detection and prevention in multiplayer online games. Blockchain technology is a decentralized product of distributed systems, featuring consensus mechanisms, immutability, security, data persistence, transparency, and scalability.

2 Related Work

Since the publication of the seminal papers in blockchain area [9] (Bitcoin) and [18] (Ethereum) various works have explored blockchain-based architectures for Massively Multiplayer Online Games. For example, in [10] the authors introduced GiNA, a blockchain-based gaming scheme leveraging packet transfer schemes for security and authenticity. The authors of [7] proposed a blockchain-based cheat prevention and robustness mechanism for Massively Multiplayer Online Game. In [15] the authors presented a decentralized authoritative multiplayer architecture, focusing on cheat detection at protocol and architecture levels. The authors of [25] introduced a blockchain consensus model based on the Bryllite Consensus Protocol, supporting a hyper-connected Massively Multiplayer Online Game ecosystem and enabling user participation through Proof of Participation. In [19,20,24] the authors proposed Proof of Play, a consensus model for blockchain-based Peer to Peer gaming systems, showcasing a serverless match-based online blockchain game, Infinity Battle. However, none of these works proposed a generic architecture for Massively Multiplayer Online Games agnostic to a specific blockchain and none of them address narrative games. Blockchain technology is not universally suitable for all Massively Multiplayer Online Game genres; only a select few meet its requirements [1,2,21] due to the discrepancy between latency requirements for MMOG and validation time needed for each block publication in blockchains. However, narrative adventure games played in real-time, where actions are spaced by brainstorming phases, align well with the flow of time in blockchain architecture. Their latency and Action Per Minute values closely match current blockchain metrics like transactions per second (TPS) and block confirmation time.

Our Contribution. We propose Challenger, a blockchain-based peer-to-peer architecture for narrative games. We detail the API of the necessary services and examine cheating scenarios to test the resilience of services and the impact of attacks on the Challenger architecture. Interestingly, our design is agnostic to particular blockchains. Any blockchain that supports smart contracts can be used as an underlying layer.

3 Challenger: Modular Decentralized Blockchain-based Architecture for Narrative Games

3.1 Narrative Online Games

Narrative adventure games resemble interactive movies and visual novels, presenting real-time, pre-scripted scenes that change based on player interaction. These games feature branching narratives, where player choices influence events, creating a personalized story. Gameplay elements, such as conversation trees, puzzles, and Quick Time Events, support story immersion. In a narrative game context, inspired by Detroit: Become Human [5], the player assumes a detective role, investigating a crime scene. The crime scene serves as the level, with evidence found representing progress items. Exploring the crime scene and finding evidence moves the investigation forward, with different story branches based on the evidence found. The DAG (directed acyclic graph) in Fig. 1 shows a level with various possible scenarios. The player starts at the left end, with starting points at nodes a, b, or c, depending on in-level actions. The level ends at the right, with different realization scenarios represented by leaves i, l, m, q, r, and s.

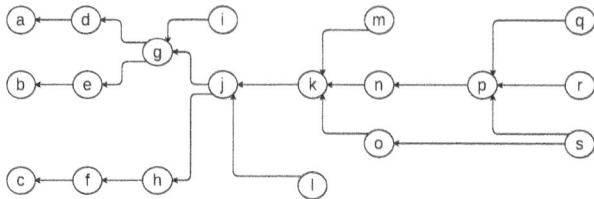

Fig. 1. Chapter scheme for a narrative game

Intermediate nodes between start and end nodes represent interactive game sequences where the player interacts with the game. These interactions may include quest resolution, research periods, action sequences, or multiple-choice discussions. The player's actions and choices alter the level's outcome. For instance, leaf i is an end scenario accessible only if the player started at node a or b. The node chain to access leaf i is either a, d, g, i or b, e, g, i. It is impossible to activate leaf i from starting node c. Choosing a leaf on the DAG selects a possible scenario end for the current level. Players can return to a previous level to unlock actions for other scenarios on subsequent levels. Once an action or scenario is completed, it cannot be revisited unless Recovery service is called following a path block identified by Conflict service. This means the user must restart at a specific previous level to begin the next level as desired, having made the correct choices to achieve the desired starting node (a, b, or c).

The game state saved in the blockchain represents a path from the beginning of the level to a leaf of the DAG (Fig. 1) (e.g., a, d, g, i or a, d, g, j, k, n, p, r or c, f, h, j, k, o, s). The distributed ledger monitors the game, detects wrong behaviour, and provides a global log for analyzing behaviour and adapting the game experience. Each verification service call is recorded on the blockchain. Storage service saves local progress within the level, focusing on level-up information from a to b.

3.2 Challenger Architecture

This architecture relies on blockchain technology, utilizing its data structure to retrieve the history of operations recorded on the blockchain. In narrative games, this means game states and transitions are written on the blockchain. Unlike traditional client-server architectures, where game progress is stored either on the server or the client-both imposing computational burdens that can impact client-side performance and server scalability-the Challenger architecture uses the blockchain for storage and employs a peer-to-peer network for more scalable exchanges. This decentralized approach enhances both scalability and surveillance. Decentralization eliminates single points of failure, enhancing resilience and security. Peer-to-peer networks can handle larger volumes of data without centralized bottlenecks, and blockchain's immutable ledger provides a transparent record of operations. However, designing and maintaining decentralized systems can be more complex than traditional architectures, and blockchain operations can be slower and more resource-intensive, leading to higher costs. Non-blockchain alternatives include Trusted Execution Environments (TEEs), which are secure areas in processors that run code in an isolated environment, offering high security and reducing the need for extensive cryptographic proofs. However, they have limited scalability and depend on hardware. Distributed consensus protocols, which are algorithms ensuring agreement among distributed systems, offer enhanced fault tolerance and flexibility in design but can result in slower consensus times and complex implementation. Cryptographic methods, such as zero-knowledge proofs and secure multi-party computation, provide strong privacy guarantees and reduced trust assumptions, but they come with high computational overhead and complexity in integration.

The Challenger architecture (Fig. 2) consists of nine essential services. Each peer provides all essential services, but some services are local, while others are distant. Local services include Membership (Algorithm 1), Publication (Algorithm 3), Conflict (Algorithm 4), Storage (Algorithm 7), Anomaly (Algorithm 9), and Orchestration ([6]). Distant services are Verification (Algorithm 2), Recovery (Algorithm 6), Choice (Algorithm 5), and Misbehaviour (Algorithm 8), see all services [6].

Challenger presents seven different scenarios, which describe the basic exchange between Orchestration and the architecture. The different use cases and their respective within the services presented in Fig. 2 are:

- Process for registering: 1a, 2a, 3a, 4a
- Process for altering the game state
  - Conflict (Algorithm 4): 5b, 6b, 7b, 8b, 9b, 10b, 11b
  - Choice (Algorithm 5): 5c, 6c, 7c, 8c, 9c, 10c, 11c, 12c, 13c, 14c, 15c, 16c, 17c
  - Recovery (Algorithm 6)

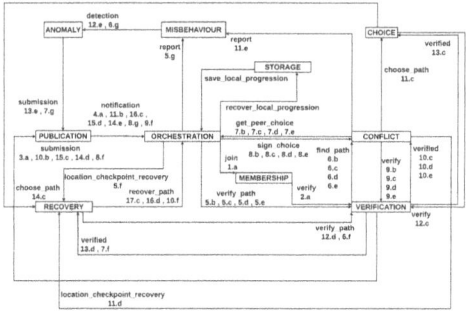

Fig. 2. Architecture Major component

- request by Conflict service (5d, 6d, 7d, 8d, 9d, 10d, 11d, 12d, 13d, 14d, 15d, 16d)
- request by the user (Algorithm 6): 5f, 6f, 7f, 8f, 9f, 10f
- Process for reporting misconduct (Algorithm 8)
  - request by Conflict service (5e, 6e, 7e, 8e, 9e, 10e, 11e, 12e, 13e, 14e, 15e)
  - request by a user (5g, 6g, 7g, 8g)

Services and Application Programming Interfaces are summarised, see [6].

4 Challenger Services in Detail

We discuss the implementation of the services, Fig. 2. For each service, we provide a pseudocode representation of the service's implementation, an overview of its architecture, and a sequence diagram demonstrating a specific use case. This approach helps to clearly illustrate the functionality and operation of each service, see [6].

4.1 Process for Registering

Membership service. Membership service facilitates the initial user connection to the game by assigning a unique user identifier (id_user) and game identifier (id_game) in exchange for the client identifier. These IDs are necessary for game participation and are generated using the client identifier as a seed. The user follows steps 1a, 2a, 3a, and 4a (Fig. 2) to utilize Membership service and obtain the IDs. Once the IDs are generated, Orchestration service informs the user of its assigned IDs. These IDs can either be stored locally or queried each time the user connects to the game. For this service, we assume that each tuple of (id_user, id_game) is stored locally in the user application.

Algorithm 1. Membership Service

```
1:  Local variable :
2:  IDENTIFICATION a table of (id_user, id_game) clients register
3:  Function :
4:  - generate (integer): based on integer generates a random integer
5:  - add (integer 1, integer 2): add a row of arguments in the IDENTIFICATION table
6:  - remove (integer 1, integer 2): remove the row including arguments of IDENTIFICATION table
7:  Upon receiving Join(id_client) from Orchestration do
8:      if id_client not in IDENTIFICATION then :
9:          id_user = Hash(generate(id_client))      ▷ generate id_user based on id_client, this allow a mapping between
            id_client and id_user, in order to be able to identify user's id_client
10:         add(id_user, id_game)                    ▷ add id_user and id_game to the table of register
11:         deliver (id_user, id_game) to Orchestration
12:         deliver (id_user, id_game) to Publication service
13:     else :
14:         deliver (id_user, id_game) to Orchestration
15:     endif
16: enddo
17: Upon receiving Unsubscribe(id_user, id_game) from Orchestration do :
18:     if (id_user, id_game) in IDENTIFICATION then :
19:         remove (id_user, id_game)
20:     else :
21:         deliver NO_EXISTENT_USER_ID to Orchestration
22:     endif
23: enddo
```

- membership.join(id_client): join is called, and the client's ID (id_client) is used as a seed to generate the user ID (id_user).
- publication.submission((id_user, id_user, current_level, next_level): submission is called to submit the newly generated player IDs to the ledger.
- orchestration.notification(new_publication_on_ledger): the user receives a notification to update the local storage of users with the new IDs.
- orchestration.update(): the user updates his local storage

Once the IDs have been successfully verified and sent to Publication service, the user's Orchestration receives a notification from both services. This allows other users to update their available user table and informs them of the new client's IDs, ensuring that all users are up-to-date with the latest information.

Verification Service. Verification service ensures the validity of a user's request to progress to the next level by evaluating if the transition from the current level meets specific conditions. It utilizes local storage to retain game state headers and minimal-level information for this purpose. The primary objective of Verification service is to filter legitimate requests from illegitimate ones. If the progression from one game state to another is recorded as a local variable and follows the logical path of the game's different states, progression is considered legitimate. Conversely, if the progression deviates from the logical path, it may be indicative of misbehaviour or a cheating attack. The verification service is designed to detect and prevent such instances, ensuring that all level advancements are valid and adhere to the game's established rules. We analyze the verification process and its various scenarios, assuming that the Verification call made by Orchestration will be successful and that all components are functioning correctly. We examine different conflict cases, such as when a user faces multiple choices when a user delegates a choice to Choice service, and when a user is blocked and must recover an anterior stage of the game to proceed. The verification process involves three services, as depicted in Algorithm 2:

- verification.verify_path((id_user, id_user, current_level, next_level): verify_path is called to determine the legitimacy of the level-up by examining the different game states. The call to verification.verify_path can be made by:
  - conflict.find_path(id_user, id_game, current_level, targeted_level)
  - choice.choose_path (id_game, current_level)
  - recovery.recovery_checkpoint (recovery_checkpoint_location)
- publication.submission((id_user, id_user, current_level, next_level): submission is called to write the change of level from the current one to the next as proof of level-up.
- orchestration.notification(new_publication_on_ledger): notification is called to update the new local level of the user.
- orchestration.update(): the user updates his local storage

Verification service reads the blockchain to assess the legitimacy of the level-up between the different game states. A comparison is made between the requested game state and the one found within the blockchain. If not, a local comparison is performed between the game states stored locally within Verification service and the requested level. The verification process algorithm, as illustrated in Algorithm 2, has a Verification service that first evaluates the legitimacy of the current level of the user requesting a level-up. Based on the result, users can either advance to the next level or call the Conflict service to find a path from their current level. This scenario indicates that the user's current position is legitimate, but the next level is unreachable due to insufficient game progress.

Publication Service. Publication service holds the exclusive right to write on the blockchain and is thereby the sole service capable of updating the game's stage within the ledger. This service records the outcome of user requests, which could be derived from various services such as verification, conflict, choice, misbehaviour, or anomaly. It is important to note that Publication service is responsible only for publishing the outcome; all verification procedures to confirm the information's accuracy must be completed beforehand. Upon publication by Publication service and the subsequent ledger update, users can access the blockchain to refresh their local cache. Algorithm 3 illustrates Publication service algorithm, which outlines several scenarios where the submission is invoked to publish.

4.2 Process for Altering the Game State

Conflict Service. Conflict service is employed to resolve two primary issues: scenario ambiguity and a blocked scenario.

- Scenario ambiguity can be addressed in two ways:
  - The first approach involves presenting the choice to the user and requesting his decision.

Algorithm 2. Verification service

1: Local variable :
2: ALL_GAME_STATE table of all game states inside the game, it is used to verify the validity of the stage of the game when a client initiates a request to level up to the next level.
3: Function :
4: - check(game_state) :
5: verify if all actions done until the current state of the game is legit
6: - advance(game_state_1, game_state_2) :
7: verify if the level up from game_state_1 to game_state_2 is legit.
8: **Upon** receiving Verify_path(id_user, id_game, current_level, next_level) from the Conflict, Choice, Recovery, application **do** :
9:    **if** check(current_level) == SUCCESS **and** advance(current_level, next_level) == SUCCESS **then** :
10:       **deliver** submission(current_level, next_level) to Publication service
11:    **elif** check(current_level) == SUCCESS **and** advance(current_level, next_level) == FAILURE **then** :
12:       **deliver** find_path(id_user, id_game, current_level) to Conflict service
13:    **elif** check(current_level) == FAILURE **and** advance(current_level, next_level) == SUCCESS **then** :
14:       **deliver** Report(id_user, id_game, current_level, next_level) to Misbehaviour service
15:    **else** :
16:       **deliver** Report(id_user, id_game, current_level, next_level) to Misbehaviour service
17:    **endif**
18: **enddo**
19: check(current_level): The idea is to use a recursive function to verify from the last block to the block where id_user and id_game of the client appear for the first time. The condition to stop the function and to unstuck it is to find the block where the client initialized its game.
20: check(current_level) will call check(precedent_level_before (current_level)), and this one will call check(precedent_level_before (precedent_level_before (current_level))) and so on, until check calls id_user and id_game.
21: The process of stacking is the verification itself. If the stack goes without any issues, the current stage of the game is legit.
22: advance(current_level, next_level): Verify if the request to level up from current_level to next_level is within the ALL_GAME_STATE table. If this is the case, the request is legit; otherwise, there is a call to Conflict service.

Algorithm 3. Publication Service

1: Function :
2: - write (object) :
3: writes in the distributed ledger object
4: **Upon** receiving submission(id_user, id_game, current_level, next_level) from Verification service **do** :
5:    write(id_user, id_game, current_level, next_level) ▷ write the progression of id_user in id_game from current_level to next_level
6: **deliver** Notification (New_publication_on_ledger) to Orchestration service
7: **enddo**
8: **Upon** receiving submission(id_user, id_game, current_level, sign_client_choice) from Conflict service **do** :
9:    write(id_user, id_game, current_level, sign_client_choice)
10: **deliver** Notification (New_publication_on_ledger) to Orchestration service
11: **enddo**
12: **Upon** receiving submission(id_user, id_game, current_level, Recovered_path) from Conflict service **do** :
13:    write(id_user, id_game, current_level, Recovered_path)
14: **deliver** Notification (New_publication_on_ledger) to Orchestration service
15: **enddo**
16: **Upon** receiving submission(id_user, id_game, current_level, Chosen_path) from Choice service **do** :
17:    write(id_user, id_game, current_level, Chosen_path)
18: **deliver** Notification (New_publication_on_ledger) to Orchestration service
19: **enddo**
20: **Upon** receiving submission(Log_anomaly) from Anomaly service **do** :
21:    write(Log_anomaly)
22: **enddo**
23: write(id_user, id_game, current_level, Result_path): write what is given in argument in the blockchain. The argument of function write() can be the level up from current_level to next_level, the decision sign by the client, a recovered path proposed by Conflict service, or a path randomly drawn by the blockchain.
24: write(Log_anomaly): update player's IDs that are designed as cheaters.

- The second approach entails deciding an algorithm that selects a path for the user.
- In the case of a blocked scenario, the only solution is to recover a previous game stage, specifically one where the scenario is ambiguous. This intersection of scenarios allows the player to alter the outcome of the blocked scenario.

A scenario intersection can be understood as a game state where multiple scenarios are possible, and a change in gameplay can occur if all requirements for a specific scenario are fulfilled. The conflict resulting from multiple choices is resolved by the user's decision, following sequence 5b, 6b, 7b, 8b, 9b, 10b, 11b in Fig. 2. This scenario illustrates a case study where a user encounters a choice of path and selects one when prompted by Conflict service. The user's choice is authenticated using their private key and submitted to Publication. During the Conflict process (Algorithm 4), all potential paths the user can take are calculated. This step serves as a preventive measure for Recovery service or Choice service, as (a) The user may be on a path leading to a dead-end, in which case Recovery is immediately initiated from a level offering more choices. (b) The user opts to use Choice, and these paths represent the possible directions the user can take within the current level. These paths are forwarded to Choice service to randomly select one based on the user's current level and paths already in the blockchain through user submissions. [6] describes Conflict service's sequence diagram.

Choice Service. Choice service is invoked when a user decides to allow the blockchain to determine the path they will take. The set of paths from which one will be selected for the user, known as SET_OF_PATH, depends on the paths already present in the blockchain for the current level. Within the Choice service, the blockchain is read, and all paths previously taken by other users to level up from the current level are gathered in a set called BLOCKCHAIN_PATH. A new set of paths, INTERESTING_PATH, is created by subtracting BLOCKCHAIN_PATH from SET_OF_PATH. Choice service then selects a path for the user from this INTERESTING_PATH set. Choice process follows the sequence 5c, 6c, 7c, 8c, 9c, 10c, 11c, 12c, 13c, 14c, 15c, 16c, 17c Fig. 2 and involves the following services: Verification requests level up post and initiates Conflict service; Conflict detects multiple paths and seeks a decision from the user; Orchestration signs the user's decision using their private key; Choice chooses a random path from the blockchain; Publication submits level up with the proposed Choice path; Orchestration updates the user's local level. A choice service sequence diagram is describe in [6].

Recovery Service. The recovery service is responsible for restoring a previous state of the game. It receives instructions on which game stage to recover to proceed with the recuperation. There are two ways to invoke Recovery service:

- Direct call by users: In case they have forgotten their last level and want to recover the entire level without considering any progress.
- Call by Conflict service: When no path is found during the Conflict service's path-finding process. In this case, Conflict reads the blockchain to find a path ambiguity and saves its location as a checkpoint for Recovery to execute.

Algorithm 4. Conflict Service

1: Service Conflict is called when a problem is detected, the purpose of this service is to determine the type of the problem and send it to the right service for a specific treatment.
2: Local variable :
3: ALL_GAME_STATE_STEP_BY_STEP table of all the game states step by step and arranged by hierarchically level.
4: LOG_ORCHESTRATION table of all requests to orchestration service
5: Function :
6: - following (current_level) :
7: returns a set of all possible following paths starting from current_level
8: - find (current_level) :
9: find a past branching from current_level, where an over scenario can be made
10: **Upon** receiving find_path (id_user, id_game, current_level, next_level) from Verification service **do** :
11:     set_of_path = following (current_level) ▷ return a set of all the possible following paths starting from current_level
12:     **if** set_of_path is empty **then** : ▷ there is no path starting from the current_level, call of Recovery service to recover at a precedent level
13:         find (current_level)   ▷ find the branching from where an over scenario can be made
14:         **deliver** location_recovery_checkpoint to Recovery service
15:     **else** :   ▷ there is a at least one path
16:         **if** set_of_path == 1 **then**:   ▷ there is only one and unique path which derives from the current_level
17:             **if** unique_path == next_level **then**:   ▷ the path the client wishes to follow is the same as the one he is allowed to take
18:                 **deliver** submission (id_user, id_game, current_level, unique_path) to Publication service
19:             **else**:   ▷ this means that the unique path the user has is different from the one he is currently on
20:                 **if** submission(id_user, id_game, current_level, unique_path) **in** LOG_ORCHESTRATION :
21:                       **deliver** submission(id_user, id_game, current_level, unique_path) to Misbehaviour service
22:                 **else**
23:                       **deliver** submission(id_user, id_game, current_level, unique_path) to Orchestration service
24:                 **endif**
25:         **if** set_of_path > 1 **then**:   ▷ this mean that the client can choose between at least 2 different paths,
26:             ▷ the first solution is to ask the point of view of the user and the second solution is to call Choice service which will choose randomly a path for the client
27:             **deliver** get_peer_choice (id_user, id_game, current_level, set_of_path or random_choice) to Orchestration ▷ the user is free to make the choice he wishes to follow
28:             ▷ the user has only access to the set_of_path paths without knowing the rest of the possible scenario
29:         **endif**
30:     **endif**
31: **enddo**
32: **Upon** receiving get_peer_choice (unknow_decision) from Orchestration **do** :
33:     **if** unknow_decision == CLIENT_CHOICE **then** :
34:         **deliver** submission (id_user, id_game, current_level, CLIENT_CHOICE) to Publication service
35:     **elif** unknow_decision == RANDOM_CHOICE **then** :
36:         **deliver** Choose_path (id_user, id_game, current_level, RANDOM_CHOICE) to Choice service
37:     **elif** unknow_decision == CONTINUE **then**:   ▷ client continues on the same scenario until he will be blocked to call Recovery service
38:         **deliver** submission (id_user, id_game, current_level, CONTINUE : next_level) to Publication service
39:     **elif** unknow_decision == RECOVERY **then**: ▷ client calls Recovery service to find a branch from where he will be able to change the current_level he currently is on
40:         **deliver** location_recovery_checkpoint to Recovery service
41:     **endif**
42: **enddo**
43: following (current_level): The objective is to locate all the leaf nodes in a Directed Acyclic Graph (DAG). Starting from an arbitrary node in the DAG, the function aims to identify all the leaves based on the current position of the node in the scenario. A depth-first search algorithm can be employed to find all the leaf nodes.
44: finds (current_level): The function finds searches for an intersection of the scenario that is anterior to the current node. In other words, it identifies a parent node of the current node with more than one child node. These child nodes represent the intersection within the scenario that determines the ending storyline of the client. To find all specific nodes, a breadth-first search algorithm can be used.

We focus on the second scenario involving Conflict, see [6]. Recovery process follows sequence 5d, 6d, 7d, 8d, 9d, 10d, 11d, 12d, 13d, 14d, 15d, 16d of Fig. 2 and involves the following services: Verification requests level-up verification and initiates Conflict service; Conflict: No potential path is found, so a checkpoint is determined to recover a previous game state. The conflict then calls Recovery to recover the checkpoint location

Algorithm 5. Choice Service

1: Local variable :
2: BLOCKCHAIN_PATH all paths registered so far given the current level within the blockchain
3: Function :
4: - which_path (current_level) :
5: returns all possible paths to leaves given the location within the current level
6: - random_choice_path (current_level) :
7: returns randomly a path not taken by most of the users
8: **Upon** receiving Choose_path (id_user, id_game, current_level, next_level) from Conflict service **do** :
9:     load BLOCKCHAIN_PATH
10:     SET_OF_PATH = which_path (current_level)
11:     random_choice_path (current_level)
12: **deliver** submission (id_user, id_game, current_level, random_blockchain_drawn) to Publication service
13: **enddo**
14:
15: which_path (current_level): is the same function as following in Conflict service, see algorithm 4
16: random_choice_path (current_level) :
17: SET_OF_PATH are all paths give recovery_current_level
18: BLOCKCHAIN_PATH are paths explored within the blockchain for a given current_level
19: INTERESTING_PATH = SET_OF_PATH minus BLOCKCHAIN_PATH
20: **return** random choice within INTERESTING_PATH

Algorithm 6. Recovery Service

1: Local variable :
2: CHECKPOINT_LOG table of all recovered locations demanded by id_user on id_game and by Conflict service to.
3: Function :
4: - add (id_user, id_game, current_level):
5: add the request in CHECKPOINT_LOG
6: - extract (level_to_recover_location) :
7: recover level_to_recover thanks to level_to_recover_location from the distributed ledger
8: **Upon** receiving Choose_path (id_user, id_game, current_level, next_level) from Conflict service **do** :
9:     add (id_user, id_game, recovery_location)
10:     extract (id_user, id_game, current_level, recovery_location)
11: **enddo**
12: add (id_user, id_game, current_level):
13: Recovery service uses a local table to store the player's IDs who request to recover a state of the game. The information stored are Players IDs and the stage of the game to recover
14: extract (id_user, id_game, current_level, requested_level) :
15: recover the requested level of id_user on id_game. Read the blockchain at current_level and search for requested_level at position recovery_location

---

and submits the level recovery location to Publication for Orchestration; Publication submits the change of level from the current one to the recovered one; Recovery locates the level to recover and sends it to Orchestration; Orchestration updates both the recovered level and its location for potential future Recovery calls due to the same player judgment error. In the Recovery Algorithm 6 process, a log of recovery requests made by users and Conflict service is maintained. This log, known as CHECKPOINT LOG, is used to monitor users' level-up progress during their game. This service helps to create a challenging game-play experience based on the requests made by Conflict to unlock users' progression. The location of the recovered game state (recovered_level) can be stored within Storage service, but for our purposes, we assume that the game state can be stored locally by users. Recovery service sequence diagram is describe in [6].

Storage Service. Storage service, Algorithm 7, enables the saving and retrieval of the current level of a user and its progression without requiring Recovery service every time. At present, Storage service is optional, as we assume that a stage of the game can

Algorithm 7. Storage Service

1: Local variable :
2: LOCAL local storage of the client
3: Function :
4: - save (id_user, id_game, current_level):
5: save the current progression
6: - get (id_user, id_game) :
7: get the last game state progression saved
8: **Upon** receiving Retrieve_local_progression (id_user, id_game) from Orchestration service **do** :
9:     get (id_user, id_game)
10:     **deliver** Recovered_local_progression
11: **enddo**
12: **Upon** receiving Save_local_progression (id_user, id_game, current_level) from Orchestration service **do** :
13:     save (id_user, id_game, current_level)
14:     **deliver** Notification (state_game_saved) to Orchestration service
15: **enddo**
16: save (id_user, id_game, current_level) : locally save the progress of id_user on id_game at current_level game state
17: get (id_user, id_game) : retrieve last game state saved of id_user on id_game

be loaded and saved within the local cache of the Orchestration service. However, if the game stage can no longer be saved locally within Orchestration, Storage service will become a critical component of this architecture.

4.3 Process for Reporting Misconduct

Misbehaviour Service. Misbehaviour service is responsible for compiling all behaviour requests made by users or the Conflict service. Its main purpose is to collect a log of requests without any filtering. Misbehaviours can range from a stubborn user repeatedly making the same mistake to trigger a Recovery service, to a user reporting another for tampering with their client code to alter a service's functionality. The detection process is primarily carried out by Conflict service, which prioritizes misbehaviour collections to ensure none are overlooked. The selection of bad behaviour is done in two steps: (1) Collect misbehaviour reports from users and detection reports from Conflict; (2) Filter by Anomaly service to differentiate between cheating behaviour and false positives. Conflict service detects suspicious behaviour, such as redundancy, back and forth, or cycles within submission requests. We describe misbehaviour detection by Conflict service. The misbehaviour detection report by a user is presented in [6]. The collection process of the log follows sequence 5e, 6e, 7e, 8e, 9e, 10e, 11e, 12e, 13e, 14e, 15e of Fig. 2 and involves the following services: Verification request path verification; Conflict: Detects of misbehaviour process; Misbehaviour: Collection of behaviour log; Anomaly filters cheating behaviour from other types; Publication submits log of anomalies; Application updates the local cache with a log of anomalies to deter users from calling the services of users identified as cheaters. The Misbehaviour Algorithm 8 collects reports made by users or Conflict service to target misbehaviour, referred to as the object of misbehaviour or the reported user ID in cases where a user succeeds in tampering with the client code. The Misbehaviour algorithm serves to collect and deliver the log of misbehaviour for further processing by the Anomaly service. Misbehavior service sequence diagram is available in [6].

Algorithm 8. Misbehaviour Service

1: Local variable :
2: LOG_behaviour table of all misbehaviour detected by Conflict service or reported by users
3: function :
4: - add (id_user, id_game, object_of_misbehaving, current_level, next_level):
5: register report
6: **Upon** Receiving Report (id_user, id_game, object_of_misbehaving, current_level, next_level) from Conflict service **do** :
7:      add (id_user, id_game, object_of_misbehaving, current_level, next_level)
8:      **deliver** Detection (LOG_behaviour) to Anomaly service
9: **enddo**
10: **Upon** Receiving Report (id_user, id_game, id_user_reported, object_of_misbehaving) from Orchestration service **do** :
11:      add (id_user, id_game, id_user_reported, object_of_misbehaving)
12:      **deliver** Detection (LOG_behaviour) to Anomaly service
13: **enddo**
14: add (id_user, id_game, id_user_reported, object_of_misbehaving) :
15: and
16: add (id_user, id_game, object_of_misbehaving, current_level, next_level) :
17: compiles the table of misbehaviour, the process focuses on collecting the report, and filtering processing will be done by Anomaly service.

Algorithm 9. Anomaly Service

1: Local variable :
2: LOG_ANOMALY table of all anomalies detected
3: Function :
4: - detection (log_behaviour):
5: filter log_behaviour to determine cheating behaviour
6: **Upon** receiving Detection (log_behaviour) from Misbehaviour service **do** :
7:      detection (log_behaviour)
8:      **update** LOG_ANOMALY
9:      **deliver** submission (LOG_ANOMALY) to Publication service
10: **enddo**
11: detection (log_behaviour) :
12: analysis of the misconduct to determine real cheating behaviour from stubborn or unwise game-play. LOG_ANOMALY works as a reference for cheating attacks, the log helps to identify behaviour that seems to be a cheat. LOG_ANOMALY must be constantly updated to predict potential cheating scheme

Anomaly Service. Anomaly service acts as a filter to differentiate between genuine cheating attacks and false positives. It utilizes a reference dataset, LOG ANOMALY, to identify and classify behaviour, which represents cheating behaviour exhibited by users. After filtering, LOG ANOMALY is submitted to Publication, and an updated log of cheating users is maintained to prevent others from experiencing suspicious outcomes when calling their services. In the case where a user directly reports misbehaviour to another user, there is a trust issue that must be addressed. The Anomaly process, as depicted in Fig. 2, involves the following services: Misbehaviour reports misbehaviour; Anomaly filters cheating attacks from false positives; Publication submits the anomaly log; Application updates and avoids cheating users. Anomaly filter detection Algorithm 9, takes a log of misbehaviour collected by trusted Conflict services and legitimate reports from altruistic users as input. To filter the misbehaviour log, Anomaly uses a local table of cheating behaviour and reads the blockchain to detect suspicious activity. However, the table of the cheating log used as a reference is biased towards identifying specific patterns. An alternative approach to the filtering problem is to consider the distance between altruistic and rational users from cheating users, shifting the focus from patterns to behavioural distance.

4.4 Challenger Resilience to Cheating

The attacks originate from a combination of studies by Yahyavi et al. [23] and Webb et al. [16] on the classification of cheating attacks. Yahyavi et al. [23] categorize attacks based on their nature, such as interruption of information dissemination, illegal game

Table 1. Vector of cheats ineffective against Challenger

Cheat description	Cheating vector	Type of cheat	Altruism required to counter cheating
Impersonation: steal credentials of valuable account	Generate ID client to match id_user and id_game or steal id_user and id_game	(in game layer; unauthorized information access)	none required: secure by design, the pair (id_user,id_game) is unique for each id_client. A common issue would be to have already someone using the id_user for the same game with a different value of id_game
Theft of a personal item: steal item of id_user on id_game	Extract for the ledger information on personal items	(ledger layer, unauthorized information access)	none required: secure by design, every game state is sign with id_user and id_game of the user's id_user who is playing id_game
Replay cheat: replay a previous state of the game	target verification.verify_path to break Verification during the comparison between the current state and the previous one of the user	(protocol layer, interruption information dissemination)	none required: secure by design, every change in state of game is writing with in the ledger, verification service detect any discontinuity in change of game state
Consistency cheat: a Cheating user act between Byzantine and Altruist to blur the lines of his behaviour	target misbehaviour.report and verification.verify_path in order to publish invalid information on the ledger	(protocol layer, interruption information dissemination)	at least 1 altruist is needed to filter with anomaly.detection() if one user is a real Cheater or not
Suppress correct cheat: suppress a correct state of game once written on the ledger	target publication.submission to break Publication after writing on the ledger	(protocol layer, interruption information dissemination)	none required: secure by design, once a game state, verified or not, is written on the ledger the information is immutable. The case where a game state is not verified will be study in the following attack: corrupt the ledger
Undo: repudiation of a game state	target publication.submission to damage the verification's algorithm	(protocol layer, interruption information dissemination)	None required: secure by design, a state of game can't be cancel, once written by publication.submission, it's stay immutable on the ledger
time cheating: lying at the time a game state is made	target verification.verify_path to ruin Verification during the comparison between the current state and the tampered time level one	(protocol layer, interruption information dissemination	at least 1 Altruist is need to deny verification_path call made by Cheaters
Escaping: cut internet link or shut down IT equipment	target recovery.recovery_checkpoint() to damage the process of retrieving the previous state of game	(infrastructure layer, interruption information dissemination)	non required: secure by design, recovery.recovery_checkpoint() read the ledger to find the latest valid game state writing by publication.submission(). Every state is writing from membership request, to change game state, to misbehaviour, to recovery
Information exposure: information which are not supposed to be disclosed are available due to the transparency on the ledger	exploit the transparency of the ledger to extract useful information	(ledger layer, unauthorized information access)	none required: secure by design, information are available because of the transparency of the ledger. However, only the state of the game and by whom can be read from the ledger, the requirement to unlock such state of game are not disclosed.

actions, and unauthorized access to information. Webb et al. [16] classify attacks based on the level at which they occur: game level, application level, protocol level, and infrastructure level. Initially, we draw inspiration from these classifications to determine Challenger's resilience, then examine cheating vectors specific to the Challenger architecture [16]. Table 1 summarizes the cheats for which Challenger is resilient. Challenger is designed to be resilient against a range of cheating attacks by leveraging its blockchain-based architecture and decentralized approach. Cheating attacks can include interruption of information dissemination, illegal game actions, unauthorized access to information, and attacks occurring at various levels (game, application, protocol, infrastructure). The Challenger architecture uses blockchain to maintain an immutable record of game states and transitions, ensuring that all actions are transparent and verifiable by any user in the network. This transparency and decentralization make it difficult for malicious users to alter game states without detection. The system assumes ideal communication conditions, where peer-to-peer communication links are reliable and not compromised by malicious users. However, it does consider the potential malicious behavior of players, including attempts to corrupt services or exploit the blockchain. Challenger's resilience is further enhanced by service separation, requiring user requests to be validated by another user, and decentralized surveillance, which allows any user to verify another user's actions through the game state history provided by the blockchain. In summary, Challenger's architecture provides robust resilience against a wide range of cheating attacks by using a combination of blockchain technology and decentralized peer-to-peer verification. This approach ensures that game states are secure, transparent, and verifiable, mitigating the risk of malicious behavior affecting the integrity of the game.

5 Conclusion

In this paper, we propose a modular blockchain-based architecture for peer-to-peer narrative games implementing services using smart contracts. The modular architecture addresses specific services such as membership, publication, anomaly detection, and game state recovery. We focus on narrative games due to their compatibility with the blockchain's current performance in transactions per second and validation blocks. Our architecture is resilient to a broad range of cheating behaviours. The subsequent phase involves extending the architecture to encompass all game categories. Achieving this will necessitate implementing a consensus algorithm capable of facilitating event scheduling at a high transaction rate.

Acknowledgements. The work presented in this document has received funding from the EU Horizon Europe research and innovation Programme under Grant Agreement No. 101070118.

References

1. Bamakan, S.M.H., Motavali, A., Bondarti, A.B.: A survey of blockchain consensus algorithms performance evaluation criteria. Expert Syst. Appl. **154**, 113385 (2020)
2. Belchior, R., Vasconcelos, A., Guerreiro, S., Correia, M.: A survey on blockchain interoperability: past, present, and future trends. ACM Comput. Surv. (CSUR) **54**(8), 1–41 (2021)
3. Carlini, E., Ricci, L., Coppola, M.: Integrating centralized and P2P architectures to support interest management in distributed virtual environments. Tech. Rep., Istituto di Scienza e Tecnologie dell'Informazione (ISTI), CNR, Pisa, Italy (2012)
4. Chanda, S., Star, S.: Contouring e-doping: a menace to sportsmanship in e-sports. Turk. Online J. Qual. Inq. **12**(8), 966–981 (2021)
5. Detroit becom human (2023). https://www.quanticdream.com/fr/detroit-become-human
6. Chan Yip Hon, B., Zaghdoudi, B., Potop-Butucaru, M., Tixeuil, S., Fdida, S.: Challenger: blockchain-based massively multiplayer online game architecture. Cryptology ePrint Archive (2024). https://eprint.iacr.org/2024/726
7. Kalra, S., Sanghi, R., Dhawan, M.: Blockchain-based real-time cheat prevention and robustness for multi-player online games. In: Proceedings of the 14th International Conference on Emerging Networking Experiments and Technologies, pp. 178–190 (2018)
8. Li, D., Liang, H., Chu, J.: A more efficient secure event signature protocol for massively multiplayer online games based on P2P. In,: International Forum on Mechanical, Control and Automation (IFMCA 2016), pp. 291–299. Atlantis Press (2016)
9. Nakamoto, S.: Bitcoin: a peer-to-peer electronic cash system (2009). http://www.bitcoin.org/bitcoin.pdf
10. Patel, N., Shukla, A., Tanwar, S., Kumar, N., Rodrigues, J.J.P.C.: GiNA: a blockchain-based gaming scheme towards ethereum 2.0. In: ICC 2021-IEEE International Conference on Communications, pp. 1–6. IEEE (2021)
11. Plumb, J.N., Kasera, S.K., Stutsman, R.: Hybrid network clusters using common gameplay for massively multiplayer online games. In: Proceedings of the 13th International Conference on the Foundations of Digital Games, pp. 1–10 (2018)
12. Prather, J., Nix, R., Jessup, R.: Trust management for cheating detection in distributed massively multiplayer online games. In: 15th Annual Workshop on Network and Systems Support for Games (NetGames), pp. 1–3. IEEE (2017)
13. Sharma, K., Mukhopadhyay, A.: Cyber-risk management framework for online gaming firms: an artificial neural network approach. Inf. Syst. Front. 25, 1757–1778 (2023). https://doi.org/10.1007/s10796-021-10232-7
14. Tian, Y., Chen, E., Ma, X., Chen, S., Wang, X., Tague, P.: Swords and shields: a study of mobile game hacks and existing defenses. In: Proceedings of the 32nd Annual Conference on Computer Security Applications, pp. 386–397 (2016)
15. Tošić, A., Vičič, J.: A decentralized authoritative multiplayer architecture for games on the edge. Comput. Inform. **40**(3), 522–542 (2021)
16. Webb, S.D., Soh, S.: Cheating in networked computer games: a review. In: Proceedings of the 2nd International Conference on Digital Interactive Media in Entertainment and Arts, pp. 105–112 (2007)
17. Webb, S.D., Soh, S., Trahan, J.L.: Secure referee selection for fair and responsive peer-to-peer gaming. SIMULATION **85**(9), 608–618 (2009)
18. Wood, G.: Ethereum: a secure decentralised generalised transaction ledger. Ethereum Project Yellow Paper **151**(2014), 1–32 (2014)
19. Wu, F., Yuen, H.Y., Chan, H., Leung, V.C.M., Cai, W.: Facilitating serverless match-based online games with novel blockchain technologies. ACM Trans. Internet Technol. **23**(1), 1–26 (2023)

20. Wu, F., Yuen, H.Y., Chan, H.C.B., Leung, V.C.M., Cai, W.: Infinity battle: a glance at how blockchain techniques serve in a serverless gaming system. In: Proceedings of the 28th ACM International Conference on Multimedia, pp. 4559–4561 (2020)
21. Wu, M., Wang, K., Cai, X., Guo, S., Guo, M., Rong, C.: A comprehensive survey of blockchain: from theory to IoT applications and beyond. IEEE Internet Things J. **6**(5), 8114–8154 (2019)
22. Yahyavi, A., Huguenin, K., Kemme, B.: Interest modeling in games: the case of dead reckoning. Multimedia Syst. **19**, 255–270 (2013)
23. Yahyavi, A., Kemme, B.: Peer-to-peer architectures for massively multiplayer online games: a survey. ACM Comput. Surv. (CSUR) **46**(1), 1–51 (2013)
24. Yuen, H.Y., Wu, F., Cai, W., Chan, H.C.B., Yan, Q., Leung, V.C.M.: Proof-of-play: a novel consensus model for blockchainbased peer-to-peer gaming system. In: Proceedings of the 2019 ACM International Symposium on Blockchain and Secure Critical Infrastructure, pp. 19–28 (2019)
25. Yun, J., et al.: MMOG user participation based decentralized consensus scheme and proof of participation analysis on the bryllite blockchain system. KSII Trans. Internet Inf. Syst. (TIIS) **13**(8), 4093–4107 (2019)

Agent-Driven BFS Tree in Anonymous Graphs with Applications

Prabhat Kumar Chand[1(✉)], Manish Kumar[2], and Anisur Rahaman Molla[1]

[1] Indian Statistical Institute, Kolkata, Baranagar, India
pchand744@gmail.com, molla@isical.ac.in
[2] Indian Institute of Technology, Madras, Chennai, India

Abstract. Breadth-First-Search (BFS) trees serve a pivotal role in designing efficient graph algorithms due to their efficacy in traversing and exploring graph structures with a systematic layer-by-layer approach. This paper introduces an agent-based novel approach for constructing a BFS tree on an arbitrary anonymous graph G with n nodes and m edges using $k \geq n$ autonomous mobile agents. In this paper, we provide algorithms for BFS tree construction for different starting configurations and demonstrate their applications. Our main result considers the *dispersed* starting configuration (i.e., each node is occupied by a single agent at the start) and takes $O(D\Delta)$ rounds to execute, where D is the diameter and Δ is the highest degree of G. The algorithm assumes the knowledge of a *root* node for the BFS tree. We further continue our investigation for BFS tree construction with two other classical configurations, namely, rooted configuration and arbitrary configuration (with and without the knowledge of *root*) of the agents with some other follow-up configurations for $k > n$. In addition, the paper demonstrates the application of the BFS tree construction methodology in tasks like - checking a graph for bipartiteness and gathering agents into a single node, a fundamental task in distributed robotics.

Keywords: Breadth First Search Tree · Mobile Agents · Distributed Network Algorithms · Time Complexity · Memory Complexity · Bipartite Graph · Gathering · Distributed Graph Algorithms

1 Introduction

Autonomous agents have emerged as a prominent area of research due to their capacity for independent action, facilitating decentralized decision-making and task allocation, thereby enabling their utilization across a wide array of distributed applications. In this paper, we model the workspace for the agents as simple connected anonymous graphs, where the agents compute decentralized tasks. Such models prove particularly advantageous in recommendation systems, social network analysis, route planning for self-driving cars, search engines, and bioinformatics, among others. On the other hand, Breadth-First-Search (BFS) trees serve a significant role in graph traversal and graph

---

M. Kumar—The author did some of the work during his stay at Indian Statistical Institute Kolkata.

exploration. BFS trees provide significantly shorter access time to different nodes of the graphs as compared to a Depth-First-Search due to its level-by-level traversal approach. In addition, BFS allows for better parallelization over DFS. These advantages allow the agents to do specific distributed tasks more efficiently.

BFS tree based applications have been used in different applications across different distributed models. In [24], the authors used a BFS tree based parallel algorithm for finding strongly connected components of a graph that efficiently works on large multi-core platforms over large-scale networks. Similarly, BFS tree is useful in executing memory-efficient graph exploration [23], sub-graph enumeration in directed graphs [17], and dispersion of autonomous agents in a graph [14, 15].

In general, agent-based BFS tree algorithms present distinctive challenges. For example, in a rooted configuration, where all agents start at the $root$ node, managing the distribution of agents level by level becomes increasingly intricate due to the unpredictability of the required number of agents at each level. Consequently, agents may need to shuttle back and forth to accurately allocate the precise number of agents needed at each level. As the agents delve deeper into the graph, the requirement of such back-and-forth movements escalates exponentially. As explored in [14], dispersing the agents across a graph using the BFS traversal requires $O(\Delta^D)$ rounds. We address these challenges by dispersing the agents across the graph before initiating the BFS tree computation. While BFS traversals offer advantages for parallel computations, synchronizing agent movements and accurately computing trees without conflicts presents an additional hurdle. To overcome this, we first evaluate Δ, the highest degree of the underlying graph.

1.1 Our Contributions

In this paper, we propose a method for constructing a Breadth-First Search (BFS) tree of a graph G utilizing $k \geq n$ autonomous agents, for different scenarios, based on the initial configuration and the number of the agents in the graph. Additionally, we show two follow-up applications of the constructed BFS tree: verifying graph bipartiteness and gathering all mobile agents to a singular node of the graph (also called the *gathering* problem).

Let G be a simple, connected anonymous graph with n nodes, m edges, maximum degree Δ, and diameter D. Let λ be the highest ID among the k agents. Let ℓ denote the number of initial clusters in the arbitrary starting configuration. We list our results below.

(i) *Results of BFS Tree Construction in various settings*(Table 1)
(ii) **Applications:** After the construction of the BFS tree for the graph G, the agents can further apply it to the following:
   1. **Checking if G is bipartite -** $k \geq n$ agents can verify if G is bipartite using an additional $O(D + \Delta)$ rounds.
   2. **Gathering -** All the $k \geq n$ agents can be gathered at the $root$ node of G in $O(D)$ rounds post the BFS tree construction.

Table 1. Complexities of BFS tree construction for different starting configurations with $O(\log n)$ bits of memory. $^*O(n \cdot \log n)$ bits of memory required per agent. In Algorithm 4, the agents need to know the parameters n, D, ℓ, Δ and λ. In Algorithm 5, the agents need to know n, Δ and λ. Other Algorithms do not require the knowledge of any global parameters.

Algorithm	Agents	root	Initial Config.	Time
1	n	Known	$dispersed$	$O(D\Delta)$
2	n	Known	$rooted$	$O(n\log(\Delta) + D\Delta)$
3	n	Known	$arbitrary$	$O(m + D\Delta)$
4	n	Unknown	$arbitrary$	$O(m + \ell(\Delta\log(\lambda) + n) + D\Delta)$
5	n	Unknown	$arbitrary$	$O(m + D\Delta\log(\lambda))^*$
6	$k > n$	Unknown	$rooted$	$O(n\log(\Delta) + D\Delta)$
7	$k > n$	Unknown	$arbitrary$	$O(m + D\Delta)$

1.2 Related Works

Some of the earliest known studies on distributed breadth-first-search algorithms were conducted by Cheung [10] and Gallager *et al.* [5,13] in the 1980s. Cheung employed a layer-by-layer approach to create a BFS from a given root, with the starting vertex assigned a layer number of 0. In [5], the authors addressed the distributed BFS algorithm for a local asynchronous point-to-point communication network, modeled by an undirected graph. They proposed two algorithms. The first algorithm had a communication complexity of $O((E + V^{1.5})\log V)$ (later improved in [3]) and a time complexity of $O(V^{1.5}\log V)$, where V and E denotes the number of nodes and edges of the graph respectively. The second one, a recursive version of the first algorithm, had communication and time complexity of $O(E \cdot 2^{\sqrt{\log V \log \log V}})$ and $O(V \cdot 2^{\sqrt{\log V \log \log V}})$, respectively. Frederickson addressed a related problem of the shortest path for a planar distributed network in [12], focusing on communication efficiency. In [19], Makki proposed an improved distributed algorithm that utilizes parallelism (visiting neighboring nodes in parallel) and enhanced synchronization techniques to create a BFS of an asynchronous network with a time complexity of $2 \cdot l$, where l is the maximum height of the BFS tree. The algorithm used $2(V - 1)$ messages to accomplish this. In [11], Chow *et al.* presented an experimental BFS implementation for large graphs consisting of billions of edges distributed over several machines. They employed $2D$ graph partitioning for the graph, where, in addition to assigning each vertex to one processor ($1D$ partitioning), each edge was also owned by one processor. The $2D$ partitioning method yielded better efficiency (both in theory and experiments) when the graph had a large average degree compared to the $1D$ partitioning. Yoo *et al.* in [27] also presented a distributed breadth-first search (BFS) scheme that scales for random graphs with up to three billion vertices and 30 billion edges. They also compared the performance based on the partitioning method over different kinds of random graphs. Additional works on scalable BFS algorithms for large-scale machines can be found in [6,7,18,26].

In [2,4], Awerbuch *et al.* described an algorithm (called *STRIP-EXPLORE*) for an agent to perform graph exploration using BFS in $O(E + V^{1.5})$ rounds on an arbitrary undirected graph. The agent's goal is to explore the graph with the constraint of returning to the root at certain intervals (called piecemeal exploration). In [20], the authors proposed an algorithm design that divides the whole graph into several clusters and then assigns respective agents at each cluster to perform the breadth-first search sequentially. Their time complexity for producing the BFS for the graph using k agents is $O(k \cdot (V + E))$. In [15], Kshemkalyani et al. used a BFS-based method to solve the *dispersion* problem (situating the agents in the graph into distinct nodes) of $k \leq n$ agents. In the local communication model (where agents can only communicate when they are at the same node), they provided a BFS-based algorithm with a time complexity of $O(D\Delta(D + \Delta))$ rounds, when all agents start from a single node. In the other case, when agents are arbitrarily placed at the start, their BFS-based dispersion takes $O((D+k)\Delta(D+\Delta))$ rounds, but it assumes the global communication model (where agents can communicate with each other at any time irrespective of their position in the graph). Both algorithms required the agents to have a memory of $O(\log D + \Delta \log k)$ bits. These results were significant improvements upon the previous exponential complexity of $O(\Delta^D)$ in [14]. Here D and Δ are respectively the diameter and highest degree of a node in the graph. The primary objective of these algorithms was to achieve dispersion from various initial configurations by employing the BFS technique, contrasting with traditionally used DFS methods.

In our work, we either assume a *dispersed* stating configuration or we first perform a dispersion of the mobile agents as an initial sub-routine. We emphasize on the construction of BFS rather than dispersing the agents by BFS. Dispersion of mobile agents, introduced by Moses Jr et al. in [1] has been receiving much attention in recent times owing to its adaptability in recent agent-based works [8,9,21]. A detailed account of dispersion algorithms for various model set-ups can be found in [22,25] and references therein.

2 Model and Problem Definition

2.1 Model

Graph: We have an underlying graph $G(V, E)$ which is connected, undirected, unweighted and anonymous with $|V| = n$ nodes and $|E| = m$ edges. The nodes of G do not have any distinguishing identifiers or labels. The nodes do not possess any memory and hence cannot store any information. The degree of a node $v \in V$ is denoted by $\delta(v)$ and the maximum degree of G is Δ. Edges incident on v are locally labelled using port numbers in the range $[0, \delta(v) - 1]$. A single edge connecting two nodes receives independent port numbering at either end. The edges of the graph serve as *routes* through which the agents can commute. Any number of agents can travel through an edge at any given time.

Mobile Agents: We have a collection of $k \geq n$ agents $\mathcal{R} = \{r_1, r_2, \ldots, r_n, \ldots, r_k\}$ residing on the nodes of the graph. Each agent has a unique ID and has finite bits of memory to store information (we bound the number of agents to $k \leq n^{c_1}$ and their IDs to n^{c_2}, where $c_1, c_2 (c_2 \geq c_1)$ are arbitrary constants). An agent cannot store the whole graph structure information within its limited memory. An agent retains its memory as long as needed and it can be updated as required. Two or more agents can be present (*co-located*) at a node or pass through an edge in G. However, an agent is not allowed to stay on an edge. An agent can recognise the port number through which it has entered and exited a node. The agents do not have any visibility beyond their (current) location at a node. An agent at node v can only see the adjacent ports (connecting to edges) at v. Only the collocated agents at a node can sense each other and exchange information. An agent can transfer all the information stored in its memory in a single round.

Communication Model: We consider a synchronous system where the agents are synchronized to a common clock and the local communication model, where, only co-located agents (i.e., agents at the same node) can communicate among themselves.

Time Cycle: Each agent r_i, on activation, performs a $Communicate - Compute - Move$ (CCM) cycle as follows.

- **Communicate:** r_i may communicate with other agents at the same node.
- **Compute:** Based on the gathered information and subsequent computations, r_i may perform all manner of computations within the bounds of its memory.
- **Move:** r_i may move to a neighboring node using the computed exit port.

Starting Configuration: In this paper, we assume three different starting configurations for the k agents.

- **Rooted Initial Configuration:** All the k agents start from a designated node called the *root* node.
- **Arbitrary Initial Configuration:** The agents are placed arbitrarily in small clusters across different nodes of the graph and represent the most generalized starting configurations for the agents.
- **Dispersed Initial Configuration:** In this configuration, each node of the graph G has at least one agent stationed in it at the start. For $k = n$, there is exactly one agent at each node of the graph.

An agent can perform the CCM task in one time unit, called *round*. The **time complexity** of an algorithm is the number of rounds required to achieve the goal. The **memory complexity** is the number of bits required by each agent to execute the algorithm.

2.2 Problem Definition

Definition 1. *Consider an n-node arbitrary anonymous simple connected graph G. We study the complexity of constructing a Breadth-First-Search (BFS) tree for G using $k \geq n$ mobile agents based upon*

1. *the starting configuration of the agents (rooted, arbitrary or dispersed),*
2. *whether the root of the BFS tree is known,*
3. *whether $k = n$ or $k > n$.*

3 Preliminaries

In this section, we briefly describe some subroutines that we use in our algorithms. The first one is a near-linear depth-first search (DFS) traversal from [25] that allows k agents to disperse across the graph, from the *rooted* configuration in $O(k \cdot \log(\tau))$ rounds, where $\tau = \min\{k, \Delta\}$. The second one is a procedure (from [8,9]) that allows two agents on neighboring nodes to meet each other if required.

3.1 ROOTED DISPERSION IN $O(k \log(\tau))$ ROUNDS

For this, the k agents start at the root and explore the graph G in a DFS manner. However, contrary to the existing DFS algorithms, the unsettled agents at a particular node do not sequentially search each outgoing port, rather they use parallelization to visit the ports of a node simultaneously. To achieve this, first, an agent from the set of unsettled agents visits a neighboring node, if it finds a settled agent there, it brings the settled agent along to the original node. Now, the two agents can simultaneously explore the rest of the ports to find an empty one. Each time, the agents are unsuccessful in finding an empty node, the number of 'helping' agents keeps doubling. Therefore, agents can search all the outgoing ports in logarithmic time with each such search taking $log(\tau)$ rounds where $\tau = \min\{k, \Delta\}$. So, at each $log(\tau)$ step the agents either find a new empty node to settle or can execute a back-track. Since the number of movements (back-track and forward) combined, is bound by $O(k)$. Therefore, the dispersion completes in $O(k \log(\tau))$ rounds.

3.2 PROCEDURE_MYN (MEET-YOUR-NEIGHBOR)

Since the port ordering of nodes is different, it can be tricky to ensure that two agents on neighboring nodes meet. Also, it is difficult to time the movement of agents and guarantee that two neighbors meet without access to a global clock. Since, it can be essential for two agents to pass information to each other, arranging ways to ensure such a meeting can be beneficial. PROCEDURE_MYN helps ensure that an agent can communicate with all its neighbors at least once when required. We use the pairing procedure PROCEDURE_MYN to ensure that during a scan for neighbors, an agent meets all its neighbors. For this, the algorithm essentially exploits the bits representing the IDs of the agents. Let λ denote the largest ID among all the n agents. Therefore, the agents use a $\log(\lambda)$ bit field to store the IDs. PROCEDURE_MYN runs in phases. Each phase consists of Δ rounds and there are a total of $\log(\lambda)$ phases. Each phase corresponds to a bit in the field (with agents having IDs less than $\log(\lambda)$ bits padding the rest with 0s). The steps in a phase are simple, starting with the rightmost bit, if the bit is 1, the agent uses Δ rounds to visit all its neighbors. If the bit is 0, the agent waits at its node for visitors. Since all agents have unique IDs, for any two pairs of neighboring agents, there exists at least one round in which the agents have different bits and meet. Clearly, the procedure takes no more than $O(\Delta \log(\lambda))$ rounds to ensure that an agent meets with all its neighbors.

4 BFS Tree Construction *Dispersed Configuration, $k = n$*

In this section, we describe a BFS tree construction algorithm for $k = n$ agents, initially placed in a *dispersed* configuration, and the *root* of the BFS tree is pre-defined. The algorithm executes in two phases. In the first phase, the agents compute Δ, the highest degree of a node in the graph G. In the second phase, we construct the BFS tree of G from the given *root* using the acquired value of Δ.

We first provide a list of variables that are used by each agent r_i during the execution of the algorithm.

1. ID - stores the ID bits of an agent. An $O(\log n)$ bit of memory space is used for the purpose.
2. *parent* - stores the *port* number from which an agent r_j finds r_i and r_i becomes the *child* of r_j. Initially *parent* $= \perp$.
3. *child* - stores the outgoing *port* number through which r_i exited its own node to move to a neighboring node to find a previously unvisited agent. Initially *child* $= \perp$
4. *completed* - a boolean variable, initially set to *false*, which takes a value *true* if and only if, each of its neighboring nodes (except *parent*) has been visited and no new unvisited neighboring node is left.
5. *level* - initially -1, it represents the *level* of r_i in a tree with respect to the *root* agent which has *level* $= 0$
6. *visitor* - a variable set to 1, if r_i is a visitor to another node from its own node. When r_i is at its home node, the *visitor* value is 0.

We denote the *root* agent as r^* and use the notation r^j to denote an agent at a *level* j with respect to a tree from the *root*.

4.1 Phase 1: Knowing the Value of Δ

The agent at the *root* node r^* begins the algorithm by visiting each of its neighboring nodes. As r^* visits each child one by one, it immediately instructs each of its children r_i^1 to visit their own children. As and when each r_i^1 receives this instruction from its parent for the first time, it starts visiting its own child nodes. Consider an agent r_i^j at the jth level who has received instruction from its parent to visit its children. Now the following cases may arise:

1. r_i^j finds a new unvisited agent (with *parent* $= \perp$) in its adjacent node - r_i^j sets the new agent as its *child* and similarly, the new agent stores the appropriate *parent* pointer to r_i^j.
2. r_i^j finds that some of its adjacent nodes are empty - In such case, r_i^j returns to its original node, marks the port as visited, and continues exploring the graph through the other available ports.
3. r_i^j finds multiple agents on one of its adjacent nodes.
   (a) The original resident of the node is present at the node (whose *visitor* $= 0$) - In such a case, the agent that has the least level (tie is broken using lower ID) becomes the parent. If r_i^j is not the selected agent, it returns to its original node and marks the node as visited.

(b) The original resident of the node is absent at the node - In such case, all agents are visitors and all of them return to their original home node.
4. If r_i^j receives an instruction from an agent to visit its neighbour for the second or consequent times, it ignores any such request.

If some agent r_i^j has no children or all of its children have already been visited (except the parent), it sets its $completed$ value to $true$ and sends the degree value of its node to its parent. Now, the parent of r_i^j waits till it gets a $completed$ message from each of its children and simultaneously collects the maximum degree information from all of its children (whose $completed = true$), compares it with its own degree, and sends the maximum to its parent along with the message $completed = true$. Once an agent has received the maximum degree of information from all of its children, it continues to move and inform the same to its parent. When the $root$ receives the maximum degree information from all of its children, it compares it with its own degree and thereby establishes the value of the maximum degree of the graph G, Δ. Now each agent has established the child-parent relationship with its appropriate neighbors. Thereafter, the $root$ propagates (downcast) the value of Δ throughout the graph using the constructed tree. Every agent in the graph is now acquainted with the maximum degree of the graph Δ.

Now all the agents have the value of Δ and we execute the next phase of constructing the BFS tree from the $root$. One may notice that the tree formed during the computation of the maximum degree (Δ) may not form a BFS tree.

4.2 Phase 2: Constructing a BFS Tree

Now, the agents have the prior knowledge of Δ and they create a BFS tree from the $root$. The $root$ starts the algorithm by visiting each of its neighbors. The $root$ marks the appropriate ports leading to each of its neighbors as its child ports. Simultaneously, when a new agent (a probable child) gets a visit from its parent for the first time, the child sets its parent port accordingly. To maintain synchronicity between the agents at each level, each agent is equipped with a variable $r_i.level$, which is initially set to -1. The $root$ sets its level to 0. During the first visit of $root$ to its children, each of its children r_i^1 set their $level$ as $r_i^1.level \leftarrow root.level + 1$. Now, each of the agents at level 1 waits for 2Δ rounds before proceeding further. By that time, it is guaranteed that $root$ had visited each of its children. Now, with the end of the first 2Δ rounds, the agents at $level = 1$ begin to explore their neighbors in search of potential children. Consider the situation, where after $2\Delta j$ rounds, all agents at level j have received the instruction from their parents to start exploring their respective children. Let an agent r_i^j at $level\ j$ start exploring its neighbors and move to a node v. Then, the following cases may arise:

1. r_i^j finds out an agent r at v with $r.level = -1$ - It marks r as its child, and simultaneously r marks r_i^j's incoming port as its parent port. r sets $r.level \leftarrow r_i^j.level + 1$
2. r_i^j finds multiple agents at v
   (a) The original resident of v, r is present at the node (whose $visitor = 0$) - r accepts the request for becoming a child of the visitor agent which has the least

ID. In case, r_i^j is that particular agent, it updates its child pointers accordingly and the newly discovered agent sets its parent port and $level \leftarrow r_i^j.level + 1$. Notice that all the multiple agents have the same level in the BFS tree due to the synchronization of the levels. If r_i^j is not the selected agent, it returns back to its original node and marks the node as visited.
   (b) The original resident of the node is absent at the node - In such case, all agents are visitors and all of them return to their original home node.
3. r_i^j finds v to be empty - r_i^j returns to explore the other neighborhoods. An empty node implies that the resident agent of that particular node is at the same level as r_i^1.
4. r_i^j finds an agent r that is already assigned a non-negative level - r_i^1 ignores r and returns back to its home node for further exploration.

During the latter stage of the execution of the algorithm, if

1. r_i^j receives an instruction from an agent to visit its neighbors for the second or consequent times, it ignores any such request or, if it
2. receives a visit from an agent with the same or lower $level$ as itself, r_i^1 ignores such an agent and continues exploration.

Now, as the algorithm continues to execute, after each 2Δ round, we have a new level of the BFS being created.

When an agent uses up all the available ports for exploration, it sets its $completed = true$ and informs its $parent$ agent about the completion. As and when an agent receives the completion information from all its children, it marks its own $completed = true$ and similarly informs its parent agent about the same. As soon as the $root$ receives the completion information from all its children, it terminates the algorithm and sends the termination information across all agents via the tree.

Lemma 1. *With the execution of Phase 2, the agents correctly create a BFS tree for the graph G.*

Proof. Since an agent always ignores any repeat request for becoming a $child$ node, algorithms in both Phase 1 and Phase 2 always create a tree substructure of the graph G. Let T be the tree generated by the agents after Phase 2. Let u be any node of the graph and $P(root = v_1, v_2, \ldots, v_k, v_{k+1}, \ldots, u = v_h)$ be the path from $root$ to u in T. Since the algorithm explores the graph level-by-level, it explores all the nodes at level k before moving on to nodes at level $k + 1$, ensuring that it finds the shortest path to each node from the $root$. Therefore, the path P represents the shortest path from $root$ to u. Hence, T is a BFS tree. □

Lemma 2. *Phase 2 takes $O(D\Delta)$ rounds to construct the BFS tree.*

Proof. In Phase 2, each level is completed in $O(\Delta)$ rounds during the construction of the BFS tree. Furthermore, the height of the BFS tree is $O(D)$. Therefore, BFS tree construction takes $O(D\Delta)$ rounds. As the agents continue to construct the BFS tree, some agents might have already completed visiting their children. These agents keep moving to their parents to inform them about their completion. The time for transmitting this completion information by all agents to the root can take at most $O(D\Delta)$ rounds, although most of this time overlaps with the BFS construction phase. Hence, the algorithm achieves completion within $O(D\Delta)$ rounds. □

Lemma 3. *Phase 1 requires $O(D\Delta)$ time to compute the Δ.*

Proof. We first establish that any agent at a distance d from the *root* gets visited within $O(d\Delta)$ rounds, using induction on d.

- $d = 1$: The *root* informs all its adjacent nodes in 2Δ rounds to explore their respective children.
- $d = i$: We assume that all agents at a distance i have been visited in $2i\Delta$ rounds.
- $d = i + 1$: With the beginning of the $2i\Delta + 1$ round, all agents at a distance i that has already been visited from the *root*, so, the agents at distance i can begin instructing their children for exploration (some may have already initiated this process). Therefore, by the end of $2i\Delta + 2\Delta$ rounds, it is guaranteed that all agents at a distance $i + 1$ from the *root* have been visited.

Since the distance between *root* and any arbitrary agent is $\leq D$, it can be guaranteed that all the n agents must have received the exploration instruction from their parents by the end of $2D\Delta$ rounds and hence the lemma.

Alternatively, it may be seen that the algorithm in Phase 2 runs identically to the BFS tree algorithm in Phase 2, except we additionally have waiting times in Phase 2. So, the running time of Phase 1 outperforms the running time of Phase 2. □

Remark 1 (Child Pointers). To efficiently manage the storage of child node pointers, the agent employs the following strategy: Upon encountering a new child node, it stores the pointer to that specific child in the memory of the previously discovered child. Specifically, if $r_{s_1}, r_{s_2}, \ldots, r_{s_t}$ represent the consecutive children of parent node r, the pointer to r_{s_1} is stored at r, the pointer to r_{s_2} is stored at r_{s_1}, the pointer to r_{s_3} in r_{s_2}, and so forth. This approach ensures organised and accessible storage of child node connections within the system while minimising the memory requirement at each agent.

Lemma 4 (Memory Complexity). *Each agent requires an $O(\log n)$ bits of memory to execute the algorithm.*

Proof. To execute the algorithm, the agents need to store the *port* numbers for *child* and *parent* pointers needing an $O(\log \Delta)$ memory space. This helps to keep the memory requirement for storing the *child* pointers to $O(\log \Delta)$ bit space. For the IDs, the agent requires $O(\log n)$ bits. Other variables require a constant number of bits. Therefore, each agent would require a $O(\log n)$ bits of memory to execute the algorithm. □

Combining lemmas from 1 to 4, we have the following result.

Theorem 1. *Given an arbitrary simple connected graph G with n nodes m edges, maximum degree Δ and diameter D. Then, a BFS tree can be constructed in $O(D\Delta)$ rounds from the root node when such a node is known as a prior and the n agents begin in a dispersed initial configuration with $O(\log n)$ bits of memory per agent. The agents do not require any prior knowledge about any global parameters.*

Remark 2 (Rooted Configuration). If all the agents start from a single node in a rooted initial configuration, a BFS tree with *root* from the node hosting the minimum ID agent can be constructed in $O(n \log \Delta + D\Delta)$ rounds, after performing *dispersion* in $O(n \log \Delta)$ rounds using the dispersion algorithm in [25].

5 BFS Tree Construction *Arbitrary Configuration, $k = n$*

In this section, we describe an algorithm to create a BFS tree when the n agents start arbitrarily as ℓ clusters across the graph G. Our algorithm runs in three stages. In the first stage, the agents perform a dispersion so that each node is occupied uniquely by a single distinct agent. This can be achieved in $O(m)$ rounds using the dispersion algorithm proposed in [16] by Kshemkalyani *et al.* for the arbitrary configuration. In the second stage, a leader agent is elected among the n agents which leads the BFS tree creation procedure in the final stage. Details and proofs of time complexities of Phase 1 and 2 can be found in [16] and [9] respectively.

5.1 Phase 1: Dispersion of Mobile Agents

The agents disperse using a method from Kshemkalyani [16], where each cluster starts its own DFS process. If two DFS processes meet, the one with more settled agents absorbs the other, a process called "subsumption". After dispersion, there might be multiple independent DFS trees and each such DFS tree is identified with its unique label ($treelabel$), which the tree obtains from one of its settled agent's IDs. The dispersion algorithm takes $O(m)$ rounds, and to ensure coordination, agents delay the leader election protocol by $cn\Delta$ rounds from the start of dispersion, with c being a large constant. To create the BFS tree, we elect a global leader agent that functions as a *root* and adapt Algorithm 4.2.

5.2 Phase 2: Leader Election

First, we make sure all agents meet their neighbors using PROCEDURE_MYN. When agents with different IDs meet, they share their $treelabel$, updating to the lower value if necessary. After PROCEDURE_MYN, agents in each DFS send their updated $treelabel$ to their DFS root. The $root$ waits for $O(n)$ rounds as it receives different $treelabel$ values from different parts of its DFS tree, then decides on the lowest $treelabel$, sending it down to all nodes via the DFS tree (*down-casting*), updating each node with the lowest $treelabel$ value. This marks the end of a phase. After the end of ℓ such phases, it is guaranteed that each of the n agents in G now has a consistent $treelabel$ value. After the protocol, the agent with the global minimum $treelabel$ becomes the leader, identified as $r^\star$.

5.3 Phase 3: BFS Tree Construction

Now, the node with the elected leader becomes the *root* of the BFS tree. At this point, we have a *dispersed* configuration of agents with *root* of the BFS tree known, thereby replicating the similar configuration of agents as in Sect. 4. The agents now follow the exact protocol from Sect. 4.2 to construct a BFS tree from the *root* for the graph G.

Combining Phase 1 and 2, we can state the following lemma. The detailed proofs can be found in [9, 16].

Lemma 5. *Dispersion and Leader Election in Phase 1 and Phase 2 collectively takes $O(m) + O(\ell(\Delta \log(\lambda) + n))$ rounds.*

Theorem 2. *Given an arbitrary simple connected graph G with n nodes m edges, maximum degree Δ and diameter D. Then, a BFS tree can be constructed in $O(m + \ell(\Delta \log(\lambda) + n) + D\Delta)$ rounds from the elected root node when the n agents begin in an* arbitrary *initial configuration, with $O(\log n)$ bits of memory per agent.*

Proof. Till the leader election stage, the algorithm takes up $O(m)+O(\ell(\Delta \log(\lambda)+n))$ rounds. In the final Phase 3, BFS tree is constructed similarly as in Sect. 4.2 taking an additional $O(D\Delta)$ rounds. □

Remark 3. **Arbitrary Initial Configuration, $root$ Known:** In this case, the agents first perform a *dispersion*. Since the $root$ of the BFS tree is known, the $root$ agent becomes the leader and completes the BFS tree from the $root$ using the algorithm described in Sect. 5.3. In this case, the completion time for the algorithm is $O(m + D\Delta)$ rounds.

Further Reduction in Time Complexity: We can further reduce the time complexity for constructing BFS tree for arbitrary configuration, when the $root$ is unknown. This can be achieved using additional $O(n \cdot \log n)$ bits of memory per agent. This method requires the initial knowledge parameters n, Δ and λ.

For this, we use an array of size n, with each field of length $\log n$ bits to store the ID of agents. We first disperse the agents in $O(m)$ rounds. Post dispersion, each agent keeps visiting each of its neighbors using PROCEDURE_MYN till each of them gets updated with the ID of the least ID agent. In one round, each agent visits each of its neighbors and stores the ID of the visited agents and the least ID among them. In the second round, each agent again similarly visits its neighbor, but this time copying out the updated list of visited agents from its neighbors into its own memory and updating the least ID agent. So, by the second round, each agent, through its neighbors, gets a list of all the neighbors within a distance of 2 from its own node. The algorithm stops once it gets updated with the list of all n agents. Since all agents from any nodes are reachable within a distance of D (diameter), each agent can collect the list of all n agents using D executions of PROCEDURE_MYN. Therefore, the algorithm takes $O(D\Delta \log \lambda)$ rounds to select the minimum ID agent as their leader. Once the leader is elected, the algorithm takes additional $O(D\Delta)$ rounds to create the BFS tree.

Lemma 6. *When equipped with $O(n \cdot \log n)$ bits of memory per agent, a BFS tree can be constructed in $O(m + D\Delta \log \lambda)$ rounds from the elected root node when the n agents begin in an* arbitrary *initial configuration.*

6 BFS Tree Construction, $k > n$

In this section, we will adapt the algorithms developed in the preceding sections to situations where the number of agents (k) exceeds the number of nodes (n) in the graph G.

6.1 Rooted Configuration

In the rooted configuration, all the agents start at a specific node (*root*) and perform DFS using the protocol described in [25]. It positions the k agents across G with one agent at each node. The remaining $k - n$ agents eventually backtrack and gather at the *root*. Once the *root* agent has all its ports visited, and the last remaining exploratory agents return to the *root*, the DFS protocol is terminated. The $k - n$ unsettled agents at the *root* are now excluded from the subsequent algorithm. The dispersion completes in $O(n \cdot \log \Delta)$ rounds.

Now, the next phase of the algorithm starts with n agents dispersed across the graph. The algorithm now follows the exact procedure as described in 4.2, to first compute the value of Δ and then build the BFS tree of the graph G from the *root*.

6.2 Arbitrary Configuration

When the agents begin arbitrarily as multiple clusters (we assume ℓ clusters) across G, we first disperse the agents. To do this, we adapt the dispersion protocol from [16]. Although the new algorithm provided in [25] for arbitrary starting configuration performs better, we find the algorithm in [16] has two other important advantages that may be easily reaped for $k > n$ - (i) termination guarantee and (ii) immediate leader election.

Following the algorithm in [16], the agents start to disperse across the graph, in parallel from each of the ℓ clusters. The agents independently execute the DFS protocol from each cluster. This creates ℓ DFS tress beginning from the ℓ clusters at the initial stage. As the DFSs grow and meet other DFSs, the DFSs with a lower number of settled agents get subsumed by the DFSs having a higher number of settled agents. When a DFS gets subsumed, all its agents (settled and unsettled) are collected at the head of the subsuming DFS, which then keeps parking the agents one by one onto the empty nodes according to its DFS traversal. As the number of agents in our case is greater than the number of nodes, we have two particular advantages. First, as there are more agents than nodes, the unsettled agents from some DFS will always keep finding other agents from different DFSs, keep absorbing them and eventually, there will be a single master DFS that will subsume all the other smaller DFSs. Finally, the master DFS (which now acts as a single DFS for G), just like the rooted case, will have all the excess unsettled agents collected at its DFS *root*. This ends the dispersion phase which takes $O(m)$ rounds. The second advantage is that, since the number of DFSs is reduced to one, electing a leader r^* can be done immediately. The settled agent at the *root* of the final DFS becomes the leader. Now, the leader constructs the BFS tree for G with given *root* using the technique described in Sect. 4.

Below we state the main theorem of this section for the *rooted* and *arbitrary* initial configuration of the agents.

Theorem 3. *Given an arbitrary simple connected graph G with n nodes m edges, maximum degree Δ and diameter D. Then,*

1. *a BFS tree can be constructed in $O(n \log \Delta + D\Delta)$ rounds from the root node when the $k > n$ agents begin in an* rooted *initial configuration.*

2. a BFS tree can be constructed in $O(m + D\Delta)$ rounds from the elected root node when the $k > n$ agents begin in an arbitrary *initial configuration in multiple clusters.*

7 Applications

7.1 Bipartite Graph

In this section, we use the BFS tree constructed (in the previous sections) by the mobile agents to check whether the n-node graph G on which the $k(\geq n)$ agents are operating is *bipartite* or not. To verify whether G is bipartite or not, we verify whether G is 2-colorable or not. Notice that a bipartite graph can be partitioned into two sets such that no two vertices in the same set are adjacent. Thereafter, we can assign the same color to the same set of nodes. Similarly, a 2-colorable graph can be partitioned into two sets based on their colors. Vertices of one color form one set, and vertices of the other color form the second set. Since no edges exist between vertices of the same color, the graph is bipartite.

Consider the graph G with its BFS tree, say T. Each agent r_i knows its level w.r.t to the *root* of the tree T, Δ and D of the graph during the BFS tree construction. Furthermore, each even-level agent sets their color $white$ and odd-level agents set their color $black$. To check whether two adjacent agents have the same color, even level agents visit their neighbors one by one based on port numbering (in ascending order) which takes twice the time of their degree, i.e., 2Δ rounds. If an agent finds all its neighbors having the other color, then it sets the decision bit to 1. If an agent r_i finds its neighboring agent with the same color or finds it empty, i.e., having the neighbor at the same level which implies having the neighbor of the same color, then the agent r_i sets its decision bit to 0. Similarly, odd-level agent follows the process and set their decision bit accordingly, which takes another 2Δ rounds. After 4Δ rounds, the leaf agent, say r_l, of the T visit to their parent and provide the decision value. The parent of r_l performs the logical AND (&) operation of all the received decision bits with its own decision bit and visits to their parent. This process is repeated iteratively and takes D rounds to send their collective decision to the *root* of T. *root* performs the logical AND operation of all the received bits with its own bit. If the *root* has the value 0 after performing the logical AND operation, then the graph is not 2-colorable, otherwise, the graph is 2-colorable. This whole process takes $4\Delta + D$ rounds. Now each agent returns back to their position and informs their children who visited their parent earlier and were waiting for the decision. This process takes further D rounds to convey the colorability of the graph to all agents. Therefore, the time required to check whether the graph is 2-colorable or not (bipartite or not) is $2D + 4\Delta$.

From the above discussion, we have the following results.

Lemma 7. *The identification of bipartite-ness of G post BFS tree construction takes $O(D + \Delta)$ rounds.*

7.2 Gathering of Agents

In this section, we describe a method of gathering $k \geq n$ agents using a BFS tree. Gathering is the process of collecting all mobile agents into a specific node within a finite amount of time. To perform gathering, we first disperse the mobile agents and create a BFS tree with a designated *root*. In case, a node has multiple agents post dispersion, the agent with the least ID among the agents in the node becomes their representative. After the construction of the BFS tree (or when such a tree is already available), gathering of agents requires an additional $O(h)$ rounds where h is the height of the BFS tree.

The gathering begins with agents at leaf nodes of the BFS tree moving to their respective *parent* nodes. Leaf nodes are those nodes in the BFS tree that have no *child* pointers. Now, a specific agent r_i, situated at a node u does the following:

1. Waits for all its *child* nodes to arrive at u with their own group of gathered agents.
2. Once all the *child* agents, along with their respective collection gathers at u, r_i along with all the gathered agents move to its *parent* node.

The algorithm ends as soon as all the agents gather at the *root*. The agents need additional $O(h)$ rounds to gather at the *root* and since, $h = O(D)$, we have the following lemma.

Lemma 8. *The gathering of* $k \geq n$ *agents placed across the nodes of G takes* $O(D)$ *rounds post the BFS tree construction.*

8 Conclusion and Future Works

In this paper, we studied the complexity of creating a Breadth-First-Search tree using agents for different starting configurations. We provided a BFS tree construction algorithm for dispersed configuration assuming the prior knowledge of the BFS tree's *root*, which operates in $O(D\Delta)$ rounds and consumes $O(\log n)$ bits of memory per agent. Expanding upon this framework, we extended our methodology to accommodate other starting configurations, considering both exactly n or more than n agents. Finally, we provided two applications for the BFS tree construction methodology - one, to identify if a graph is bipartite and the other, to gather all the agents into a single node. Post BFS tree construction, these algorithms run in $O(D + \Delta)$ and $O(D)$ rounds respectively.

It would be interesting to establish lower bounds for the above computations in terms of both time complexity and memory per agent. Furthermore, the efficiency of the problem in the faulty agent model can be an interesting investigation for the future.

References

1. Augustine, J., Moses, Jr., W.K.: Dispersion of mobile robots: a study of memory-time tradeoffs. In: ICDCN (2018)
2. Awerbuch, B., Betke, M., Rivest, R., Singh, M.: Piecemeal Graph Exploration by a Mobile Robot. Massachusetts Institute of Technology (1995)
3. Awerbuch, B., Gallager, R.: A new distributed algorithm to find breadth first search trees. IEEE Trans. Inf. Theory **33**(3), 315–322 (1987)
4. Awerbuch, B., Betke, M., Rivest, R.L., Singh, M.: Piecemeal graph exploration by a mobile robot. Inf. Comput. (1999)

5. Awerbuch, B., Gallager, R.G.: Distributed BFS algorithms. In: FOCS (1985)
6. Beamer, S., Buluç, A., Asanovic, K., Patterson, D.: Distributed memory breadth-first search revisited: enabling bottom-up search. In: IPDPS (2013)
7. Buluç, A., Madduri, K.: Parallel breadth-first search on distributed memory systems. In: SC 2011 (2011)
8. Chand, P.K., Das, A., Molla, A.R.: Agent-based triangle counting and its applications in anonymous graphs. arXiv preprint arXiv:2402.03653 (2024)
9. Chand, P.K., Molla, A.R., Sivasubramaniam, S.: Run for cover: dominating set via mobile agents. In: Georgiou, K., Kranakis, E. (eds.) ALGOWIN 2023, pp. 133–150. Springer, Cham (2023). https://doi.org/10.1007/978-3-031-48882-5_10
10. Cheung, T.Y.: Graph traversal techniques and the maximum flow problem in distributed computation. IEEE Trans. Softw. Eng. (1983)
11. Chow, E., Henderson, K.W., Yoo, A.: Distributed breadth-first search with 2-d partitioning. In: LLNL Technical Report (2005)
12. Frederickson, G.N.: A single source shortest path algorithm for a planar distributed network. In: STACS 1985 (1985)
13. Gallager, R.: Distributed minimum hop algorithms. M.I.T. Technical Report (1982)
14. Kshemkalyani, A.D., Ali, F.: Efficient dispersion of mobile robots on graphs. In: ICDCN (2019)
15. Kshemkalyani, A.D., Molla, A.R., Sharma, G.: Dispersion of mobile robots using global communication. J. Parallel Distribut. Comput. (2022)
16. Kshemkalyani, A.D., Sharma, G.: Near-optimal dispersion on arbitrary anonymous graphs. In: OPODIS (2021)
17. Levinas, I., Scherz, R., Louzoun, Y.: BFS-based distributed algorithm for parallel local-directed subgraph enumeration. J. Complex Netw. (2022)
18. Liu, C.H.: Optimization communication for BFS based on 1d-partition. J. Phys. Conf. Ser. **1684**(1), 012125 (2020)
19. Makki, S.: Efficient distributed breadth-first search algorithm. Comput. Commun. **19**(8), 628–636 (1996)
20. Palanisamy, V., Vijayanathan, S.: Cluster based multi agent system for breadth first search. In: ICTER (2020)
21. Pattanayak, D., Bhagat, S., Gan Chaudhuri, S., Molla, A.R.: Maximal independent set via mobile agents. In: ICDCN (2024)
22. Pattanayak, D., Sharma, G., Mandal, P.S.: Dispersion of mobile robots in spite of faults. In: SSS (2023)
23. Ryu, H., Chung, W.K.: Local map-based exploration using a breadth-first search algorithm for mobile robots. Int. J. Precision Eng. Manuf. **16**(10), 2073–2080 (2015)
24. Slota, G.M., Rajamanickam, S., Madduri, K.: Bfs and coloring-based parallel algorithms for strongly connected components and related problems. In: IPDPS (2014)
25. Sudo, Y., Shibata, M., Nakamura, J., Kim, Y., Masuzawa, T.: Near-linear time dispersion of mobile agents. arXiv preprint arXiv:2310.04376 (2023)
26. Ueno, K., Suzumura, T., Maruyama, N., Fujisawa, K., Matsuoka, S.: Efficient breadth-first search on massively parallel and distributed-memory machines. Data Sci. Eng. **2**(1), 22–35 (2017)
27. Yoo, A., Chow, E., Henderson, K., McLendon, W., Hendrickson, B., Catalyurek, U.: A scalable distributed parallel breadth-first search algorithm on bluegene/l. In: SC 2005 (2005)

Some New Results With k-Set Agreement

Carole Delporte-Gallet[1(✉)], Hugues Fauconnier[1], and Mouna Safir[1,2]

[1] IRIF, Univeristé Paris Cité, Paris, France
{cd,hf,safir}@irif.fr
[2] College of Computing, Université Polytechnique Mohammed VI Benguerir, Benguerir, Morocco

Abstract. In this article, we investigate the solvability of k-set agreement among n processes in distributed systems prone to different types of process failures. k-set agreement allows each process to propose a value and decide a value such that at most k different values are decided by the correct processes, in such a way that, if all the correct processes propose the same value v, they will decide v. We specially explore two scenarios: synchronous message-passing systems prone to up to t Byzantine failures of processes, and asynchronous shared memory systems prone to up to t crash failures. Our goal is to address the gaps left by previous works [4,8,15] in these areas. In the message passing system with Byzantine failures we enriched the system with authentication, we present an algorithm that ensures k-set agreement in only two rounds, with no constraints on the number of faults t, with k determined as $k \geq \lfloor \frac{n}{n-t} \rfloor + 1$, and an optimal algorihtm ensuring k-set agreement in $t+1$ rounds for $k \geq \lfloor \frac{n}{n-t} \rfloor$. While in the crash asynchronous shared memory systems, we introduce an algorithm that ensure k-set agreement when $n > 2t$ for $k \geq \lfloor \frac{n-t}{n-2t} \rfloor + 1$, and an impossibility result for $k \leq \lfloor \frac{n-t}{n-2t} \rfloor - 1$.

Keywords: Byzantine failures · Crash failures · Distributed systems · k-set agreement · Shared memory · Authentication · Message Passing

1 Introduction

The consensus problem is an abstraction of many coordination problems in a distributed system that can suffer process failures. Roughly speaking, the consensus problem is to have processes of a distributed system agree on a common decision. Because of the many practical problems that can be reduced to this simple primitive, consensus has been thoroughly studied. We refer the reader to [18] for a detailed discussion of consensus. Motivated by the significance of consensus, researchers have explored variations of the problem to investigate the boundaries of what is possible and impossible. One such variation is the k-set consensus [5], which relaxes the safety conditions of consensus to allow for a

---

The authors have been supported by the ANR French projects DUCAT (ANR-20-CE48-0006).

© The Author(s), under exclusive license to Springer Nature Switzerland AG 2024
A. Castañeda et al. (Eds.): NETYS 2024, LNCS 14783, pp. 83–99, 2024.
https://doi.org/10.1007/978-3-031-67321-4_5

set of decision values with a cardinal of up to k (compared to $k = 1$ in consensus). The k-set agreement problem has been widely studied in the field of distributed computing [16]. Beyond the practical interest of this problem, particularly regarding fault-tolerant distributed computing, one of the main reasons behind the focus on the k-set agreement problem is the fact that it can be used to define and compare computational power properties of systems.

In the k-set agreement, each process must decide on a value such that no more than k different values are decided by processes. In addition, the processes must guarantee a validity condition that characterizes which decision values are allowed as a function of the input values and whether failures occur. Regarding k-set agreement in asynchronous models, one of the most famous (and difficult) results is the extension of the consensus impossibility result to the impossibility of the k-set agreement [3,10,17] when at least k processes may fail.

In synchronous models with crash failures, k-set agreement is solvable for all k. But interestingly, this (imperfect) agreement on more than one value will divide the complexity in the number of rounds needed to solve the k-set agreement: as proved in [6], $\lfloor t/k \rfloor + 1$ rounds of communication are necessary and sufficient to solve k set agreement with no more than t faulty processes. Note that these results depend on the chosen validity condition.

In this work, we aim to investigate the solvability of k-set agreement in distributed systems prone to different types of failures with the validity condition ensuring that if all correct processes have the same initial v all correct processes decide v. Specifically, we focus on two scenarios: synchronous message-passing systems prone to Byzantine failures and asynchronous shared memory systems prone to crash failures. Concerning Byzantine failures we consider models with authentication in which messages may be signed by processes with unforgeable signatures. Most of the results concerning general Byzantine failures are already shown in [4,8,15], where in [15] the authors investigated the k-set agreement with Byzantine failures in an asynchronous system both in message passing and shared memory models. Our objective is to address gaps left by previous works in these areas and provide insights into the solvability of k-set agreement under specific failure models and give some results in terms of round complexity.

We present two algorithms ensuring k-set agreement in a synchronous Byzantine message passing model enriched with authentication, first, an algorithm that works in two rounds and solves k-set for $k \geq \lfloor \frac{n}{n-t} \rfloor + 1$, for any value of t, then another algorithm ensuring optimality on the number k, that spans $t + 1$ rounds and guarantees k-set agreement for $k \geq \lfloor \frac{n}{n-t} \rfloor$. This algorithm leverages n instances of the Terminating Reliable Broadcast (TRB), where the delivered value represents the proposed value for the set agreement. This result is interesting: if k is the optimal value for k-set agreement, we have $t + 1$ rounds to achieve the k-set but only 2 rounds for the $(k + 1)$-set. That means for example that only 2 rounds are needed for the 2-set agreement. Note also that these results apply to crash failure models with the validity property ensuring that if all the correct processes propose the same value that value is decided. Our results, in addition to those presented in [11,14], further advance the solvability of k-set agreement in a Byzantine message passing system with authentication.

The authors in [15] also studied the solvability of k-set agreement in an asynchronous shared memory system prone to crash failures. They left a small gap when $n > 2t$ and for $k = t + 1$ when $n \leq 2t$. To address the first gap, we propose an algorithm that ensures k-set agreement for $k \geq \lfloor \frac{n-t}{n-2t} \rfloor + 1$ and proves the impossibility result for $k \leq \lfloor \frac{n-t}{n-2t} \rfloor - 1$, the only gap remaining in this case is when $k = \lfloor \frac{n-t}{n-2t} \rfloor$.

Our algorithm uses an instance of a snapshot primitive, where the result of the snapshot is stored as a vector, and then each process performs computations on that vector. This approach helps us achieve the desired k-set agreement while considering the constraints imposed by the system's asynchronous nature and crash failures.

In summary, our work contributes to the understanding of k-set agreement in distributed systems, providing valuable insights into the solvability of this problem under specific failure models. We address important gaps in existing research and offer practical solutions to achieve k-set agreement in both synchronous and asynchronous distributed systems with different types of failures. The rest of the paper is organized as follows: Sect. 2 presents the model and the preliminaries, Sect. 3 presents an only two rounds algorithm for k-set Agreement for $k \geq \lfloor \frac{n}{n-t} \rfloor + 1$ and a $t+1$ rounds algorithm for $k \geq \lfloor \frac{n}{n-t} \rfloor$ in synchronous message passing model with Byzantine failures and authentication, Sect. 4 presents the result in the asynchronous shared memory model. Finally, Sect. 5 concludes the paper and discusses future research directions.

2 Preliminaries

In this section, we provide a detailed explanation of the communication model and failure models used in our study, as well as an overview of two essential primitives, the Terminating Reliable Broadcast (TRB), and the Snapshot primitive.

2.1 Communication Model

We consider a distributed system, which is made up of a set of n distributed and interconnected computing units, or *processes*. We assume that the set of processes is static, and is denoted by $\Pi = \{p_1, p_2, \ldots, p_n\}$, where each p_i represents a distinct process. The processes are communicating either by message passing or shared memory.

Message Passing Model. In the *message passing model*, the processes communicate by *sending* and *receiving* messages through channels between processes. We consider that the channel is *reliable*: Neither message loss, creation, modification, nor duplication. A reliable channel is crucial for maintaining consistency and ensuring coordinated actions among different processes. Each channel is assumed to be *bidirectional* (it can carry messages in both directions).

In *synchronous* message passing model, the messages' delays are known by all processes.

In the synchronous model, processes operate with predictable timing. We can build on this to create a system using synchronous rounds. For the synchronous rounds, processes work in successive rounds, each round is composed of three consecutive steps, such that:

1. Each (correct) process sends a message to all the processes,
2. Each (correct) process receives the messages sent to it during the current round.
3. Each (correct) process executes its local computation (involving its current local state and the set of messages it received).

Shared Memory Model. In the *shared memory model*, each process has its own dedicated register, these registers mainly allow two operations: *read* and *write*. Communication between processes occurs when one process reads the register of another. Thus, to share information, a process writes in its own register, knowing that other processes can read that register. We assume that a write operation is completed fully and is not corrupted.

2.2 Failure Models

Furthermore, the system can be susceptible to process failures. We first start by defining a correct process, it is a process that behaves exactly as specified by the algorithm, its behavior is consistent with the specification. When a process is not correct it is said to be faulty. We distinguish two types of process failures, crash failures, and Byzantine failures. The first failure is where a process simply stops its execution. The second type is where a process may arbitrarily deviate from its protocol specification. Note that a crash is a special case of Byzantine failure. We assume that t is the number of faulty processes in the system with $1 \leq t \leq n - 1$. Assuming that runs are infinite, a faulty process that crashes in a run makes a finite number of steps.

2.3 Two Useful Primitives

In Sects. 3 and 4 we present algorithms that solve k-set agreement. Our solutions rely mainly on two primitives **Terminating Reliable Broadcast (TRB)** [12] for Byzantine failure with authentication and the **Snapshot** primitive [1] for the shared memory model.

Terminating Reliable Broadcast. In Sect. 3, we detail our algorithm which uses the Terminating Reliable Broadcast (TRB) as a foundational primitive. In this Section, we will give a reminder of the TRB.

A TRB protocol typically organizes the system into a sending process and a set of receiving processes, which includes the sender itself.

The goal of the protocol is to transfer a message from the sender to the set of receiving processes, at the end of TRB a process will "deliver" a message by passing it to the application level that invoked the TRB protocol. We consider the message sent by the sending process as its initial value.

In order to tolerate arbitrary failures, the TRB protocol is enriched with authentication so that the ability of a faulty process to lie is considerably limited. If a correct process detects that the sender is faulty, the delivered message then is a "sender faulty" message. This protocol works for any number of faulty processes.

Consider a set of value V, and a special value SF (for sender faulty). A TRB protocol is a protocol of broadcast value with a process p being the sender, and making a *TRB-bcast(m,p)* for some $m \in V$. All the correct processes deliver a value m by a *TRB-deliver(p)*, where p is the sender of the message m, in such a way to satisfy the following properties:

- **Termination.** Every correct process delivers some message.
- **Validity.** If the sender, p, is correct and broadcasts a message m, then every correct process delivers m.
- **Integrity.** A process delivers a message at most once, and if it delivers some message $m \neq SF$, then m was broadcast by the sender.
- **Agreement**. If a correct process delivers a message m, then all correct processes deliver m.

Snapshot. The snapshot object was introduced in [1] as a shared data structure allowing concurrent processes to store information in a collection of shared registers. It can be seen as an initially empty set, which can then contain up to n values (one per process). This object provides two operations denoted *update*() and *snapshot*(). The invocation *update*(m) by a process p_i writes in process p_i's register the value m. The invocation *snapshot*() by a process p_i reads all process p_j's register and returns its content, which we denote as $view_i$.

We consider an atomic snapshot object i.e. the snapshot object satisfies the following properties:

- **Termination.** The invocation of *snapshot*() or *update*() by a correct process terminates.
- **Atomicity Property.** The snapshot and update operations are atomic, meaning that they appear to execute instantaneously and they satisfy the sequential specification of the snapshot.

The snapshot object satisfies the following property, and it is applicable only when the code of each process starts with updating its local value first and then can have any number of invocations to take a snapshot.

- **Inclusion Property.** (1) When a process p_i takes a snapshot, the resulting view $view_i$ includes the local value of p_i, and (2) If a snapshot by p_i (getting a resulting view $view_i$) occurs before a snapshot by p_j (getting a resulting view $view_j$), then $view_i$ is a subset of $view_j$.

2.4 k-Set Agreement

In k-set agreement, each process must decide on a value such that no more than k different values are decided by correct processes. More precisely, let V be a finite set of at least $k + 1$ values. Each process has an *initial* value v in V and we say that each process *proposes* v to the k-set Agreement. Each process has to irrevocably *decide* on a value in V. The decided values must satisfy the following properties.

- **Validity.** If all the correct processes propose the same initial value v, no correct process decides a value different from v.
- **Agreement.** At most k different values are decided by the correct processes.
- **Termination.** Eventually, all the correct processes decide.

We say that an algorithm solves k-set Agreement in a system of n processes with at most $t < n$ failures of processes, if all the executions in this system satisfy these properties. Note that only the correct processes have to decide.

Several non-equivalent validity properties for k-set agreement have been proposed and argued [15]. The validity considered here is generally the one used in the Byzantine case. More recently, [7] argues on the possibilities and impossibilities of various validity in the context of consensus.

Remark that the validity property given here is stronger than the validity property generally given for crash failures in which a decided value has only to be one of the initial value of a process (correct or faulty). Hence, in some cases, a decided value would come from a faulty process, which can be acceptable when processes are not malicious as with crash failures. Moreover, in the Byzantine case, it is not clear what is the initial value of a Byzantine process (any value, no value?), and such a weak validity condition would lead to deciding any value in all cases.

Note that, if applied to the crash failure model, it could also be interesting from a practical point of view to force the decided value when all correct processes propose the same value.

3 Authenticated Synchronous Message Passing Model

In this section, we explore k-set agreement in a message-passing model with authentication. In fact, all these results apply to crash failure models too. Our focus is on ensuring reliable communication between processes through the exchange of **authenticated** messages in the TRB algorithm. Each received message is signed by the sender, guaranteeing its authenticity.

In the first step, we present a k-set agreement algorithm in two rounds, with no constraints on the number of failures t. But with a value of k such that $k \geq \lfloor \frac{n}{n-t} \rfloor + 1$. In a second step, we give an optimal algorithm concerning the value of k for $k \geq \lfloor \frac{n}{n-t} \rfloor$, where this algorithm needs $t + 1$ rounds.

3.1 A Two Rounds k-Set Agreement

We first present a two rounds algorithm, that ensures k-set Agreement for $k \geq \lfloor \frac{n}{n-t} \rfloor + 1$, this is an authenticated algorithm where the messages sent by processes are signed. This prevents any faulty process from forging the signature of a correct process or misrepresenting the value sent by a correct process.

The Algorithm

Algorithm 1 ensures k-set agreement for $k \geq \lfloor \frac{n}{n-t} \rfloor + 1$, where the processes exchange their messages in two rounds. A process p_i in the first round sends its signed initial value v_i and receives every other process' correct signed initial value, it stores them in a vector V_i, and in the second round, it signs its vector and sends it to every other process and receives from every p_j a signed vector V_j if any.

```
 1  Initialization: V_i vector of decision of size n initialized to ⊥
 2  forall w, j ≠ i do
 3  |   M_i[j][w] ← ⊥
 4  end
 5
    Input: M_i[i][i] = V_i[i] ← v_i
    /* ------------ round 1 -------------------- */
 6  Send the signed value M_i[i][i] to all the processes ;
 7  if  p_i receives v_j, correctly signed from p_j then  M_i[i][j] ← v_j;
    /* ------------ round 2 -------------------- */
 8  Send the vector V_i = M_i[i][*] to all the processes;
 9  if  p_i receives a vector V correctly signed from p_j then  M_i[j] ← V;
    /* ------------ at the end of round 2 ------------------ */
10  for j ← 1 to n, with j ≠ i do
11  |   w = M[i][j];
12  |   if  w =⊥ then
13  |   |   V_i[j] =⊥
14  |   else
15  |   |   V_i[j] = w;
16  |   |   for ℓ ← 1 to n, with ℓ ≠ i do
17  |   |   |   if M_i[ℓ][j] ≠⊥ then  if M_i[ℓ][j] ≠ w then V_i[j] =⊥ ;
18  |   |   |   ;
19  |   |   end
20  |   end
21  end
    /* -------- Decision at the end of round 2 ---------- */
22  if p_i finds in V_i, n − t values equal to v_i then
23  |   decide v_i;
24  else
25  |   decide ⊥;
26  end
```

Algorithm 1: Solving k-set agreement in an authenticated Byzantine synchronous message passing model. Code for p_i.

Proof of the algorithm

Each process manages a local matrix $M_i[1..n][1..n]$, such that if v_i is the value proposed by p_i, where $M_i[i][i]$ is v_i signed ($v_i : p_i$) by p_i, and all the other entries are initialized to $\bot$. In the first round each p_i sends $M_i[i][i]$ to all the processes and assigns to $M_i[i][j]$ the value it receives from p_j if correctly signed. It is important to note that if p_i receives a value v_j from p_j, it can only come from p_j and not from any other source.

Then at the second round, each process p_i broadcasts its signed $M_i[i][*]$ vector and the received vectors from other processes are used to update the matrix M_i as follows: p_i receives from p_j the signed vector V that it stores it in $M_i[j][*]$ if correctly signed. After this round, process p_i compares the values of each column. If it detects that a process has sent two different values to two different processes, it sets its value in V_i to $\bot$, where V_i is considered the decision vector. To guarantee the Validity property, if p_i finds $n-t$ values in V_i that are equal to its own initial value v_i, it decides on v_i as the agreed value. Otherwise, it decides on $\bot$.

Lemma 1. *Let p_i be a correct process with matrix M_i, and let p_ℓ and p_j be two processes. If $M_i[i][j] \neq M_i[\ell][j]$, and $M_i[\ell][j] \neq \bot$, then p_j is Byzantine.*

Proof. By contradiction, let us suppose that p_j is correct and sends the same value to everyone, thanks to the authentication, p_j's message cannot be forged or lied about, and then all the processes in Π will have the same view on p_j' value, and all the correct processes will relay the same message sent by p_j, a Byzantine process either relay nothing or the same message sent by p_j.

Lemma 2 (Validity). *If all the correct processes propose the same value, they decide that value.*

Proof. Consider a set C consisting of correct processes that propose the value v. Since we have at most t faulty, C consists of at least of $n-t$ correct processes. To satisfy the validity property, all correct processes must decide on v. By the end of the second round, all correct processes will have at least $n-t$ values in their vector that are equal to v. Thus, in Line 17 of the algorithm, when a correct process observes this condition, it will decide on the value v.

Lemma 3 (Agreement). *At most $\lfloor \frac{n}{n-t} \rfloor + 1$ values are decided.*

Proof We first prove that no more than $\lfloor \frac{n}{n-t} \rfloor$ different values from $\bot$ are decided.

First, note that a Byzantine process may lie about another Byzantine process' value, in this case, we have two different values in the same column, and then a correct process analyzing its matrix will set that value to $\bot$.

Let p_ℓ be a Byzantine process that sends two distinct values, to two correct processes in the first round, since the lines of the correct processes are equal in all the matrices, all the correct processes will detect that p_ℓ is Byzantine, and set its value to $\bot$ in line 18.

Now we suppose that p_ℓ does not send two distinct values to two correct processes in the first round, but sends v_ℓ to one and nothing to the other. In this case, at the end of the second round, let us suppose two correct processes p_i and p_j with respectively V_i and V_j as decision vectors. Either the two processes have $V_i[\ell] = V_j[\ell]$ or one of them has $\bot$ and the other v_ℓ.

From all the above, the worst case scenario is when p_ℓ a Byzantine process is acting like a correct, in this case, when a correct process p_i is deciding its initial value, the occurrence of v_i in V_i has to be $n-t$. Thus, we can have up to $\lfloor \frac{n}{n-t} \rfloor$ groups of size $n-t$ with different values, since a Byzantine process cannot belong to a set of processes proposing v and another set of processes proposing v'.

In conclusion, we have at most $\lfloor \frac{n}{n-t} \rfloor$ decided values plus the $\bot$.

Lemma 4 (Termination). *All the correct processes decide.*

Proof. All the correct processes will execute the two rounds, and decide at the end of the second round.

By the above lemmas, we get the following theorem.

Theorem 1. *Algorithm 1, ensures k-set Agreement in an authenticated message passing system with Byzantine failures for $k \geq \lfloor \frac{n}{n-t} \rfloor + 1$ in two rounds.*

3.2 k-Set Agreement Optimal Concerning The Value k

In this subsection, we present an optimal algorithm, in terms of set agreement, solving k-set agreement in the presence of up to t Byzantine processes when:

$$\lfloor \frac{n}{n-t} \rfloor \leq k.$$

To achieve this level of agreement, we are constrained to use more than two rounds. The algorithm incorporates a primitive that operates over $t+1$ rounds. Once again, there are no limitations on the number of failures t for the TRB.

This algorithm uses n instances of the Terminating Reliable Broadcast (TRB), where each process broadcasts its proposed value for the set-agreement by TRB. For our algorithm, we will implement the authenticated TRB primitive for n instances, where the ith instance of TRB corresponds to the run instance where process p_i is the sender in TRB.

The Algorithm

Algorithm 2 ensures k-set agreement for $k \geq \lfloor \frac{n}{n-t} \rfloor$. When $TRB\text{-}bcast(v_i, p_i)$ is called, process p_i is the sender in the TRB algorithm; it stores its proposed value in the vector L_i. On the call of $TRB\text{-}deliver(q)$, where process p_i is not the sender in the TRB algorithm, it stores the delivered value broadcasted by process q in $L_i[q]$.

```
 1  Initialization: L_i vector initialized to ⊥
    /* --------- Phase 1 -------------------              */
 2  TRB-bcast(v_i,p_i):
 3  L_i[p_i] ← v_i ;
 4  foreach q ∈ Π do
 5      TRB-deliver(q):
 6      L_i[q] ← m;
 7  end
    /* --------- Phase 2 -------------                    */
 8  if p_i finds in L_i, n − t values identical to v_i then
 9      decide v_i
10  else if p_i finds in L_i a value v repeated n − t then
11      decide v;
12  else
13      decide ⊥;
14  end
```

Algorithm 2: Solving k-set agreement in Byzantine Synchronous Message passing model. Code for p_i.

Proof of the Algorithm

Every process p_i holds a vector L_i initialized to $\bot$. n instances of TRB are started, one per process, with each process p_i being the sender in the instance i.

Every process p_i records in vector L_i the messages delivered from the other processes.

At the end of Phase 1, after each process sets its vector L_i, from the validity and agreement properties of the TRB, even if we have in the system Byzantine processes, all the vectors of correct processes will be equal, and if all the correct processes propose the same value, we will have at least $n-t$ values equal to their initial value.

This ensures the Validity of the k-set agreement, at the end of Phase 2, they will decide that value in line 9.

At the end of the n instances of TRB, all the correct processes have the same L. Thus, in phase 2, each correct process p_i, decides from L_i, by either finding $n-t$ values equal to its initial value, or any value repeated $n-t$ times, if not decides $\bot$. We will see in the following lemma that if a process decides $\bot$, then no other correct process decides a value different from $\bot$.

Lemma 5. *Let p_i and p_j be two correct processes that run Algorithm 2, we have $L_i = L_j$, at the end of Phase 1.*

Proof. From the agreement of the TRB [2.3], we have that if a correct process delivers a value m, that value is delivered by all the correct processes, the delivered message is stored in the vectors of correct processes, then all the correct processes will have the same value in their vector.

Hence, from the above Lemma we conclude that at the end of phase 1, all the correct processes have the same view on L.

Lemma 6. *The vector L contains the initial value broadcast by correct processes.*

Proof. Let L be the vector L_i of a correct process p_i, from Lemma 5, all the correct processes have the same L. Since in Phase 1, every correct process p_i stores its initial value in L_i in line 2, then every initial value broadcast by a correct process p_i is in L.

Lemma 7. *If a correct process p_i decides a value v different from $\bot$, no other correct process will decide $\bot$.*

Proof. Let p_i be a correct process that decides on the value v in Phase 2. This implies that p_i has found at least $n - t$ instances of the value v in L_i. Consider another correct process p_j. From Lemma 5, given that the vectors L_i and L_j are equal for all correct processes, p_j will also find at least $n - t$ instances of the value v. Thus, every correct process will either decide its initial value in line 9 or decide v in line 11.

Lemma 8. [Validity] *If all the correct processes propose the same value, they decide this value.*

Proof. Let C be a set of correct processes that propose v, from Lemmas 5 and 6 we have at least $n - t$ values equal to v in L, then in line 9, all the correct processes will find that condition and decide v.

Lemma 9. [Termination] *All the correct processes decide.*

Proof. All the correct processes will execute the two phases and will decide at the end of Phase 2.

Lemma 10. [Agreement] *At most $\lfloor \frac{n}{n-t} \rfloor$ values are decided by correct processes.*

Proof. By Lemma 7, if a correct process decides $\bot$, all the correct processes will decide that value. Thus, exactly one value is decided. And if a correct process decides a value different from $\bot$, it decides a value that have a frequency of at least $n - t$.

We suppose that the correct processes decide on a specific number of distinct values α. Given that each of the α values must appear at least $n - t$ times in L for a decision to be made, the total count of these appearances is $\alpha(n - t)$. This count cannot exceed the total number of the processes in the system, we have $\alpha(n-t) \leq n$, leading to $\alpha \leq \lfloor \frac{n}{n-t} \rfloor$. From Lemma 5, no correct process will decide $\bot$.

Theorem 2. *In a Byzantine synchronous message passing model, Algorithm 2 ensures k-set agreement in $t + 1$ rounds with $k \geq \lfloor \frac{n}{n-t} \rfloor$.*

Lemma 11. *When $\frac{n}{n-t} \geq 2$ it is impossible to achieve $\lfloor \frac{n}{n-t} \rfloor - 1$ Set-Agreement.*

Proof. Let's suppose we organize the n processes into, sets C_i of size $n - t$ with $i = 1, \ldots, \lfloor \frac{n}{n-t} \rfloor$, and a set K, with K being the remaining processes of size $n - (n - t)\lfloor \frac{n}{n-t} \rfloor$. Let us suppose we are in the execution α, where all the processes in the sets C_i are correct, and the processes in the set K crash. In each set C_i the processes propose v_i, a process $p \in C_1$ will decide v_1: because this execution is equivalent for p to the execution β where the processes of C_1 are correct and proposes v_1 and the processes of the other sets including K are Byzantine (Note that the size of $C_2 \ldots C_n + K$ is $n - (n - t) = t$). In both executions in order to ensure validity p should decide v_1.

If we do that for every set C_i, each set will decide a value and we will have $\lfloor \frac{n}{n-t} \rfloor$ decided value.

By the above Lemmas, we get the following Theorem:

Theorem 3. *In a Byzantine synchronous message passing model, Algorithm 2 is an optimal algorithm when $\frac{n}{n-t} \geq 2$, for $k \geq \lfloor \frac{n}{n-t} \rfloor$.*

4 Crash Failures Asynchronous Shared Memory

In this section, we present an algorithm that operates in an Asynchronous Read-Write (Shared Memory) setting, specifically designed to handle crash failures. This algorithm applies to a system consisting of n processes, among which up to t processes may crash. It is known that in the asynchronous system, there is no algorithm for solving consensus when the system is subject to crash failures [9]. The authors of [15] investigate the k-set agreement in an asynchronous system, exploring several variations of the problem definition by varying the validity condition and the system model. In our case, we are interested in the following validity: *if all the correct processes propose the same value, that value is decided.* They presented an impossibility result.

Theorem 4. *[15] In the Shared Memory/Crash model, there is no protocol for solving k-set agreement when $t \geq \frac{n}{2}$ and $t \geq k$.*

And a possible one:

Theorem 5. *[15] In the Shared Memory/Crash model, there exist two protocols that can solve k-set agreement, one for $t < \frac{k-1}{2k}n$, and the other for $k > t + 1$.*

They left a small gap between their possibility and impossibility results. In this section, we managed to find an algorithm for the case for $t < \frac{k-1}{2k-1}n$, which is equivalent to $k > \frac{n-t}{n-2t}$. Our algorithm uses the snapshot primitive, in a look-alike first phase of a round then exploiting the result returned by the snapshot each process makes a decision. The snapshot helps with handling with the system asynchrony as the algorihtm periodically records snapshots of the shared memory state. These snapshots represent a consistent view of the system at a specific point in time, capturing the values of all shared variables.

The Algorithm

Algorithm 3 solves k-set agreement for $k \geq \lfloor \frac{n-t}{n-2t} \rfloor + 1$. If a process receives at least $n - t$ values it moves to a decision-making step, since we are in an asynchronous system, processes can not wait indefinitely, as a process cannot distinguish between a correct process that is slow and a process that crashes.

```
   Data: Initial value m
 1 Initialization: X_i and L_i vectors initialized to ⊥;
 2 x_i = 0, Shared variable: S.snapshot initialized to ⊥;
 3 S.update(m);
 4 while |j, L_i[j] ≠ ⊥ | < n − t do
 5 |   L_i ← S.snapshot();
 6 end
 7 X_i ← L_i; /* Last snapshot                                            */
 8 x_i ← ♯ of values ≠ ⊥ in X_i;
 9 if p_i finds in X_i, at least x_i − t values equal to initial value m then
10 |   decide m ;
11 else if p_i finds in X_i, at least x_i − t values equal to any value v then
12 |   decide v;
13 |   labeldec1
14 else
15 |   decide ⊥;
16 end
```

Algorithm 3: Solving k–set agreement in a Crash Asynchronous Shared Memory Model: Code for p_i.

Proof of the Algorithm

First we assume that $n > 2t$. We consider a snapshot object S, each process p_i starts by updating its register by $S.update(m)$ with the value m its initial value, then invokes $S.snapshot()$ and stores its view in a vector L_i of size n initialized to $\perp$, as long as the number of $\perp$ is greater than $n - t$, the processes repeat the invocation of the snapshot. At the end of all the invocations, the vector L_i is stored in X_i. Then in line 8, p_i computes x_i the number of values different from $\perp$, then if in X_i it finds at least $x_i - t$ values equal to its initial value it decides that value, else a value v that appears $n - t$ times since or $\perp$ in other case. As $n > 2t$, $x_i - t$ is strictly greater than 0.

The snapshots are ordered by inclusion order with X_i being the snapshot of p_i, line 7.

Let α_v be the number of occurrences of v in X.

Let p_i be the process that gets the smallest snapshot X_i among all the snapshots in line 7.

Lemma 12. *No correct process decides a value v if $\alpha_v^i < x_i - t$.*

Proof. Let p_j be a correct process, by definition of p_i, $X_j \geq X_i$. Let us suppose by contradiction that p_j decides v. Then $\alpha_v^j \geq x_j - t$.

Since $X_i \leq X_j$:

$$\alpha_v^j - \alpha_v^i \leq x_j - x_i \Rightarrow \alpha_v^j - x_j \leq \alpha_v^i - x_i$$
$$\text{Since } \alpha_v^i < x_i - t \qquad (1)$$
$$\text{Then } \alpha_v^j - x_j < -t \Rightarrow \alpha_v^j < x_j - t$$

Contradicting the fact that $\alpha_v^j \geq x_j - t$.

Lemma 13. *If all the correct processes propose the same value, that value is decided.*

Proof. Let us suppose that all the correct processes propose the same value v. Let ℓ be a correct process, by the algorithm $x_\ell \geq n-t$. We have at most t values from the faulty process, thus at least $x_\ell - t$ values from correct processes. As $n > 2t$, $x_\ell - t > 0$. Then process ℓ will decide v.

Lemma 14. *At most $\lfloor \frac{n-t}{n-2t} \rfloor + 1$ values are decided by correct processes.*

Proof. If $\frac{n-t}{n-2t}$ is an integer: Let p_i be the process that gets the smallest snapshot X_i among all the snapshots in line 7. Since $n > 2t$ and $x_i - t > 0$ from Lemma 12, a value v can only be decided if $\alpha_v^i \geq x_i - t$.

In X_i, there can be at most $\frac{x_i}{x_i - t}$ different values v such that $\alpha_v^i \geq x_i - t$. Therefore, we have at most $\frac{x_i}{x_i - t}$ decided values from processes with the smallest snapshot. Since $n - t \leq x_i \leq n$ and $\frac{x_i}{x_i - t}$ is a decreasing function, the maximum number of different values decided is obtained when $x_i = n - t$. Thus, $\frac{n-t}{n-2t}$ is the maximum number of decided values from correct processes with the smallest snapshot.

Let p_j be a correct process with $X_j > X_i$. Suppose p_j decides v_j, a value different from the $\frac{n-t}{n-2t}$ values decided by the processes with the smallest snapshot. This contradicts Lemma 12. Therefore, p_j will either decide a value from the $\frac{n-t}{n-2t}$ values or bottom if the conditions in lines 10 and 10 are not fulfilled.

If $\frac{n-t}{n-2t}$ is not an integer: Similary to the integer case, we have at most $\lfloor \frac{x_i}{x_i - t} \rfloor$ different values from $\bot$ that can be decided by the processes with the smallest snapshot plus $\bot$. Thus, $\lfloor \frac{n-t}{n-2t} \rfloor + 1$ is the maximum number of decided values from correct processes with the smallest snapshot. Let p_j be a correct process with $X_j > X_i$. Suppose p_j decides v_j, a value different from the $\lfloor \frac{n-t}{n-2t} \rfloor$ values decided by the processes with the smallest snapshot. Smilary to the case where $\frac{n-t}{n-2t}$ is an integer, p_j will either decide one of the $\lfloor \frac{n-t}{n-2t} \rfloor$ different values or $\bot$.

In both cases, we have at most $\lfloor \frac{n-t}{n-2t} \rfloor + 1$ decided values.

Lemma 15. *All the correct processes will eventually decide.*

Proof. The number of failures is at most t, we have then at least $n - t$ correct processes, which means that each correct process will scan at least $n - t$ registers and decide.

By the above Lemmas, we get the following Theorem.

Theorem 6. *In a Crash Asynchronous Shared Memory model, when $k \geq \lfloor \frac{n-t}{n-2t} \rfloor + 1$, and $n > 2t$, Algorithm 3 ensures k-set agreement.*

Theorem 7. *In a Crash Asynchronous Shared Memory model. If $n > 2t$, there is no Algorithm that can solve k-set agreement for $k \leq \lfloor \frac{n-t}{n-2t} \rfloor - 1$.*

Proof. Due to space constraints, we only provide the proof for the case where $\frac{n-t}{n-2t}$ is an integer. However, the proof in the non-integer case follows a similar approach.

Let us partition $n - t$ processes into $\frac{n-t}{n-2t}$ subsets $g_1, g_2, \ldots, g_{\frac{n-t}{n-2t}}$ of size of at least $n - 2t$. As $n > 2t$ there is at least one process in each set g_i. Let T be the remaining processes We consider a run α, where for each g_i, all the processes propose their initial value v_i. Let τ be the time at which all processes of $\Pi - T$ decide in α. Before τ, all the processes in g_i propose v_i, while the remaining processes t do not take any step.

Let α_1 be a run, where after τ, for each g_i, with $i > 1$, the processes in g_i crash, and the remaining T, have an initial value v_1 and begin the execution of their algorithm after τ. In this execution the processus of g_1 may be correct, to ensure validity have to decide v_1.

As $n > 2t$, there is at least one process p_1 in g_1 that cannot distinguish between α and α_1, thus decides the same value v_1 in both runs.

Generalizing the same argument,t for every g_i in α. There are at least $\frac{n-t}{n-2t}$ different decided values.

Our results almost resolve the solvability of k-set agreement in a crash-prone asynchronous shared memory model when $n > 2t$, as show in Fig. 1, the only remaining case is $k = \lfloor \frac{n-t}{n-2t} \rfloor$, and the remaing case for $n \leq 2t$ is when $n \leq 2t$ for $k = t + 2$.

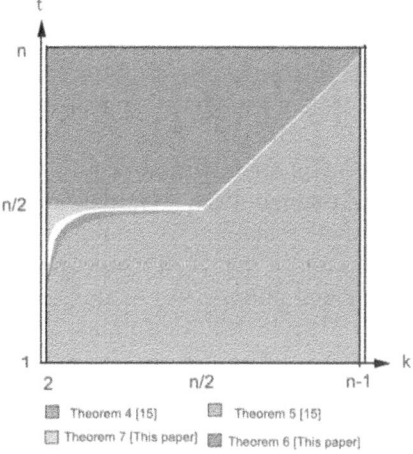

Fig. 1. k-set agreement in a shared memory crashed model.

4.1 Special Case: Crash Asynchronous Message Passing Model

As mentioned above, it is shown in [2], that any wait-free algorithm based on atomic, single-writer (and multi-writer) multi-reader registers can be automatically emulated in message-passing systems, provided that at least a majority of the processes are correct, and the reverse is always true whatever the value of t [13].

From Theorem 6 and Theorem 7, we have the following Theorem.

Theorem 8. *In a crash Asynchronous Message Passing Model, when $n > 2t$ we have an algorithm ensuring k-set agreement for $k \geq \lfloor \frac{n-t}{n-2t} \rfloor + 1$ and an impossibly result when $k \leq \lfloor \frac{n-t}{n-2t} \rfloor - 1$.*

5 Conclusion

In this study, we have contributed to the understanding of k-set agreement in distributed systems, particularly focusing on scenarios with different types of failures. We addressed and filled certain gaps left by previous works such as [8,15], providing valuable insights into the solvability of the problem.

In the context of the Synchronous Message Passing model with Byzantine failures and authentification, we presented two algorithms that achieve k-set agreement. The first algorithm ensures $k \geq \lfloor \frac{n}{n-t} \rfloor + 1$ in just two rounds, demonstrating its efficiency and practicality. On the other hand, the second algorithm achieves optimality, ensuring $k \geq \lfloor \frac{n}{n-t} \rfloor$ in $t+1$ rounds.

We also present an algorithm for the Asynchronous Shared Memory model with crash failures, when $n > 2t$, which solves k-set agreement for $k \geq \lfloor \frac{n-t}{n-2t} \rfloor + 1$, and an impossibility result for $k \leq \lfloor \frac{n-t}{n-2t} \rfloor - 1$, the only gap remaining when $k = \lfloor \frac{n-t}{n-2t} \rfloor$.

Furthermore, we extend this previous result by leveraging the equivalency of the models. The Shared Memory model is equivalent to the Message Passing model when $n > 2t$.

Although certain gaps remain open, our aim is to provide answers and establish a comprehensive understanding of the solvability of k-set agreement in both asynchronous and synchronous systems. We emphasize the importance of the validity property, which guarantees that if all correct processes propose the same value, that value will be decided upon.

The main contribution of this article are summarized in Table 1 :

Table 1. Summary of results

Authenticated Byz. Synch MP			Crash Asynch SM	
Condition	nb rounds	Results	Condition	Results
$k \geq \lfloor \frac{n}{n-t} \rfloor + 1$	2	[Algo 1]	$n \leq 2t$ and $t \geq k$	Impossible [15]
$k \geq \lfloor \frac{n}{n-t} \rfloor$	$t+1$	[Algo 2]	$k > \frac{n}{n-2t}$	[15]
$k \leq \lfloor \frac{n}{n-t} \rfloor - 1$ Impossible and $n \leq 2t$		[Th 3]	$k > t+1$	[15]
			$n > 2t$ $k \leq \lfloor \frac{n-t}{n-2t} \rfloor - 1$	Impossible [Th 7]
			$n > 2t$ $k \geq \lfloor \frac{n-t}{n-2t} \rfloor + 1$	[Algo 3]

Acknowledgments. The authors want to thank the referees for their constructive comments that helped them improve the presentation of the article.

References

1. Afek, Y., Dolev, D., Attiya, H., Gafni, E., Merritt, M., Shavit, N.: Atomic Snapshots of Shared Memory, vol. 40, pp. 1–13 (1990). https://doi.org/10.1145/93385.93394
2. Attiya, H., Bar-Noy, A., Dolev, D.: Sharing memory robustly in message-passing systems. J. ACM **42**(1), 124–142 (1995). https://doi.org/10.1145/200836.200869
3. Borowsky, E., Gafni, E.: Generalized FLP impossibility result for t-resilient asynchronous computations. In: Proceedings of the Twenty-Fifth Annual ACM Symposium on Theory of Computing, 16–18 May 1993, San Diego, pp. 91–100. ACM (1993)
4. Bouzid, Z., Imbs, D., Raynal, M.: A necessary condition for byzantine k-set agreement. Inf. Process. Lett. **116**(12), 757–759 (2016)
5. Chaudhuri, S.: More choices allow more faults: Set consensus problems in totally asynchronous systems. Inf. Comput. **105**(1), 132–158 (1993)
6. Chaudhuri, S., Herlihy, M., Lynch, N.A., Tuttle, M.R.: Tight bounds for k-set agreement. J. ACM **47**(5), 912–943 (2000). https://doi.org/10.1145/355483.355489
7. Civit, P., Gilbert, S., Guerraoui, R., Komatovic, J., Vidigueira, M.: On the validity of consensus. In: Oshman, R., Nolin, A., Halldórsson, M.M., Balliu, A. (eds.) Proceedings of the 2023 ACM Symposium on Principles of Distributed Computing, PODC 2023, Orlando, 19–23 June 2023, pp. 332–343. ACM (2023), https://doi.org/10.1145/3583668.3594567
8. Delporte-Gallet, C., Fauconnier, H., Raynal, M., Safir, M.: Optimal algorithms for synchronous byzantine k-set agreement. Theor. Comput. Sci. **973**, 114098 (2023). https://www.sciencedirect.com/science/article/pii/S0304397523004115
9. Fischer, M.J., Lynch, N.A., Paterson, M.: Impossibility of distributed consensus with one faulty process. J. ACM **32**(2), 374–382 (1985)
10. Herlihy, M., Shavit, N.: The asynchronous computability theorem for t-resilient tasks. In: Proceedings of the Twenty-Fifth Annual ACM Symposium on Theory of Computing, 16–18 May 1993, San Diego, pp. 111–120. ACM (1993)
11. Lamport, L., Shostak, R., Pease, M.: The byzantine generals problem. ACM Trans. Program. Lang. Syst. **4**(3), 382–401 (1982)
12. Lorenzo, A.: Consensus and Reliable Broadcast (2006). http://www.cs.utexas.edu/users/lorenzo/corsi/cs371d/08F/notes/week8.pdf
13. Lynch, N.A.: Distributed Algorithms. Elsevier (1996)
14. Pease, M.C., Shostak, R.E., Lamport, L.: Reaching agreement in the presence of faults. J. ACM **27**(2), 228–234 (1980). https://doi.org/10.1145/322186.322188
15. Prisco, R.D., Malkhi, D., Reiter, M.K.: On k-set consensus problems in asynchronous systems. IEEE Trans. Parallel Distributed Syst. **12**(1), 7–21 (2001). https://doi.org/10.1109/71.899936
16. Raynal, M.: Fault-tolerant agreement in synchronous message-passing systems. Synth. Lect. Distrib. Comput. Theory **1**(1), 1–189 (2010)
17. Saks, M., Zaharoglou, F.: Wait-free k-set agreement is impossible: the topology of public knowledge. SIAM J. Comput. **29**(5), 1449–1483 (2000)
18. Turek, J., Shasha, D.: The many faces of consensus in distributed systems. Computer **25**(6), 8–17 (1992). https://doi.org/10.1109/2.153253

A Domain Specific Language for Testing Distributed Protocol Implementations

Cezara Dragoi[1], Srinidhi Nagendra[2,3(✉)], and Mandayam Srivas[3]

[1] ENS, INRIA, Paris, France
[2] IRIF, Universite Paris Cite, CNRS, Paris, France
nagendra@irif.fr
[3] Chennai Mathematical Institute, Chennai, India

Abstract. Large-scale, fault-tolerant, distributed systems are the backbone for many critical software services. Since they must execute correctly in a possibly adversarial environment with arbitrary communication delays and failures, the underlying algorithms are intricate. In particular, achieving consistency and data retention relies on intricate consensus (state machine replication) protocols. Ensuring the reliability of implementations of such protocols remains a significant challenge because of the enormous number of exceptional conditions that may arise in production. We propose a methodology and a tool called Netrix for testing such implementations that aims to exploit programmer's knowledge to improve coverage, enables robust bug reproduction, and can be used in regression testing across different versions of an implementation. As evaluation, we apply our tool to a popular proof of stake blockchain protocol, Tendermint, which relies on a Byzantine consensus algorithm, a benign consensus algorithm, Raft, and BFT-Smart. We were able to identify deviations of the implementation from the protocol specification and validate corrections on an updated implementation. Additionally, we were able to confirm the presence of known bugs in previous versions.

1 Introduction

Large-scale, fault-tolerant, distributed systems are the backbone of many critical software services. The underlying protocols are intricate as they have to ensure correct behavior in the presence of concurrent asynchronous message exchanges and failures. In particular, *consensus protocols* are used to guarantee data retention and consistency and form the bedrock of storage systems such as Cassandra and Redis, or Blockchain systems based on proof-of-stake models. Bugs in these implementations have had significant real world consequences and ensuring correctness of these implementations remains a significant challenge, precisely because of the enormous number of exceptional conditions that may arise in production. Consensus protocols are designed to tolerate faults that can be (1) benign such as replica crashes, network partitions, message drops, replays, or (2) Byzantine, where replicas can behave arbitrarily, coordinate or lie. Given a distributed protocol implementation, the number of possible executions is large even if the number of inputs (client requests) is small. This is an instance of the infamous state explosion problem. The number of interleavings grows exponentially in the number of replicas and the number of failures.

In this work, we explore a space of tradeoffs where a developer can test protocol implementations. On one end, fully automated tools allow developers to search the state space. While these tools are protocol agnostic and require minimal effort, they are unreliable in reproducing results and can get lost in the large state space. On the other end, a skilled developer can craft intricate executions which control all the non-determinism. While the second approach can be time-consuming and require expertise, we get reliably reproducible results. We propose a framework where developers provide lighthouses to guide the search for automated tools, thereby controlling the tradeoff.

Prior work on testing distributed protocol implementations focuses extensively on *exhaustive enumeration* or *random sampling* of executions for a fixed set of client requests, e.g., [1,5,12,16,19,20,22,23,26,27]. Existing works tackle the state space explosion by imposing bounds such as the number of steps in an execution, the time frequency of network partitions [1], the number of periods in which a replica is isolated from the rest [14], the number of events for which all possible orderings must be covered (bug depth) [22] etc. Shrinking the search space using such bounds decreases exploration time in the case of exhaustive enumeration and increases the effectiveness of random sampling. Jepsen [1] and PCTCP [8,22] are the prominent random sampling techniques. Both Jepsen and PCTCP have been effective in discovering bugs in production systems. However, the main drawback with the approaches is that they are unreliable in reproducing bugs. For example, the probability that the PCTCP algorithm [22] catches a bug of depth d is roughly, at least $1/n^d$ where n is a bound on the size of the executions (number of exchanged messages). While this probability reduces exponentially only with respect to the bug depth d, it can still become exceedingly small when executions are production scale, e.g., in the order of thousands of events, and d has a reasonable value, e.g., 10. As we show in our experimental evaluation (Sect. 5), such values of d are to be expected when searching for "interesting" executions that are not necessarily bugs but deviations from an abstract model for instance, or (bounded) liveness related bugs.

We present Netrix, a domain specific language (DSL) with a networking infrastructure for programmer guided exploration of large-scale distributed systems. Netrix enables the programmer to write high-level scenario based tests as opposed to low-level packed manipulation with existing tools. The DSL allows the programmer to specify only the required event constraints as a set of *filters*, thereby allowing existing randomized techniques such as PCTCP to explore the residual non determinism. The filters that make up a unit test are of the form, "if-then", akin to Match-Action table entries in a network device. The "if" condition can relate to the type of the message or the number of messages already delivered to a destination, and the "then" part defines a set of messages to forward to a certain destination. The latter allows for message corruption, duplication, or arbitrary delays (defining that set of messages to be empty). In addition, the developer can monitor properties using a *state machine*. Our unit tests improve reproducibility, as opposed to ad-hoc methods for controlling the schedule, e.g., by introducing network partitions for a fixed period or sleep cycles. Netrix's unit tests are aimed at regression testing different versions of an implementation and therefore, the unit tests help developers confidently develop and deploy new features without fear of breaking existing behavior.

Netrix's central server is implemented in the go programming language and receives events and messages over RPC. As a consequence, developers can test implementations written in any programming language by changing the communication primitives of the implementation. We evaluated Netrix on several production implementations of protocols that solve for the consensus problem. In particular, we instrumented an open-source implementation of the Raft [21] protocol, the Tendermint [7] protocol and BFT-Smart [6,24]. Using Netrix, we were able to (1) write unit tests to explore behaviors that are not commonly observed in production environments, including known bugs (2) demonstrate behaviors where the implementation deviates from the protocol specification, and (3) run tests on multiple versions of the implementation thereby checking corrections for the observed deviations. The tests for Tendermint allowed developers to gain confidence in the correctness of the implementation and write unit tests for planned changes.

2 Our Approach

A distributed system that Netrix tests consist of a set of replicas that send/receive messages according to the protocol. An execution in such a system is characterized by a sequence of events which are message sends/receives or other internal steps such as start/end a timer. Figure 1 illustrates the architecture of Netrix applied to a 4-node distributed system. All replicas run the same implementation augmented with a communication adapter that sends all events and messages to Netrix and receives messages from Netrix.

Netrix determines the order in which messages are received by replicas using two mechanisms. The first and default mechanism is a randomized exploration algorithm (in our case PCTCP) for sampling executions of a distributed system. Second, Netrix receives as input a unit test written by a developer. The unit test processes the events as a stream and determines the messages to be delivered at each step. A unit test can, for instance, block delivery of a message based on event A and deliver the message upon observing a later event B. These blocked messages are not seen by the random exploration algorithm. Additionally, a unit test can also introduce fictitious messages which simulate Byzantine behaviors (e.g., where replicas send messages that are not prescribed by the protocol). A unit test consists of a set of filters to control message delivery and an assertion defined by a state machine. We introduce a domain-specific language that is embedded in go to specify filters and assertions. Filters allow developers to introduce specific faults such as dropping messages, reordering, or replaying messages. If no filters are specified, the delivery of messages is controlled entirely by the random exploration algorithm.

To explain the structure of filters and assertions, we use the Practical Byzantine Fault Tolerance (PBFT) [9] protocol as a running example for the rest of

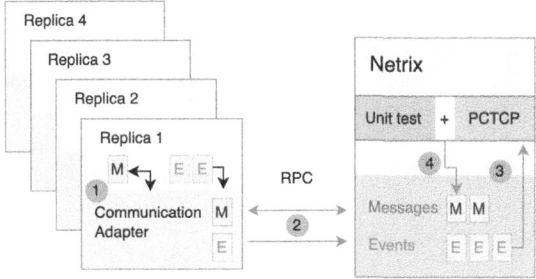

Fig. 1. Netrix architecture (1) The replicas submit events, send/receive messages to a communication adapter. (2) The adapter talks to Netrix via RPC. (3) The events and messages drive unit tests. (4) Unit tests decide which messages to deliver

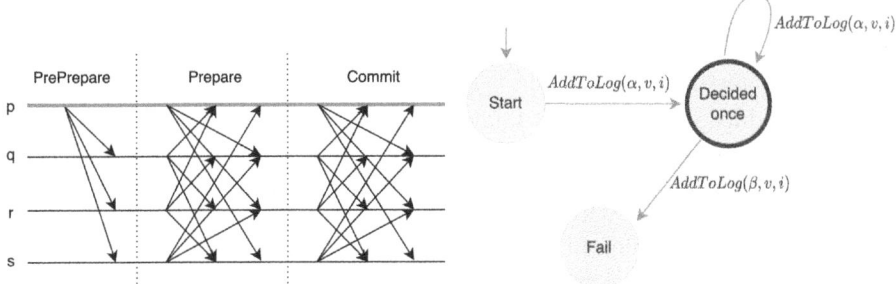

Fig. 2. PBFT normal case execution with p as leader.

Fig. 3. Event driven state machine for assertions. Related to adding an entry α to log at index i in view v. Fail if a different entry β is added at the same index.

the paper. PBFT solves consensus in the presence of Byzantine faults. For a distributed system of n replicas, PBFT can tolerate $f < \frac{n}{3}$ byzantine replicas. Replicas go through a sequence of rounds of communication called views. In each view v, one replica is chosen to be the leader, and the remaining replicas are identified as backups. Figure 2, illustrates the "normal" execution of the protocol (no faults and instantaneous message delivery). Each view is split into three phases, (1) The PrePrepare phase coordinated by the leader p for a client request α, (2) Upon receiving PrePrepare messages, replicas broadcast Prepare messages and, (3) Upon receiving $2f + 1$ replicas Prepare messages, replicas broadcast a Commit message. When a replica receives $2f + 1$ Commit messages, it adds the request to its log. Additionally, For every request α that the client sends, the replicas keep a timer. When $2f + 1$ replica's timer expires, the replicas initiate a ViewChange and transition to the next view $v + 1$.

The correctness of PBFT relies on the property that no two replicas decide to add different requests to their log for a given index i in any given view. Developers can write state machines to specify this property. Figure 3 illustrates the state machine for the safety property that no two replicas add different requests α, β to the same log index "i". The transitions between states are labelled by a condition on an event. In this case, AddToLog(α,v,i) is a condition that is satisfied on the event indicating a replicas decision to add a request "α" to the log at index "i" in view "v". The first time we observe such an event for a client request "α" we transition to an accepting "Decided Once" state. If we observe an event indicating a decision for a different client request "β" for the same index "i" then we transition to a fail state.

Example 1. *Drop* Prepare *messages of view v to one specific replica p*

```
If(IsMessageOfView(v)
.And(IsMessageType(Prepare))
.And(MessageTo(p))
).Then(DropMessage())
```

Unit tests that contain no filters capture executions with arbitrary communication delays and faults (network partitions can be simulated with "infinite" delays), but no Byzantine faults. The order in which messages are delivered are entirely in the control of the underlying random exploration algorithm. Filters can be used to introduce specific delays, faults whose probability of being exposed by a random exploration algorithm is very low, or to introduce fictitious messages that simulate Byzantine faults. For instance, we can drop Prepare messages to one replica p and check if the property stated above still holds. Example 1 describes the corresponding filter.

The filters provides a tradeoff to the developers. Writing unit tests where more expressive tests (in terms of number of filters) provide better probabilistic guarantees. On the other hand, broader exploration of the execution space can be achieved with smaller tests. Furthermore, in Sect. 5, we associate filters with a distance score based on the number of messages between the actual position in a synchronous execution and the expected position after re-ordering. We show experimentally that filters that exceed a certain distance threshold are necessary to constrain the execution space to observe the desired property. The distance measure can help developers in making the right tradeoff decisions.

We present the syntax and the semantics of the filters and of the state machine in Sect. 4 (along with the instrumentation effort). The next section formalizes the semantics of a protocol with Netrix.

3 System Model

We formalize the semantics of a Netrix unit test for a protocol as a product between a transition system modeling the executions of the protocol with a set $\mathcal{R}$ of replicas ($|\mathcal{R}| = n$) and a transition system modeling a monitor that controls the delivery of messages to the replicas and asserts some property. The latter is an abstract representation of Netrix unit tests whose syntax is presented in Sect. 4. We characterize the capability of the monitor to restrict the protocol behavior by showing that it can be programmed to reproduce precisely any set of executions that differ only in the order of concurrent computation steps (not related by the standard happens-before relation).

The set $\mathcal{R}$ of replicas exchange messages during the execution of the protocol. A message m is a tuple $(\mathcal{R} \times \mathcal{R} \times \mathcal{V}_m \times \mathcal{T}_m)$, where $\mathcal{V}_m$ denotes the set of possible message values and $\mathcal{T}_m$ denotes the set of possible message types. Any set $M \subseteq \mathcal{M}$ of messages can be partitioned based on the replica the message is intended to $M[r] = M \cap (\mathcal{R} \times \{r\} \times \mathcal{V}_m \times \mathcal{T}_m)$ where $r \in \mathcal{R}$.

An execution of a protocol at a replica can be characterized by a sequence of events. Events can correspond to sending or receiving a message, or an internal computational step. For example, in PBFT an internal step can be committing a value or changing the view. An event e is a tuple $(\mathcal{R} \times \mathcal{T}_e \times \mathcal{V}_e)$, where $\mathcal{T}_e = \{send, receive, internal\}$ is the set of event types and $\mathcal{V}_e \supseteq \mathcal{M}$ is the set of possible event values. We say $\mathcal{E}$ is the set of all events.

Protocol Transition System. In a protocol, we represent each replica as a transition system $(\Sigma_p, s_p^0, \delta_p, F_p)$ where

- Σ_p is the set of replica states as defined by the protocol with the initial state $s_p^0 \in \Sigma_p$
- $\delta_p : \Sigma_p \times (\mathcal{M} \cup \{\bot\}) \rightharpoonup \Sigma_p \times \mathcal{E}$ is the (partial) transition function of the replica. Each transition emits an event. Internal steps are represented with transitions $\delta_p(s, \bot)$ while receiving a message m is represented with a transition $\delta_p(s, m)$. We assume that internal steps and message receive steps cannot be enabled in the same state, i.e. from any state $s \in \Sigma_p$ if $\delta_p(s, \bot)$ is defined, then $\delta_p(s, m)$ for any $m \in \mathcal{M}$ is not defined.
- $F_p \subseteq \Sigma_p$. For any state $s \in F_p$, δ_p is not defined from s. Final states allows us to restrict the length of an execution in each replica.

For example, in PBFT, the set of states is a valuation of the local variables (index, view, etc.) with the initial state as both index and view being 0. A replica in PBFT can transition to a leader state and emit the corresponding event.

A protocol $\mathcal{P}$ is a product of $|\mathcal{R}| = n$ replica transitions systems. The configuration of the protocol is denoted by $C = (E, pool, states, messages)$ where,

- $E = (e_0, e_1, \cdots)$ is a sequence of events $e_i \in \mathcal{E}$. This serves as a queue of events where replicas push new events to be consumed by the monitor (as it will be clear when defining the monitor transition system below).
- $pool \subseteq \mathcal{M}$ is the set of messages in transit between different replicas
- $states$ maps each replica r to a state in Σ_p
- $messages$ maps each replica r to a sequence of messages $(m_0, m_1, \cdots)$ with $m_i \in \mathcal{M}[r]$. This sequence is used as an inbound queue that replicas use to process incoming messages

Figure 4 refers to the transition rules between two configurations of the protocol. The rule PROTOCOL captures all transitions related to message sends, receives and internal steps of the protocol. The NETWORK rule adds messages from the pool to a replica's inbound message queue $messages[r]$. Additionally, the ADVERSARY rule models adversarial (Byzantine) behavior where the message

$$\frac{(E, pool, states, messages) \xrightarrow{e \in \mathcal{E}} (E', pool', states', messages')}{(E, pool, states, messages) \longrightarrow (E', pool', states', messages')} \text{ Protocol}$$

$$\frac{messages[r] = \sigma \quad m \in pool[r]}{(E, pool, states, messages) \xrightarrow{network} (E, pool \setminus \{m\}, states, messages[r \to \sigma.m])} \text{ Network}$$

$$\frac{M \subseteq \mathcal{M}}{(E, pool, states, messages) \xrightarrow{adversary} (E, M, states, messages)} \text{ Adversary}$$

Fig. 4. Transition rules of a protocol. For a function $f : A \to B$, we use $f[a \to b]$ to denote a function $f' : A \to B$ where $f'(a) = b$ and $f'(a') = f(a')$ for all $a' \neq a$.

pool is transformed arbitrarily. The ADVERSARY rule allows arbitrary manipulation of the message pool for two reasons. One, any byzantine behavior is meaningfully observed only through the messages. Two, generic about the constraints on the number of byzantine actors, traditional constrains of only f byzantine actors are related only to specific protocols.

We define an execution ρ as a sequence of transitions between configurations from the initial configuration $C_0 = ((), \phi, states_0, messages_0)$ with $\forall r \in \mathcal{R}$, $states_0[r] = s_p^0$ and $messages_0[r] = ()$. An execution ρ is *complete* if all replicas have reached final states. ($\forall r, states_k[r] \in F_p$).

The *history* of an execution ρ is the tuple $H_\rho = (E_\rho, <_\rho)$ where E_ρ is the set of events in ρ ordered by the standard (partial) happens-before order $<_\rho$. Formally, $E_\rho = \{e \mid \exists l_i \in \rho, l_i = e\}$. We will use $e \in E_\rho$ and $e \in H_\rho$ interchangeably to denote an event exists in a history. For two events $e_1, e_2 \in E_\rho$, we say $e_1 <_\rho e_2$ if (1) e_1, e_2 are emitted by the same replica, and e_1 occurred before e_2 in ρ, (2) e_1 is a send event and e_2 is the matching receive event, i.e., $e_1 = (m.from, send, m)$ and $e_2 = (m.to, receive, m)$, or (2) (transitive closure) there exists e_3 such that $e_1 <_\rho e_3$ and $e_3 <_\rho e_2$. Also, we define $M_\rho = \{m \mid (m.to, receive, m) \in E_\rho\}$ as the set of messages delivered to the replicas in the execution.

Monitor Transition System. Netrix includes a central monitor that receives all communication from the replicas and is able to control the delay of delivered messages or send new messages by itself as a way to model Byzantine faults. The monitor is also used to assert some property. The central monitor is driven by the events emitted by the replicas. At each step, the monitor can decide to block a certain message from being delivered or to deliver some set of messages based on the current event and context (monitor state). We define the monitor transition system as a tuple $\mu = (\Sigma_\mu, s_\mu^0, \delta_\mu, F_\mu)$ where

- Σ_μ is the set of possible monitor states with s_μ^0 as the initial state
- $\delta_\mu : \Sigma_\mu \times \mathcal{E} \rightharpoonup \Sigma_\mu \times 2^\mathcal{M} \times \mathbb{B}$ is the transition function which accepts the current state and event, and transitions to a new state along with a set of messages to be delivered and a Boolean value in $\mathbb{B} = \{\bot, \top\}$ which in the case

of a send event signals whether the message is blocked (if ⊤) or available for delivery (if ⊥). If the message is blocked in order to be delivered later, then it can be stored in the state of the monitor until delivery. δ_μ encapsulates the semantics of executing the filters and state machine for a given unit test.
- $F^M \subseteq \Sigma_\mu$ is the set of accepting states (used to signal some property being satisfied)

A configuration of the monitor is defined by $C = (E, bl, ubl, messages, s)$ where

- E is a sequence of events as described in the protocol transition system. Here it serves the purpose of an event queue for the monitor to consume.
- bl is the set of blocked messages, ubl is the set of unblocked messages
- $messages$ maps each replica to a sequence of messages as in the protocol transition system
- $s \in \Sigma_\mu$ is a monitor state

Figure 5 describes the MONITOR transition rule. The rule invokes the transition function δ_μ with the head of the event queue E and the current monitor state as input and returns the new state, a set of messages to deliver, and a possibly updated set of blocked messages. The delivered messages are added to the respective replica's inbound message queues and the monitor state is updated.

$$E = e.E'$$
$$\delta_\mu(s, e) = (s', M, b)$$
$$\forall r.\ messages'(r) = messages(r).M[r]$$
$$bl' = \begin{cases} bl \cup (b?\{m\} : \emptyset), \text{if } e = (\_, send, m) \\ bl, \text{otherwise} \end{cases}$$
$$ubl' = \begin{cases} ubl \cup (b?\emptyset : \{m\}), \text{if } e = (\_, send, m) \\ ubl, \text{otherwise} \end{cases}$$

$$(E, bl, ubl, messages, s) \xrightarrow{monitor} (E', bl', ubl', messages', s')$$

Fig. 5. Monitor transition rule ($cond?v_1 : v_2$ is interpreted to v_1 if $cond$ is true and v_2, otherwise).

Product Transition System. The asynchronous product of the two transition systems, that of the protocol $\mathcal{P}$ and the monitor μ defines the set of executions admitted by a unit test (that will be explored by Netrix). The protocol transition system takes steps which publish events that are consumed by steps of the monitor. In turn, the monitor controls the messages that are consumed by the replicas in the protocol transition system. A configuration of the product transition system is $C = (E, pool, states, messages, bl, ubl, s)$:

- E, $pool$, $states$ and $messages$ are defined as in the protocol transition system.
- bl is the set of blocked messages controlled by the monitor.
- ubl is the set of unblocked messages released by the monitor and s is the monitor state.

Figure 6 defines the transition rules for the product transition system. Steps can be either INTERNAL, SEND, RECEIVE from the protocol transition system (transitions labeled by events $e \in \mathcal{E}$), a step in the monitor transition system MONITOR, or a variation of the NETWORK rule (NETWORK-NB) which adds a *non-blocked* message to a replica's inbound message queue. Note that a monitor step can deliver a set of messages (add them to replica inbound queues) which have been either sent by replicas in the past (these messages were blocked by the monitor and stored in its state) or fictitious messages (corresponding to Byzantine behavior). Therefore, a monitor step simulates a (possibly-empty) sequence of NETWORK and ADVERSARY steps from the protocol transition system.

$$\frac{(E, pool, states, messages) \xrightarrow{e \in \mathcal{E}} (E', pool', states', messages')}{(E, pool, states, messages, bl, ubl, s) \longrightarrow (E', pool', states', messages', bl, ubl, s)} \text{ PROTOCOL}$$

$$\frac{(E, bl, ubl, messages, s) \xrightarrow{monitor} (E', bl', ubl', messages', s')}{(E, pool, states, messages, bl, s) \longrightarrow (E', pool, states, messages', bl', ubl', s')} \text{ MONITOR}$$

$$\frac{messages[r] = \sigma \quad m \in ubl[r] \quad m \in pool[r]}{(E, pool, states, messages, bl, ubl, s)} \text{ NETWORK-NB}$$
$$\longrightarrow (E, pool \setminus \{m\}, states, messages[r \to \sigma.m], bl, ubl \setminus \{m\}, s)$$

Fig. 6. Transition rules of product system

A run of the product system $\rho = C_0 \xrightarrow{l_0} C_1 \xrightarrow{l_1} \cdots \xrightarrow{l_{k-1}} C_k$ is a sequence of transitions as above. A run is accepting if the monitor's state in the last configuration is a final state, i.e., $C_k^M.s \in F^M$. The set of accepting states of the monitor models the success or failure of a unit test. Netrix uses a randomized exploration algorithm in order to explore the non-determinism introduced by NETWORK-NB transitions.

On the Expressivity of the Monitor. We give a characterization of the monitor's capability to restrict the protocol behavior. We show that as an extreme case, the monitor can restrict the protocol to produce a *single* history for a complete execution, i.e., all the complete executions in the product transition system have the same history.

We state our result as a relation between the histories produced in a product transition system and the history of a given complete protocol execution ρ. Histories of possibly incomplete executions of the product transition system are not necessarily equal to the history of ρ but only a *prefix*. The prefix relation $\preceq$ between two histories $H_1 = (E_1, <_1)$ and $H_2 = (E_2, <_2)$ is defined as usual, i.e., $H_1 \preceq H_2$ if (1) Downward closure: $E_1 \subseteq E_2$ and for every event $e \in E_1$ and $e' \in E_2$, $e' <_2 e \Rightarrow e' \in E_1 \wedge e' <_1 e$, and (2) Preserving happens before: For two events $e, e' \in E_1$, $e <_1 e' \Leftrightarrow e <_2 e'$.

Theorem 1. *For any complete run ρ in the protocol $\mathcal{P}$, there exists a monitor μ such that, for all runs ρ' in the product transition system of $\mathcal{P}$ and μ, $H_{\rho'} \preceq H_\rho$*

To prove Theorem 1, we construct a monitor to reproduce *exactly one* history. In practice however, a developer writes unit tests to reproduce one of a set of histories. Consider a unit test of PBFT where a developer is interested in executions such that Commit messages are delivered to a replica before Prepare messages, without restricting the order between messages of the same type. Our DSL allows a developer to program such constraints as a unit test into the monitor's transition function δ_μ and hence observe the exact expected behavior. We defer a more elaborate discussion to Sect. 4.

4 Netrix Unit Tests

Instrumentation. Protocol implementations contain communication APIs to facilitate sending/receiving messages. To test the implementation using Netrix, one needs to augment the communication APIs with a Shim. The Shim sends messages to Netrix central server thereby giving it control to decide the order of messages delivered. To aid the instrumentation effort of writing a Shim, we provide language specific libraries (currently in Go and Java). Since Netrix is protocol agnostic, each message is recorded as a sequence of bytes. To read the contents of the messages in the unit tests, the developer needs to provide a serialization and deserialization adapter.

Domain Specific Language. A unit test in Netrix is represented by a TestCase object. To create a TestCase, developers should invoke NewTestCase which accepts the test case name, a timeout duration, the state machine and the filters. The filters are created by invoking NewFilterSet and filters.AddFilter will add more filters of the form If(*condition*).Then(*actions*) to the test. We define a *Condition* as a function that accepts an event, a context object and returns a boolean. Similarly, we define *Action* as a function that accept an event, a context object and returns a set of messages. In addition to filters, a TestCase accepts a state machine (created by invoking NewStateMachine). To recall, the state machine encodes a generic safety property. The transitions are labelled with a *condition* and states can be accepting.

Netrix takes a step for each event in the EventQueue. At each step, we execute the filters similar to a switch case. We check the conditions in the sequential order of the filters and invoke the corresponding actions when a filter condition returns true. When none of the filter conditions match, the event is passed to the random exploration algorithm. Additionally, we deliver messages scheduled by the random exploration algorithm at each step. At the same time, the state machine takes a step for every event. If at the end of the iteration, the state machine is in an accepting state then we consider that iteration of the unit test to be a success and fail otherwise. The state machine is reset to the initial state at the start of every iteration. The above algorithm is the concrete implementation of δ_μ in Sect. 3.

The core of the DSL defines generic *conditions* (with boolean connectives) and *actions* that are protocol agnostic. We believe, the filters in combination with the `Context` key-value state allow for describing complex message interleavings. For example, to deliver only a specific number of messages (e.g. 3) of type `Prepare` to a replica p, the developer has to write only two filters. First, to count and deliver if count is less than 3

```
If(IsMessageType("Prepare")
  .And(IsMessageTo("p").And(Count("delivered").Lt(3)))
  .Then(Count("delivered").Incr, DeliverMessage))
```

and second similar one, to drop when the count is greater than or equal to 3. Here, the counter is stored in an auxillary key-value store `Context`. Similarly, messages can be stored in the context using `MessageSet` primitives to facilitate reordering. In general, the *conditions* read from the `Context` and actions modify the contents of the `Context`.

Since *conditions* and *actions* are functions, it is possible to augment the DSL with protocol specific functions. In Sect. 2 (Example 1 and Fig. 3), we refer to PBFT specific conditions such as `AddToLog`(α, v, i) and `IsMessageOfView`(v). Augmenting the DSL is mandatory to change the contents of the messages as the message contents are specific to the implementation. The augmentations aid in writing unit tests incrementally and to build a corpus of standard tests.

5 Case Studies

Using our DSL we write unit tests for three open source protocol implementations, **Tendermint**[1] [7] (version v0.34.3), **Raft**[2] [21] (version v3.5.2) and **BFTSmart**[3]. They are production implementations of popular consensus algorithms and are used in a wide variety of applications. The Tendermint protocol is a Byzantine consensus algorithm inspired by PBFT and is the backbone of the cosmos network[4]. We test the official implementation of Tendermint written in Go. Similarly, BFTSmart [6,24] implements in Java a Byzantine consensus algorithm. It is used to build key-value stores and distributed file systems. Raft is a popular benign consensus protocol that tolerates crash failures. We test the Go implementation that is used in many cloud services such as `etcd` and distributed graph databases such as `dgraph`.

The instrumentation effort aided by our language specific libraries needed to test these implementations is very little and is evident in the size of the instrumented code added - 600 LOC for Tendermint codebase of 150kLOC, 120LOC for Raft codebase of 16kLOC and 150LOC for BFTSmart codebase of 16kLOC. All our code is available publicly[5]

---

[1] https://github.com/tendermint/tendermint.
[2] https://github.com/etcd-io/etcd/tree/main/raft.
[3] https://github.com/bft-smart/library.
[4] https://cosmos.network.
[5] https://github.com/netrixframework.

For the three implementations, we write a total of 34 unit tests. As shown in Table 1, in 27 out of 34 unit tests, we are able to constrain the executions explored to those specified by the unit test. Each unit test is run for 100 iterations. We encode the constrainment criteria in the state machine that accompanies the test and indicate a successful outcome when the state machine succeed. Furthermore in the case of Tendermint, we find 4 instances where the implementation deviates from the protocol specification. One of these instances leads to a liveness bug where a lagging process does not catch up to the remaining process. These deviations were acknowledged by the Tendermint team and duly fixed. We demonstrate additional benefits to testing using Netrix, (1) the unit tests are concise and easy to write - unit tests have on average 2.5 filters, (2) the unit tests help with regression testing - We were able to run the tests on multiple versions of the implementation with little or no changes, (3) Netrix can be used to test implementations written in any language - we test implementations written in Java (BFTSmart) and Go (Raft, Tendermint) and finally (4) the constrained exploration with unit tests allow the developer to gain confidence even when no bugs are found like in the case of Raft and BFTSmart

To contrast Netrix with a randomized testing algorithms, we ran PCTCP on all three implementations. It fails to capture any of the new bugs/deviations in Tendermint or known bugs in Raft. We believe that the developers intuition is key to catching bugs. However, writing many unit tests requires time and effort/expertise and it is important to balance the tradeoffs. In our case, developer effort translates to number of filters in a unit test. We define a notion of *filter distance* to encode the significance of a filter in a unit test and experimentally show that PCTCP can do the work of shorter distance filters.

Filter Distance. From our unit tests, we identified three categories the filters can be grouped into—(1) **Byzantine** - Filters that introduce Byzantine behavior, (2) **Drop** - Filters that drop messages, (3) **Reorder** - Filters that reorder messages. The Reorder filters can be grouped into pairs. Ones that capture the message and store it in a set and ones that release the messages stored in a set. Filter distance is defined for a pair of capture-release filters and can be determined syntactically. The distance for byzantine filters is inf by definition and a drop filter is essentially a reorder filter where the release filter releases messages at the end of the execution. Therefore, we define the metric only for reorder filters. Recall that in consensus protocols, messages are associated with rounds/phases. We define the filter distance as the number of messages between the capture and release filter in a normal execution of the protocol (without any faults). For example, if the capture filter corresponds to messages of round r and the release filter corresponds to message of round $r + 2$. The distance is then $2n$ where n (linear in number of processes) messages are sent each round. We observe that PCTCP fails to explore executions where the re-orderings are beyond $O(n)$ distance. However, the filters with short distance measures (1–2 communication rounds) are not crucial and PCTCP is able to explore the respective re-ordering. Therefore, the developer can forego writing these filters.

Table 1. List of unit tests. The table lists unit tests grouped by the protocol. The columns are number of filters, state machine states, LOC and outcomes in number of iterations that successfully caught the interesting scenario/bug. For the tests (*) indicates new bugs and (^) indicates replicating known bugs

Name	#F	#S	LOC	Outcomes	Name	#F	#S	LOC	Outcomes
Tendermint					Raft				
ExpectUnlock*	3	5	90	41/100	Liveness^	5	3	64	15/100
Relocked*	4	5	115	53/100	LivenessNoCQ^	5	3	64	100/100
LockedCommit*	3	5	85	100/100	NoLiveness^	5	3	33	100/100
LaggingReplica*	3	4	71	100/100	ConfChangeBug^	5	2	94	55/100
ForeverLaggingReplica*	5	5	89	100/100	DropHeartbeat	2	3	69	100/100
RoundSkip	3	4	74	90/100	DropVotes	1	3	44	80/100
BlockVotes	2	3	55	33/100	DropFVotes	1	2	57	100/100
PrecommitInvariant	1	3	68	100/100	DropAppend	1	3	81	100/100
CommitAfterRoundSkip	3	3	82	36/100	ReVote	2	3	54	74/100
DifferentDecisions	8	3	180	20/100	ManyReVote	2	4	64	92/100
NilPrevotes	2	3	61	99/100	MultiReVote	2	4	60	81/100
ProposalNilPrevote	1	3	56	56/100	BFTSmart				
NotNilDecide	2	2	49	100/100	DPropForP	2	3	60	81/100
GarbledMessage	1	2	68	30/100	DPropSame	2	2	40	100/100
HigherRound	1	3	91	37/100	DropWrite	1	2	30	100/100
					DropWriteForP	1	2	33	89/100
					ExpectNewEpoch	1	2	28	94/100
					ExpectStop	1	2	38	100/100
					ByzLeaderChange	3	2	46	89/100
					PrevEpochProposal	2	3	53	99/100

Unit Test Methodology. To describe unit test scenarios for the three protocols, we referred to the protocol specification, proofs of the protocol and personal interaction with the developer teams (in the case of Tendermint). Here we describe some general methodology that could be applied to other protocols to write unit test scenarios. While the specification and proof allow us to write tests systematically, interactions with the developer team were aimed at writing tests target for under-tested parts of the code.

The protocol specification allows us to describe and encode the state machine for scenarios without any failures. Alternatively, trying to cover all lines of the protocol specification also leads to test scenarios. For example, consider the following lines from the Tendermint protocol specification

```
Upon (f+1) messages from a higher round r
    Transition to round r
```

To simulate this scenario, we isolate one replica p and do not deliver any messages from round 0. We then force the remaining replicas to move to round 1. According to the protocol specification, after receiving $f+1$ messages from the round 1, the isolated replica transitions to round 1. Specifically, we found that the Tendermint implementation fails this unit test and the isolated replica fails to catch up the other replicas immediately. The Tendermint team has acknowledged the bug.

Protocol Proofs. Apart from the protocol specification, the developer can derive test scenarios from the proofs of the protocols. For example, consider the following inductive invariants used in the proof of the Tendermint protocol[6]:

$$v \neq nil \land \exists p.precommitted(p,r,v) \rightarrow$$
$$\exists quorum. \forall p. p \in quorum \rightarrow prevoted(p,r,v)$$

This formula states that if a replica p `Precommits` a non nil value v in round r, then a quorum of validators should have sent `Prevote` messages for v in round r. This is an implication of the form $A \rightarrow B$, and the corresponding unit test contains filters to ensure $\neg B$, i.e., a quorum of replicas do not `Prevote` on the `Proposed` value, and a state machine that reaches the fail state if it observes A, i.e., it observes a `Precommit` from any validator.

Our corpus of unit tests for Tendermint and Raft are compact. Furthermore, they serve as a base repository of common filters that can be used to write more unit tests as the implementation evolves. As mentioned in Sect. 5, we extend the DSL to define *conditions* and *actions* specific to Tendermint. Our extensions prove to be useful in writing short unit tests due to their reusability. Some common extensions are `IsMessageFromRound`, `IsVoteForProposal`, `IsVoteFromPart` etc.

6 Related Work

Testing implementations of distributed systems has received considerable attention over the recent years. Probabilistic Concurrency Testing with Chain Partitioning (PCTCP) [22,23] provides precise probabilistic guarantees about observing every possible order between a fixed number of events. The Jepsen tool [1] makes it possible to introduce benign faults randomly with a certain frequency, which provides very little control over the outcome of a test. Observing a bug or not depends on the interaction between the fault injection frequency and the scheduler which is not controllable. Jepsen has demonstrated its success empirically by finding bugs in well known systems such as Cassandra [17] and Redis [18]. Similarly, developers also use simulation-based testing where they run many heavily instrumented replica instances on a single machine and randomly introduce message drops or network partitions. This process can be enhanced with simulated virtual clocks to speed up or slow down replicas [2]. Both Jepsen and PCTCP does not offer any control over the executions that are explored. Furthermore, unlike in our approach, these techniques cannot explore executions that include byzantine failures.

---

[6] https://github.com/tendermint/spec/tree/master/ivy-proofs.

MoDist [26], SAMC [19] and CrystalBall [25] adopt model checking techniques to test distributed systems implementations and exhaustively explore the execution space. These techniques require that tests be run for hours on compute intensive hardware (48 full machine days with SAMC). They cannot deal with Byzantine faults. Moreover, differently from these works, Netrix makes it possible to program the amount of asynchrony or faults in the executions, which simplifies the process of root causing and debugging potential violations.

Our work is inspired by Concurrit [15], which enables a similar scenario-based testing approach for *multi-threaded* concurrent programs. It introduces a DSL that enables developers to define tests where they can control the scheduling between threads with a minimal instrumentation effort. This DSL is specific to multi-threading and very different compared to Netrix's DSL which is specific to testing distributed protocol implementations. GFuzz [13] applies the idea of exploring different message orderings between concurrent go channels and has demonstrated success in finding concurrency bugs in actual implementations. P# [11] is an actor based programming language that allows developers to write asynchronous systems. P# is embedded in the C# programming language and is accompanied by a systematic concurrency testing framework. Similar to GFuzz, P# explores arbitrary event orderings between the actors to find concurrency bugs. However, both GFuzz and P# do not allow describing specific scenarios.

Our DSL primitives are motivated by specification languages for protocols. DISTAL [10] programs are a sequence of *Upon* clauses. Each *Upon* is followed by a predicate on the state of the protocol and current message. Similar to our DSL, DISTAL predicates contain counting, sets of messages and comparing message types. ModP [13] language allows protocol designers to describe and test a model of the protocol. Similar to DISTAL, ModP machines contains a sequence of *on* event handlers that modify the state of the machine. The *on* handlers are followed by predicates similar to DISTAL. ModP also generates code for testing the programs. While these are effective in finding bugs in a *model* of a protocol, the results however do not help in testing production implementations. The main reason they do not help in production environments is because model checkers do not scale when applied directly on implementation of large systems. Moreover most model-checkers that work at the programming language level, are not even applicable to this application domain, as they focus on primitives for shared memory and not message passing [3,4]. Therefore our DSL provides the only guided way to do exploration of the execution space on implementations.

7 Conclusion

Distributed systems suffer from complex and intricate bugs. Existing tools adopt a black box testing approach and rely on either systematic or probabilistic exploration of possible executions. We propose a more guided scenario-based unit testing approach where developers program and reuse tests aided by probabilistic exploration techniques to obtain better bug reproducibility. To facilitate this, we introduce a domain specific language to describe unit tests and define its syntax and semantics. Furthermore, we build an open source tool Netrix that is based on the domain specific language. We use Netrix to instrument and test Tendermint [7], Raft [21] and BFTSmart [6,24]. Our unit tests are effective in capturing deviations from the specification in the implementations. Furthermore, we demonstrate the re-usability of the tests by running them on different versions of the implementations and checking the bug fixes made in the implementation. A possible future extension would be to leverage the protocol proofs to automatically generate tests.

Acknowledgements. We thank the anonymous reviewers for their constructive feedback that shaped the paper to its current form. We also thank the developers of Informal Systems who helped evaluate the approach on Tendermint. The work was partially supported by the Interchain foundation.

References

1. Jepsen (2020). https://jepsen.io
2. Viewstamped Replication made famous (2020). https://github.com/coilhq/viewstamped-replication-made-famous
3. . Rust Shuttle Model checker (2021). https://github.com/awslabs/shuttle
4. Kotlin Lincheck (2023). https://github.com/Kotlin/kotlinx-lincheck
5. Abdulla, P.A., Aronis, S., Jonsson, B., Sagonas, K.: Optimal dynamic partial order reduction. In: Jagannathan, S., Sewell, P. (eds.) The 41st Annual ACM SIGPLAN-SIGACT Symposium on Principles of Programming Languages, POPL '14, San Diego, CA, USA, 20–21 January 2014, pp. 373–384. ACM (2014). https://doi.org/10.1145/2535838.2535845
6. Bessani, A.N., Sousa, J., Alchieri, E.A.P.: State machine replication for the masses with BFT-SMART. In: 44th Annual IEEE/IFIP International Conference on Dependable Systems and Networks, DSN 2014, Atlanta, GA, USA, 23–26 June 2014, pp. 355–362. IEEE Computer Society (2014)https://doi.org/10.1109/DSN.2014.43
7. Buchman, E., Kwon, J., Milosevic, Z.: The latest gossip on BFT consensus. CoRR arxiv:1807.04938 (2018)
8. Burckhardt, S., Kothari, P., Musuvathi, M., Nagarakatte, S.: A randomized scheduler with probabilistic guarantees of finding bugs. SIGARCH Comput. Archit. News **38**(1), 167–178 (2010) https://doi.org/10.1145/1735970.1736040
9. Castro, M., Liskov, B.: Practical byzantine fault tolerance. In: Proceedings of the Third Symposium on Operating Systems Design and Implementation, OSDI 1999, pp. 173–186. USENIX Association, USA (1999)
10. Delgado, P.: Distal: Domain-specific language for implementing distributed algorithms (2012). http://infoscience.epfl.ch/record/187164
11. Deligiannis, P., Donaldson, A.F., Ketema, J., Lal, A., Thomson, P.: Asynchronous programming, analysis and testing with state machines. SIGPLAN Not. **50**(6), 154–164 (2015). https://doi.org/10.1145/2813885.2737996
12. Deligiannis, P., et al.: Uncovering bugs in distributed storage systems during testing (not in production!). In: Brown, A.D., Popovici, F.I. (eds.) 14th USENIX Conference on File and Storage Technologies, FAST 2016, Santa Clara, CA, USA, 22–25 February 2016, pp. 249–262. USENIX Association (2016). https://www.usenix.org/conference/fast16/technical-sessions/presentation/deligiannis

13. Desai, A., Phanishayee, A., Qadeer, S., Seshia, S.A.: Compositional programming and testing of dynamic distributed systems. Proc. ACM Program. Lang. **2**(OOPSLA) (2018). https://doi.org/10.1145/3276529
14. Dragoi, C., Enea, C., Ozkan, B.K., Majumdar, R., Niksic, F.: Testing consensus implementations using communication closure. Proc. ACM Program. Lang. **4**(OOPSLA), 210:1–210:29 (2020). https://doi.org/10.1145/3428278
15. Elmas, T., Burnim, J., Necula, G., Sen, K.: Concurrit: a domain specific language for reproducing concurrency bugs. In: Proceedings of the 34th ACM SIGPLAN Conference on Programming Language Design and Implementation, PLDI 2013, pp. 153–164. Association for Computing Machinery, New York (2013). https://doi.org/10.1145/2491956.2462162
16. Killian, C.E., Anderson, J.W., Jhala, R., Vahdat, A.: Life, death, and the critical transition: Finding liveness bugs in systems code (awarded best paper). In: Balakrishnan, H., Druschel, P. (eds.) 4th Symposium on Networked Systems Design and Implementation (NSDI 2007), Cambridge, Massachusetts, USA, 11–13 April 2007, Proceedings. USENIX (2007). http://www.usenix.org/events/nsdi07/tech/killian.html
17. Kingsbury, K.: Jepsen: Cassandra (2013). https://aphyr.com/posts/294-call-me-maybe-cassandra
18. Kingsbury, K.: Redis-raft 1b3fbf6 (2020). https://jepsen.io/analyses/redis-raft-1b3fbf6
19. Leesatapornwongsa, T., Hao, M., Joshi, P., Lukman, J.F., Gunawi, H.S.: Samc: semantic-aware model checking for fast discovery of deep bugs in cloud systems. In: Proceedings of the 11th USENIX Conference on Operating Systems Design and Implementation, OSDI 2014, pp. 399–414. USENIX Association (2014)
20. Lukman, J.F., et al.: Flymc: highly scalable testing of complex interleavings in distributed systems. In: Candea, G., van Renesse, R., Fetzer, C. (eds.) Proceedings of the Fourteenth EuroSys Conference 2019, Dresden, Germany, 25–28 March 2019, pp. 20:1–20:16. ACM (2019). https://doi.org/10.1145/3302424.3303986
21. Ongaro, D., Ousterhout, J.: In search of an understandable consensus algorithm. In: 2014 USENIX Annual Technical Conference (USENIX ATC 14), pp. 305–319. USENIX Association, Philadelphia (2014). https://www.usenix.org/conference/atc14/technical-sessions/presentation/ongaro
22. Ozkan, B.K., Majumdar, R., Niksic, F., Befrouei, M.T., Weissenbacher, G.: Randomized testing of distributed systems with probabilistic guarantees. Proc. ACM Program. Lang. **2**(OOPSLA) (2018). https://doi.org/10.1145/3276530
23. Ozkan, B.K., Majumdar, R., Oraee, S.: Trace aware random testing for distributed systems. Proc. ACM Program. Lang. **3**(OOPSLA), 180:1–180:29 (2019). https://doi.org/10.1145/3360606
24. Sousa, J., Bessani, A.N.: From byzantine consensus to BFT state machine replication: A latency-optimal transformation. In: Constantinescu, C., Correia, M.P. (eds.) 2012 Ninth European Dependable Computing Conference, Sibiu, Romania, 8–11 May 2012, pp. 37–48. IEEE Computer Society (2012). https://doi.org/10.1109/EDCC.2012.32
25. Yabandeh, M., Knezevic, N., Kostic, D., Kuncak, V.: Crystalball: Predicting and preventing inconsistencies in deployed distributed systems. In: Rexford, J., Sirer, E.G. (eds.) Proceedings of the 6th USENIX Symposium on Networked Systems Design and Implementation, NSDI 2009, Boston, MA, USA, 22–24 April 2009, pp. 229–244. USENIX Association (2009). http://www.usenix.org/events/nsdi09/tech/full_papers/yabandeh/yabandeh.pdf

26. Yang, J., et al.: Modist: transparent model checking of unmodified distributed systems. In: Proceedings of the 6th USENIX Symposium on Networked Systems Design and Implementation, NSDI 2009, pp. 213–228. USENIX Association (2009)
27. Yuan, X., Yang, J., Gu, R.: Partial order aware concurrency sampling. In: Chockler, H., Weissenbacher, G. (eds.) CAV 2018. LNCS, vol. 10982, pp. 317–335. Springer, Cham (2018). https://doi.org/10.1007/978-3-319-96142-2_20

Tool Augmented LLMs for Big Data Analysis

Mohammed Ali Essabri[1,2](✉), Jamal Rebii[1], and Mohammed Erradi[2]

[1] Henceforth Rabat, Rabat, Morocco
`j.rebii@henceforth.ma`
[2] ENSIAS University Mohamed V of Rabat, Rabat, Morocco
`mohammed.erradi@ensias.um5.ac.ma`, `mohammedali_essabri@um5.ac.ma`

Abstract. Recent advancements in artificial intelligence, have been driven by the development of Large Language Models (LLMs). Following the emergence of these models, the field has witnessed remarkable progress, paving the way for unprecedented innovations. Despite these advancements, the application of LLMs in real-world systems faces challenges due to the diverse range of tools and environments, necessitating innovative approaches for practical deployment. A critical focus has been on enhancing LLMs' text-oriented question-answering capabilities through interaction with tools and APIs, aiming to reduce hallucinations and boost performance. In this paper we explore LLMs' capability for handling and learning tools for Big Data Analysis. We propose a pipeline and a methodology for developing LLMs that can interface with complex big data environments. By achieving this, we significantly lower the barriers to entry for non-expert users, enabling them to leverage big data analytics and visualization tools without requiring prior knowledge of the database type or the tools' implementation details.

Keywords: Artificial Intelligence · Large Language Models · Tool Augmented Language Modeling · Big data analysis · Intelligent queries

1 Introduction

In recent years, artificial intelligence (AI), with a particular focus on natural language processing (NLP), has seen rapid advancements primarily through the development of Large Language Models (LLMs) [2]. These models have significantly enhanced our capacity to process and generate language in ways that closely resemble human capabilities, establishing themselves as cornerstone technologies in AI research [5,14–16]. Despite these advances, applying LLMs to real-world systems presents numerous challenges, mainly due to the wide array of tools and environments involved. This diversity results in a complex integration landscape, highlighting the need for innovative approaches to bridge the gap between theoretical progress and practical deployment.

In facing these challenges, a pivotal area of focus has been to refine the text-oriented question-answering capabilities of LLMs through their interaction with tools and APIs [9–11,13], aiming to mitigate the hallucinations problem and improve their benchmark performance. This exploration has led to the emergence of two principal strategies for integrating tools with LLMs. The first involves fine-tuning LLMs to learn the use of specific tools, by leveraging synthetic datasets [7,10]. The second strategy, in-context learning [7–9], employs prompt-based demonstrations to teach LLMs tool usage, offering a more adaptable solution capable of accommodating new tools.

In this paper we explore the capability of LLMs for handling and learning tools for a new horizon tasks, namely Big Data Analysis. We propose a pipeline where such LLM could operate, and a methodology for developing LLMs that interfaces with complex big data environments. In this approach, we aim to provide a more adaptable and intelligent AI system to interact with big data environments by making the interaction easier while addressing complex tasks.

2 Preliminaries

2.1 Database

Our work utilizes a graph-structured data stored in Neo4j DBMS, comprising YouTube videos (Fig. 1). This data includes nodes representing videos, comments, and users, along with various features like content and creation dates, connected through several types of relationships. This rich structure allows for the extraction of insightful visualizations critical for our analysis.

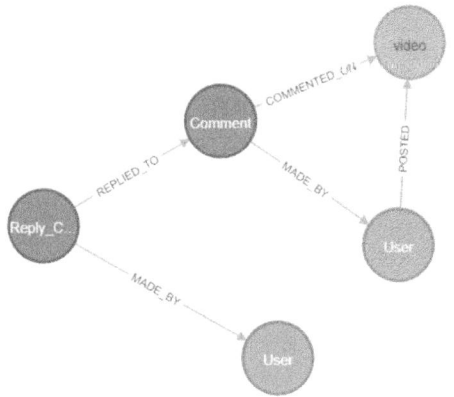

Fig. 1. Data Model with three types of nodes.

2.2 Tools

To enable the LLM to generate visualization plots, we developed a suite of tools designed to output specific plots based on given inputs. The model is tasked with overcoming two main challenges: identifying the appropriate tool for a given task and determining the correct input for that tool. We mainly employ six distinct visualization tools: **Distribution, Correlation Matrix, Word Cloud, Box Plot, Violin Plot**, and **Pie Chart**, these tools are designed to be fully independent, allowing for their application across various databases and facilitating easier generalization.

3 Approach

Our approach centers on creating an LLM capable of translating non-expert user requests into database-compatible queries and employing various visualization tools to fulfill those requests. As depicted in Fig. 2 the process involves teaching the LLM to transform English language requests into specific database queries, select the suitable visualization tool, and pass the correct arguments for generating responses .

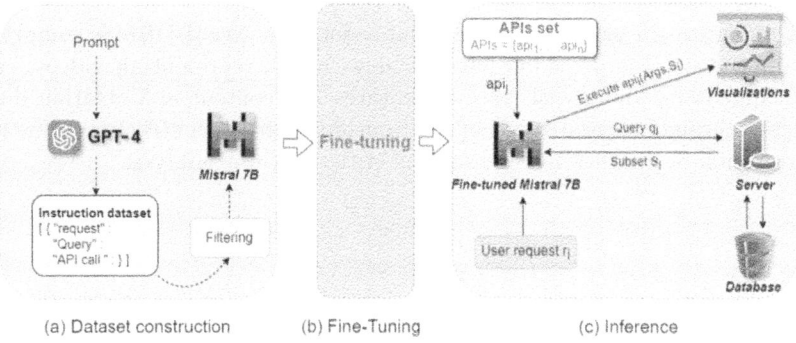

Fig. 2. Three phases of constructing our big data analyzer LLM: constructing a fine-tuning dataset using GPT-4 [5], fine-tuning the model then inference. During inference, the model is integrated into a pipeline where it receives a request and returns an output containing a query that is sent to the database server and an API call that is executed after receiving the query results.

3.1 Dataset Construction:

To fine-tune the model for the mentioned tasks, a fine-tuning dataset $D = \{R, Q, C\}$ is needed, where R contains user requests $R = \{r_1, \ldots, r_n\}$, queries $Q = \{q_1, \ldots, q_n\}$, and API calls with the passed arguments $C = \{c_1, \ldots, c_n\}$. To generate this dataset, we prompted GPT-4 [5], The prompt includes APIs descriptions, descriptions of database architecture, and some well-chosen examples written by humans. This process requires minimal human supervision and can be easily extended to new databases and new visualization APIs.

The generated data is then filtered by executing the queries and API calls and remove the non-executable instructionsas shown in Fig. 2(a). Here is an example of a generated sample:

{"request" : "What are the dominant languages in the videos?",
"query" : "MATCH (v : Video) RETURN v.language",
"API_call" : "plot_distribution([result['v.language'] for result in results])"}

3.2 Fine Tuning:

After sampling and filtering the generated queries and API calls, we obtain a new dataset $D' = \{R', Q', C'\}$. Then, we merge the remaining queries and API calls with the requests to create the fine-tuning dataset $D^* = \{S_1, \ldots, S_n\}$, where for each S_i in D^* :

$$S_i = \text{"request:"} + r_i + \text{"query:"} + q_i + \text{"API\_call:"} + c_i \tag{1}$$

This dataset is used to fine-tune the model using the LoRA approach [4].

3.3 Inference:

After fine-tuning, the model is integrated into a pipeline with the database server and the tool set as shown in Fig. 2(c). When a user sends a request, the model generates an output containing a query q^* and an API call with arguments c^*. The query is then sent to the server, which returns a subset S that is also passed with the arguments of the API as indicated in the call c^*. Finally, the call is executed to return a visualization.

4 Experiments

For the dataset construction, we prompted GPT-4 [5] and MISTRAL-8x7b [3] to generate two datasets of 1000 Instructions. The prompt includes a description of the tools, the database architecture, and some human-written examples. After executing all the queries and tool calls, we filtered out the non-executable Instructions.

Table 1. Generated Instructions filtering.

LLM	Generated Instructions	Executable Queries	Executable API Calls
GPT-4	1000	756 (75.6%)	678 (67.8%)
mistral-8x7b	1000	456 (45.6%)	390 (39.6%)

As illustrated in Table 1, since GPT-4 is the best-ranked LLM in tools usage based on the Berkeley Function-Calling Leaderboard [12], it generates a more accurate dataset.

In the evaluation phase on the testing set generated by GPT-4, our fine-tuned model achieved a **100%** accuracy for database querying and a **90%** accuracy for API calls. However, for some human written indirect requests (20 requests), the model achieved about **75%** accuracy for database querying and **60%** accuracy for API calls.

For the inference, the model receives the tools description and data architecture as context, and we specify its output format as follows:

$$\{\text{``Query}: \ldots..$$
$$\text{API\_call}: \ldots..\text{''}\}$$

Then the query and API call are extracted from the model output and executed, as shown in Fig. 3.

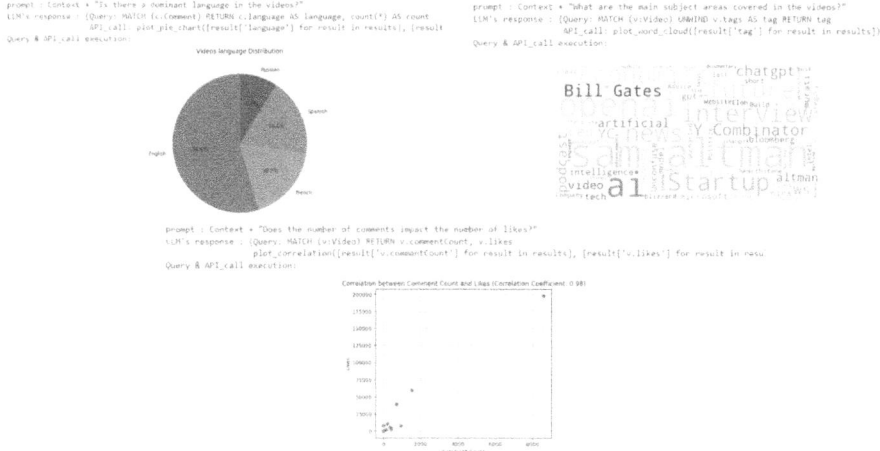

Fig. 3. Inferring Indirect Requests with Fine-Tuned MISTRAL-7b

5 Conclusion

Our findings underscore the utility of Large Language Models in big data analysis, expressing remarkable results. As future works, we plan to optimize our architecture further and enhance model performance through self-verification methods, aiming to minimize synthetic data noise and increase model reliability. Additionally we aim to explore the ability of our model to generalize by testing a more variety of database structures and data visualization tools.

References

1. Jiang, A.Q., et al.: Mistral 7B. arXiv preprint arXiv:2310.06825 (2023)
2. Vaswani, A., et al.: Attention is All you Need. In: Neural Information Processing Systems (2017)
3. Jiang, A.Q., et al.: Mixtral of Experts. arXiv preprint arXiv:2401.04088 (2024)
4. Hu, J.E., et al.: LoRA: low-rank adaptation of large language models. arXiv preprint arXiv:2106.09685 (2021)
5. Achiam, J., et al.: OpenAI. GPT-4 Technical Report (2023)
6. Paranjape, B., et al.: ART: automatic multi-step reasoning and tool-use for large language models. arXiv preprint arXiv:2303.09014 (2023)
7. Guu, K., et al.: Retrieval augmented language model pre-training. In: International Conference on Machine Learning. PMLR (2020)
8. Yao, S., et al.: React: synergizing reasoning and acting in language models. arXiv preprint arXiv:2210.03629 (2022)
9. Qin, Y., et al.: Tool learning with foundation models. arXiv preprint arXiv:2304.08354 (2023)
10. Schick, T., et al.: Toolformer: language models can teach themselves to use tools. Adv. Neural Inf. Process. Syst. **36** (2024)
11. Thoppilan, R., et al.: Lamda: language models for dialog applications. arXiv preprint arXiv:2201.08239 (2022)
12. Berkeley Computer Science Department. Gorilla Leaderboard. https://gorilla.cs.berkeley.edu/leaderboard.html
13. Parisi, A., Zhao, Y., Fiedel, N.: Talm: tool augmented language models. arXiv preprint arXiv:2205.12255 (2022)
14. Touvron, H., et al.: Llama: open and efficient foundation language models. arXiv preprint arXiv:2302.13971 (2023)
15. Chowdhery, A., et al.: Palm: scaling language modeling with pathways. J. Mach. Learn. Res. **24**(240), 1–113 (2023)
16. Brown, T., et al.: Language models are few-shot learners. Adv. Neural Inf. Processing Syst. **33**, 1877–1901 (2020)

Static Data Race Detection via Lazy Sequentialization

Bernd Fischer[1], Giulio Garbi[2,3(✉)], Salvatore La Torre[3], Gennaro Parlato[2], and Peter Schrammel[4]

[1] Stellenbosch University, Stellenbosch, South Africa
bfischer@sun.ac.za
[2] University of Molise, Pesche, Italy
{giulio.garbi,gennaro.parlato}@unimol.it
[3] University of Salerno, Fisciano, Italy
slatorre@unisa.it
[4] Diffblue Ltd, Oxford, UK
peter.schrammel@diffblue.com

Abstract. We present a new symbolic static data race detection algorithm, which is defined as a code-to-code translation that injects code to monitor any accesses to shared memory locations. We implemented this algorithm in the LaDR tool as an extension of an existing lazy sequentialization schema which works well when used in tandem with bounded model checkers. We evaluated LaDR on the benchmarks from the data race demonstration category of SV-COMP 2024, and on `safestack`, a lock-free data structure that contains a rare ABA-related bug. LaDR finds more data races than all other tools participating in SV-COMP 2024, and is the only tool that can find a data race in `safestack`.

Keywords: Data races · Static analysis · Lazy sequentialization

1 Introduction

A *data race* occurs if different computations in a concurrent system access the same memory location "at the same time" (i.e., in arbitrary order but immediately following each other) and at least one of the two accesses is a write access. Bugs caused by data races are often extremely difficult to detect manually, due to their non-deterministic nature; therefore, a large number of different data race detection tools have been developed to help developers in debugging.

Traditionally, most tools use *dynamic* techniques, where the target program is instrumented and executed to produce an execution which is then analyzed for races; for example, Eraser [24] tracks the set of locks held for each memory access, while ThreadSanitizer [26] tracks the order of memory accesses and synchronization operations throughout the program execution. Since they observe real program executions over concrete inputs, dynamic techniques only analyze feasible behaviors, and all identified data races can happen in practice (i.e., they report no *false positives*). However, they may miss data races (i.e., report *false negatives*) as a result of poor test suites.

Static techniques construct and analyze an execution model without actually executing the target program. In principle, static techniques can be *sound* (i.e., never report false positives) or *complete* (i.e., never report false negatives), but in practice precise execution models become too complex for the analysis, and the techniques often use a number of different abstraction methods, balancing soundness and completeness. For example, Locksmith [22] uses lock state analysis, sharing analysis, correlation inference, and escaping and linearity checks.

SAT-based symbolic execution and model checking convert a program into a model in form of a logical formula that is satisfiable if and only if the program violates a given specification. Their performance has improved substantially in the recent past. Retargeting them to data race detection has thus become a viable alternative. We follow this approach here and describe a precise data race detection tool based on bounded model checking; more specifically, we develop and implement on top of the Lazy-CSeq sequentialization [12,13] a code-to-code translation schema that rewrites a concurrent program into a bounded non-deterministic sequential program such that data races can be detected by assertion checking. This sequentialized program is processed by a backend verification tool that constructs a logical formula that is satisfiable iff the original program contains a data race. The non-determinism in the original program is reflected in underconstrained variables in the constructed formula.

Our schema uses a flag for each shared memory location to indicate that location is involved in a data race, and injects control code that manipulates these flags. The flags are non-deterministically set on a write (reflecting the fact that this could be the write-part of the race), and checked on each other write or read (reflecting the fact that this could be the second part of the race). The non-determinism simplifies our design because we do not need to maintain complex data structures, and can be handled efficiently by the SAT solver.

We implemented this schema in the LaDR data race detection tool for C programs that use the pthreads-library as concurrency mechanism, using the bounded model-checker CBMC [4,8] as backend verifier. LaDR is sound but incomplete, due to the bounding of programs, but it performs very well over the SV-COMP 2024 data race benchmarks. It finds the highest number (183 out of 232) of data races, outperforming the three best performing tools in this category at SV-COMP 2024. It is also the only tool that can find a data race in safestack, a lock-free data structure that contains a rare ABA-related bug.

2 Bounded Multi-threaded Programs

Like bounded model checking [4], we focus on bug detection. We thus work with *bounded* programs, which are syntactically guaranteed to terminate after a bounded number of steps, e.g., through the absence of loops, recursion, and goto-statements representing backward jumps. Unbounded programs can be bounded through a series of simple code-to-code transformations such as loop unwinding, function inlining, and function cloning [6].

$$P \;::=\; (dec;)^* \, (\texttt{void}\, f_i\, () \,\{(\texttt{static?}\, dec;)^* \, stm\})_{i=0,\ldots,n}$$
$$dec \;::=\; typ\, v \mid \texttt{thread}\, t \mid \texttt{mutex}\, m$$
$$typ \;::=\; typ* \mid typ\,[exp] \mid \texttt{int}$$
$$stm \;::=\; seq; \mid con; \mid \{stm^+\}$$
$$seq \;::=\; \texttt{assume}(exp) \mid \texttt{assert}(exp) \mid \texttt{goto}\, l \mid l\texttt{:skip} \mid \texttt{if}(exp)\, stm \,\texttt{else}\, stm \mid exp$$
$$con \;::=\; n:stm \mid \texttt{return} \mid t\texttt{=create}\, f_i() \mid \texttt{join}\, t \mid \texttt{lock}\, m \mid \texttt{unlock}\, m$$
$$exp \;::=\; lval = exp \mid exp\,,\,exp \mid exp\, \texttt{OP}\, exp \mid exp\,?\,exp:exp \mid \&lval \mid lval \mid const \mid (\texttt{*})$$
$$lval \;::=\; lval\,[exp] \mid *lval \mid v$$

Fig. 1. Syntax of bounded multi-threaded programs

LaDR supports the full C language, but we illustrate our code-to-code translation schema using a simple, multi-threaded imperative language with mutex locking and unlocking operations for thread synchronization. Its grammar is shown in Fig. 1; here m denotes a mutex, t a thread variable, v a program variable, l a non-numeric label, and n a numeric label. Program variables can be integers, pointers, or (multidimensional) arrays, in arbitrary combination.

A *bounded multi-threaded program* comprises a list of declarations of *global* (or *shared*) variables and a list of parameterless *thread functions* f_i that in turn each comprise a list of *local* variable declarations and a (block) statement stm.

Shared and static local program variables, including pointers and individual array elements, are initialized to 0; non-static ones remain uninitialized and non-deterministically assume an arbitrary value (denoted by (*)) until they are explicitly assigned. Mutexes must be declared globally and are initially free.

A *sequential statement seq* can be an assume- or assert-statement, a conditional statement, a goto- or a labeled skip-statement, which serves as jump target, or an expression, which is evaluated for its side effects. A *concurrent statement con* can be a labeled statement of the form $n:stm$ where stm is either an unlabeled concurrent statement or a sequential statement that accesses the shared memory, a return-statement, a thread creation or join operation, or a mutex lock or unlock operation. A thread creation statement t = create $f_i()$ spawns a new thread from f_i. A thread join statement join t suspends the executing thread until the thread identified by t has executed its last statement. Thread variables must be initialized by a create-statement before they can be accessed by a join-statement. Lock and unlock statements respectively acquire and release a mutex, with the usual blocking behavior.

Expressions exp can contain side effects in the form of *assignment expressions* $v = e$, which compute the memory location denoted by the lvalue x, evaluate e and write its value into the computed location, and return the value of e. *Comma expressions* e_1, e_2 explicitly sequence expression evaluation, i.e., they first evaluate e_1 for its side effects but discard its value, then evaluate e_2 and return its value. We also model arbitrary strict operators OP, lazy evaluation in the form of *conditional expressions* $e_1 ? e_2 : e_3$, which first evaluate the guard expression e_1 and, depending on the result, evaluate and return either e_2 or e_3, and the address-of operator &.

We assume that a valid program P satisfies the usual well-formedness conditions, and that its execution does not involve the application of any operator to illegal arguments (e.g., division by zero). The last statement in the body of each function must be its single `return`-statement. All concurrent statements in a function as well as its first and last statement must be labeled with a numerical label n, such that the labels in each function start from 0 and increase by 1 according to the statement order; any other label of the program must be non-numerical. We call any statement with a numerical label a *visible statement*. This structure is required by the lazy sequentialization to simulate context-switching and can be established easily by code-to-code transformations.

In the *interleaving semantics*, a concurrent execution is defined as the interleaving of the individual thread executions. A sequence of consecutively executed statements from one thread is called a *context*. A *round* contains one (possibly empty) context from each thread. We assume that all threads are scheduled in each round in the same fixed order; other schedules can be simulated using additional rounds and empty contexts.

A *data race* occurs in a bounded multi-threaded program P if there is an execution in P where two different threads can access the same shared memory location at the "same time" and at least one of these is a write to this shared location. In the interleaving semantics, a data race is captured if these two accesses occur respectively at the end (i.e., in the last executed visible statement) of one context and at the beginning (i.e., in the first executed visible statement) of the following context in the computation. Since these two accesses are not synchronized there is always another computation that interleaves the two accesses in the reversed order but still keeps one after the other (possibly by increasing the number of contexts). In the following, we thus assume without loss of generality that the write occurs always first in the interleaving.

3 Lazy Sequentialization

Sequentialization [17,23] is a general program analysis technique that transforms concurrent programs into non-deterministic sequential programs such that the reachability of program states is preserved. It can be implemented as a code-to-code translation, which allows us to build tools for the analysis of multi-threaded programs by reusing existing tools for sequential programs.

The *lazy sequentialization* translation (LS) [12,13] has been specifically designed to work well in combination with SAT-based bounded model checking tools (in particular CBMC), and thus fits our approach well. LS was designed for reachability checking, and does not directly support data race detection. The main contribution of this paper is to extend LS to detect data races efficiently through the use of a shadow memory (see Sect. 4). This section gives an overview of the aspects of LS that are relevant to this extension. Figure 2 illustrates the complete translation; the code fragments in red are added for the data race detection and can be ignored for now.

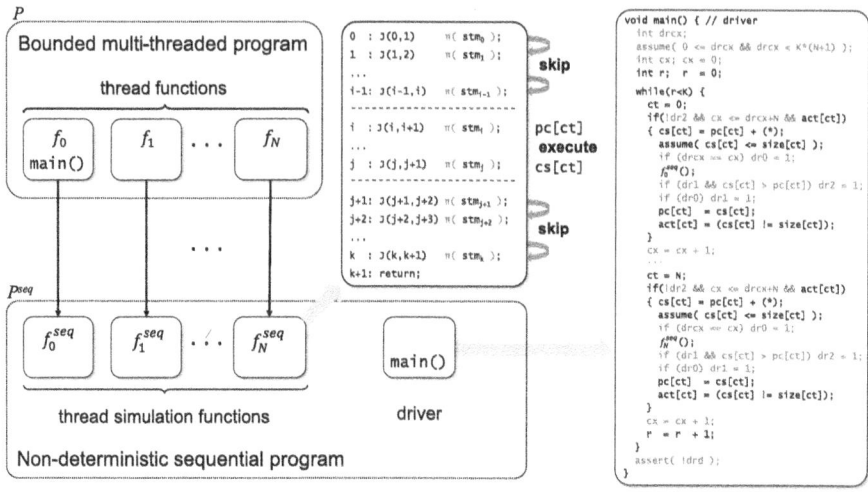

Fig. 2. Code-to-code translation overview

We assume that P is a bounded multi-threaded program with $N+1$ thread functions $f_0, f_1, \ldots, f_N$, where f_0 denotes P's main function, and that it contains N create-statements using each $f_1, \ldots, f_N$ exactly once as thread function; P thus spawns at most N threads. The corresponding sequential program P^{seq} is formed by a new function main and a *thread simulation function* f_i^{seq} for each thread function f_i in P. LS assumes the interleaving semantics, and simulates the programs in a round-robin fashion up to a given number of rounds K $>$ 0.

We use pc and cs to store the numerical labels respectively at the beginning and the end of each context; size to store the largest numerical label for each thread function f_i; act to track the active (i.e., created but not yet terminated) threads (initially only act[0] is set to true, as f_0^{seq} corresponds to the main function of P); and ct to store the numerical identifier of the thread being currently simulated.

Main Driver. In each loop iteration the new main simulates a (possibly empty) context of each active thread f_{ct} of P by calling the corresponding simulation function f_{ct}^{seq} for ct $\in [0, N]$ (see Fig. 2). Specifically, for each active thread, it

- non-deterministically guesses the numerical label of the next context-switch and stores it in cs[ct];
- ensures that this value is within the appropriate bounds;
- calls the thread simulation function f_{ct}^{seq} to simulate the thread ct from pc[ct] through to cs[ct];
- stores cs[ct] in pc[ct] (which is used in the next round to resume the computation); and
- sets act[ct] to false if cs[ct] is the label of the return-statement, which means that the simulation of the thread is terminated.

Thread Translation. The main driver repeatedly calls each f_{ct}^{seq} to simulate the non-deterministically selected context. Each f_{ct}^{seq} must therefore (i) maintain the thread-local state between the consecutive calls, and (ii) execute *only* the statements between pc[ct] and cs[ct]. The first is achieved simply by changing the storage class of the thread-local variables to static (which is more efficient than snapshotting the thread memory), while the second is achieved by injecting control code that suppresses the execution of statements not within the range. More specifically, the control code forces f_{ct}^{seq} to jump over each individual visible statement whose label is smaller than the stored label of the current context's resumption point or larger than its end point. This mechanism can be implemented in a way that avoids complex branching in the control flow by exploiting the consecutive natural numbers used as labels on the visible statements, and so leads to simpler formulas. Specifically, right after each numerical label i (except for the last one), a conditional jump of the form is injected in front of the original

$$\texttt{if(pc[ct]>}i \texttt{ || } i\texttt{>=cs[ct]) goto } j; \qquad \text{(J macro)}$$

statement. Note that the injected condition becomes false iff the control is between pc[ct] and cs[ct], so that exactly the same statements as in the original thread are executed by f_{ct}^{seq}. The translation always calls the J-macro with literal arguments i and $i+1$ (see Fig. 2). In effect, each f_{ct}^{seq} jumps (in multiple hops) to the saved position pc[ct] in the code, resumes its execution until the visible statement with the label cs[ct] of the next context-switch is reached, and jumps (again in multiple hops) to the final return-statement. Figure 2 illustrates this.

We omit details of LS that are not essential for our data race instrumentation, including the handling of control-flow branching and the simulation of synchronization routines. These details can be found in [12,13].

4 Symbolic Data Race Detection Schema

In this section, we describe our LaDR data race detection scheme. It is implemented as a code-to-code translation on top of LS (see Sect. 3) and uses the symbolic shadow memory API provided by CBMC-SSM. We first give a high-level overview of our translation before we discuss details of the extension to LS (shown in red in Fig. 2).

Overview. In the interleaving semantics, we can split a data race detection into two distinct phases (cf. Sect. 2):

Phase 1: We non-deterministically select a context C_1 in which the execution of the last visible statement of C_1 updates a shared location ℓ.

Phase 2: We check whether the first visible statement of the next (non-empty) context C_2 of another thread accesses ℓ; if so, a data race involving ℓ occurs.

In contrast to deterministic methods, which manipulate large and complex data structures that store the status of each memory location in order to detect data races, we rely on the schedule non-determinism, which frees us from having to encode these data structures at the formula level, and thus results in a more scalable solution.

We implement the two phases on top of LS by injecting *control code* into the main driver and *rewriting* the statements and expressions in the thread functions. The statement rewriting is represented in Fig. 2 by the function π described below. The injected control code implements a finite state machine that identifies the contexts C_1 and C_2, and tracks the phases. Statement rewriting injects code in the form of comma expressions to set the shadow memory bit for each update to the shared memory when in Phase 1, and to query the shadow memory for each access to the shared memory and to possibly flag that a data race has occurred when in Phase 2.

We use the following auxiliary global variables which are set according to the following invariants:

dr0 is set to **true** right before C_1 is simulated, indicating that Phase 1 started;
dr1 is set to **true** right after C_1 has been simulated, indicating that Phase 1 is completed;
dr2 is initialized to **false** and set to **true** as soon as C_2 is executed, indicating that Phase 2 is completed; and and thus no more contexts need to be simulated;
drd is initialized to **false** and set to **true** when a data race is detected.

Only drd is modified in the thread simulation functions while dr0, dr1, and dr2 are only updated in the main driver. This keeps the generated formulas compact.

Shadow Memory. In the LaDR scheme, we need to determine whether the shared memory location at a given address has been updated by a thread or not. For efficiency reasons, we keep this information as flags in a *shadow memory*, which is a separate data structure that is invisible to the analyzed program but can be accessed efficiently through its original memory addresses.

More specifically, we use the shadow memory as implemented in CBMC-SSM [8], an extension of CBMC [4]. Its shadow memory associates a *bit field* with each byte of memory. We assume that all bit fields are initialized to **false** and then manipulate them via the following API functions:

set_sm(*addr*, *val*) sets to *val* the bit fields of all memory bytes whose memory addresses are between *addr* and *addr* + sizeof(*T*), where *T* is the type of the object at *addr*.
get_sm(*addr*) returns the disjunction of all bit field values corresponding to all memory locations whose addresses are between *addr* and *addr* + sizeof(*T*).

Main Driver. We now describe the changes made to the main driver of LS. Since we simulate K contexts for each of the $N+1$ threads, we identify contexts by integers from 0 to $K \cdot (N+1) - 1$, increasing in the order in which they are simulated. We declare and constrain a fresh local variable drcx, to non-deterministically select the context C_1 through its numerical identifier. The simulation follows the same line as LS, with the difference that a thread is simulated only if it is active, *and* Phase 2 has not been completed yet (i.e., !dr2 holds). We also require that at most N threads have been scheduled since Phase 1 has been completed (i.e., cx<=(drcx+N) holds). This prevents the main driver from executing a function when Phase 1 is completed but Phase 2 has not started within the following N contexts, which allows us to abort schedules that can be captured by others, and avoids false positives (i.e., write and read are contained in the same thread). A final assert-statement is injected into the main driver to force failure when a data race is found. The extra code in the main driver maintains the invariants stated above for the auxiliary global variables.

Thread Translation. The thread simulation functions keep the same structure as in LS, since the extension only adds code (in form of comma expressions) at the level of expressions. This is captured by the translation function π in Fig. 2.

Translation Modes. An expression may require different translations, depending on its usage in the code, similar to but not exactly following the usual lvalue/rvalue distinction. For example, the occurrence of a shared variable x requires the injection of data race detection code if the *content* of its memory location is accessed in a read (e.g., in an arithmetic expression $x + y$) or write operation (e.g., in an assignment of the form $x = 0$) but not if only the address of its location is accessed (e.g., in an address-operation $\&x$). Moreover, when we rewrite expressions, we may need to duplicate sub-expressions, but without duplicating any side effects (i.e., memory writes) they can have. We achieve this in the usual way by hoisting the evaluation of side-effecting sub-expressions into comma expressions. We distinguish the four different modes below, and use $[\![e, M]\!]$ to denote the translation of an expression e in mode M:

ACC indicates that the value of the expression is used to access a memory location; if it is an lvalue, it may thus be involved in a data race and we instrument it with data race detection code.
NACC indicates that the value of the expression is not used to access the memory; if the expression itself is an lvalue, we thus do not instrument it with data race detection code. However, its sub-expressions may be instrumented.
WSE is used to access the value of the expression, without executing its side effects, if any. We require that any side effects have already been hoisted out and executed in the preceding part of a comma expression. If the original expression is an lvalue, the resulting expression is also an lvalue that identifies exactly the same memory location as the original one.
PRE is only used to handle the case of the translation of array expressions; it is used essentially to keep track of the ACC/NACC mode in the translation of the sub-expressions.

The Translation Function π. Function π is composed of two parts. The first part, which is injected only for visible statements, checks whether the execution is at the end of the non-deterministically guessed context C_1 (for Phase 1) or at the begin of the context C_2 (for Phase 2). The result of these checks are stored in the global variables P1 and P2. The second part (denoted by $[\![stm]\!]$) injects the data race control code into the expressions occurring in the statements stm; Fig. 3 illustrates this transformation down to the level of the expressions (which include assignments).

Hence, for a visible statement stm with the numerical label j of a thread i, $\pi(stm)$ is defined as follows:

```
P1 = (j == cs[i]-1) && dr0 && !dr1;
P2 = (j == pc[i])   && dr1;
```
$[\![stm]\!]$

The conditions $j == \mathrm{cs}[i]\text{-}1$ and $j == \mathrm{pc}[i]$ hold if j is the label of the last and the first visible statement of the current context of thread i, respectively. The other conjuncts in the assignment for P1 identify the current context of i as C_1 since dr0 && !dr1 means that Phase 1 has started but not finished yet. Similarly, dr1 identifies the current context of i as C_2; in fact, as soon as the control returns to the main driver, dr2 is set to true and no more contexts are simulated (see Fig. 2). P1 and P2 are set to false at any other visible statements. For non-visible statements, no code is injected and the statement is left unchanged.

$$
\begin{aligned}
&[\![\texttt{assume}(e)]\!] &&\triangleq \texttt{assume}(([\![e,\mathsf{ACC}]\!]\,,\,[\![e,\mathsf{WSE}]\!])) \\
&[\![\texttt{assert}(e)]\!] &&\triangleq \texttt{assert}(([\![e,\mathsf{ACC}]\!]\,,\,[\![e,\mathsf{WSE}]\!])) \\
&[\![e]\!] &&\triangleq [\![e,\mathsf{ACC}]\!] \\
&[\![\texttt{goto }l]\!] &&\triangleq \texttt{goto } l \\
&[\![l\texttt{:skip}]\!] &&\triangleq l\texttt{:skip} \\
&[\![\texttt{if}(e)\ stm\ \texttt{else}\ stm]\!] &&\triangleq \texttt{if}(([\![e,\mathsf{ACC}]\!]\,,\,[\![e,\mathsf{WSE}]\!]))\ [\![stm]\!]\ \texttt{else}\ [\![stm]\!] \\
&[\![\texttt{return}]\!] &&\triangleq \texttt{return}
\end{aligned}
$$

Fig. 3. Translation of statements

The data race detection code that we inject differs for the two phases. In Phase 1, we update the shadow memory and inject code of the form

$$\texttt{P1 \&\& set\_sm(\&}[\![e,\mathsf{WSE}]\!]\texttt{, true)} \tag{Ph1}$$

whenever there is a write access to the shared memory location corresponding to e. Note that this relies on C's short-circuit evaluation of the conjunctions, so that the second conjunct is not evaluated if P1 is false and thus the shadow memory is (correctly) not updated if the statement is not at the end of the non-deterministic selected context C_1.

In Phase 2, we query the shadow memory to update the variable drd, and inject code of the form

$$\text{P2 \&\& (drd = (drd || get\_sm(\&}[\![e, \text{WSE}]\!])))\tag{Ph2}$$

whenever there is a read or write access to the shared memory location corresponding to e. Again, due to short-circuit evaluation, drd is updated only if P2 holds (i.e., the execution is at the beginning of context C_2); likewise, drd is never updated once it has been set to true. Hence, drd is set to true only if a write access to the location is recorded in the shadow memory. However, since the shadow memory is updated only at the end of the context C_1, this implies that the write access and the second access can happen immediately adjacently in the multi-thread program, i.e., that there is a data race on this location.

Expression Translation. Figure 4 shows the detailed expression translation rules. For simplicity, we assume that all lvalues identify shared memory locations; for local memory locations, the data race detection code of the form (Ph1) and (Ph2) must be omitted from the translation rules.

ACC and WSE are the only translation modes that are used by the statement translation (see Fig. 3). Consequently, these are the only modes where we start the expression translation. The NACC mode comes into play only when no access to the shared memory can occur through the corresponding lvalue (e.g., the operand of a reference expression), or when this is accounted for elsewhere by the translation (e.g., the left-hand side of an assignment). The PRE mode only occurs in the translation of prefixes of array expressions. The cases not shown in Fig. 4 cannot occur in well-formed expressions.

Figure 4(a) shows the translation for assignment expressions, i.e., expressions of the form $e_1 = e_2$. In all modes but WSE, the translation unfolds as follows:

1. We generate the side effects of the left part e_1 in NACC mode. Here, the write access to the shared memory is annotated in the next part of the rewriting process, eliminating the need to reconsider this location for data race detection purposes.
2. We then generate the side effects of the right part e_2 in ACC mode, accounting for potential accesses to the shared memory.
3. If in Phase 1, we annotate the shadow memory of the assigned location; for this we use an expression of the form (Ph1).
4. If in Phase 2 and a write access to e_1 was already annotated into the shadow memory, we update drd; for this we use an expression of the form (Ph2).
5. Finally, we simulate the assignment without generating further side effects.

In WSE mode, we just rewrite the expression to $[\![e_1, \text{WSE}]\!]$ since all side effects of the original expression have been accounted for at this point.

Figure 4(b) shows the translation for the comma expressions of the form e_1 , e_2. In ACC and PRE, we rewrite the entire expression again as a comma expression, with the first sub-expression being e_1 rewritten in ACC mode to

(a)	$[\![e_1 = e_2, \text{ACC/NACC/PRE}]\!]$	$\hat{=} [\![e_1, \text{NACC}]\!], [\![e_2, \text{ACC}]\!], \text{P1 \&\& set\_sm(\&}[\![e_1, \text{WSE}]\!], \text{true}),$
		$\text{P2 \&\& drd = (drd || get\_sm(\&}[\![e_1, \text{WSE}]\!])), [\![e_1, \text{WSE}]\!] = [\![e_2, \text{WSE}]\!]$
	$[\![e_1 = e_2, \text{WSE}]\!]$	$\hat{=} [\![e_1, \text{WSE}]\!]$
(b)	$[\![e_1, e_2, \text{ACC}]\!]$	$\hat{=} [\![e_1, \text{ACC}]\!], [\![e_2, \text{ACC}]\!]$
	$[\![e_1, e_2, \text{PRE}]\!]$	$\hat{=} [\![e_1, \text{ACC}]\!], [\![e_2, \text{PRE}]\!]$
	$[\![e_1, e_2, \text{WSE}]\!]$	$\hat{=} [\![e_2, \text{WSE}]\!]$
(c)	$[\![e_1 \text{ OP } e_2, \text{ACC/PRE}]\!]$	$\hat{=} [\![e_1, \text{ACC}]\!] \text{ OP } [\![e_2, \text{ACC}]\!]$
	$[\![e_1 \text{ OP } e_2, \text{WSE}]\!]$	$\hat{=} [\![e_1, \text{WSE}]\!] \text{ OP } [\![e_2, \text{WSE}]\!]$
(d)	$[\![e_1 ? e_2 : e_3, \text{ACC}]\!]$	$\hat{=} ([\![e_1, \text{ACC}]\!], [\![e_1, \text{WSE}]\!]) ? [\![e_2, \text{ACC}]\!] : [\![e_3, \text{ACC}]\!]$
	$[\![e_1 ? e_2 : e_3, \text{PRE}]\!]$	$\hat{=} ([\![e_1, \text{ACC}]\!], [\![e_1, \text{WSE}]\!]) ? [\![e_2, \text{PRE}]\!] : [\![e_3, \text{PRE}]\!]$
	$[\![e_1 ? e_2 : e_3, \text{NACC}]\!]$	$\hat{=} ([\![e_1, \text{ACC}]\!], [\![e_1, \text{WSE}]\!]) ? [\![e_2, \text{NACC}]\!] : [\![e_3, \text{NACC}]\!]$
	$[\![e_1 ? e_2 : e_3, \text{WSE}]\!]$	$\hat{=} [\![e_1, \text{WSE}]\!] ? [\![e_2, \text{WSE}]\!] : [\![e_3, \text{WSE}]\!]$
(e)	$[\![e_1[e_2], \text{ACC}]\!]$	$\hat{=} [\![e_1, \text{PRE}]\!], [\![e_2, \text{ACC}]\!],$
		$\text{P2 \&\& drd = (drd || get\_sm(\&}[\![e_1, \text{WSE}]\!] [[\![e_2, \text{WSE}]\!]]))$
	$[\![e_1[e_2], \text{NACC/PRE}]\!]$	$\hat{=} [\![e_1, \text{PRE}]\!], [\![e_2, \text{ACC}]\!]$
	$[\![e_1[e_2], \text{WSE}]\!]$	$\hat{=} [\![e_1, \text{WSE}]\!][[\![e_2, \text{WSE}]\!]]$
(f)	$[\![v, \text{ACC/PRE}]\!]$	$\hat{=} \text{P2 \&\& drd = (drd || get\_sm(\&}v))$
	$[\![v, \text{NACC}]\!]$	$\hat{=} \text{(void) 0}$
	$[\![v, \text{WSE}]\!]$	$\hat{=} v$
(g)	$[\![*e, \text{ACC/PRE}]\!]$	$\hat{=} [\![e, \text{ACC}]\!], \text{P2 \&\& drd = (drd || get\_sm(}[\![e, \text{WSE}]\!]))$
	$[\![*e, \text{NACC}]\!]$	$\hat{=} [\![e, \text{ACC}]\!]$
	$[\![*e, \text{WSE}]\!]$	$\hat{=} *[\![e, \text{WSE}]\!]$
(h)	$[\![\&e, \text{ACC/NACC}]\!]$	$\hat{=} [\![e, \text{NACC}]\!]$
	$[\![\&e, \text{WSE}]\!]$	$\hat{=} \&[\![e, \text{WSE}]\!]$
(i)	$[\![const, \text{ACC/NACC}]\!]$	$\hat{=} \text{(void) 0}$
	$[\![const, \text{WSE}]\!]$	$\hat{=} const$

Fig. 4. Translation of expressions

account for potential accesses to shared memory. The second sub-expression, e_2, is rewritten in the same mode as the original comma expression. In WSE mode, we simply rewrite the comma expression as e_2 in WSE mode.

Figure 4(c) shows the translation for expressions the form $e_1 \text{ OP } e_2$. These expressions are rewritten as expressions of the same type. Specifically, in ACC and WSE mode, we pass on the sub-expression the same mode since the overall value is computed by the values of the two expressions. Thus, we rewrite both e_1 and e_2 respectively in ACC mode and WSE mode. In PRE mode, we adopt the same rewriting as in ACC mode, as it represents the scenario when the bottom of the recursion is reached during the rewriting of an array expression.

Figure 4(d) shows the translation for the conditional expression. In all modes but WSE, we replace expression e_1 with a comma expression in which we evaluate e_1 in ACC mode to accommodate potential memory access within e_1, thus ensuring the production of side effects. Then, we generate the same value as the original expression by a rewriting it in WSE mode. For e_2 and e_3 we rewrite them by keeping the starting translation mode. In WSE mode, we just pass the translation function in WSE mode to the three sub-expressions.

Figure 4(e) shows the translation for *array expressions* of the form $e_1[e_2]$. According to the grammar given in Fig. 1, array expressions are generated by yielding an index at each step and then recursing over the prefix. At the bottom of the recursion an expression evaluating to the starting address of the array elements is generated. This expression gives an lvalue, which can lead to an access to the memory if the expression is not constant. Furthermore, the evaluation of each index can lead to an access to the memory while the intermediate prefixes do not. The translation rules are designed accordingly. In the ACC mode, we translate e_1 (i.e., the prefix of the array expression) in PRE mode, then e_2 (i.e., the index generated at the current recursion step) in ACC mode, and finally we inject code of the form (Ph2) to check a possible data race on $e_1[e_2]$. In NACC and PRE modes, $e_1[e_2]$ does not count as an access to the shared memory and thus the portion of code to check for a possible data race is omitted. In WSE mode, we just pass the translation function in WSE mode to the two sub-expressions.

Figure 4(f) shows the translation for *identifier expressions* v, e.g., the name of a scalar or pointer variable. Since this cannot have any side-effects, we return in WSE mode the original identifier. In ACC mode we just need to update drd by injecting code of the form (Ph2). The same code is injected in PRE mode. In the NACC mode we rewrite v to (void) 0 (recall that NACC means that v is not used to access the data).

Figure 4(g-h) shows the translation for the expressions of the forms $*e$ and $\&e$. In the WSE mode, we simply apply the translation function recursively over the operator. The PRE mode may occur only for $*e$, and for these expressions we apply the same translation both in PRE and ACC modes: first we generate the side-effects of e in ACC mode (since e may contain pointer variables), and then we update drd by checking Phase 2 for the location of $*e$. In all remaining cases, we just generate the side-effects of e. For expressions of the form $\&e$, the rewriting of e is done in NACC mode since in these expressions the lvalue yield by e is not used to access memory locations.

Figure 4(i) shows the translation for *constant expressions const*. Since this expression has no side effects and does not contribute to data races, we rewrite it to (void) 0 in both ACC and NACC modes and to *const* itself in WSE mode.

The given translation rules can be safely simplified by removing the rewriting of a sub-expression in ACC, NACC, and PRE modes if we can deem that there are no side-effects and no shared memory location is accessed. We have adopted this simplification and few more optimizations in our implementation.

5 Experimental Evaluation

We compared our LaDR data race detection tool with the leading contenders from the recent *13th Software Verification Competition* (SV-COMP 2024).[1]

---

[1] https://sv-comp.sosy-lab.org.

SV-COMP is the premier venue for evaluating the performance of verification tools for C and Java programs using a comprehensive suite of established benchmarks. The competition is organized into categories and subcategories based on the specific properties to be verified for the programs. In SV-COMP 2024, the c/NoDataRace-Main subcategory concerns data race detection. Three tools emerged as top performers in this subcategory: Sv-sanitizers (based on ThreadSanitizer, see Sect. 1 for more details), Dartagnan [18], and Deagle [10] (see Sect. 6 for more details). We evaluated LaDR's data race detection capabilities against these three tools. The evaluation covered both the established c/NoDataRace-Main benchmarks and a real-world benchmark, safestack, known for its particularly rare ABA-related bug.

Experimental Setup. Each experiment was run on a dedicated Google Compute Engine of type n2-custom-2-16384. This configuration provides two vCPUs running at 2.80GHz with 16GB of memory, running Ubuntu 22.04. We used the runexec tool from the BenchExec suite [1] to manage the individual experiments. Similar to SV-COMP 2024, runexec automatically terminates tool executions exceeding pre-defined memory or time limitations. For the experiments, we installed the follwoing tools on each machine: LaDR (replication package available at https://doi.org/10.5281/zenodo.10826274), Dartagnan, Deagle, and Sv-sanitizers.[2] We mirrored the competition settings of SV-COMP 2024 by allocating 15 min and 12 GB of RAM per experiment.

SV-COMP Benchmarks. The SV-COMP 2024 data race category offers a rich evaluation ground with 1013 benchmarks. These benchmarks average around 60 lines of code (excluding libraries) and represent a diverse set of concurrency constructs and can exhibit significant complexity. We focused our comparison on the 232 benchmarks with data races, since LaDR is designed as a data race detection tool, rather than a data race freedom proving tool.

We ran LaDR with a loop unwinding bound and round bound large enough to expose the data races, according to the usual bounded model checking practices. Other tools were executed using their respective competition scripts. LaDR performs very well on these benchmarks, and returns the highest number of correct results (183 out of 232), followed by Dartagnan (165), Deagle (145) and Sv-sanitizers (144). To validate the soundness of LaDR reports, we additionally ran it on the SV-COMP 2024 benchmarks that were classified as data race free. Notably, LaDR produced only one false data race report, but we believe that this benchmark is in fact incorrectly classified.

Safestack. safestack is a real world benchmark implementing a lock-free stack designed for weak memory models [31]. It contains a very rare ABA-related bug that requires at least three threads and five context-switches for exposure under the SC semantics (although only four context-switches under TSO or PSO), while typical real-world concurrency bugs require at most three context-switches

---

[2] Reproducibility packages for Dartagnan, Deagle, and Sv-sanitizers can be found on the SV-COMP 2024 web page: https://sv-comp.sosy-lab.org/2024/systems.php.

to manifest themselves [19]. `safestack`, for this reason, presents a nontrivial challenge for concurrency analysis tools.

LaDR is the only tool we are aware of that can automatically find this data race: it takes 24 min and 4 s on the test machine to find the data race under the SC semantics, using the minimal necessary loop unwinding and round bounds. Deagle crashes during the analysis, while Dartagnan, PorSE, and Sv-sanitizers did not find the bug in 12 h.

6 Related Work

Concurrent Program Sequentialization. The idea of sequentializing concurrent programs for analysis purposes was first proposed by Qadeer and Wu [23] and then generalized to capture an arbitrary number of context switches by Lal and Reps [17]. Several other sequentializations were proposed in the literature [3,7,16,20,27,28]. However, to the best of our knowledge, only two other approaches have used sequentialization to detect data races. Qadeer and Wu [23] adapted their sequentialization to data races involving only one given memory location. The sequentialization we propose here does not have such restriction and works for general aliasing. Like us, Coto et al. [5] have extended Lazy-CSeq to detect data races. However, their implementation stores the target address of each shared variable write in auxiliary variables and explicitly compares these on each read and write to check for a race, leading to large formulas. Moreover, they incorrectly identify some simultaneous read-accesses as data races. In SV-COMP 2024, they found the data race in 39 benchmarks over the 232 ones that had it, while they reported 295 false alarms over the 781 race-free benchmarks.[3]

Bounded Data Race Model Checkers. Dartagnan [18] is a bounded model checker that can perform the analysis under several weak memory models which can be in passed as input parameters. Although it is not a pure data race detector, it has participated in the data race detection category at SV-COMP 2024 by taking as input a sequential consistency model.

Deagle [10] computes a logical formula that captures the happens-before ordering of the shared memory accesses and thus detects data races as loops in such ordering. The inter-thread behaviors are encoded by a logical formula that captures the happens-before relations among the shared memory accesses and the intra-thread behaviors by a propositional formula. The analysis is done by passing the overall formula to an SMT solver.

Automata-Based Tools. Several members of the Ultimate model checker family have also participated successfully in the data race detection category at SV-COMP 2024. Ultimate Automizer [11] is the basic tool in this family. It is based on an automata-theoretic approach to software verification that can check safety properties. Ultimate Taipan [9] combines trace abstraction with abstract interpretation on path programs. Ultimate GemCutter [15] is based on the CEGAR paradigm and integrates the classical CEGAR generalization with orthogonal

---

[3] https://sv-comp.sosy-lab.org/2024/.

generalization across interleavings. All these approaches encode data race detection in a more general framework than ours but their underlying automata-based algorithms are quite different from our approach.

Data Race Freedom Provers. Goblint [29] is a static analyzer for multi-threaded C programs that can perform data race detection. It uses a sound concurrency abstraction, based on privatization, and combines different pointer and value analyses which enable it to handle a wide range of locking schemes, including locks allocated dynamically as well as locks stored in arrays.

One of the most common techniques for race prevention is to protect any access to a shared memory location with locks. Locksmith [22] is a static analysis tool that discovers data races by checking whether this property is violated. There have also been other techniques developed following this idea [2,14,29,30]. They differ in the locking structures they can address, the accuracy of the detection, the need for user annotations, and the reduction of false alarms. The approach we propose here is more general in the sense that we do not search only for data races that can arise from careless lock usage and we do not require user annotations as some of these approaches do.

Tools Based on Symbolic Execution. PorSE [25] combines partial-order reduction techniques with symbolic execution to handle data non-determinism, and is implemented as an extension of KLEE. This tool has found race conditions in memcached and GNU sort, showing that the technique scales to industrial-size benchmarks. However, since KLEE explores execution paths individually, it usually struggles to find rare bugs that only manifest themselves in few executions, as shown by our experiments.

7 Conclusions and Future Work

We introduced a new static approach to detect data races in multi-threaded programs based on the LS sequentialization schema. We use a flag for each shared memory location which is non-deterministically set on a write and checked on each other access. The non-determinism allows us to inject simple control code that manipulates these flags.

Our experiments show that our approach outperforms the other static methods on the SV-COMP 2024 benchmarks. LaDR is also the only tool that finds the very rare data race in the safestack benchmark. Our results for this benchmark also confirm the general intuition that methods based on bounded model-checking are more suitable for deep and rare bugs in concurrent programs.

We have also tried to extend our approach to perform the analysis in parallel, following the schema from [21]. However, preliminary experiments have shown that the scalability of this approach is only partially improved by our parallelization scheme. We believe that data abstraction techniques can reduce the size of the formulas computed by the underlying bounded model-checker and so improve efficiency. The key will be to balance and reduce the different sources of non-determinism and the number of processors available for the analysis.

Acknowledgments. This work was partially supported by AWS 2021 Amazon Research Awards, INDAM-GNCS 2024, FARB 2021-2024 grants Università degli Studi di Salerno, VITALITY Ecosystem, Spoke 1 MEGHALITIC (E13C22001060006) under the NRRP MUR program funded by the EU - NGEU, and the Google Cloud Research Credits program with the award GCP19980904.

Disclosure of Interests. The authors have no competing interests to declare that are relevant to the content of this article.

References

1. Beyer, D., Löwe, S., Wendler, P.: Reliable benchmarking: requirements and solutions. Int. J. Softw. Tools Technol. Transf. **21**(1), 1–29 (2019). https://doi.org/10.1007/S10009-017-0469-Y
2. Blackshear, S., Gorogiannis, N., O'Hearn, P.W., Sergey, I.: RacerD: compositional static race detection. Proc. ACM Program. Lang. **2**(OOPSLA), 144:1–144:28 (2018). https://doi.org/10.1145/3276514
3. Chaki, S., Gurfinkel, A., Sinha, N.: Efficient verification of periodic programs using sequential consistency and snapshots. In: Formal Methods in Computer-Aided Design, FMCAD 2014, Lausanne, Switzerland, 21–24 October 2014, pp. 51–58. IEEE (2014). https://doi.org/10.1109/FMCAD.2014.6987595
4. Clarke, E., Kroening, D., Lerda, F.: A tool for checking ANSI-C programs. In: Jensen, K., Podelski, A. (eds.) TACAS 2004. LNCS, vol. 2988, pp. 168–176. Springer, Heidelberg (2004). https://doi.org/10.1007/978-3-540-24730-2_15
5. Coto, A., Inverso, O., Sales, E., Tuosto, E.: A prototype for data race detection in CSeq 3. In: TACAS 2022, Part II. LNCS, vol. 13244, pp. 413–417. Springer, Cham (2022). https://doi.org/10.1007/978-3-030-99527-0_23
6. Currie, D.W., Hu, A.J., Rajan, S.P.: Automatic formal verification of DSP software. In: Micheli, G.D. (ed.) Proceedings of the 37th Conference on Design Automation, Los Angeles, CA, USA, 5–9 June 2000, pp. 130–135. ACM (2000). https://doi.org/10.1145/337292.337339
7. Emmi, M., Qadeer, S., Rakamaric, Z.: Delay-bounded scheduling. In: Ball, T., Sagiv, M. (eds.) Proceedings of the 38th ACM SIGPLAN-SIGACT Symposium on Principles of Programming Languages, POPL 2011, Austin, TX, USA, 26-28 January 2011, pp. 411–422. ACM (2011). https://doi.org/10.1145/1926385.1926432
8. Fischer, B., La Torre, S., Parlato, G., Schrammel, P.: CBMC-SSM: bounded model checking of C programs with symbolic shadow memory. In: 37th IEEE/ACM International Conference on Automated Software Engineering, ASE 2022, Rochester, MI, USA, 10–14 October 2022, pp. 156:1–156:5. ACM (2022). https://doi.org/10.1145/3551349.3559523
9. Greitschus, M., Dietsch, D., Heizmann, M., Nutz, A., Schätzle, C., Schilling, C., Schüssele, F., Podelski, A.: Ultimate Taipan: trace abstraction and abstract interpretation. In: Legay, A., Margaria, T. (eds.) TACAS 2017, Part II. LNCS, vol. 10206, pp. 399–403. Springer, Heidelberg (2017). https://doi.org/10.1007/978-3-662-54580-5_31
10. He, F., Sun, Z., Fan, H.: Deagle: an SMT-based verifier for multi-threaded programs (Competition Contribution). In: TACAS 2022, Part II. LNCS, vol. 13244, pp. 424–428. Springer, Cham (2022). https://doi.org/10.1007/978-3-030-99527-0_25

11. Heizmann, M., et al.: Ultimate Automizer and the search for perfect interpolants. In: Beyer, D., Huisman, M. (eds.) TACAS 2018, Part II. LNCS, vol. 10806, pp. 447–451. Springer, Cham (2018). https://doi.org/10.1007/978-3-319-89963-3_30
12. Inverso, O., Tomasco, E., Fischer, B., La Torre, S., Parlato, G.: Bounded model checking of multi-threaded C programs via lazy sequentialization. In: Biere, A., Bloem, R. (eds.) CAV 2014. LNCS, vol. 8559, pp. 585–602. Springer, Cham (2014). https://doi.org/10.1007/978-3-319-08867-9_39
13. Inverso, O., Tomasco, E., Fischer, B., La Torre, S., Parlato, G.: Bounded verification of multi-threaded programs via lazy sequentialization. ACM Trans. Program. Lang. Syst. **44**(1), 1:1–1:50 (2022). https://doi.org/10.1145/3478536
14. Kahlon, V., Sinha, N., Kruus, E., Zhang, Y.: Static data race detection for concurrent programs with asynchronous calls. In: van Vliet, H., Issarny, V. (eds.) Proceedings of the 7th joint meeting of the European Software Engineering Conference and the ACM SIGSOFT International Symposium on Foundations of Software Engineering, 2009, Amsterdam, The Netherlands, 24–28 August 2009, pp. 13–22. ACM (2009). https://doi.org/10.1145/1595696.1595701
15. Klumpp, D., et al.: ULTIMATE GEMCUTTER and the axes of generalization. In: TACAS 2022, Part II. LNCS, vol. 13244, pp. 479–483. Springer, Cham (2022). https://doi.org/10.1007/978-3-030-99527-0_35
16. La Torre, S., Madhusudan, P., Parlato, G.: Reducing context-bounded concurrent reachability to sequential reachability. In: Bouajjani, A., Maler, O. (eds.) CAV 2009. LNCS, vol. 5643, pp. 477–492. Springer, Heidelberg (2009). https://doi.org/10.1007/978-3-642-02658-4_36
17. Lal, A., Reps, T.W.: Reducing concurrent analysis under a context bound to sequential analysis. Formal Methods Syst. Des. **35**(1), 73–97 (2009). https://doi.org/10.1007/s10703-009-0078-9
18. Ponce-de-León, H., Furbach, F., Heljanko, K., Meyer, R.: DARTAGNAN: bounded model checking for weak memory models (Competition Contribution). In: TACAS 2020, Part II. LNCS, vol. 12079, pp. 378–382. Springer, Cham (2020). https://doi.org/10.1007/978-3-030-45237-7_24
19. Musuvathi, M., Qadeer, S.: Iterative context bounding for systematic testing of multithreaded programs. In: Ferrante, J., McKinley, K.S. (eds.) Proceedings of the ACM SIGPLAN 2007 Conference on Programming Language Design and Implementation, San Diego, California, USA, 10–13 June 2007, pp. 446–455. ACM (2007). https://doi.org/10.1145/1250734.1250785
20. Nguyen, T.L., Fischer, B., La Torre, S., Parlato, G.: Lazy sequentialization for the safety verification of unbounded concurrent programs. In: Artho, C., Legay, A., Peled, D. (eds.) ATVA 2016. LNCS, vol. 9938, pp. 174–191. Springer, Cham (2016). https://doi.org/10.1007/978-3-319-46520-3_12
21. Nguyen, T.L., Schrammel, P., Fischer, B., La Torre, S., Parlato, G.: Parallel bug-finding in concurrent programs via reduced interleaving instances. In: Rosu, G., Penta, M.D., Nguyen, T.N. (eds.) Proc. of the 32nd IEEE/ACM International Conference on Automated Software Engineering, ASE 2017, Urbana, IL, USA, October 30 - November 03, 2017, pp. 753–764. IEEE Computer Society (2017). https://doi.org/10.1109/ASE.2017.8115686
22. Pratikakis, P., Foster, J.S., Hicks, M.: LOCKSMITH: Practical static race detection for C. ACM Trans. Program. Lang. Syst. **33**(1), 3:1–3:55 (2011). https://doi.org/10.1145/1889997.1890000
23. Qadeer, S., Wu, D.: KISS: keep it simple and sequential. In: Pugh, W.W., Chambers, C. (eds.) Proc. of the ACM SIGPLAN 2004 Conference on Programming

Language Design and Implementation 2004, Washington, DC, USA, 9–11 June 2004, pp. 14–24. ACM (2004). https://doi.org/10.1145/996841.996845
24. Savage, S., Burrows, M., Nelson, G., Sobalvarro, P., Anderson, T.E.: Eraser: a dynamic data race detector for multithreaded programs. ACM Trans. Comput. Syst. **15**(4), 391–411 (1997). https://doi.org/10.1145/265924.265927
25. Schemmel, D., Büning, J., Rodríguez, C., Laprell, D., Wehrle, K.: Symbolic partial-order execution for testing multi-threaded programs. In: Lahiri, S.K., Wang, C. (eds.) CAV 2020. LNCS, vol. 12224, pp. 376–400. Springer, Cham (2020). https://doi.org/10.1007/978-3-030-53288-8_18
26. Serebryany, K., Potapenko, A., Iskhodzhanov, T., Vyukov, D.: Dynamic race detection with LLVM compiler. In: Khurshid, S., Sen, K. (eds.) RV 2011. LNCS, vol. 7186, pp. 110–114. Springer, Heidelberg (2012). https://doi.org/10.1007/978-3-642-29860-8_9
27. Tomasco, E., Inverso, O., Fischer, B., La Torre, S., Parlato, G.: Verifying concurrent programs by memory unwinding. In: Baier, C., Tinelli, C. (eds.) TACAS 2015. LNCS, vol. 9035, pp. 551–565. Springer, Heidelberg (2015). https://doi.org/10.1007/978-3-662-46681-0_52
28. Tomasco, E., Nguyen, T.L., Fischer, B., La Torre, S., Parlato, G.: Using shared memory abstractions to design eager sequentializations for weak memory models. In: Cimatti, A., Sirjani, M. (eds.) SEFM 2017. LNCS, vol. 10469, pp. 185–202. Springer, Cham (2017). https://doi.org/10.1007/978-3-319-66197-1_12
29. Vojdani, V., Apinis, K., Rõtov, V., Seidl, H., Vene, V., Vogler, R.: Static race detection for device drivers: the Goblint approach. In: Lo, D., Apel, S., Khurshid, S. (eds.) Proceedings of the 31st IEEE/ACM International Conference on Automated Software Engineering, ASE 2016, Singapore, 3–7 September 2016, pp. 391–402. ACM (2016). https://doi.org/10.1145/2970276.2970337
30. Voung, J.W., Jhala, R., Lerner, S.: RELAY: static race detection on millions of lines of code. In: Crnkovic, I., Bertolino, A. (eds.) Proceedings of the 6th joint meeting of the European Software Engineering Conference and the ACM SIGSOFT International Symposium on Foundations of Software Engineering, 2007, Dubrovnik, Croatia, 3–7 September 2007, pp. 205–214. ACM (2007). https://doi.org/10.1145/1287624.1287654
31. Vyukov, D.: Bug with a context switch bound 5. https://social.msdn.microsoft.com/Forums/en-US/91c1971c-519f-4ad2-816d-149e6b2fd916/bug-with-a-context-switch-bound-5?forum=chess (2010). Accessed 17 Aug 2022

Algebraic Computations in Anonymous VANET

Dariusz R. Kowalski[1], Miguel A. Mosteiro[2(✉)], and Austin Powlette[2]

[1] Augusta University, Augusta, GA, USA
DKOWALSKI@augusta.edu
[2] Pace University, New York, NY, USA
{mmosteiro,ap26302n}@pace.edu

Abstract. In the area of development of AI/ML applications in Vehicular Adhoc Networks (VANET), a highly dynamic environment, efficient algebraic distributed computations are of utmost importance. On the other hand, there is a growing concern about privacy of users/drivers. One of the solutions is to perform computations assuming anonymity of the users. There is already a large amount of work on this topic in the general Anonymous Dynamic Network model, however the obtained theoretical guarantees are not suitable for very large-scale networks, such as VANET. In this work, we propose an anonymous algebraic computation framework tailored for VANET, called Anonymous Vehicular Adhoc Networks (A-VANET). We introduce heuristic changes to the Restricted Methodical Counting (RMC) protocol aiming to speed up performance in A-VANET with respect to the theoretical bounds in general Anonymous Dynamic Networks. We evaluate this protocol on traces of taxi trips in New York City extracted from publicly available data from 2013, and on a highway traffic environment modeled by a set of path graphs. Both inputs are highly dynamic including also recurrent disconnections.

Our results show that, for the parameter combinations tested and for networks with good expansion, RMC is sub-quadratic and even linear under some conditions. Therefore, even the theoretical upper bound proved as a function of connectivity parameters is loose by a factor of more than n^7. These results show the promise of further exploring the question of what is the optimal running time for algebraic computations in A-VANET and other practically-motivated Anonymous Dynamic Networks with limited messages, memory and disconnections.

Keywords: Vehicular Ad-hoc Networks · Algebraic Computations · Anonymous Dynamic Networks

1 Introduction

Algebraic distributed computations are important components of various types of applications to Vehicular Adhoc Networks (VANET). They are also particularly challenging to implement efficiently, due to high dynamicity and limited resources available in VANET. Additionally, due to the massive network size and privacy concerns, it is desirable to keep the VANET users anonymous. There is a large body of work on algebraic computations in Anonymous Dynamic Networks (ADN). (See [12,14] and the references therein.) However, algorithms in such model are not well-scallable and thus not suitable for restricted large networks such as VANET. In this work, we present an anonymous algebraic computation framework tailored for VANET, which we call Anonymous Vehicular Adhoc Networks (A-VANET).

Recently, in [13] a protocol termed Restricted Methodical Counting (RMC) was included as a building block of a Congested Clique emulator on Anonymous Dynamic Congested Systems with Opportunistic Connectivity. RMC performs algebraic computations in a network where the messages among nodes as well as internal memory of each node are limited to $O(\log n)$ bits. Moreover, the network is not required to be connected continuously, as long as connectivity is achievable over time. Admitting network disconnection is crucial for VANETs, since vehicles cannot be assumed to be in range of other vehicles all the time, whereas small message size and memory are fundamental on inexpensive devices.

RMC is simple[1], works with restricted resources, and it is resilient to network disconnections. However, its current theoretical analysis applies to adversarial dynamicity (that is, arbitrarily-fast movement of nodes) which is too pessimistic for VANETs. Even with dynamicity parameterized, RMC has time complexity $\widetilde{O}(n^{1+2\mathcal{T}(1+\epsilon)}/(\ell i_{\min}^2))$, for any $\epsilon > 0$, where ℓ is a number of distinguished nodes used by RMC,[2] $i_{\min}$ is the minimum isoperimetric number of the dynamic network topology, and $\mathcal{T}$ is a connectivity parameter. On the other hand, the only lower bounds known are the trivial $\Omega(\mathcal{D})$, where $\mathcal{D}$ is the dynamic network diameter, and $\Omega(\log n)$ if $\mathcal{D}$ is constant [4]. That is, there is still a (possibly large) polynomial gap between these bounds.

In this work, we focus on the experimental evaluation of RMC on A-VANET. Our hypothesis is that RMC trends (polynomial running times, in particular) are as predicted by theory, but the constants and actual polynomial degrees could be much lower than the theoretical bounds. Also, we expect significant speed-ups for real traffic, thus we heuristically introduce changes aimed to identify under which conditions this speed-up is maximized. The details follow.

Our Contributions. In this work, we study heuristic improvements aimed at speeding up RMC when run on dynamic topologies motivated by A-VANET and IoT. We evaluate experimentally heuristic modifications of RMC for different input topologies and parameter combinations as follows.

---

[1] By "simple" we mean that the algorithm does not require complex data structures or complex calculations over them. In a nutshell, RMC is a simple arithmetic calculation to update a value (the potential) repeated iteratively, followed by conditionals to decide when that value has reached some range. This type of algorithm is sometimes called a "light implementation".

[2] In case of VANET, these could be even static access points located in selected places, or company cars.

In VANETs nodes are vehicles and "neighborhood" is defined by directly reachable vehicles (i.e., by direct or indirect wireless communication, where the latter could be with use of some embedded forwarding devices). In this work, the network topology is extracted from real traces of taxi trips in NYC, where proximity is determined by the street locations. Additionally, we consider path topologies (simulating highways) with short reachability among nodes.

The extraction of input network topologies from real world traces of traffic, is a technical challenge in itself, given the massive data source available.

Our study shows that in networks with good expansion properties (which, apparently, A-VANETs are) the heuristic RMC is overwhelmingly faster than the worst-case theoretical running time of RMC, confirming our hypothesis. We observe that for NYC taxi traffic data RMC is sub-quadratic, whereas on highway traffic it is mildly above quadratic. Moreover, under some conditions, we observe that for NYC taxi traffic data RMC is linear, whereas on highway traffic it is mildly above linear.

These results show that RMC is much more efficient than the (very pessimistic) theoretical running time of $\widetilde{O}(n^{1+2\mathcal{T}(1+\epsilon)}/(\ell i^2))$ would indicate, while preserving RMC's simplicity and resilience to disconnections, even in a very restrictive environment where memory and message size are harshly limited. Indeed, for $\mathcal{T} = 5$ (as in our taxi graphs), optimal isoperimetric number $i \in \Theta(n)$ (as in ideal complete graph), and constant number of distinguished vehicles/devices ℓ, the theoretical upper bound becomes $\widetilde{O}(n^{9+10\epsilon})$. That is, our heuristic framework is more than a factor of n^7 faster.

In gossip-based algorithms (such as RMC) the information is disseminated by slowly sharing fractions of it with neighbors. Hence, the time to complete the dissemination is lower bounded by the network diameter. Therefore, our A-VANET topologies are more pessimistic than other models used in the VANET literature based on unit disc graphs [7,17,20,23], or even more sophisticated models considering signal-propagation constrains [9,17,21].

Roadmap. The rest of the paper is organized as follows. Related work is discussed in Sect. 2. The model and an overview of the RMC algorithm are given in Sects. 3 and 4. The details of our experimental setup and a discussion of the obtained results can be found in Sect. 5. We conclude this study and discuss open problems in Sect. 7.

2 Related Work

The literature related to VANETs is vast, focusing in various issues such as security, privacy, communication, and others (cf. surveys in [3,10]). Some of that work has focused on more optimistic network models such as unit disc graphs [7,17,20,23], and models considering signal-propagation constrains [9, 17,21]. However, for dynamic environments with restricted resources, such as A-VANET, a more pessimistic model is needed. Some works [15,16] studied scheduling in VANETs of "line topology", or paths, as we also consider in the present work. Much of that work is related to high level problems, leaving aside fundamental problems such as computing the network size.

The closest related work is [13] where a protocol termed Restricted Methodical Counting (RMC) was included as a building block of a Congested Clique emulator on Anonymous Dynamic Congested Systems with Opportunistic Connectivity. RMC performs algebraic computations in a network where the messages among nodes, as well as internal memory of each node, are limited to $O(\log n)$ bits. Moreover, the network is not required to be connected continuously, as long as connectivity is achievable over time. Thus, it is applicable to A-VANETs. The study in [13] is only theoretical and adversarial, that is, overly pessimistic.

Work related to aggregate computations in other ad-hoc networks models is abundant (e.g. [1,6]). To the best of our knowledge, ours is the first experimental study of distributed algebraic computations in an environment with memory, communication, and connectivity restrictions as in A-VANETs.

3 Preliminaries

Model. Our model is an application to VANETs of the restrictions in the Anonymous Dynamic Congested Systems with Opportunistic Connectivity [13]. We call it *Anonymous Vehicular Adhoc Network (A-VANET)*.

An A-VANET is composed by a set V of n mobile network nodes with computation and communication capabilities. Motivated by privacy concerns, we aim for algorithms that do not use node identifiers (IDs).

The set of nodes is partitioned in ℓ *counted* nodes and $n-\ell$ *uncounted* nodes, where $0 < \ell < n$. The number ℓ is known to all nodes. As shown in [14,18] these assumptions are necessary to carryout algebraic computations deterministically in anonymous dynamic networks without knowing n. Within each partition, nodes are indistinguishable. The algorithm studied in this work includes two different programs: one for counted nodes and another for uncounted nodes. Each node gets one of these two programs installed before network deployment.

Time is slotted in *rounds* of communication. For each round t, the network topology is modeled with a graph $G_t = (V, E_t)$, where E_t is the set of communication links among network nodes available during round t. In each round t, every node $i \in V$ is able to transmit a *message* to *all* nodes $j \in V$ such that $(i,j) \in E_t$, called *neighbors*.[3] Communication links are symmetric, that is, $(i,j) \in E_t \Rightarrow (j,i) \in E_t$.

The set of communication links may change arbitrarily from round to round, even allowing disconnection within some limits. Our evolving network-topology model is a $\mathcal{T}$-connected time-evolving graph (also called *temporal graph* throughout indistinctively), defined as follows.

---

[3] Mobility and anonymity prevent the nodes from sending destination-oriented messages.

Definition 1. *An evolving graph $\mathcal{G}$ is $\mathcal{T}$-connected if, for any sequence of constituent graphs $G^{(t+1)}, G^{(t+2)}, \ldots, G^{(t+\mathcal{T})}$, $t \geq 0$, the union graph $G_{\cup_t} = \left(V, \cup_{i=1}^{\mathcal{T}} E^{(t+i)}\right)$ is connected.*

We assume that n is initially unknown. Due to lack of IDs, nodes also do not know their neighbors. Moreover, due to mobility, each node does not know even the number of its neighbors before receiving messages from them. We label the nodes throughout the presentation for clarity and sake of evaluation – the nodes have only access to the messages sent by neighbors. As shown in [13], algebraic computations are not possible in anonymous dynamic networks without knowledge of $\mathcal{T}$. Thus, we assume that nodes know $\mathcal{T}$. No other node knowledge other than $\mathcal{T}$ and ℓ is assumed in this work.

As in [13], each message is limited to $O(\log n)$ bits, and the internal memory of each node is also limited to $O(\log n)$ bits. Nodes do not know these limits either.[4]

Nodes and communication links, as defined in evolving graph $\mathcal{G}$, do not fail.

Algorithms. We consider distributed algorithms that run under the model defined above. Network nodes start up and execute their programs synchronously without centralized control. We evaluate algorithm performance in rounds of communication, given that, in comparison, memory access and local computations take negligible time.

Problem. As shown in [12] and references therein, algebraic computations can be carried out having an algorithm that computes the number of network nodes. Thus, we focus on the following problem.

Definition 2. *The Counting Problem is solved by an algorithm $\mathcal{A}$ if, after completing its execution, all network nodes obtained the size of the network n and stop.*

4 Heuristic Restricted Methodical Counting

In this section, we overview the main ideas underlying RMC and we specify our heuristic modifications. We refer the reader to [13] for further details on RMC.

RMC is organized in epochs, each associated with some estimate k of the network size. Thanks to synchronization mechanism guaranteed by the algorithm, k is the same for all nodes. Initially k is set to $\ell + 1$ because $\ell < n$. From each epoch to the next one k grows exponentially until $k \geq n$ (which is detected without knowing n of course), and from that point a binary search is done until $k = n$.

---

[4] In practice, more memory and more communication may become available as nodes require them, but keeping them below the limit n in all rounds is the job of the algorithm.

Algorithm 1: Centralized simulation of counted and uncounted nodes running our heuristic RMC; The only knowledge used by nodes is ℓ: the number of counted nodes, and $\mathcal{T}$: the input connectivity parameter. E is the set of links in the referred round (unknown to nodes, number of neighbors learned after receiving messages). k is the running estimate of network size (same for all nodes thanks to dissemination of status in Line 24). Vectors ρ, **s** and **Φ** correspond to accumulators, status and potentials of each node, respectively. The heuristic changes with respect to the original RMC are the exponents $speedup_p$ and $speedup_r$ (in red, lines 5 and 6) tuned during simulations depending on the input graph.

```
 1  γ ← 1.01              // RMC parameter fixed, γ = 1 + ε for any ε > 0
 2  k ← ℓ + 1
 3  repeat                                                        // epoch
 4      s ← ⃗probing
 5      p ← 2k^(γ−speedup_p) log k^γ / ℓ
 6      r ← k^(2+2Tγ−speedup_r)
 7      for each node i do
 8        ⌊ if counted then Φ[i] ← 0, ρ[i] ← 0 else Φ[i] ← ℓ
 9      for phase = 1 to p do
10          for round = 1 to r do
11              for each node i do                       // potential update
12                  concurrently
                    Φ[i] ← Φ[i] + ∑_{j:(i,j)∈E} (⌊k^γ Φ[j]⌋ k^{−2γ} − ⌊k^γ Φ[i]⌋ k^{−2γ})
13              for each node i such that s[i] ≠ probing or
                  ∃j : (i, j) ∈ E : s[j] ≠ probing or |{j : (i, j) ∈ E}| ≥ d do
14                ⌊ s[i] ← low, Φ[i] ← ℓ                          // k < n
15          for each node i do
16              if phase = 1 and Φ[i] > ℓ(1 − ℓk^{−γ}) then
17                ⌊ s[i] ← low, Φ[i] ← ℓ                          // k < n
18              if counted and s[i] = probing then
19                ⌊ ρ[i] ← ρ[i] + Φ[i], Φ[i] ← 0
20          for each counted node i such that s[i] = probing do
21              if (k − ℓ)(1 − k^{−γ}) ≤ ρ ≤ (k − ℓ)(1 + k^{−γ}) then s[i] ← done  // k = n
22              if ρ[i] < (k − ℓ)(1 − k^{−γ}) then  s[i] ← high    // k > n
23            ⌊ if ρ[i] > (k − ℓ)(1 + k^{−γ}) then  s[i] ← low     // k < n
24          for d rounds do
25              for each uncounted node i such that ∃j : (i, j) ∈ E : s[j] ≠ probing do
26                ⌊ concurrently s[i] ← s[j]
27          update k according to s by exponential or binary search
28  until s = ⃗done
29  return k
```

To decide whether the size estimate k is small, large or $k = n$, nodes maintain a *status* that is changed according to a locally stored value called *potential*.

The potential at each node changes because each node shares iteratively fractions of it. Under some conditions, this technique, known as *gossip*, gets the potential converging to the average throughout the network [2,6,8,11,22]. In congested anonymous dynamic networks (such as our A-VANET model) messages are limited to $O(\log n)$ bits. Thus, in each iteration RMC truncates the fractions of potential shared to $c \log k$ bits, for some constant $c > 0$, leaving the remainder of the truncation at the sharing node.

Each counted node starts an epoch with no potential and each uncounted node with potential ℓ. After enough number of rounds, the potentials at nodes converge to the average. Then, the counted nodes move their potential to a separate accumulator. Continuing this process, most of the $(n - \ell)\ell$ total potential is accumulated at the ℓ counted nodes, but not knowing the network size the convergence time can be only computed as a function of k. That is, the accumulated potential may not give the correct size if $k \neq n$. Hence, instead, each node decides $k \lesseqgtr n$ comparing its current potential with some functions of k, and changes its status as needed. The final decision when $k = n$ is made by the counted nodes, and then broadcasted to the uncounted nodes.

Aiming to reduce the running time of RMC on A-VANET, we have heuristically changed some of the algorithm parameters, such as number of iterations and various thresholds. Our goal was to identify experimentally all possible changes that may reduce the running time in A-VANET while maintaining correctness of the computation. Therefore, we kept increasing speed-ups until RMC crashed or returned a wrong answer. The most impactfull change in this sense was to reduce the number of rounds and the number of phases (see Algorithm 1).

Specifically for NYC taxi traffic data, with respect to the original RMC, we obtained that dividing the number of rounds r by $k^{11.1}$, and the number of rounds p by $k^{0.1}$, RMC is still correct in all executions, while increasing further those exponents makes RMC produce an incorrect output or run indefinitely for most executions. The introduced heuristics reduce the overall running time on NYC taxi traffic data to less than quadratic for a constant number of counted nodes and linear for a linear number of counted nodes.

5 Simulations

The goal of our simulations is to evaluate experimentally heuristic improvements of RMC on A-VANET. RMC is the only simple algorithm in the literature that tolerates restricted memory, message size, and it is resilient to disconnections. For this simulations we additionally simplify it (from its general topologies version) and we adjusted it to A-VANET.

Simulator. We introduced a series of modifications to RMC for centralized simulation. Potentials, accummulated potentials, and status at the beginning of round t are maintained in vectors $\boldsymbol{\Phi_t}$, ρ, and $\mathbf{s_t}$ respectively, where each component i of such vectors corresponds to node i. Nodes labels are only used for this bookkeeping but not used by the algorithm to compute the network size (recall that nodes are anonymous). Alarms and other details are handled as updates of vectors. Further details of the modifications of RMC for simulation purposes, including our heuristic modifications, can be seen in Algorithm 1. Counted and uncounted nodes execute the same algorithm, with selected parts executed only by one type of node (see Lines 8, 18–19, 20–23, and 25 in Algorithm 1).

Traces of NYC Taxi Traffic. In order to create a series of graphs to input into the simulator, we created a process that generates the necessary graphs from NYC taxi traffic data publicly available [19]. To do this, we used a tool known as the Simulation of Urban Mobility (SUMO) [5] to create vehicular networks. To build a vehicular network, SUMO needs a road network and a set of routes. SUMO includes a feature called Netconvert to create such road networks. To create our road network based on Manhattan streets, we used Netconvert to transform an OpenStreetMap file of Manhattan into road network file. To obtain the latter, we used an API called OpenStreetMap Overpass to generate a georeferenced osm file corresponding to Manhattan. SUMO includes a process to download a city using OpenStreetMap. This process performs a series of queries into the OSM Overpass API. With the road network realized, we created the routes. We used Duarouter to map latitude-longitude coordinates as start and endpoint destinations to the geo-referenced map of Manhattan. Manhattan taxi traffic data from 2013 was used as the input for Duarouter to create the routes. The traffic data was parsed for latitude-longitude with a custom made Python script to convert data from csv to xml format. This Python script utilized the Pandas library to manipulate the data to a suitable format and then it was written to a new xml file. Unfortunately, the taxi traffic data was too large to parse through all at once, so a csv splitting tool called Split was used to slice the data into files that contained 1000 trips each. The Python script was then adapted to iterate through any number of files and convert them to a corresponding xml file. Then, the road network generated from Netconvert and the xml traffic data were fed into Duarouter to create a rou.xml file corresponding to the set of routes. Afterwards, we run SUMO with its Bluetooth function activated, the road network and the Manhattan taxi traffic routes. The simulation output was an xml file that marked the communication between cars when they came into proximity with each other. It also noted their interaction time and when the cars stopped interacting. Additionally, for the purpose of scaling, a batch script was created that would automatically take any number of xml traffic data files, run them through Duarouter with the Manhattan road network and return the corresponding rou.xml file. Furthermore, the batch script would continue the process by running SUMO with the Bluetooth feature enabled, the rou.xml file and the Manhattan road network. This process creates any number of xml files representing the interactions between cars. We then created another custom Python script that would strip away the xml components of any number of files and turn them into csv files which could be used for our RMC simulator as input time-varying graphs.

We used the 1000 files so generated iteratively in our simulator, one for each round. That is, each of the 1000 files including the interactions of 1000 Bluetooth identifiers (that is, cars) was used as the set of links for each round. For simulations on network sizes $n < 1000$ we simply discarded the links including identifiers larger than n.

We analyzed the connectivity of the traffic graphs concluding that over the 1000 graphs the average number of connected components was approximately 78. Nevertheless, folding those constituent graphs in groups of 5 we obtained that each graph resulting from a group has just one connected component. We conclude from this analysis that $\mathcal{T} = 5$ on average for this input.

Highway Traffic. We also evaluate our heuristic RMC simulating highway traffic with a set of paths topology. Given that A-VANET's neighborhoods are defined by reachability among vehicles, a path topology models a pessimistic short-range scenario for information dissemination. Disconnection among paths in the set model sections of the highway without vehicles.

Thus, we generated cycles with 10 disconnections placed at random, that is, a set of 10 paths. We used each set of paths so generated as a new topology for every 10 rounds of communication. Given the randomness on placing the disconnections along the cycle, we conclude that on average the connectivity parameter of this input is $\mathcal{T} = 11$.

In general, anonymous dynamic network nodes may change position arbitrarily in such path. However, cars in a highway do not move arbitrarily fast. Thus, instead, we introduced the dynamicity locally. Specifically, the dynamicity in these networks is obtained by shuffling the nodes at random within each connected path.

In gossip-based algorithms (like RMC) the information is disseminated by slowly sharing fractions of the information with neighbors. Hence, the time to complete the dissemination is lower bounded by the network dynamic diameter. Therefore, our highway topologies are more pessimistic than others that have been used in the A-VANET literature (e.g. unit disc graphs).

Input Parameters. The main parameters of our simulations were the size of the network $n = \{128, 256, 500, 600, 700, 800, 900, 1000\}$, the number of counted nodes $\ell = \{30, n/4 - 1\}$, and the average-connectivity parameter $\mathcal{T} = \{1, 2.5, 5, 11\}$.

For the number of rounds, the number of phases, and other parameters of RMC, we replaced approximations to the parameters in Corollary 1 in [13], as well as the constants in the asymptotic notation. Specifically, a constant factor 2 for the $O(\log n)$ bits truncation of messages, a constant factor 1 for the asymptotic upper bound on the number of rounds, and parameter $\epsilon = 0.01$, yielding

$$r \in O\left(n^{2+2\mathcal{T}(1+\epsilon)}\right) \Rightarrow r = n^{2+2\mathcal{T}(1+\epsilon)} = n^{2+2.02\mathcal{T}}$$

$$p = \frac{2k^{1+\epsilon}\ln k^{1+\epsilon}}{\ell} = \frac{2.02 k^{1.01}\ln k}{\ell}$$

Simulations Platform. We implemented our heuristic RMC simulation in Java 8. The simulations were carried out on a Linux cluster, known as HPCmaster, owned by Seidenberg School of CSIS at Pace University. The specifications are Intel®Xeon®CPU X5450 @ 3.00GHz, 2GB RAM, 150GB HD, running Debian 8×64.

We run various instances of the simulator in parallel to speedup our experiments. Notice that we did not use the parallelism features of the cluster to simulate the communication among nodes given that the simulator is centralized. Using the cluster to simulate the communication among nodes would not provide any additional insight given that the potential unreliability of the communication in A-VANET is modeled by the changing topology.

6 Discussion of Results

All the presented results reflect the average behavior over multiple executions of the simulator. The discussion and plots that follow correspond to a subset of cases, but similar results were obtained for others. We evaluated the performance in number of taken communication rounds.

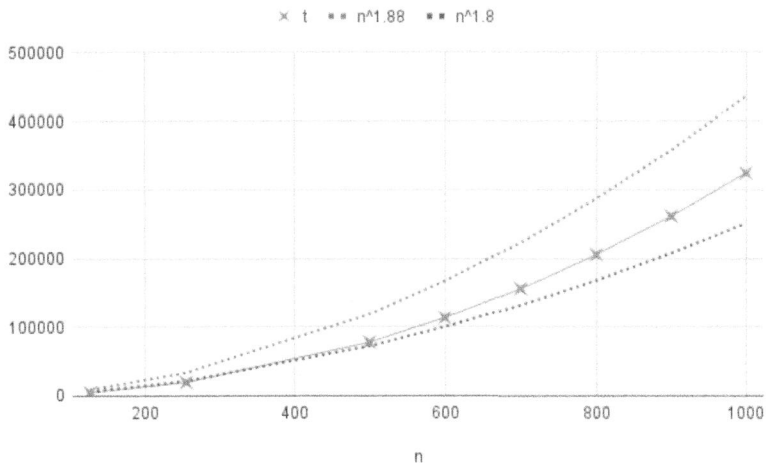

Fig. 1. NYC taxi traffic input for $\ell = 30$ and $\mathcal{T} = 5$. Dotted lines correspond to functions of n bounding the running time.

Figures 1 and 3 show the number of rounds as n grows for the NYC taxi traffic input for constant $\ell = 30$ and $\ell = n/4 - 1$ respectively. As explained

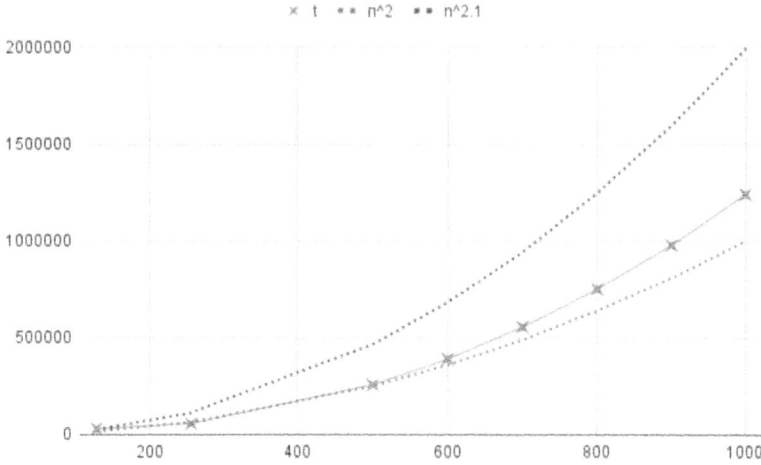

Fig. 2. Highway input for $\ell = 30$ and $\mathcal{T} = 11$. Dotted lines correspond to functions of n bounding the running time.

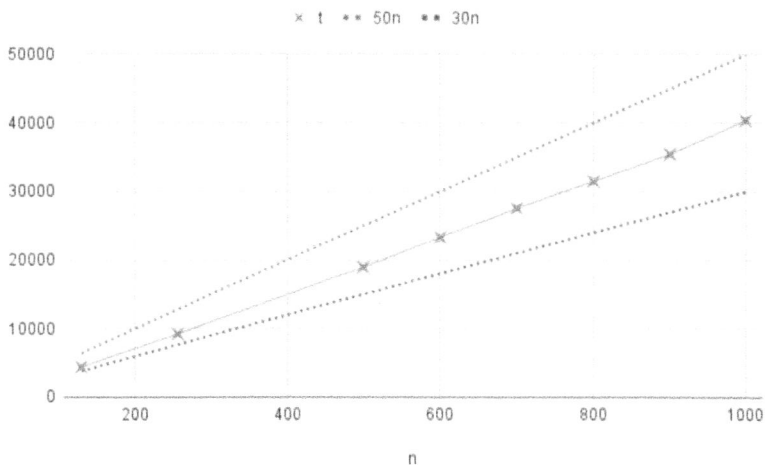

Fig. 3. NYC taxi traffic input for $\ell = n/4 - 1$ and $\mathcal{T} = 5$. Dotted lines correspond to functions of n bounding the running time.

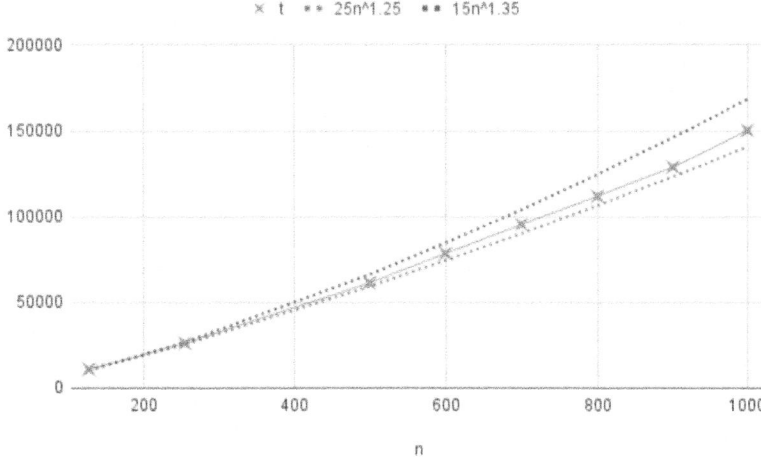

Fig. 4. Highway input for $\ell = n/4-1$ and $\mathcal{T} = 11$. Dotted lines correspond to functions of n bounding the running time.

above our graph analysis yielded $\mathcal{T} = 5$, on average, for this temporal graph input.

Figures 2 and 4 on the other hand show the number of rounds as n grows for the highway traffic input for constant $\ell = 30$ and $\ell = n/4 - 1$ respectively. As explained above, on average this temporal graph input has $\mathcal{T} = 11$.

Our main observations follow.

- Our experimental study confirms our hypothesis that in networks with good expansion properties (such as A-VANETs) the heuristic RMC is overwhelmingly faster than the worst-case theoretical running time of RMC. We observe that for NYC taxi traffic data, the heuristic RMC is sub-quadratic, whereas on highway traffic it is mildly above quadratic (see Figs. 1 and 2), both for constant ℓ.

  Having a constant number of counted nodes yields stronger results, as knowing ℓ does not reveal any information about n. Nevertheless, we have simulated the case of linear ℓ because anyway not enough information is revealed as the constant is unknown. For $\ell = n/4 - 1$ we observe that for NYC taxi traffic data RMC is linear, whereas on highway traffic it is mildly above linear (see Figs. 3 and 4).

  These results show that RMC is indeed much more efficient than the (very pessimistic) theoretical running time of $\widetilde{O}(n^{3+2\mathcal{T}(1+\epsilon)}/\ell)$, while preserving RMC's simplicity and resilience to failures, even in a very restrictive environment where memory, message size, and connectivity are harshly limited.

- Recall that the experimental approach was to increase the speed-ups until the answer of the algorithm becomes incorrect. We observed in our experiments a threshold behavior: up to the obtained speed-up, in 100% of the executions

the computation is correct, whereas for speed-ups above the threshold, almost all computations are incorrect.
- We did not observe a significant impact on the asymptotic running time as a function of n by the variety of other parameters tested: frequency of topology changes, number of cycle disconnections, and not even connectivity parameter $\mathcal{T}$ in the case of NYC taxi traffic graph, where smaller $\mathcal{T}$ was obtained by merging the constituent graphs of the temporal graph in groups. Notice that merging constituent graphs is equivalent to adding links between nodes that are otherwise not connected directly, which in turn produces an effect similar to the increase of the communication range of nodes.
- We also observed an interdependence between the number of phases p and the number of counted nodes ℓ, beyond their mathematical dependence (i.e. $p = 2k^{1+\epsilon} \ln k^{1+\epsilon}/\ell$). In fact, a significant reduction on the number of phases for a constant ℓ would require to increase the number of counted nodes to maintain correctness, but if ℓ is constant such increase is not feasible.

7 Conclusions

In this work, we studied experimentally heuristic improvements of the RMC protocol [13] for algebraic computations in A-VANET.

Our input A-VANETs were generated from real traces of traffic data extracted from New York City taxi trips. We also simulated highway traffic using input networks whose topology corresponds to sets of paths. Both are temporal graphs including disconnections.

The contribution of our experimental speedup of RMC is two-fold. On one hand it shows that for networks with good expansion the time savings are very large. So much so that even the theoretical upper bound of $\widetilde{O}(n^{1+2\mathcal{T}(1+\epsilon)}/(\ell i^2))$ proven as a function of isoperimetric number i in [13] is too pessimistic. Indeed, for $\mathcal{T} = 5$ (as in our taxi graphs), optimal isoperimetric number $i \in \Theta(n)$ (complete graph), and constant ℓ that upper bound becomes $\widetilde{O}(n^{9+10\epsilon})$. That is, faster by a factor bigger than n^7.

Surprisingly, there was little impact of the connectivity parameter T in the asymptotic running time as a function of n for traffic data. Given that the smaller values of T were obtained by merging the original graphs, the effect is similar to increase the range of the nodes. These observations indicate that in A-VANETs the strength of the wireless signal (and so, the range) may not be that important, as long as the temporal graph is reasonably well-connected. If so, we could save energy by reducing the power of transmissions, and maybe even speed up the execution since shorter signal wavelength yields typically faster information transfer. A deeper study of this aspect is left for future work.

Our study also shows that one can tune some parameters of the algorithm to find the best time performance, should the topology or other characteristics of the network be known.

These results show the promise of further exploration of the question of what is the optimal running time for algebraic computations in A-VANET and other practically-motivated Anonymous Dynamic Networks with limited messages, memory, and connectivity. Indeed, further improvement of time performance and non-trivial lower bounds are the most important open directions.

Acknowledgments. This study was partially funded by Pace Univ. SRC and Kenan Awards.

Disclosure of Interests. The authors have no competing interests to declare that are relevant to the content of this article.

References

1. Almeida, P.S., Baquero, C., Farach-Colton, M., Jesus, P., Mosteiro, M.A.: Fault-tolerant aggregation: flow-updating meets mass-distribution. Distrib. Comput. **30**(4), 281–291 (2017). https://doi.org/10.1007/S00446-016-0288-5
2. Boyd, S., Ghosh, A., Prabhakar, B., Shah, D.: Randomized gossip algorithms. IEEE/ACM Trans. Networking **14**(SI), 2508–2530 (2006)
3. Cooper, C., Franklin, D., Ros, M., Safaei, F., Abolhasan, M.: A comparative survey of VANet clustering techniques. IEEE Commun. Surv. Tutorials **19**(1), 657–681 (2016)
4. Di Luna, G.A., Baldoni, R.: Investigating the cost of anonymity on dynamic networks. CoRR arXiv:1505.03509 (2015)
5. Eclipse Foundation: Simulation of urban mobility (2024). https://eclipse.dev/sumo/
6. Fernández Anta, A., Mosteiro, M.A., Thraves, C.: An early-stopping protocol for computing aggregate functions in sensor networks. J. Parallel Distrib. Comput. **73**(2), 111–121 (2013)
7. Fiore, M., Härri, J.: The networking shape of vehicular mobility. In: Proceedings of the 9th ACM International Symposium on Mobile Ad Hoc Networking and Computing, pp. 261–272 (2008)
8. Ghosh, B., Muthukrishnan, S.: Dynamic load balancing by random matchings. J. Comput. Syst. Sci. **53**(3), 357–370 (1996)
9. Gozalvez, J., Sepulcre, M., Bauza, R.: Impact of the radio channel modelling on the performance of VANet communication protocols. Telecommun. Syst. **50**(3), 149–167 (2012)
10. Hasrouny, H., Samhat, A.E., Bassil, C., Laouiti, A.: VANet security challenges and solutions: a survey. Veh. Commun. **7**, 7–20 (2017)
11. Kempe, D., Dobra, A., Gehrke, J.: Gossip-based computation of aggregate information. In: Proceedings of the 44th Annual IEEE Symposium on Foundations of Computer Science, pp. 482–491 (2003)
12. Kowalski, D.R., Mosteiro, M.A.: Polynomial counting in anonymous dynamic networks with applications to anonymous dynamic algebraic computations. J. ACM **67**(2), 1–7 (2020)
13. Kowalski, D.R., Mosteiro, M.A.: Efficient distributed computations in anonymous dynamic congested systems with opportunistic connectivity. CoRR arXiv:2202.07167 (2022)
14. Kowalski, D.R., Mosteiro, M.A.: Polynomial anonymous dynamic distributed computing without a unique leader. J. Comput. Syst. Sci. **123**, 37–63 (2022). https://doi.org/10.1016/J.JCSS.2021.07.002

15. Kowalski, D.R., Nussbaum, E., Segal, M., Milyeykovski, V.: Scheduling problems in transportation networks of line topology. Optim. Lett. **8**(2), 777–799 (2014). https://doi.org/10.1007/s11590-013-0613-x
16. Kowalski, D., Nutov, Z., Segal, M.: Scheduling of vehicles in transportation networks. In: Vinel, A., Mehmood, R., Berbineau, M., Garcia, C.R., Huang, C.-M., Chilamkurti, N. (eds.) Nets4Cars/Nets4Trains 2012. LNCS, vol. 7266, pp. 124–136. Springer, Heidelberg (2012). https://doi.org/10.1007/978-3-642-29667-3_11
17. Meireles, R., Ferreira, M., Barros, J.: Vehicular connectivity models: from single-hop links to large-scale behavior. In: 2009 IEEE 70th Vehicular Technology Conference Fall, pp. 1–5. IEEE (2009)
18. Michail, O., Chatzigiannakis, I., Spirakis, P.G.: Naming and counting in anonymous unknown dynamic networks. In: Higashino, T., Katayama, Y., Masuzawa, T., Potop-Butucaru, M., Yamashita, M. (eds.) SSS 2013. LNCS, vol. 8255, pp. 281–295. Springer, Cham (2013). https://doi.org/10.1007/978-3-319-03089-0_20
19. NYC Taxi & Limousine Commission: TLC trip record data (2024). https://www.nyc.gov/site/tlc/about/tlc-trip-record-data.page
20. Pallis, G., Katsaros, D., Dikaiakos, M.D., Loulloudes, N., Tassiulas, L.: On the structure and evolution of vehicular networks. In: 2009 IEEE International Symposium on Modeling, Analysis & Simulation of Computer and Telecommunication Systems, pp. 1–10. IEEE (2009)
21. Protzmann, R., Schu, B., Radusch, I.: The influences of communication models on the simulated effectiveness of v2x applications. In: 2010 IEEE Vehicular Networking Conference, pp. 102–109. IEEE (2010)
22. Rabani, Y., Sinclair, A., Wanka, R.: Local divergence of markov chains and the analysis of iterative load-balancing schemes. In: Proceedings of the 39th IEEE Annual Symposium on Foundations of Computer Science, pp. 694–703 (1998)
23. Viriyasitavat, W., Bai, F., Tonguz, O.K.: Dynamics of network connectivity in urban vehicular networks. IEEE J. Sel. Areas Commun. **29**(3), 515–533 (2011)

Federated Learning for Enhanced Medical Image Analysis

Sanaa Lakrouni[✉], Slimane Bah, and Marouane Sebgui

Smart Communication Research Team, Mohamedia School of Engineers, University Mohammed V in Rabat, Rabat, Morocco
sanaalakrouni@research.emi.ac.ma, {slimane.bah,sebgui}@emi.ac.ma

Abstract. As artificial intelligence (AI) algorithms continue to advance, researchers have leveraged deep neural networks to address a range of challenges in the medical field. These models require a large-scale dataset and high-quality annotated data for model generalization, which is a major challenge in imaging data due to their limited availability in healthcare institutions. Additionally, it is primarily challenging to work with private patient data and share it with an external entity due to the privacy concerns. These challenges of the traditional centralized learning have led to a more efficient decentralized approach. This approach involves training with a diverse range of data from various domains, which are required to enhance model performance. Hence, many researchers have adopted Federated learning as an emerging paradigm to collaboratively train a machine learning model among multiple healthcare institutions without sharing their local private data. However, medical datasets are sourced from different medical institutions; hence they are often acquired by different protocols, scanner types, data modalities, and from different patient populations. Thus, it is inherently heterogeneous which degrades the global model performance in the federated setting. In this paper, we explore the key motivation for using federated learning in the healthcare field and discuss the challenges posed by the diversity and data heterogeneity of medical data from various institutions. Additionally, we present recent works that help mitigate the non-iid data issue in federated learning. Furthermore, we empirically evaluate the federated learning algorithms alongside centralized learning and one site learning using a benchmark medical dataset. Our analysis demonstrates that the adoption of advanced methods in FL enables us to effectively mitigate the data heterogeneity issue while leveraging data privacy and large-scale datasets within the medical domain.

Keywords: Federated Learning · Healthcare field · Artificial intelligence

1 Introduction

The remarkable advancements in artificial intelligence, particularly in the form of deep learning models characterized by billions of parameters, have led to effective solutions for numerous healthcare challenges such as radiology and pathology. Breast cancer ranks as the most commonly detected cancer globally. Consequently, much research has illustrated the state of the art in breast cancer classification, contributing significantly to early detection efforts [1]. Accordingly, these deep learning models require access to extensive datasets. They depend on large and sufficient data samples that enable successful deep learning algorithms to gain valuable insights and improve performance. However, developing such models in the medical field requires a large-scale imaging dataset. AI algorithms process this data to identify abnormalities in mammograms and MRI scans, to achieve effective performance. Nonetheless, the acquisition of medical datasets at a single location remains challenging. Thus, the availability of medical data for machine learning research is often insufficient and constrained [2]. Furthermore, to train these models effectively and improve their generalizability, a diverse range of data from various domains is required. Acquiring such data from different sources can be complicated due to privacy constraints. Medical data is subject to legal constraints under patient confidentiality, where individual patients and hospitals have continuous concerns about sharing their private information with an external entity. Hence, these regulations restrict the potential of machine learning models to leverage a variety of datasets from different institutions and collaboratively train models from various sources [3]. To address this issue, many researchers have shared medical imaging data anonymously to prevent patient identification. However, even anonymized data can be vulnerable, in [4] authors were able to reconstruct real images from MRI samples, highlighting a potential infringement of patient privacy. Although various methods exist to address privacy concerns related to medical data in centralized learning, sharing imaging datasets with a remote cloud remains inefficient due to their large size, which can lead to increased latency [5].

These challenges encourage authors to adopt an alternative decentralized approach. Federated learning, which is a collaborative training paradigm, aims to train a machine learning model among K clients. Each client trains its local model with its private local data, then shares these updates to a remote server for global aggregation. This approach trains a global model and leverages data privacy by not sharing the client's data to the cloud. Furthermore, it allows training on large-scale datasets from multiple healthcare institutions, which can improve model performance.

This approach, however, presents a challenge of data heterogeneity since medical data is acquired from different devices and equipment. This diversity can be seen in several ways, including different image modalities, a prominent number of negative samples, and variance in image intensity profiles among different institutions. This heterogeneity leads to the creation of non-identical and independently distributed (non-IID) datasets across healthcare sites, which can degrade the global model performance in the training phase [6].

In this paper, we investigate the potential of multi-site training among multiple healthcare institutions with federated learning. We highlight the challenge of data heterogeneity in medical datasets. We further evaluate advanced federated learning methods and algorithms that tackle data heterogeneity, yielding consistent results. Hence, our contributions are as follows:

- We emphasize the complexities in leveraging machine learning within healthcare field due to the inherent data heterogeneity.
- We conduct a review of existing approaches aimed at mitigating data heterogeneity in federated learning within the medical field.
- We propose our methodology to mitigate domain shift across medical institutions to reduce client drift in FL and we propose our general solution.
- We empirically evaluate the efficacy of advanced federated learning algorithms. Our findings show a significant impact of data heterogeneity on the model's performance within healthcare data. Furthermore, we demonstrate how advanced FL algorithms can overcome this issue, thus enhancing performance.

The paper is organized into the following sections: Sect. 1, we provide a comprehensive definition of heterogeneity in the medical field, its motivation, and the challenges it presents within federated learning. In Sect. 2 we present the review of the existing literature on federated learning, its applications in the medical field, and how it addresses data heterogeneity issues. Further in Sect. 3 we explore the concept of domain shift in Federated Learning (FL) and its connection to client drift, which degrades model performance we introduce our methodology that leverages transformers and self-supervised learning (SSL) to address domain shift and straggler issues. Furthermore, in Sect. 4 we train a CNN algorithm to evaluate empirically the federated learning algorithm with centralized and one site learning using the Bloodmnist dataset under non-IID data conditions. Finally in Sect. 5 we conclude by discussing the benefits of adopting a decentralized approach within the medical field to address data privacy concerns, improve multi-site training performance, and tackle data heterogeneity in medical datasets.

1.1 Heterogeneity of Medical Image Analysis

Deep learning models depend on large, diverse, and high-quality datasets containing thousands to millions of data points to achieve optimal performance [7]. However, these datasets can rarely be found in individual medical institutions. This can be due to the limited number of patients at individual sites, and the availability of data-generating devices in hospitals may be insufficient and vary from one to another. For instance, certain healthcare institutions possess advanced equipment, while others lack access to such resources. This variability can pose challenges in data acquisition within healthcare settings, especially for individual one-site training. Furthermore, creating high-quality labeled medical imaging datasets, especially for supervised learning, is often an extensive, costly, and time-consuming process that requires the participation of multiple experts and radiologists [8]. Consequently, these datasets are unlikely to be freely accessible due to their potential business value. Moreover, the patient examinations and routine screening in hospitals often produce datasets with a high number of negative samples [9]. This limited representation of positive samples in these datasets presents a challenge for training a robust machine learning model. Thus, acquiring data from multiple healthcare institutions offers a potential solution to cope with these challenges. Given the significance of developing robust machine learning models for medical diagnosis, it is important to employ a diverse and varied training dataset that captures a wide range of input characteristics [10]. This improves the reliability of models that can generalize across different patient populations and heterogeneous datasets acquired from different devices encountered in real-world medical settings. However, in traditional centralized learning models, we often train from a single domain, while in real-world settings, machine learning models can be deployed to other institutions where data comes from a different domain and follows a different data distribution. Therefore, training collaboratively from different data institutions can help the model generalize to the data distribution of multiple institutions. However, most healthcare organizations typically do not have access to such extensive amounts of data. Medical data is often isolated, requiring the transfer of individual data from multiple institutions to a distant server. This remains an obstacle due to the sensitivity of medical data, which is often subject to strict privacy regulations [11]. Moreover, sharing all the client's data to the cloud for training requires an extensive amount of communication and resource/energy demand, leading to inefficiency in terms of latency and bandwidth, especially for imaging analysis. Thus, keeping medical data private and training locally is required.

For most researches, adopting a decentralized approach can overcome the aforementioned challenges in the medical field. Federated learning has recently emerged to establish a privacy-preserving training among multiple medical sites, it trains a machine learning model in parallel across K clients, each client trains locally its model on its own local dataset. Then, the participants share their local parameters with a remote server. The server performs a global aggregation to compute a global parameter, which is the average summation of all the previous clients' parameters. It then broadcasts the global parameter back to the participants for further local updates. The process iterates for T iterations until the model converges and achieves sufficient accuracy. Despite that clients only share local parameters, there are plenty of researches that tackle data privacy in federated learning. In [12] authors acknowledge that private information can still be leaked from client's uploaded parameters, they propose NbAFL, a method that adds artificial noise using differential privacy (DP) techniques to client parameters on the client-side before sharing them for aggregation.

FL has demonstrated its potential in solving many healthcare tasks such as Breast Cancer Histopathological Image Classification [2] and Tumor Segmentation [5], It tackles data privacy and data heterogeneity among clients' datasets, further leveraging a larger-scale medical imaging dataset in the training process. However, the key challenge in federated learning within the medical field is the non-IID nature of medical data across different institutions. The decentralized approach still suffers from data heterogeneity in real world applications, hence the non-iid distribution of local datasets can harm the performance of the global model in federated learning yield to performing poorly in a subset of clients [13].

In the healthcare field, we aim to train collaboratively a global model among multiple medical institutions. Their local datasets are often acquired from different devices, a variety of equipment such as scanner type, protocols, and from different system vendors, which produce images that significantly differ in terms of intensity profiles. This introduces a change in the data distribution across clients' data [14]. This heterogeneity can occur in various forms: 1) some hospitals may contain more data than small hospitals or community clinics (quantity skew). 2) Further some hospitals may have more data at early stage than in the severe stage (e.g. label distribution skew). 3) Features distribution skew: images from different sites acquired from different devices, from different modalities and from different populations. Although in real-world scenarios we rarely consider these assumptions, they lead to many challenges during the deployment of medical machine learning models. These mentioned challenges result in the rise of client drift in the FL setting, which degrades model performance. Recent research has focused on mitigating client drift through various techniques.

2 Related Work

With the rapid development of data-driven medical applications, research on federated learning in the medical field is growing rapidly to address data heterogeneity and privacy concerns. In the federated learning setting, the key objective is to solve the global objective $F*$ to achieve a lower loss for all clients. Each client tends to minimize its local objective within its local data. However, when training data are sampled from a non-IID distribution, each client's local update can differ and converge towards different local optima. This increases the variance between the estimated client's update and the global update, leading to client drift under non-IID data. in [14] the authors propose SCAFFOLD to tackle data heterogeneity in FedAvg algorithm, it is a new Stochastic Controlled Averaging algorithm that mitigate the client drift. The algorithm aims to reduce the variance between the clients objective and the global objective and performs a client-variance-reduction by adding a new term to correct the local update and bring them to be closer to the centralized updates. This new weighted sum of local parameters tends towards the true global optimum. The authors compared SCAFFOLD to FedAvg using non-iid data and showed that their method performed the best. However, they evaluate their method with a logistic regression, while most state-of-the-art algorithms in real medical applications employ deep learning models. In [15] the authors introduce (MOON) to tackle data heterogeneity. This method used the contrastive learning to reduce the distance between the global representation and the local representation, while increasing the distance between the current local model and the previous local model to reduce client drift. The proposed method modifies the local loss function of the FedAvg of each client during each local update. After receiving the global model weight from the server, the algorithm extracts the representations of the current local update (i.e. $z = R_{w_i}^t(x)$), the global model $z(glob)$, and the previous local model $z(prev)$. The local model is then updated to minimize the new local objective, which is the sum of the supervised loss and the contrast loss: $l = l(const) + l(sup)$. The authors investigated the impact of local epochs on test accuracy. Training local models with just one epoch resulted in lower accuracy across all approaches. MOON, however, demonstrated superior performance, achieving 63% accuracy. As the number of epochs increased to 5, the accuracy improved. However, exceeding 5 epochs led to a drop in accuracy for all algorithms, this can be due to client drift. Performing more local updates can cause local models to diverge from the global model as they become increasingly fitted to their local datasets.

Deep learning models require extensive datasets to learn efficiently. However, in the medical field, this poses an obstacle due to limited and often unavailable high-quality labeled data. Creating such datasets with medical images is a demanding task, given rise to the Label deficiency challenge. This issue refers to the lack of sufficient high-quality labeled data in medical imaging datasets. In [16], the authors propose a self-supervised (FL) framework to leverage unlabeled medical imaging data. The method learn visual representation and patterns from unlabeled local datasets with federated learning self-supervised pre-training using the BEiT method. During training, for each image on each client, the algorithm computes the encoder layer (a ViT), outputting an encoded representation of the image patch, then feed the decoder with the previous encoded representations for all image patches to reconstruct the visual tokens located at the masked patches. The encoder and decoder are trained with the local data at each client to optimize the local loss function. Clients then share their local encoder and decoder to the server for the aggregation. The server sends back the global encoder and decoder to the clients. When the FL pre-training finished, only the global encoder is saved. In federated fine-tuning, clients initialize their local encoder with the pre-trained global encoder and feed it to a linear classifier for the image classification task.

While these works address data heterogeneity, particularly focusing on the class distributions among clients, the medical field frequently encounter feature distribution shift across clients' data. This diversity is evident in imaging datasets, where variations in pixel intensity and contrast can be observed. Notably, there are few works that focus on addressing this specific issue with FL. In [17] the authors propose the HarmoFL method to address the issue of feature distribution shift and mitigate both client and global drifts. HarmoFL employs amplitude normalization for each image using a fast Fourier transform (FFT) in the frequency space. This harmonizes low-level features across client data, reducing client drift among them. The harmonized features are then shared with the server. Additionally, the algorithm encourages suitable clients to aggregate, particularly those with flat optima by utilizing adversarial training to generate a new perturbation term in the weight space. This perturbation term encourages clients to reach a flat optimum, hence reducing the variation in loss among clients. This adjustment ensures that the global model will not be distracted by divergent local optima, ultimately reducing global drift. Within the healthcare system, medical institutions can be grouped and collaborate by forming federations, each including multiple institutions. However, in this scenario, a central server to govern these federations is absent. Consequently, traditional algorithms like FedAvg and MOON would be ineffective. To address this challenge, [18] proposed MetaFed, an algorithm that facilitates federated learning among federations using Knowledge Distillation. MetaFed focuses on exchanging common knowledge across federations. Each federation trains a local model on its own data, calculating the new local objective $l_i^{total} = \frac{1}{n_i^{train}} \sum_{(x,y) \in D_i^{train}} l_{cls}(f_i; x, y) + \lambda l_{dist}(g_{tea}, g_i; x)$, it combines classification Loss l_{cls} and the Knowledge Distillation Loss l_{dist}. This term encourages the current federation's model g_i to learn from the previously trained federation's model g_{tea} and to fully extract all the common knowledge from each federation, λ is an hyper-parameter controls the trade-off of knowledge transfer. Hence, the current federation exchange its model to the next federation. The previous federation acts as the teacher, while the current one acts as the student. This iterative process helps the accumulation of shared knowledge across the federations without the need of a central server, resulting in a final model (f) with enhanced knowledge (Fig. 1).

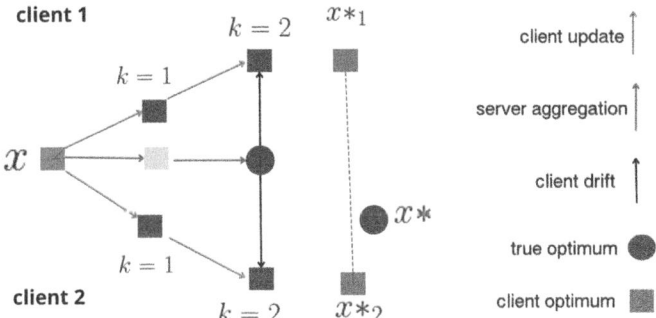

Fig. 1. Client drift concept is illustrated using FedAvg with two clients, each performing two local training steps (N = 2, K = 2). client 1 (represented in blue) updates its local model parameters towards its own optimal state (orange square,then the server in FedAvg averages all local updates during training. This averaging process can lead the global model to the average sum of local updates instead of to the true optimum x*. (Color figure online)

3 Methodology

Federated learning (FL) offers a promising approach for training machine learning models on medical imaging data while preserving patient privacy. However, the inherent heterogeneity of medical imaging data across institutions presents a significant challenge. This heterogeneity, arising due to variations in imaging devices, protocols, and acquisition systems, leads to the rise of domain shift across healthcare institutions. Domain shift is a phenomenon where the distribution of the source domain (data used for training) differs from the target domain (data where the model will be deployed) [19].

FL leverages data from diverse medical datasets at each healthcare institution, representing different domains. During local updates, models learn features specific to their own data distribution. Consequently, during FL training, these local updates diverge, tending towards their local optima to fit the specific features of their local data. This divergence in local updates hinders the convergence of the global model towards an optimal solution. The difference between the average sum of these divergent local updates and the true optimum of the global model leads to client drift [20]. Client drift significantly degrades the performance of the FL model and slows the convergence.

Several existing approaches address domain shift in FL with medical imaging data, Batch normalization (BN) layers [21] are a common technique to mitigate covariate shift in centralized learning. In [22] the authors propose FedBN, which add BN layers locally at each client and averages them globally. However, their effectiveness in federated settings with severe non-IID data distributions remains limited [23]. Domain adaptation techniques aim to reduce domain shift between institutions. For instance, Unsupervised Domain Adaptation (UDA) methods [9] mitigate feature skew among medical sites. This methods address this issue by aligning the feature space of data from different sites with adversarial learning, where a source and target feature extractor are trained for each pair of sites. Additionally, a domain discriminator is employed for each site to distinguish between the source and target feature distributions. Within the (FL) framework, the global server aggregates the weights of the locally trained models, leveraging the knowledge from each site despite domain variations. However, sharing latent representations among medical sites during training raises privacy concerns and incurs additional communication rounds between clients.

We propose a novel FL framework to address data heterogeneity within medical imaging data. We leverage recent advancements in Vision Transformers (ViTs) [24], which have demonstrated superior performance compared to traditional Convolutional Neural Networks (CNNs) in FL settings with image data. Further we perform a self-supervised learning (SSL) technique specifically designed for medical images, MoCo-CXR [25]. Unlike standard instance discrimination methods that struggle with the inherent anatomical similarities in medical images, MoCo-CXR focuses on learning context-aware representations. This is achieved by training an encoder-decoder network to reconstruct the original image region from its augmented version. This process encourages the model to capture fine-grained details like intensity, shape, boundary, and texture within the local context, leading to more discriminative and diverse features to distinguish between medical images. Our approach tackles client drift by learning domain-agnostic representations with SSL. These representations are robust to variations in data distributions across institutions, while leveraging ViTs to enhance client accuracy. Moreover, recent works address data heterogeneity in FL for medical imaging, they often rely on the traditional synchronous approach, where all clients share their local parameters with the server simultaneously. This approach suffers from the straggler problem. This occurs when slower clients delay the model update process, forcing faster clients to wait. To address this, we propose a novel notification-based approach based on Stale Synchronous Parallelism (SSP) [26]. Instead of passively waiting for all clients to finish, the server actively notifies participating institutions to communicate their local parameters periodically. This approach offers several advantages: We acknowledge that the optimal number of local epochs can vary across clients due to differences in hardware capabilities or data size, this allows for maximizing the global model performance while respecting hardware limitations. Furthermore, the framework will encourage clients to share their latest local parameters rather than waiting for local training to finish, to avoids unnecessary delays due to stragglers. Moreover faster clients can contribute more training iterations, leading to a more efficient and scalable FL framework for medical imaging data.

4 Experiment

In this section we empirically evaluate three federated learning algorithms FedAvg, FedProx and MetaFed to centralized learning and the one site learning under non-iid setting using BloodMnist dataset. Our primary goal is to illustrate the significant role that data heterogeneity plays in the training of machine learning models within a federated setting, we observe that severe heterogeneity across clients lead to the degradation of the model performances. Further we investigate advanced methods and algorithms of FL that tackle non-iid data issue in federated learning. Our results show that MetaFed attained a high accuracy and concurred the centralized learning, hence preserved data privacy and tackled the data heterogeneity of medical imaging data, furthermore we observe that the three federated learning algorithms outperformed the one site learning (e.g., base algorithm) even when data is iid.

In this experiment we train a Convolutional neural network (CNN) algorithm for automatic classification of peripheral blood cells dataset, it contains 17,092 images of individual cells for a multi classification with eight classes. Each image has a shape of 360×363 pixels, which is resized to 256×256 pixels for training. We evaluate the test accuracy and the loss error of five algorithms: FedAvg, FedProx, MetaFed, the Base algorithm and centralized learning. Moreover, to simulate the base algorithm that consist of training a local model on each client without sharing it with a central server. Hence, the dataset is divided into five equals parts, ensuring each client has the same data size. Centralized learning, in contrast, involves training the entire dataset with the SGD (Stochastic Gradient Descent) algorithm.

The CNN architecture consists of five convolutional layers. Each convolutional layer is followed by a batch normalization layer, a ReLU activation layer, and a max pooling layer. Finally, a SoftMax function is applied. We configure

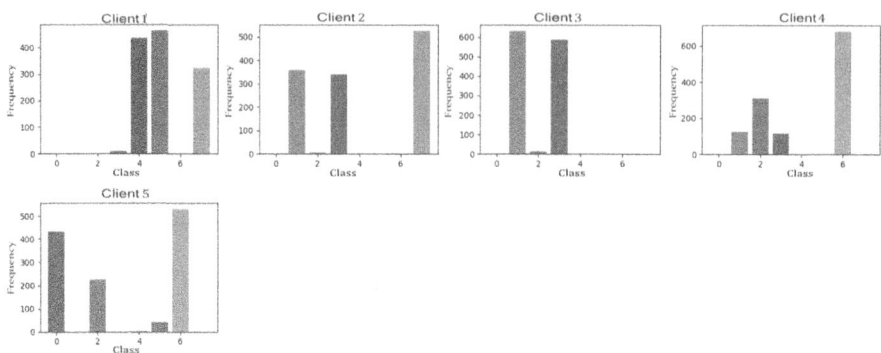

Fig. 2. Data distribution sampled with Dirichlet distribution from 8 classes across 5 clients, when $\alpha = 0.01$.

the same hyperparameter settings for all federated algorithms and centralized learning: the batch size is set to $N = 32$, the learning rate is set to $l = 1e-2$ and the cross-entropy for the loss function. The number of filters is increased from 16 in the initial layers to 64 in the later layers, allowing the network to learn increasingly complex features. We train the federated learning algorithms for 300 iterations while in centralized learning the model attained his highest accuracy started from the 80 ith iteration. In federated learning algorithms, five clients participate in each training iteration. Before sending local parameters for global aggregation, the default number of local training steps is set to 1. To simulate data heterogeneity, we sample non-IID datasets across different clients using a Dirichlet distribution.

$$p_j = p_{j,1}, \ldots . p_{j,N} \sim \mathrm{Dir}_N(\alpha) \tag{1}$$

For j classes, we randomly partition the datasets among the K clients. Where each client k get a partition of the dataset containing $p_{j,k}$ samples of class j. The parameter alpha α controls the distribution of data across clients, e.g., when α is smaller the data across clients is more heterogeneous. Figure 2 depicts the distribution of data among 5 clients under severe heterogeneity ($\alpha = 0.01$). It is evident that each client possesses a different number of training samples for each class. Additionally, it is noticeable that certain clients are lack training samples for certain classes which emphasis the severe data heterogeneity present across healthcare institutions in real-world scenarios. Thus to address the non-iid issue in Federated learning we train FedAvg and FedProx algorithms with different α value for 300 iterations, to sample non-iid datasets among clients we sample 5 local datasets with $\alpha = 0.1$ while the iid client datasets are sampled randomly, Fig. 3 illustrate a significant difference in the training loss between sampled datasets. Notably, datasets drawn from an (iid) distribution exhibit lower error loss compared to non-iid datasets with higher error. This translates to a 15% reduction in the algorithm's error function when data is iid compared to non-iid (alpha = 0.1), this deference is due to client drift, where each local model trains on a different data distribution. In extreme cases, some clients may lack entire classes present in others' datasets as shown in Fig. 2, each client optimizes based on its limited data, the resulting local optimum significantly deviates from the global optimum, however when data is iid we observe that the two algorithms converge faster this can be associated to the decrease in client-drift.

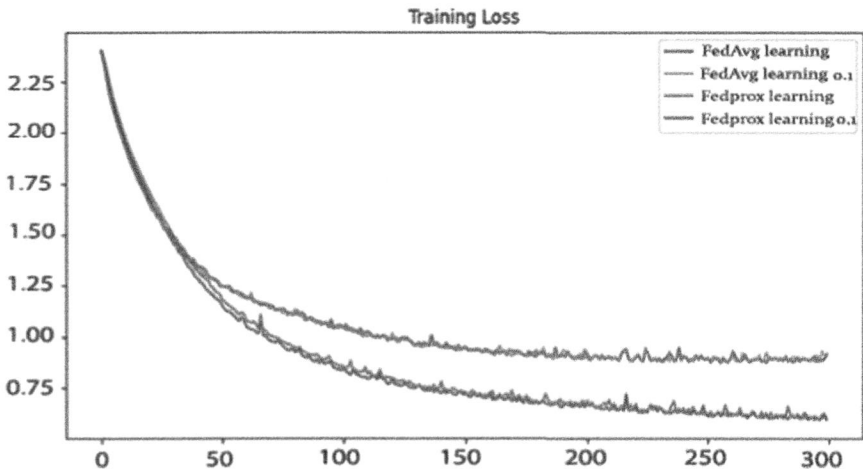

Fig. 3. The training error for algorithms FedAvg, FedProx when data across clients is non-iid $\alpha = 0.1$ and iid in 300 iteration

Table 1. Accuracy Test of three federated learning algorithms and centralized learning and the base algorithm when data is IID (e.g.: $\alpha = 1$).

Algorithm	Accuracy
FedAvg	93.85%
FedProx	93.33%
MetaFed	95.18%
SGD	95.48%
Base	82.52%

To empirically compare federated learning, one-site learning, and centralized learning, we train and evaluate three federated algorithms (FedAvg, FedProx, and MetaFed). Their test accuracy are presented in Table 1. The best accuracy is achieved by MetaFed algorithm when data is iid while the centralized learning outperformed it by 0.30% in the test accuracy, the results also show that the proposed federated learning algorithms has outperformed and exceeds the one

Table 2. Accuracy Test of Algorithms When the Alpha Parameter of the Dirichlet Distribution Changes.

Algorithm	Alpha	Accuracy
FedAvg	0.1	91.69%
	0.01	80.11%
FedProx	0.1	90.29%
	0.01	82.22%
Base	0.1	75.14%
	0.01	74%

site learning by 11% this can be attributed to the limited data in each client without share it for the global aggregation therefore the local model cannot well generalize, furthermore we evaluate the three federated algorithm with different data heterogeneity levels, hence the clients datasets are sampled with different α the results are illustrated in Table 2 show that when $\alpha = 0.01$ the MetaFed accuracy it always better than FedProx and FedAvg when data is non-iid, while FedProx outperforms FedAvg when $\alpha = 0.01$, hence FedAvg computes just the aggregation of the local parameters in the server, while FedProx solve the issue by correcting the global aggregation to maintain the data heterogeneity.

5 Conclusion

In this paper we address the challenge of data heterogeneity across medical institutions. We advocate for a decentralized approach where hospitals and clinics can collaboratively train a global model without sharing local data in a central location. This approach prioritizes privacy concerns while still leveraging the benefits of training on a larger-scale medical dataset. However, as our analysis demonstrates, the inherent heterogeneity of healthcare data across institutions poses a significant challenge. Each healthcare institution typically collects data independently, resulting in high variations between hospitals. We empirically show that this severe heterogeneity consistently harms model performance. We observe that advanced algorithms like MetaFed can outperform single-site learning while concurrent decentralized training. In our work, we explore the potential of Vision Transformers (ViTs) due to their potential to effectively handling medical imaging data. Additionally, we incorporate Self-Supervised Learning (SSL) techniques that allows to learn world representation without the human supervision from unlabeled data. We focus to address the challenge of limited labeled medical datasets and take the unique characteristics of medical imaging data enhancing its robustness to data heterogeneity. Furthermore, given that medical institutions independently collect and manage their data and models, we explore strategies to address the straggler problem during training. This problem arises when some institutions experience delays, potentially slowing the entire process. Our goal is to develop methods that compensate for the trade-off between performance and communication costs.

References

1. Tariq, M., Iqbal, S., Ayesha, H., Abbas, I., Ahmad, K.T., Niazi, M.F.K.: Medical image based breast cancer diagnosis: state of the art and future directions. Expert Syst. Appl. **167**, 114095 (2021)
2. Li, L., Xie, N., Yuan, S.: A federated learning framework for breast cancer histopathological image classification. Electronics **11**(22), 3767 (2022)
3. Rieke, N., et al.: The future of digital health with federated learning. NPJ Digit. Med. **3**(1), 1–7 (2020)
4. Schwarz, C.G., et al.: Identification of anonymous MRI research participants with face-recognition software. N. Engl. J. Med. **381**(17), 1684–1686 (2019)
5. Tedeschini, B.C., et al.: Decentralized federated learning for healthcare networks: a case study on tumor segmentation. IEEE Access **10**, 8693–8708 (2022)
6. Chang, Q., et al.: Mining multi-center heterogeneous medical data with distributed synthetic learning. Nat. Commun. **14**, 5510 (2023)
7. Nazir, S., Kaleem, M.: Federated learning for medical image analysis with deep neural networks. Diagnostics **13**(9), 1532 (2023)
8. Parekh, V.S., et al.: Cross-domain federated learning in medical imaging. arXiv preprint arXiv:2112.10001 (2021)
9. Jiménez-Sánchez, A., Tardy, M., Ballester, M.A.G., Mateus, D., Piella, G.: Memory-aware curriculum federated learning for breast cancer classification. Comput. Methods Program. Biomed. **229**, 107318 (2023)
10. Sarma, K.V., et al.: Federated learning improves site performance in multicenter deep learning without data sharing. J. Am. Med. Inform. Assoc. **28**(6), 1259–1264 (2021)
11. Chowdhury, A., Kassem, H., Padoy, N., Umeton, R., Karargyris, A.: A review of medical federated learning: applications in oncology and cancer research. In: Crimi, A., Bakas, S. (eds.) BrainLes 2021. LNCS, vol. 12962, pp. 3–24. Springer, Cham (2021). https://doi.org/10.1007/978-3-031-08999-2_1
12. Wei, K., et al.: Federated learning with differential privacy: algorithms and performance analysis. IEEE Trans. Inf. Forensics Secur. **15**, 3454–3469 (2020)
13. Luo, M., Chen, F., Hu, D., Zhang, Y., Liang, J., Feng, J.: No fear of heterogeneity: classifier calibration for federated learning with non-IID data. Adv. Neural. Inf. Process. Syst. **34**, 5972–5984 (2021)
14. Karimireddy, S.P., Kale, S., Mohri, M., Reddi, S., Stich, S., Suresh, A.T.: SCAFFOLD: stochastic controlled averaging for federated learning. In: International Conference on Machine Learning, pp. 5132–5143. PMLR (2020)
15. Li, Q., He, B., Song, D.: Model-contrastive federated learning. In: Proceedings of the IEEE/CVF Conference on Computer Vision and Pattern Recognition, pp. 10713–10722 (2021)
16. Yan, R., et al.: Label-efficient self-supervised federated learning for tackling data heterogeneity in medical imaging. IEEE Trans. Med. Imaging (2023)
17. Jiang, M., Wang, Z., Dou, Q.: HarmoFL: harmonizing local and global drifts in federated learning on heterogeneous medical images. In: Proceedings of the AAAI Conference on Artificial Intelligence, vol. 36, pp. 1087–1095 (2022)

18. Chen, Y., Lu, W., Qin, X., Wang, J., Xie, X.: MetaFed: federated learning among federations with cyclic knowledge distillation for personalized healthcare. IEEE Trans. Neural Netw. Learn. Syst. (2023)
19. Guan, H., Liu, M.: Domain adaptation for medical image analysis: a survey. IEEE Trans. Biomed. Eng. **69**(3), 1173–1185 (2021)
20. Shi, Y., Zhang, Y., Xiao, Y., Niu, L.: Optimization strategies for client drift in federated learning: a review. Procedia Comput. Sci. **214**, 1168–1173 (2022)
21. Ioffe, S., Szegedy, C.: Batch normalization: accelerating deep network training by reducing internal covariate shift. In: International Conference on Machine Learning, pp. 448–456. PMLR (2015)
22. Li, X., Jiang, M., Zhang, X., Kamp, M., Dou, Q.: FedBN: federated learning on non-IID features via local batch normalization. arXiv preprint arXiv:2102.07623 (2021)
23. Wang, Y., Shi, Q., Chang, T.-H.: Why batch normalization damage federated learning on non-IID data? IEEE Trans. Neural Netw. Learn. Syst. (2023)
24. Shamshad, F., et al.: Transformers in medical imaging: a survey. Med. Image Anal. 102802 (2023)
25. Taher, M.R.H., Haghighi, F., Gotway, M.B., Liang, J.: CAiD: context-aware instance discrimination for self-supervised learning in medical imaging. In: International Conference on Medical Imaging with Deep Learning, pp. 535–551. PMLR (2022)
26. Tang, Z., Shi, S., Wang, W., Li, B., Chu, X.: Communication-efficient distributed deep learning: a comprehensive survey. arXiv preprint arXiv:2003.06307 (2020)

Towards Stronger Blockchains: Security Against Front-Running Attacks

Anshuman Misra and Ajay D. Kshemkalyani[✉]

University of Illinois Chicago, Chicago, USA
{amisra7,ajay}@uic.edu

Abstract. Blockchains add transactions to a distributed shared ledger by arriving at consensus on sets of transactions contained in blocks. This provides a total ordering on a set of global transactions. However, total ordering is not enough to satisfy application semantics under the Byzantine fault model. This is due to the fact that malicious miners and clients can collaborate to add their own transactions ahead of correct clients' transactions in order to gain application level and financial advantages. These attacks fall under the umbrella of front-running attacks. In this paper, we propose causality preserving total order as a solution to this problem. The resulting blockchains will be stronger than traditional consensus based blockchains and will provide enhanced security ensuring correct application semantics in a Byzantine setting.

Keywords: Blockchain · Causal Order · Front-Running Attack · Security · Broadcast · Byzantine failure · Application Semantics · Consensus

1 Introduction

Blockchain is a shared distributed ledger that provides a tamper-proof ordered sequence of records. Bitcoin [25] was the first blockchain that provided a solution to the *double-spending problem* and revolutionized electronic money transfer. Bitcoin solves Byzantine-tolerant consensus [19] via proof-of-work. This led to the development of further blockchains that solved consensus such as Ethereum [31] that go a step further and provide smart contracts [9] that allow the blockchain to act as a *universal computer*. Smart contracts are code hosted on the blockchain that provide operations to change the state of the blockchain. Since the code is tamper-proof, a set of parties can conduct business in a transparent manner on the blockchain. Further, smart contracts provide the capability to run classic centralized applications on the blockchain in a decentralized manner, such as auctions [12] and elections [13]. As more applications are designed for blockchain, an important question that arises is—does blockchain guarantee the required semantics for these applications? In the case of peer-to-peer money transfer, the answer is yes, because total order prevents double-spending. However, total order is not enough for a decentralized auction, because a Byzantine miner can collude with a Byzantine client by informing the client of its opponents' bids prior to them being added to the blockchain. This lack of enforcement of semantics provides an opportunity to Byzantine nodes to launch a variety of attacks known as front-running attacks [11,33]. An important point to note is that blockchains preserve total ordering across transactions by utilizing consensus. This is equivalent to total order broadcast with transactions as messages. Total order broadcast and consensus protocols do not necessarily preserve causal relationships across transactions [8]. In this paper we prove that front-running attacks are essentially causality violations [18] accross transactions in the blockchain. Further, we propose utilizing causal ordering protocols enforcing strong safety [21–23] to provide an enhanced level of security in the blockchain ecosystem. Our contributions are as follows:

1. We formalize front-running attacks and prove that they are a violation of causal ordering (this is a precise characterization of front-running attacks).
2. We prove that utilizing a causal ordering protocol will enforce application semantics and make the blockchain more secure and suitable for classic centralized applications.
3. We introduce a protocol to provide security against front-running attacks by providing a causality preserving total ordering across transactions recorded in the blockchain. We term the resulting blockchain as a strong blockchain since it provides stronger security guarantees and semantics compared to traditional blockchains.
4. We prove the correctness of our protocol and analyze its intrinsic fairness properties.

2 System Model

This paper models the set of miners as a distributed system having Byzantine processes which are processes that can misbehave [19,26]. A correct process (miner) behaves exactly as specified by the blockchain protocol whereas a Byzantine process (miner) may exhibit arbitrary behaviour including crashing at any point during the execution. A Byzantine process cannot impersonate another process or spawn new processes. The distributed system is modelled as an undirected graph $G = (\mathcal{M}, H)$. Here $\mathcal{M}$ is the set of miners adding blocks to the blockchain. Let n be $|\mathcal{M}|$. H is the set of FIFO logical communication links over which miners communicate by message passing. G is a complete graph. This model is equivalent to the permissioned blockchain model [27]. Nonetheless, as can be seen by the proof of Theorem 1, our result proving that front-running attacks are causal violations holds for permissionless blockchains [25] as well. However, the solution we provide is geared towards permissioned blockchains.

The system is assumed to be synchronous, i.e., there is a known fixed upper bound δ on the message latency, and a known fixed upper bound ψ on the relative speeds of processors [10]. This is opposed to an asynchronous system, i.e., there is no upper bound δ on the message latency, nor any upper bound ψ on the relative speeds of processors [10]. Clients send their transactions to the system of miners by broadcasting a protocol message containing the transaction to the system. This message contains all the required metadata for the transaction such as gas fees and the client's identity. Next, transactions sit at each miner's mempool [28], waiting to get added to the blockchain. Clients can also be Byzantine and collude with Byzantine miners and miners can also act as clients in the system. Our protocol assumes an upper bound on the number of Byzantine miners, t with $n \geq 3t + 2$. The number of Byzantine clients is assumed to be unbounded.

Definition 1. *The happens before relation $\rightarrow$ on messages consists of the following rules:*

1. *If p_i sent or delivered message m before sending message m', then $m \rightarrow m'$.*
2. *If $m \rightarrow m'$ and $m' \rightarrow m''$, then $m \rightarrow m''$.*

Definition 2. *The causal past of message m is denoted as $CP(m)$ and defined as the set of all messages m' such that $m' \rightarrow m$.*

Definition 3. *A causal ordering algorithm must ensure the following:*

1. **Strong Safety:** *$\forall m' \in CP(m)$ such that m' and m are sent to the same (correct) process(es), no correct process delivers m before m'.*
2. **Liveness:** *Each message sent by a correct process to another correct process will be eventually delivered.*

Definition 4. *A **transaction** is a string contained in messages broadcasted to the system of miners with the intention of being recorded in the blockchain via consensus. Transactions change the state of the blockchain by executing business logic between two or more clients.*

Definition 5. *The happens before relation $\rightarrow$ on transactions is defined as follows: Given messages m_1 and m_2 containing transactions t_1 and t_2 respectively, $t_1 \rightarrow t_2$ if and only if $m_1 \rightarrow m_2$.*

Definition 6. *The causal past of transaction t is denoted as $CP(t)$ and defined as the set of all transactions t' such that $t' \rightarrow t$.*

Definition 7. *A **block** contains a sequence of totally ordered transactions and a hash of its parent block. A block is only added to the blockchain after the system of miners arrive at consensus on the contents of the block.*

Definition 8. ***Blockchain*** *is a distributed data structure consisting of a tree of blocks. Each block has only one parent (except the genesis block) and may have multiple children blocks.*

Definition 9. *A causal ordering algorithm for blockchain BT must ensure the following:*

1. **Strong Safety:** *Given transaction t, $\forall t' \in CP(t)$, t' gets recorded in BT before t.*

2. **Liveness:** Each transaction sent by a correct client eventually arrives in every correct miner's memory pool.

Definition 10. Given a blockchain BT, the **consensus chain** is a sequence of blocks $B_0, B_1, ..., B_l$ such that B_k is the parent of B_{k+1} and $tree\_depth(BT) = l$.

Definition 11. BT is a **valid blockchain** if BT contains one and only one consensus chain.

As a shorthand, we will refer to the consensus chain of a valid blockchain BT as $consensus\_chain(BT)$.

3 Front-Running Attacks

In this section we first present a broad family of attacks called front-running attacks. We formalize the attacks and prove that they are essentially an attack on causal ordering. An important point to note is that front-running attacks are executed prior to execution of the blockchain consensus protocol. Miners can view unconfirmed transactions in their memory pools and broadcast their own transactions with higher transaction fees with the intention of executing front-running attacks on unsuspecting clients. Byzantine miners can also collude with Byzantine clients to execute front-running attacks. However, without loss of generality in our proofs and solutions, we assume that miners act as clients in executing attacks. The following are illustrative examples of front-running attacks on real-world applications:

1. An honest client process p_i sends transaction t_i to the network as part of a decentralized auction. A malicious miner M reads t_i, figures out the bid value p_i wants to place for an asset being auctioned and sends its own transaction t_M with the purpose of getting into the blockchain first. This results in an unfair advantage for M in winning the auction.
2. An honest client process p_i sends a request to buy cryptocurrency (transaction t_1) at price x, where the market price y is less than x. A malicious miner M can attempt to make a profit here by adding two transactions to the block where it includes t_1:
   (a) It adds t_0 buying cryptocurrency at price y from the market. t_0 is placed before t_1. Note that the miner is exhibiting malicious behaviour in this step.
   (b) It sells cryptocurrency to p_i in transaction t_2 to p_i (placed after t_1) at price x. Note that in isolation, sending transaction t_2 is not malicious behaviour.

   This results in M making a profit by arbitraging off an honest client with a profit of $(x - y)$ per coin.

An honest miner should not look into the content of transactions in the network. Blockchains incentivize miners to go after transactions with higher mining fees to maximize profits. The blockchain protocol requires miners to be concerned with only transaction fees and not the contents of transactions. The Byzantine fault model encapsulates behaviour that does not follow the specified protocol. Therefore, such malicious miners can be modeled as Byzantine processes and Byzantine fault-tolerant protocols can be utilized to prevent such behaviour.

Observation 1. *Miners executing front-running attacks are Byzantine.*

Front-running attacks are broadly categorized as follows [30]:

1. **Displacement Attack**: A Byzantine miner reads transaction t from its memory pool and broadcasts its own transaction (copying contents of t) t' with higher transaction fees in order to record t' in the blockchain before t.
2. **Sandwich Attack**: A Byzantine miner reads transaction t_1 from its memory pool and broadcasts two transactions t_0 and t_2 with the intention of recording t_0 before t_1 and t_2 after t_1 in the same block. In this way, the Byzantine miner creates an arbitrage opportunity to make a profit.
3. **Suppression Attack**: A Byzantine miner reads transaction t from its memory pool and broadcasts a set of transactions T containing transactions with high transaction fees. This attack essentially forces t to not get recorded in the next block in the blockchain.

We now formally define front-running attacks and prove that they are causal ordering violations. Since front-running attacks are executed before consensus and are harder to execute when no forks exist, for the sake of proofs we assume without loss of generality that they are executed on valid blockchains (Definition 11).

Definition 12. *A Byzantine miner executes a **front-running attack** by reading an unconfirmed transaction t_x and broadcasting/mining its own transaction t_y with the intention of recording t_y before t_x in the consensus chain of a valid blockchain BT.*

Note that a sandwich attack consists of two transactions being sent out by the Byzantine miner. The first transaction front-runs the client's transaction as per Definition 12, while the second transaction is non-malicious in isolation. Also note that a suppression attack is simply the repeated application of Definition 12. In other words, multiple transactions are sent out by the Byzantine miner to be recorded in the blockchain before the client's transaction, ultimately forcing the client's transaction be recorded in a future block.

Theorem 1. *Front-running attacks are a violation of causal ordering.*

Proof. BT is a valid blockchain and let $C = consensus\_chain(BT)$. Let p_i broadcast m_1 (containing transaction t_1) to the system of miners. Miner M delivers m_1 and adds t_1 to its memory pool. Miner M then broadcasts m_2 (containing

t_2) with significantly higher transaction fees than m_1 (t_1), with the intention of adding t_2 to C before t_1 is added to it. If this attack succeeds, one of the following scenarios must play out:

1. Miner M' (M may be M') succeeds in adding the next block B containing t_2 to C. The new consensus chain of BT is $C' = C + B$. Eventually, t_1 gets added to $consensus\_chain(BT)$ as part of block B'. Since C' is a prefix of all future consensus chains, t_2 is ordered before t_1.
2. Miner M' (M may be M') succeeds in adding the next block B to C. B contains both t_1 and t_2 with t_2 ordered before t_1.

By Definition 12, this is a front-running attack on t_1 by M via t_2. In order to execute this attack, M delivered m_1 and broadcasted m_2. By the message order rule in Definition 1, $m_1 \to m_2$. Since t_2 is recorded in C before t_1, the contents of m_2 are consumed by the system before the contents of m_1 resulting in a strong safety violation as per Definition 3. Therefore, it is clear that a front-running attack across transactions requires a causality violation across their respective protocol messages. □

4 Background

4.1 Some Cryptographic Basics

We utilize non-interactive threshold cryptography as a means to guarantee strong safety of broadcasts [29]. Threshold cryptography consists of an initialization function to generate keys, message encryption, sharing decrypted shares of the message and finally combining the decrypted shares to obtain the original message from ciphertext. The following functions are used in a threshold cryptographic scheme:

Definition 13. *The dealer executes the generate() function to obtain the public key PK, verification key VK and the private keys SK_0, SK_1, ... , SK_{n-1}.*

The dealer shares private key SK_i with each process p_i while PK and VK are publicly available.

Definition 14. *When process p_i wants to send a message m to p_j, it executes $E(PK, m, L)$ to obtain C_m. Here C_m is the ciphertext corresponding to m, E is the encryption algorithm and L is a label to identify m. p_i then broadcasts C_m to the system of processes.*

Definition 15. *When process p_l receives ciphertext C_m, it executes $D(SK_l, C_m)$ to obtain σ_l^m where D is the decryption share generation algorithm and σ_l^m is p_l's decryption share for message m.*

When process p_j receives a cipher message C_m intended for it, it has to wait for k decryption shares to arrive from the system to obtain m. The value of k depends on the security properties of the system. It derives the message from the ciphertext as follows:

Definition 16. *When process p_j wants to generate the original message m from ciphertext C_m, it executes $C(VK, C_m, S)$ where S is a set of k decryption shares for m and C is the combining algorithm for the k decryption shares.*

The following function is used to verify the authenticity of a decryption share:

Definition 17. *When a decryption share σ is received for message m, the Share Verification Algorithm is used to ascertain whether σ is authentic : $V(VK, C_m, \sigma) = 1$ if σ is authentic, $V(VK, C_m, \sigma) = 0$ if σ is not authentic.*

4.2 Byzantine Causal Broadcast via Byzantine Reliable Broadcast

We propose a causal order broadcast algorithm for clients to send transactions to miners. Byzantine-tolerant causal broadcast is invoked as BC_broadcast(m) and delivers a message through BC_deliver(m). Under the covers, Byzantine Causal Broadcast invokes Byzantine Reliable Broadcast. These two are defined next.

Definition 18. *Byzantine Causal Broadcast (BCB) satisfies the following properties:*

1. *(BCB-Validity:) If a correct process p_i BC_delivers message m from sender(m) then sender(m) must have BC_broadcast m.*
2. *(BCB-Termination-1:) If a correct process BC_broadcasts a message m then it eventually BC_delivers m.*
3. *(BCB-Agreement or BCM-Termination-2:) If a correct process BC_delivers a message m from a possibly faulty process, then all correct processes eventually deliver m.*
4. *(BCB-Integrity:) For any message m, every correct process p_i BC_delivers m at most once.*
5. *(BCB-Causal-Order:) If $m \to m'$, then no correct process BC_delivers m' before m.*

BCB-Causal-Order is the strong safety property of Definition 3. *BCB-Termination-1* and *BCB-Agreement* imply the liveness property of Definition 3.

The Byzantine-tolerant Reliable Broadcast (BRB) [3,4] is invoked by BR_broadcast and its message is delivered by BR_deliver, and satisfies the properties given below.

Definition 19. *Byzantine-tolerant Reliable Broadcast (BRB) provides the following guarantees [3,4]:*

1. *(BRB-Validity:) If a correct process BR_delivers a message m from sender-(m), then sender(m) must have BR_broadcast m.*
2. *(BRB-Termination-1:) If a correct process BR_broadcasts a message m, then it eventually BR_delivers m.*
3. *(BRB-Agreement or BRB-Termination-2:) If a correct process BR_delivers a message m from a possibly faulty process, then all correct processes eventually BR_deliver m.*
4. *(BRB-Integrity:) For any message m, every correct process BR_delivers m at most once.*

5 Causal Ordering Protocol to Prevent Front-Running Attacks

In light of the result of Theorem 1, we present a causality preserving blockchain protocol to strengthen the security of blockchain to withstand front-running attacks under the synchronous system setting. A synchronous system can assume lock-step execution in rounds. Within a round, a process can send messages, then receive messages, and lastly have internal events; further a message sent in a round is received in the same round at all its destinations. Algorithm 1 serves as a reference point for synchronous round-based communication. Without loss of generality, we assume that all processes send their messages at the beginning of each round, all messages arrive in the same round that they are sent out and messages are delivered at the end of each round. In Algorithm 2, threshold cryptography in conjunction with the execution in rounds and Byzantine Reliable Broadcast are used to ensure strong safety + liveness. Clients broadcast transactions to the system of miners encapsulated in protocol messages via BRB. Using BRB protects against liveness attacks by Byzantine clients via *BRB-Termination-1* and *BRB-Agreement*.

Algorithm 1: Synchronous round-based message passing protocol

Data: Each process locally maintains two FIFO queues Q_s and Q_d for storing outgoing/incoming messages respectively

1 **when** round r starts:
2   broadcast all messages in FIFO order after dequeuing from Q_s
3 **when** round r ends:
4   deliver all messages in FIFO order after dequeuing from Q_d
5 **when** the application is ready to broadcast message m:
6   $Q_s.enqueue(m)$
7 **when** message m arrives:
8   $Q_d.enqueue(m)$

We present our solution called *causality preserving blockchain protocol* in Algorithm 2. Classic Blockchain consensus protocols generate a total ordering of transactions. Our protocol guarantees a stronger property, *causally consistent total ordering* of transactions. Algorithm 2 ensures that the blockchain's total ordering does not violate causality across transactions, hence ensuring application semantics in a Byzantine setting. This is why we term any blockchain following our protocol as a stronger blockchain than classic blockchains. For simplicity, we term this as a *strong blockchain* and is defined below.

Definition 20. *A **strong blockchain** BT must satisfy the following properties:*

1. BT is a valid blockchain (Definition 11)
2. $\forall t_1, t_2$ such that $t_1 \to t_2$, t_1 is recorded before t_2 in BT's consensus chain.

Algorithm 2 is agnostic to the blockchain consensus mechanism. Algorithm 2 ensures that only transactions whose causal past is already recorded in the consensus chain are allowed to be mined. In addition to blockchain-specific properties that need to be satisfied (e.g., sufficient balance, identity of client), a transaction is not considered for mining if it causally depends on one or more transactions that have not been finalized in the blockchain. Algorithm 2 only mines what we term as *safe transactions*. Safe transactions satisfy blockchain-specific properties and all transactions in their causal past are already recorded in the blockchain. Algorithm 2 only considers *safe blocks* for consensus, thereby preventing front-running attacks by maintaining causal relations across transactions. Safe transactions and safe blocks are formalized below:

Definition 21. *t is a **safe transaction** with regards to a strong blockchain BT if and only if $\forall t' \in CP(t), \exists B' \in BT$ such that $t' \in B'$ and B' is an ancestor of the block B that contains t (B may be mined in the future).*

Definition 22. *A **safe block** B only contains safe transactions.*

Note that in Algorithm 2, we construct a strong blockchain (Definition 20) using only safe blocks (Definition 22) which are in turn comprised of only safe transactions (Definition 21). However, a strong blockchain can also be constructed using *unsafe transactions*, as long as all causal dependencies of a recorded transaction are recorded before it in a previous or even the same block. In Algorithm 2 each client process p_{c_i} has access to PK (global public key), each miner process p_{M_i} has access to VK (global verification key). Each miner p_{M_i} has access to a local secret key SK_i. Each client uses a FIFO queue Q_s for outgoing protocol messages. Each miner p_{M_i}'s memory pool is denoted by a set MP. The causal past of transaction t is denoted as $CP(t)$. The set of all miners is $\mathcal{M}$. BT is the shared blockchain. B_r^i is the block proposed by miner p_{M_i} in round $r + 1$.

Algorithm 2 provides the BC_broadcast primitive to clients to protect against front-running attacks and BC_deliver to miners for extracting transactions from messages. BR_broadcast and BR_delivery are the underlying primitives implementing Byzantine reliable broadcast (BRB) [3,4]. Let β and γ denote the maximum and minimum number of rounds (sequential steps) respectively in a BRB protocol. For example, Bracha's BRB has $\beta = \infty$, $\gamma = 3$ and requires $n > 3f$ [3,4] whereas Imbs-Raynal [14] has $\beta = \infty$, $\gamma = 2$ and requires $n > 5f$. However, $\beta = \infty$ is the case when a Byzantine process initiates broadcast and the Byzantine processes do not follow the protocol in its entirety. Whenever a correct process initiates BRB, it is delivered in γ rounds. In the case of a Byzantine broadcaster, the message will either not be delivered or in case it is delivered some correct processes may deliver the message after others as we will show in Lemma 1. Although a message m sent in a round is delivered after all messages sent in previous rounds, a Byzantine miner can peek into m before its transaction is committed to the blockchain and send a causally dependent message m' in the same round to initiate a broadcast send via its own BR_broadcast. m' may be BR_delivered in the same round as m at some miners, thus leading to a

Algorithm 2: Causality Preserving Blockchain Protocol

1 **when** round r starts at client p_{c_i}:
2 **while** $Q_s.head() \neq \phi$ **do**
3     $C_m = Q_s.pop()$
4   BR_broadcast($C_m, \mathcal{M}$)

5 **when** client p_{c_i} sends m to $\mathcal{M}$ via BC_broadcast($m, \mathcal{M}$) in round r:
6 $C_m = E(PK, m, id_m)$
7 $Q_s.push(C_m)$

8 **when** round r starts at miner p_{M_i}:
9 $B = consensus(candidate\_set)$ ▷ consensus on the set of blocks delivered in the previous round
10 $candidate\_set = \phi$
11 Add B at the end of $consensus\_chain(BT)$
12 **for** all $t \in B$ **do**
13   delete t from MP
14   **for** all t' such that $t \in CP(t')$ **do**
15        $CP(t') = CP(t') \setminus t$

16 $B_r^i = \phi$
17 **for** all t in MP such that t is semantically invalid **do**
18   delete t
19 **for** all t in MP' where $MP' \subseteq MP \wedge CP(t) = \phi$ **do**
20     $B_r^i = B_r^i \cup \{t\}$ ▷ Block construction with safe transactions
21 **for** all $p_{M_j} \in \mathcal{M}$ **do**
22   send B_r^i to p_{M_j}

23 **when** B_r^j arrives at miner p_{M_i} during round r: ▷ Block created by miner p_{M_j} in round r and proposed for consensus in round $(r+1)$
24 **for** all $t \in B_r^j$ **do**
25   **if** t is semantically invalid $\vee\, CP(t) \neq \phi$ **then**
26   discard B_r^j
27 **if** B_r^j has not been discarded **then**
28     $candidate\_set = candidate\_set \cup B_r^j$ ▷ all safe blocks arriving in round r are added to candidate_set

29 **when** C_m is BR_delivered at miner p_{M_i} in round r:
30 $\sigma_i^m = D(SK_i, C_m)$
31 **for** all $p_{M_j} \in \mathcal{M}$ **do**
32   send σ_i^m to p_j in round $(r+1)$

33 **when** miner p_{M_i} receives $(2t+1)$th valid $\langle \sigma_x^m \rangle$ message by round r:
34 Store $(2t+1)$ decryption shares in set S
35 $m = C(VK, C_m, S)$
36 extract t_m from m ▷ bc_delivery(m)
37 $CP(t_m) = MP$
38 $MP = MP \cup \{t_m\}$

potential front-running attack across the transactions contained in m and m'. To prevent a Byzantine process from peeking into the transaction of a message prior to BC_delivery, the message is encrypted using threshold encryption.

Algorithm 2 consists of both miner side code and client side code divided into six *when blocks*, each in reaction to an event in the protocol. The *when block* from lines 1–4 is executed in the beginning of a round, with each client broadcasting messages it created in the previous round using BRB in a FIFO manner from a local queue containing those messages. FIFO ordering at the client in conjunction with FIFO channels ensures source order at the miners' end. The *when block* in lines 5–7 describes how clients utilize the BC_broadcast primitive provided by Algorithm 2. Clients encrypt messages using threshold cryptography and enqueue them in a local FIFO queue, ready to be sent out in the beginning of the next round. The *when block* between lines 8–22 is executed by each miner in the beginning of a round. In line 9, miners arrive at consensus on the set of blocks proposed by each miner in the previous round. These blocks are stored in a set *candidate_set*. Miners then clear *candidate_set* to make it ready to store blocks in the current round and the consensus block B is added to the blockchain. Lines 12–15 clear transactions contained in B from the miners' memory pool, MP (a set data structure containing transactions waiting to be added to the blockchain), and the causal past ($CP(t)$ keeps track of transactions in MP that need to be added to the blockchain before t) of the remaining transactions in MP. Next, the miner constructs its own block (to be sent out for consensus in the next round) with semantically valid and safe transactions (lines 16–20). In lines 21–22, miners send their blocks for consensus in the next round. The *when block* in lines 23–28 deals with incoming blocks from other miners for which consensus will be arrived at in the next round. When a miner receives a block, it checks if the block is semantically valid and makes sure all transactions in the block do not have causal dependencies on existing transactions in the memory pool. If that is the case, the block is added to *candidate_set*. The *when block* in lines 29–32 deals with miners receiving a message (containing a transaction) from a client via BR_delivery, computing their decryption shares for the message and broadcasting the decryption share in the next round. Finally, the *when block* in lines 33–38 deals with miners receiving the required number of decryption shares ($2t+1$) for decrypting a protocol message. The miners decrypt the message m in line 35 and extract the transaction t_m in line 36 (this line is BC_delivery) and store the causal past of t_m in $CP(t_m)$. Finally, t_m is added to the memory pool in line 38. For the purposes of this protocol, $CP(t)$ is treated as a dynamic set data structure, which starts off containing the entire set of transactions in the causal past of t. As each of these transactions is added to blockchain BT, it is removed from $CP(t)$. Once $CP(t) = \phi$, t is a safe transaction and is ready to be added to the blockchain.

Lemma 1. *In a system following the BRB protocol in [3], if a correct process* BR_delivers *message m in round r, it will be* BR_delivered *at all correct processes at or before round $(r+1)$.*

Proof. Let p_i be the first correct process to BR_deliver m; let it do so in round r. For this to be the case, p_i must have received at least $(2t+1)$ $READY(m)$ messages by round r. At least $(t+1)$ of the $READY(m)$ messages were sent by correct processes. Therefore, at the end of round r, all correct processes will have received at least $(t+1)$ $READY(m)$ messages. At the start of round $(r+1)$, all correct processes will broadcast $READY(m)$ and will receive $(2t+1)$ $READY(m)$ messages before the end of the round. Therefore, all correct processes will BR_deliver m at or before round $(r+1)$. □

Theorem 2. *For all transactions t_1 and t_2 in a valid blockchain BT, such that $t_1 \to t_2$, Algorithm 2 guarantees that t_1 is ordered before t_2 in BT's consensus chain.*

Proof. Consider messages m_1 and m_2 containing transactions t_1 and t_2 respectively, with $m_1 \to m_2$. From Definition 5, $t_1 \to t_2$. Let p_{m_j} (possibly Byzantine) be the sender of m_2. p_{m_j} BC_delivers m_1 and views t_1 in line 36 of Algorithm 2. The earliest that m_2 can be broadcasted to the system is in round r itself (this is Byzantine behaviour, a correct miner would broadcast m_2 in round $(r+1)$). The fastest delivery time of m_2 at any miner would be the minimum latency of BRB (γ) + decryption share latency (1 round) + sending round (r). Therefore, the earliest m_2 can be BC_delivered at any miner is at round $r_{m_2} = (r + \gamma + 1)$. Whereas the latest that m_1 is BC_delivered at any miner is $r_{m_1} = (r+2)$. This is because from Lemma 1, m_1 must be BR_delivered at all correct processes within round $(r+1)$ because it must have been BR_delivered at at least $(t+1)$ correct processes by round r for BC_delivery to be possible at p_{m_j}. And in round $(r+2)$ all correct processes will receive the required number of decryption shares, $(2t+1)$ to BC_deliver m_1 because all correct processes broadcast their decryption shares in the very next round of BR_delivering a message. Therefore, at any correct miner p_{M_l}, we have the following:

$$r_{m_1} \leq (r+2)$$
$$r_{m_2} \geq (r+\gamma+1)$$
$$r_{m_1} < r_{m_2} \text{ (since } \gamma > 1)$$

Since $r_{m_1} < r_{m_2}$, m_1 will be BC_delivered before m_2 and t_1 will be in the memory pool (MP) prior to the extraction of t_2 (lines 33–38). Therefore, when t_2 will be included in MP at all correct miners, $CP(t_2)$ will include t_1 (lines 36–38). Any block B containing t_2 will be rejected by correct miners if t_1 is not recorded in blockchain BT (lines 23–26). Consequently, no such block B can be added to the blockchain until t_1 is recorded in BT. Therefore, given $t_1 \to t_2$, t_1 will be recorded in BT prior to t_2. □

Theorem 3. *All transactions broadcasted to blockchain BT via Algorithm 2 will be added to each correct miner's memory pool MP within bounded time.*

Proof. Let client p_{c_i} send message m (containing transaction t_m) to BT via Algorithm 2 in round r. p_{c_i} sends m's ciphertext C_m via BRB in lines 1–4 to the system of miners. By *BRB-Termination-1* and *BRB-Agreement* from Definition

19, it can be seen that all correct miners will BR_deliver C_m in γ rounds (since p_{c_i} is following the protocol in Algorithm 2, BRB will terminate in γ rounds) at line 29 and broadcast their respective decryption shares in the next round in lines 30–32. In the next round all correct processes will receive the required number of decryption shares to decrypt C_m in line 33. All correct miners will proceed to decrypt message m and store its transaction t_m in MP in the same round (lines 34–38). Therefore, a transaction t_m sent in round r via Algorithm 2 will arrive at every correct miner's memory pool in round $(r + \gamma + 1)$. □

Corollary 1 follows from Theorems 2 and 3.

Corollary 1. *Algorithm 2 guarantees causal ordering as defined in Definition 9.*

Theorem 4. *Any blockchain constructed by Algorithm 2 is resilient to front-running attacks.*

Proof. Follows from Theorem 1 and Corollary 1. □

A critical observation about Algorithm 2 is that any transaction t BC_delivered in round r will be added to the causal past of every transaction BC_delivered in rounds $(r+1), (r+2), ...(r+k)$, where $(r+k)$ is the round where t is recorded to the blockchain. Consequently, any transaction t' added to the memory pool after t cannot be added to the blockchain until t is added to it. This forces miners to mine and add existing transactions in the memory pool to the blockchain in order to ensure that future transactions do not end up waiting in the memory pool, thereby preventing wastage of both resources and time. This leads us to Observation 2.

Observation 2. *Any blockchain constructed by Algorithm 2 guarantees intrinsic fairness to clients.*

6 Discussion

Front-Running Attacks. In this paper we studied front-running attacks and proved that all front-running attacks are causal ordering violations accross transactions. The reason that front-running attacks are feasible against existing blockchains is because blockchains provide a *total ordering* of transactions by solving Byzantine-tolerant consensus but do not preserve causality when building this total ordering. We conclude that solving consensus is not enough from an application semantics perspective in a Byzantine environment.

Stronger Blockchains. In light of our findings, we defined the notion of a *strong blockchain*, which is a blockchain that provides a causality-preserving total order across transactions. This eliminates the feasibility of front-running attacks by Byzantine processes and guarantees application semantics. We proposed a causal ordering protocol to be used in conjunction with the consensus protocol to build a strong blockchain. This approach is modular because it does not interfere with the consensus protocol of the blockchain. Instead, the causal ordering protocol on transactions runs prior to the consensus protocol on blocks of transactions. That is, the causal ordering protocol ensures that transactions added to blocks do not have causal dependencies in the memory pool. This makes it straightforward to incorporate causal ordering as a pre-consensus protocol to existing blockchains. Our blockchain protocol keeps track of causal dependencies of every transaction added to the memory pool of every miner. BRB ensures that all correct miners have correct knowledge of the causal dependencies. This allows our protocol to stop any transactions from being mined whose causal dependencies have not been added to the blockchain.

Related Work. Recently, a technique to make sandwich attacks unprofitable to *rational* Byzantine processes in the permissionless setting was proposed [1]. This technique involves changing the blockchain protocol itself by making random reorderings of transactions within proposed blocks. Fair ordering of transactions at the consensus level has been formalized in [6,15]. However, this approach does not completely rule out front-running attacks. Commit reveal schemes to prevent front-running attacks have been explored in [7] along with a game-theoretic analysis of the same. However, this protocol cannot prevent suppression attacks and impedes smart contract composability. The work presented in [32] works on detection of front-running attacks via a mining algorithm and presents a solution to detect the possibility of front-running attacks at the smart contract level. It also provides an experimental analysis of techniques for preventing front-running attacks. This paper is experimental and runs orthogonal to the fundamental finding in our paper. The work in [16] presents the notion of batch-order-fairness, and prevents front-running attacks as long as a pre-determined fraction of honest nodes have seen the correct transaction ordering. The work in [2] presents a consensus protocol promoting fairness of transaction ordering while utilizing threshold cryptography to prevent censorship by Byzantine nodes. Our protocol also uses threshold cryptography, which has previously been used in a probabilistic algorithm based on atomic (total order) broadcast for secure causal atomic broadcast (liveness and strong safety) in an asynchronous system [5]. This algorithm used acknowledgements and effectively processed the atomic broadcasts serially. This protocol would force miners to see transactions in a total order inhibiting parallel mining of transactions sent concurrently. Additionally, this protocol in conjunction with blockchain would solve consensus twice, wasting time and resources. More recently, threshold cryptography has been used to develop a non-deterministic multicast algorithm for causal ordering in asynchronous systems [22].

Causality Preserving Blockchain Protocol. We proposed a strong blockchain protocol and proved its correctness in this paper. Our protocol provides *deterministic* causal ordering in a synchronous communication model. Since our protocol operates in a synchronous setting, the consensus protocol will also be deterministic. Our protocol assumes that there are $(3t+1)$ miners out of which at most $(t-1)$ can be Byzantine[1]. This means that this protocol is suited for a permissioned blockchain, with a static number of miners. Our protocol has a message complexity of $O(n^2)$ and has an upper bound on latency (time for a transaction to arrive in all correct miners' memory pools) of $(\gamma + 1)$ rounds.

Asynchronous Systems. In this paper we provided a deterministic solution for synchronous systems. However, most real-world applications do not have the luxury of synchronized clocks which are essential for providing synchrony. Therefore, future work involves devising solutions for asynchronous systems. It is important to note that the result of Theorem 1 is system model agnostic and applies to all blockchain systems including asynchronous and permissionless blockchains because the proof does not assume any particular system model settings. Second, neither consensus nor causal ordering are deterministically solvable in asynchronous systems. Therefore, any solutions preventing front-running attacks by addressing the root cause—causal ordering violations—will be non-deterministic. The main takeaway for asynchronous systems that we provide in this paper is that the best solution to address the issue of front-running attacks in blockchains is to use a Byzantine-tolerant causal ordering protocol independent of the consensus mechanism. Further, a probabilistic version of Algorithm 2 can be tailored for asynchronous systems using a Byzantine-tolerant clock synchronization protocol [17,20] to approximate synchrony. Note that the clock synchronization protocol has to be chosen based on the system settings assumed by the blockchain. This task is non-trivial and is left as future work.

7 Conclusions

This paper established that causal ordering is critical for blockchain security and maintaining application semantics and provided a causal ordering solution for synchronous permissioned blockchains. To the best of our knowledge, this is the first work that addressed the *root cause* that makes front-running attacks possible, and proved that front-running attacks are causal violations. Additionally, we provided a solution that can be adopted by existing blockchains *without interfering* with the blockchain protocol. Our solution for synchronous systems is deterministic; it is not possible to develop a deterministic strong blockchain in an asynchronous system [23,24]. Our result in Theorem 1, stating that front-running attacks are causal violations is independent of the system model of our protocol. Therefore, front-running attacks are not feasible against our notion of a strong blockchain regardless of the system model assumptions (permissioned vs. non-permissioned, synchrony vs. asynchrony). Future work comprises developing protocols for strong blockchain in different system settings such as non-permissioned blockchains and blockchains with asynchronous communication.

---

[1] BRB requires an upper bound of t Byzantine processes out of $(3t+1)$ processes. In our case, the client becomes the $(3t+2)^{th}$ process in the system when broadcasting to the system of miners via BRB. In case the broadcasting client is Byzantine, correctness of the protocol can only be guaranteed when at most $(t-1)$ miners are Byzantine.

References

1. Alpos, O., Amores-Sesar, I., Cachin, C., Yeo, M.: Eating sandwiches: modular and lightweight elimination of transaction reordering attacks. arXiv preprint arXiv:2307.02954 (2023)
2. Asayag, A., et al.: A fair consensus protocol for transaction ordering. In: 2018 IEEE 26th International Conference on Network Protocols (ICNP), pp. 55–65. IEEE (2018)
3. Bracha, G.: Asynchronous byzantine agreement protocols. Inf. Comput. **75**(2), 130–143 (1987)
4. Bracha, G., Toueg, S.: Asynchronous consensus and broadcast protocols. J. ACM (JACM) **32**(4), 824–840 (1985)
5. Cachin, C., Kursawe, K., Petzold, F., Shoup, V.: Secure and efficient asynchronous broadcast protocols. In: Kilian, J. (ed.) CRYPTO 2001. LNCS, vol. 2139, pp. 524–541. Springer, Heidelberg (2001). https://doi.org/10.1007/3-540-44647-8_31
6. Cachin, C., Mićić, J., Steinhauer, N., Zanolini, L.: Quick order fairness. In: Eyal, I., Garay, J. (eds.) FC 2022. LNCS, vol. 13411, pp. 316–333. Springer, Cham (2022). https://doi.org/10.1007/978-3-031-18283-9_15
7. Canidio, A., Danos, V.: Commitment against front running attacks. arXiv preprint arXiv:2301.13785 (2023)
8. Défago, X., Schiper, A., Urbán, P.: Total order broadcast and multicast algorithms: taxonomy and survey. ACM Comput. Surv. (CSUR) **36**(4), 372–421 (2004)
9. Dickerson, T., Gazzillo, P., Herlihy, M., Koskinen, E.: Adding concurrency to smart contracts. In: Proceedings of the ACM Symposium on Principles of Distributed Computing, pp. 303–312 (2017)
10. Dwork, C., Lynch, N.A., Stockmeyer, L.J.: Consensus in the presence of partial synchrony. J. ACM **35**(2), 288–323 (1988)
11. Eskandari, S., Moosavi, S., Clark, J.: SoK: transparent dishonesty: front-running attacks on blockchain. In: Bracciali, A., Clark, J., Pintore, F., Rønne, P.B., Sala, M. (eds.) FC 2019. LNCS, vol. 11599, pp. 170–189. Springer, Cham (2020). https://doi.org/10.1007/978-3-030-43725-1_13
12. Hahn, A., Singh, R., Liu, C.C., Chen, S.: Smart contract-based campus demonstration of decentralized transactive energy auctions. In: 2017 IEEE Power & Energy Society Innovative Smart Grid Technologies Conference (ISGT), pp. 1–5. IEEE (2017)
13. Hanifatunnisa, R., Rahardjo, B.: Blockchain based e-voting recording system design. In: 2017 11th International Conference on Telecommunication Systems Services and Applications (TSSA), pp. 1–6. IEEE (2017)
14. Imbs, D., Raynal, M.: Trading off t-resilience for efficiency in asynchronous byzantine reliable broadcast. Parallel Process. Lett. **26**(04), 1650017 (2016)
15. Kelkar, M., Deb, S., Kannan, S.: Order-fair consensus in the permissionless setting. In: Proceedings of the 9th ACM on ASIA Public-Key Cryptography Workshop, pp. 3–14 (2022)
16. Kelkar, M., Deb, S., Long, S., Juels, A., Kannan, S.: Themis: fast, strong order-fairness in byzantine consensus. In: Proceedings of the 2023 ACM SIGSAC Conference on Computer and Communications Security, pp. 475–489 (2023)
17. Khanchandani, P., Lenzen, C.: Self-stabilizing byzantine clock synchronization with optimal precision. Theory Comput. Syst. **63**(2), 261–305 (2019)
18. Lamport, L.: Time, clocks, and the ordering of events in a distributed system. Commun. ACM **21**(7), 558–565 (1978)

19. Lamport, L., Shostak, R.E., Pease, M.C.: The byzantine generals problem. ACM Trans. Program. Lang. Syst. **4**(3), 382–401 (1982)
20. Malekpour, M.R.: A self-stabilizing byzantine-fault-tolerant clock synchronization protocol. Technical report (2009)
21. Misra, A., Kshemkalyani, A.D.: Solvability of byzantine fault-tolerant causal ordering problems. In: Koulali, M.A., Mezini, M. (eds.) NETYS 2022. LNCS, vol. 13464, pp. 87–103. Springer, Cham (2022). https://doi.org/10.1007/978-3-031-17436-0_7
22. Misra, A., Kshemkalyani, A.D.: Byzantine fault-tolerant causal order satisfying strong safety. In: Dolev, S., Schieber, B. (eds.) SSS 2023. LNCS, vol. 14310, pp. 111–125. Springer, Cham (2023). https://doi.org/10.1007/978-3-031-44274-2_10
23. Misra, A., Kshemkalyani, A.D.: Byzantine fault-tolerant causal ordering. In: Proceedings of the 24th International Conference on Distributed Computing and Networking, pp. 100–109 (2023)
24. Misra, A., Kshemkalyani, A.D.: Byzantine-tolerant causal ordering for unicasts, multicasts, and broadcasts. IEEE Trans. Parallel Distrib. Syst. **35**(5), 814–828 (2024). https://doi.org/10.1109/TPDS.2024.3368280
25. Nakamoto, S.: Bitcoin: a peer-to-peer electronic cash system. Decentralized business review (2008)
26. Pease, M.C., Shostak, R.E., Lamport, L.: Reaching agreement in the presence of faults. J. ACM **27**(2), 228–234 (1980)
27. Polge, J., Robert, J., Le Traon, Y.: Permissioned blockchain frameworks in the industry: a comparison. ICT Exp. **7**(2), 229–233 (2021)
28. Saad, M., et al.: Exploring the attack surface of blockchain: a systematic overview. arXiv preprint arXiv:1904.03487 (2019)
29. Shoup, V., Gennaro, R.: Securing threshold cryptosystems against chosen ciphertext attack. J. Cryptol. **15**(2), 75–96 (2002)
30. Torres, C.F., Camino, R., et al.: Frontrunner jones and the raiders of the dark forest: an empirical study of frontrunning on the ethereum blockchain. In: 30th USENIX Security Symposium (USENIX Security 2021), pp. 1343–1359 (2021)
31. Wood, G., et al.: Ethereum: a secure decentralised generalised transaction ledger. Ethereum Project Yellow Paper **151**(2014), 1–32 (2014)
32. Zhang, W., et al.: Combatting front-running in smart contracts: attack mining, benchmark construction and vulnerability detector evaluation. IEEE Trans. Softw. Eng. **49**(6), 3630–3646 (2023)
33. Züst, P., Nadahalli, T., Wattenhofer, Y.W.R.: Analyzing and preventing sandwich attacks in ethereum. ETH Zürich (2021)

Distributed Station Assignment Through Learning

Lu Dong, Miguel A. Mosteiro[✉], and Michelle Wang

Pace University, New York, NY 10036, USA
{ldong,mmosteiro,yw46356p}@pace.edu

Abstract. We study a dynamic assignment problem in a communication network where a set of mobile nodes called clients have to upload data packets to a set of static nodes called stations. Clients are restricted by a maximum delay between packet uploads, and stations by a maximum capacity at any given round of communication. The goal is to assign clients to stations in each round aiming to minimize various energy-related costs. The Station Assignment problem has been well studied from a centralized scheduling perspective. In this work we consider the application of Multi-Agent Reinforcement Learning (MARL) so that each client can self-assign to a station independently using only local information. MARL is challenging because the decisions of clients are affected by the concurrent decisions of other clients. In this work, as a step towards a better understanding of the feasibility of MARL for distributed assignment problems, we study Distributed Station Assignment experimentally applying Independent Proximal Policy Optimization (IPPO) for various scenarios.

Keywords: Station Assignment · Windows Scheduling · Multi-Agent Reinforcement Learning · Independent Proximal Policy Optimization

1 Introduction

In this work we evaluate experimentally the feasibility and performance of applying a Multi-agent Reinforcement Learning (MARL) to solve distributedly the Station Assignment (SA) Problem. In SA, data on mobile devices called clients has to be uploaded periodically to any of the static devices available, which we call stations. Efficient algorithms for SA have applications to wearable health-monitoring systems, participatory sensing [12,15], streaming services, and others.

The need of periodic, but possibly not continuous, data uploads is modeled by a parametric laxity for each client, which bounds the maximum duration a client is not transmitting to some station. The shared nature of the access to stations is modeled by that laxity and a bandwidth requirement of each client, whereas on the side of stations by a maximum capacity for each communication channel. SA is the problem of assigning clients to stations so that every client uploads its data satisfying the laxity and bandwidth constraints.

In this work we consider settings where all clients start participating in the system simultaneously, and continue indefinitely unless they fail or run out of battery. Clients may upload to different stations over time, we call that a reallocation. Due to mobility, it may be more energy efficient to reallocate a client. However, reallocation usually involves handover between stations, and possibly activation of a new channel of communication, incurring a cost that is time related and also signal related [6]. We aim to reduce the cost of reallocations, channel activations, and energy consumption. However, these goals are orthogonal. Thus, we evaluate the trade-offs between those performance metrics.

To the best of our knowledge, this is the first study of the feasibility and performance of de-centralized (i.e. distributed) MARL for SA. In fact, Multi-agent Reinforcement Learning is challenging in Distributed Computing in general. The main reason being the non-stationary environment. That is, clients choosing different policies and taking concurrent actions as the learning progresses. In other words, an action's effects may depend on the actions of the other clients. The approach to policy updating used in this work, known as Independent Proximal Policy Optimization (iPPO) [20], is aimed to cope with these challenges.

Previous Work. The closest previous work is [11], where centralized reallocation algorithms were presented for SA. A similar model, but without reallocations, was studied in [10]. We contrast our experimental results with that work. A particular case of SA, called Windows Scheduling (WS), was also studied [2,3,5,8]. In WS the bandwidth requirement of each client is the same and each channel can only serve one client at a time. A comprehensive overview of related work in WS, Scheduling, Load Balancing, Matching, and others can be found in [11].

Our Contributions. To conduct our study, we specify the application of distributed MARL to the SA problem as a Decentralized Partially Observable Markov Decision Process (Dec-POMDP) as defined in [14], which formalizes our approach. Solving Dec-POMDPs is hard and proven to be NEXP-complete [4] due to non-stationarity. Our approach to policy updating, known as iPPO [20], is aimed to cope with these challenges.

For our experimental evaluation, we consider the special case of Windows Scheduling when clients have all the same bandwidth requirement equal to channel capacity. We also mapped the location of clients to policy learning, given that distance to stations is a fundamental aspect for energy savings. Under such modeling, clients may be assumed to be static since ID's can be assigned (and reassigned) according to location. We also consider that clients have an unbounded source of data to upload. That is, they continue participating in the system for unbounded time, amortizing the learning phase into a long period of data upload. In other words, the time (and possibly initial bad performance) during the learning phase becomes negligible in the limit. So, we compare the performance of our system during the last episode of learning only.

For a variety of system parameters we evaluated the energy and reallocation competitive ratios of our solution (channel usage ratio is irrelevant for bandwidth requirement equal to channel capacity) during the last episode until most clients are deactivated by running out of battery. In comparison with previous experimental work [11], for energy usage ratio ours is the first evaluation to the best of our knowledge, and with respect to reallocations ratio we observe that our solution achieves similar reallocations ratio but with a distributed algorithm that uses only local information, in contrast with the centralized scheduler in [11]. That is, our system computes policies for SA by *distributed learning*, and those policies may be used for future clients at no additional scheduling cost for the system.

Roadmap. Section 2 includes the formal specification of our model, problem, and performance metrics. The formal specification of our approach, including the details of our algorithm, can be found in Sect. 3. The details of our simulation design, and a discussion of the results as well as some open questions can be found in Sects. 4 and 5 respectively.

2 Model and Problem

Model. We consider a communication network composed by a set V_c of n mobile nodes, called **clients**, and a set V_σ of m static nodes called base stations, or simply **stations** for short. Clients have data to upload[1] to stations. Time is slotted in **rounds** $1, 2, 3, \ldots$, and each round is further divided in a **control subround** and a **data subround**. We discretize data according to this time discretization. That is, each data subround is long enough for a client to upload one data **packet** to some station, and each control subround is long enough to exchange some (much shorter) **control messages** among clients and stations, and run some local computations (which are assumed to take negligible time in comparison with the communication). For clarity, we assume that clients do not move within a round, only in between rounds. The communication between clients and stations is limited by some requirements and restrictions as follows.

- Each client $c \in V_c$ has an ID in $[n]$ (to distinguish from stations, the ID may be prefixed with the character 'c', we omit such detail throughout for clarity). A client c may not require to upload a packet in every round, limited to a maximum delay $0 < w_c < |\tau_c|$ in rounds between two consecutive uploads, called **laxity**, and also a **bandwidth** requirement b_c for rounds when c uploads a packet.
- Each station $\sigma \in V_\sigma$ has an ID in $[m]$ (to distinguish from clients, the ID may be prefixed with the character 'σ', we omit such detail throughout for clarity), and multiple communication **channels**, each of these channels has a maximum **capacity** B_σ. We assume that each station σ has enough number of communication channels to serve all clients that upload to σ.[2]

---

[1] The problem of downloading is symmetrical.
[2] Obviously there is a physical limit on the number of channels of any station, but we assume that number to be very large because, if that number were limited, there are inputs for which the problem cannot be solved.

– Clients do not communicate among them.

Under the above definitions, each client $c \in V_c$ must upload a packet at least once within each w_c consecutive rounds. Clients may upload to different stations in different rounds, but in any given round a client may upload to at most one station (i.e., it may not upload in that round). On the other hand, the aggregated bandwidth of clients that upload to each channel of each station $\sigma \in V_\sigma$ in each round is limited to B_σ.

For algorithm specification, we define the **leftover laxity** $w_c(r)$ of client $c \in V_c$ at a given round r as the number of rounds left before the laxity of client c is violated. If a client c uploads data to a station σ in a given round r we say that c is **allocated** to σ for round r. If c uploads to station σ in a given round, and the next upload of c is to some other station $\sigma' \neq \sigma$, we say that c has been **reallocated**. Reallocations of clients to another channel within the same station are possible at no cost, while reallocations among stations incur in some **reallocation cost** ρ, which is also applied for the first allocation. We say that a station channel that has clients allocated is **active**, or **inactive** otherwise. We denote the set of channels of station σ as H_σ, and the set of active channels of station σ in round r as $H_\sigma(r)$.

We denote the **schedule of allocations** of a client c as a temporal sequence τ_c of values from the alphabet $\{0\} \cup V_\sigma \times H_\sigma$, where $\tau_c(r)$ is the rth allocation in the sequence τ_c. A **station assignment** is a set $\tau = \{\tau_1, \tau_2, \ldots, \tau_n\}$ of schedules of allocations, one for each client, that models the uploads from clients to stations. More precisely, for each client $c \in V_c$ and round r, it is $\tau_c(r) = \langle \sigma, h \rangle$ if c is scheduled to upload to channel $h \in H_\sigma$ of station $\sigma \in V_\sigma$ in round r, and $\tau_c(r) = 0$ if c does not upload in round r.

Problem. The **Station Assignment (SA)** problem is to schedule the allocation of clients to channels in stations with the purpose of uploading data under the restrictions of the model defined. Formally,

– Input:
  A set V_σ of tuples $\langle \sigma, B_\sigma \rangle$.
  A set V_c of tuples $\langle c, w_c, b_c \rangle$.
– Output:
  A set of schedules $\tau = \{\tau_c | c \in V_c\}$ such that
  $\forall c \in V_c : \forall r \in \mathbb{N} : \exists r' \in [r, r + w_c) : \tau_c(r') \neq 0$
  $\forall \sigma \in V_\sigma : \forall r \in \mathbb{N} : \forall h \in H_\sigma(r) : \sum_{c \in V_c : \tau_c(r) = \langle \sigma, h \rangle} b_c \leq B_\sigma$.

Algorithms. We study **distributed learning reallocation algorithms** for SA, structured in rounds as follows.

– In each *control subround*: each client exchanges information with all stations within range. Specifically, any information needed so that each client can decide which station to upload (if any) in the data subround that follows. Then, still during the control subround, each client broadcasts the ID of the chosen station. Knowing which clients will upload, each station activates/deactivates channels and internally reallocate clients among channels as needed.

- During each *data subround*: each client uploads a data packet to its chosen station (if any).

Performance Metric.

In previous works on SA [7,11] the model included only one station[3]. Such model was simple and expressive enough to study SA with the objective of minimizing the number of active channels and the cost of reallocating clients, but it neglects the impact on energy consumption of the spatial positions of clients when the system has many stations (which is the case in real applications). In this work, we extend those metrics to minimize also energy consumption by the clients. Thus, the global objective is to minimize the number of channels used by all stations, the reallocations of clients, and the energy consumption of all clients due to communication, minimizing implicitly the energy consumption of the system as a whole.

Given that the choice of the clients is what station to connect but not what channel inside the station, we assume that channel assignment within each station is done optimally, so that we can identify the impact of clients' choice of stations on system performance regardless of channel assignments. (For implementation, the local channel assignment subproblem can be solved by each station as in [7,11], where client arrivals and departures model the reallocation of clients among stations).

Let the energy consumed by a client c while uploading to a station σ in round r be $\epsilon d(c,\sigma,r)^\delta$, where ϵ is a scaling factor[4], $d(c,\sigma,r)$ is the Euclidean distance between the location of c and σ in round r (we drop the specification of round when clear from context), and δ is the physical medium attenuation factor. We also define $\sigma(c,r)$ to be the last station that c uploaded on or before round r, initially set to $\sigma(c,r) = 0$. Let the **weight** of a client c in round r be $1/w_c(r)$. The following notation for each round r will be used.

- For the execution of some algorithm ALG:
    - $R(ALG,r)$: set of clients being reallocated in all stations,
    - $D(ALG,r)$: set of clients departed since the last reallocation,
    - $E(ALG,r)$: set of clients uploading to all stations,
    - $\mathcal{H}(ALG,r)$: number of active channels in all stations,
    - $\mathcal{R}(ALG,r)$: weighted cost of reallocations, that is

$$\mathcal{R}(ALG,r) = \sum_{c \in R(ALG,r)} \rho/w_c(r),$$

---

[3] Indeed it had unbounded stations, each with only one channel. So it is equivalent to our model with only one station, exchanging names station-channel.

[4] The ϵ factor comprises various radio communication factors involved in physical transmission as well as the minimum signal strength required by stations to properly receive the transmissions. For clarity we assume all these factors to be the same for all clients-stations. A richer model with different ϵ's is a simple extension of our analysis.

- $\mathcal{D}(ALG, r)$: aggregated weight of clients departed since the last reallocation, that is
$$\sum_{c \in \mathcal{D}(ALG, r)} 1/w_c,$$
- $\mathcal{E}(ALG, r)$: energy consumption of all clients uploading, that is
$$\mathcal{E}(ALG, r) = \sum_{c \in \mathcal{E}(ALG, r)} \epsilon d(c, \sigma(c, r), r)^\delta.$$

- For an optimal algorithm OPT that minimizes each resource:
  - $\mathcal{H}(OPT, r)$: minimum number of active channels needed to allocate clients, which can be bounded from below by $\lceil \sum_{c \in V_c} B/(b_c w_c(r)) \rceil$ if all stations have the same capacity B,
  - $\mathcal{E}(OPT, r)$: minimum energy consumption needed to allocate clients, which can be bounded from below by $\sum_{c \in V_c} \epsilon \min_{\sigma \in V_\sigma} d(c, \sigma, r)^\delta / w_c(r)$.

Minimizing reallocation cost, number of active channels, and energy consumption simultaneously may not be possible. Indeed, the minimum reallocation cost is achieved by not reallocating any clients, but that could be costly in number of active channels and/or energy consumption. The same can be said for the other two objectives. Hence, we evaluate performance in these dimensions separately with the following metric. We say that an SA algorithm ALG achieves an (α, β, γ)-***performance*** if the following holds for any input.

$$\max_{r: E(ALG, r) \neq \emptyset} \frac{\mathcal{H}(ALG, r)}{\mathcal{H}(OPT, r)} \leq \alpha$$

$$\max_{r: R(ALG, r) \neq \emptyset} \frac{\mathcal{R}(ALG, r)}{\mathcal{D}(ALG, r)} \leq \beta$$

$$\max_{r: E(ALG, r) \neq \emptyset} \frac{\mathcal{E}(ALG, r)}{\mathcal{E}(OPT, r)} \leq \gamma.$$

These ratios are defined only for rounds when ALG reallocates or uploads data, since they would not be well-defined for other rounds. We put our metrics in perspective of similar metrics in previous work in the discussion section.

3 SA Algorithm

Our SA protocol follows the algorithmic framework specified in Sect. 2. Namely, within each round, an initial control subround where clients exchange information with stations to decide what station to upload, if any, followed by a broadcast of the ID of the chosen station. Then, clients choosing to upload to some station transmit their data packet in the data subround that follows. In this work, the choice of station to upload is done using reinforcement learning distributedly by each client. These two tasks: learning and data uploading, could be executed independently and sequentially to attain lower cost. However, the learning algorithm also involves rounds of communication, and due to laxity constraints it is not possible to hold the uploads during learning. Thus, we intertwine both tasks in one algorithm. For fair comparison with previous work, we evaluate performance computing the competitive ratios defined in previous section over rounds *after* learning while clients do not move[5].

We specify our Decentralized Multi-Agent Reinforcement Learning (Dec-MARL) approach in Sect. 3.1, our Dec-MARL implementation using Proximal Policy Optimization (PPO) to cope with Dec-MARL challenges in Sect. 3.2, and the resulting SA protocol in Sect. 3.3.

3.1 Decentralized Partially Observable Markov Decision Process

Our approach to the application of reinforcement learning to decision making in the SA problem can be formalized as a **Decentralized Partially Observable Markov Decision Process** (Dec-POMDP) as defined in [14] with the following characteristics.

– The model satisfies the Markov property, i.e. the future state of the network depends on the current state of the network and the actions clients take, instead of the whole history.
– All clients have the same goal: to upload their data within laxity and bandwidth constraints, while conserving energy and minimizing the number of active channels and reallocations cost.
– Each client has only partial/local information of the whole network due to limited range of transmissions.
– Clients do not know each other's actions, and act independently and simultaneously.

Customarily, we denote our Dec-POMDPs model as a tuple $\langle V_c, S, A, P_S, O, P_O, R, W \rangle$, where

– V_c is the set of n agents, i.e. clients.
– S denotes the state space.
– A is the joint action space.
– P_S is the state transition probability function.
– O is the joint observation space.
– P_O is the observation transition probability function.
– R is the reward function.
– W is the finite horizon, defined by the number of rounds while the movement of clients is not significant with respect to the speed of the computation.

---

[5] Clients do move in practice, but the speed of such movement is much slower than the speed of computation and communication. Hence, we can analyze the system as having periods during which clients do not move.

The joint action space $A = \times_{c \in V_c} A_c$ is defined as the Cartesian product of clients' action space, where A_c is the action space of client c. We define $a = \langle a_1, ..., a_n \rangle$ as the joint action in a given round. Similarly, the joint observation space $O = \times_{c \in V_c} O_c$ is the Cartesian product of clients' observation space, where O_c is the observation space of client c. We define $o = \langle o_1, ..., o_n \rangle$ as the joint observation in a given round. The environment starts in an initial state denoted as $s^0 \in S$, when clients obtain an initial joint observation denoted as $o^0 \in O$. A client c chooses an action a_c according to its own stochastic policy π_c that maps from observations to actions, where the action is the decision of uploading to some station, if any. We also define the joint policy in a given round as $\pi = \langle \pi_1, ..., \pi_n \rangle$. For a given round r, we denote the joint policy, joint action, the joint observation, and the state before action, as π^r, a^r, o_r, and s^r respectively. In any given round r, to reach or determine the next state s^{r+1}, we use the state transition probability function P_S to specify $P_S(s^{r+1}|s^r, a^r)$, the state transition probability. Agents then have access to a new joint observation for round $r+1$, that is o^{r+1}, where the observation probability $P_O(o^{r+1}|a^r, s^r)$ is defined by the observation transition probability function P_O. Each client c only observes its own component o_c^{r+1}.

The reward function R gives the reward for a given client of moving to a new state once an action is taken based on the current state. The reward of a client is influenced by multiple factors. Namely, the activation (or not) of a channel, the reallocation (or not) to another station, the energy consumed, and the leftover laxity. The following formulation of each of those factors corresponds to any given client $c \in V_c$ *after the action* taken in any round $r \geq 1$.

Recall that, for a constant $\delta \geq 2$ that depends on the physical medium and scaling factor $\epsilon > 0$, the energy consumption incurred by client c while uploading to station σ at distance $d(c, \sigma, r)$ in round r is

$$\epsilon d(c, \sigma, r)^\delta.$$

Recall also that $\rho/w_c(r)$ is the weighted reallocation cost of client c in round r, and that $\sigma(c, r)$ is the last station that c uploaded on or before round r, or 0 if it did not upload yet. The reallocation cost must be charged to a client c uploading to a station σ if the last station receiving an upload from c is different from σ. (The first allocation is also charged since the re-arrangement of clients/channels, if any, needed to accommodate a new client is the same as in a reallocation.) That is,

$$\left\lceil \frac{|\sigma - \sigma(c, r-1)|}{m} \right\rceil \frac{\rho}{w_c(r)}.$$

Let $X(\sigma, r)$ be an indicator variable that takes value 1 if a channel needs to be activated by σ in round r, or 0 otherwise, and let η be the fee for activating a channel. That is, the cost due to channel activation for a client c is

$$X(\sigma(c, r), r)\eta$$

For a scaling factor $\xi > 0$, we define the cost of not uploading to any station in round r as
$$\begin{cases} \xi w_c(r), & \text{if } w_c(r) > w_c/\kappa, \text{for some } \kappa \geq 2, \\ \xi/w_c(r), & \text{otherwise.} \end{cases}$$

The intended effect of this cost function is to stop clients from transmitting too early within their laxity period. Notice that the cost of not uploading is ∞ if $w_c(r) = 0$.

Then, combining all the above factors, if c uploads in round r, the reward is

$$R(c,r) = \Gamma - \left[\frac{|\sigma(c,r) - \sigma(c,r-1)|}{m}\right] \frac{\rho}{w_c(r)} + X(\sigma(c,r), r)\eta + \epsilon d(c, \sigma(c,r), r)^\delta, \tag{1}$$

whereas if c does not upload in round r it is

$$R(c,r) = \Gamma - \begin{cases} \xi w_c(r), & \text{if } w_c(r) > w_c/\kappa, \\ \xi/w_c(r), & \text{otherwise.} \end{cases} \tag{2}$$

where Γ is a positive constant larger than any cost a client may incur introduced for the purpose of implementing our protocol using standard libraries that maximize rewards. (Alternatively, we could minimize costs.) Then, the total reward of client $c \in V_c$ up to the finite horizon is $\sum_{r=1}^{W} R(c,r)$. Thus, the learning goal is to find a stochastic policy π_c that maximizes the reward up to the finite horizon W. Then, we consider time divided in phases of W rounds, and the learning mechanism is applied in each phase.

Finding optimal policies for Dec-POMDPs is hard and proven to be NEXP-complete [4]. The main reason why traditional or popular reinforcement learning algorithms fail at solving Dec-MARL effectively is the non-stationary environment. Such non-stationarity is caused by clients' different policies and concurrent actions as the learning progresses. In other words, an action's effects may depend on the actions of the other clients. Our approach to policy updating, specified in the following section, is aimed to cope with these challenges.

3.2 Proximal Policy Optimization

A number of well-known reinforcement learning methods (e.g. Monte-Carlo methods [13] and Temporal-Difference Learning [19]) are aimed to learn a *state-value function* $V_\pi(s)$ or *action-value function* $Q_\pi(s,a)$ that quantify the expected amount of future rewards we could obtain from state $s \in S$ by acting some policy π. However, given that in our application states depend on clients locations, our state space is continuous (hence, infinite) and therefore computing value functions is computationally too expensive. Even if we discretize locations the number of actions and states may be very large. Therefore, we consider instead policy gradient methods, where the policy is learned directly using only an *estimate* rather than the exact value functions. The reward function depends on this policy, and then various algorithms can be applied to optimize it for the highest reward.

In this work, to optimize the policy we specifically use the algorithm known as **Proximal Policy Optimization** (PPO) which has been presented and shown to outperform other policy gradient methods in [18]. The goal of such algorithm is to improve training stability avoiding updates that change the policy too much at one step. Specifically, for any round r, the goal is to maximize the following.

$$\pi_\theta = \arg\max_{\pi_\theta} \hat{\mathbf{E}}_r \left[L(\pi_\theta, \pi_{\theta_{old}}, a_r, s_r) \right],$$

$$L(\pi_\theta, \pi_{\theta_{old}}, a_r, s_r) = \begin{cases} \min\left(\frac{\pi_\theta(a_r|s_r)}{\pi_{\theta_{old}}(a_r|s_r)}, 1+\epsilon\right) \hat{A}_r, & \text{if } \hat{A}_r \geq 0, \\ \max\left(\frac{\pi_\theta(a_r|s_r)}{\pi_{\theta_{old}}(a_r|s_r)}, 1-\epsilon\right) \hat{A}_r, & \text{otherwise}, \end{cases}$$

where $\hat{\mathbf{E}}_r[\cdot]$ is the empirical average over a finite batch of samples starting from round r, π_θ is a stochastic policy, and $\hat{A}_r$ is an estimator of the advantage function at round r. The advantage function is $A_r(s,a) = Q_r(s,a) - V_r(s)$, where $Q_r(s,a)$ and $V_r(s)$ are the action- and state-value functions respectively.

Given that in *distributed* SA clients execute the protocol independently using only local information, we use the **Independent PPO** (IPPO) method presented in [20]. In IPPO, clients update their policies independently of other clients, estimating a variant of the advantage function based on local observations. That is, for each client $c \in V_c$ the policy update is the following.

$$\pi_\theta = \arg\max_{\pi_\theta} \hat{\mathbf{E}}_r \left[L(\pi_\theta, \pi_{\theta_{old}}, a_r(c), s_r(c)) \right], \tag{3}$$

$$L(\pi_\theta, \pi_{\theta_{old}}, a_r(c), s_r(c)) = \begin{cases} \min\left(\frac{\pi_\theta(a_r(c)|s_r(c))}{\pi_{\theta_{old}}(a_r(c)|s_r(c))}, 1+\epsilon\right) \hat{A}_r(c), & \text{if } \hat{A}_r(c) \geq 0, \\ \max\left(\frac{\pi_\theta(a_r(c)|s_r(c))}{\pi_{\theta_{old}}(a_r(c)|s_r(c))}, 1-\epsilon\right) \hat{A}_r(c), & \text{otherwise.} \end{cases}$$

The advantage function estimates are computed as in Eq. 4 in [20], using each client rewards, and estimates of the value functions as in [17]. The maximization in Eq. 3 on the other hand is computed by stochastic gradient ascent [16].

3.3 Algorithm

We present our distributed SA protocol that intertwines the learning and data upload tasks in Algorithm 1.

4 Simulations

As a first approach to the experimental evaluation of MARL in the SA problem, we simplified the model assuming that all clients have the same bandwidth requirement b and all channels have the same bandwidth capacity B, and that $b = B$. That is, each client uploading to a station uses one whole channel. In this way we focus on the problem of allocating laxities, which is orthogonal to allocating bandwidths.

Algorithm 1: SA protocol for each client $c \in V_c$. $Coord_\sigma$ are the location coordinates of station σ. $X(\sigma)$ is the value of the indicator variable $X(\sigma(c,r),r)$. w_c, b_c are as defined in the model section. T is the parametric number of iterations between policy updates (a.k.a. minibatch size).

```
 1  σ_prev ← 0
 2  w_left ← w_c
 3  π ← uniform distribution over integers in [0, m]
 4  i ← 1                                    // Minibatch iteration counter
 5  for r = 1, 2, . . . do
        // control subround
 6      x ← choose a number in [0, m] at random with probability distribution π
 7      if x ≠ 0 then
 8          broadcast ⟨c, w_c, b_c, x⟩
 9          receive ⟨σ, Coord_σ, X(c, σ)⟩ from station σ = x
10      R_i ← compute reward using Coord_σ, X(σ), σ_prev, w_left and x
        // Equations 1 and 2
11      if i = T then
12          compute advantage estimators Â_1, . . . , Â_T using R_1, . . . , R_T
            // Equation 4 in [20]
13          update π                                             // Equation 3
14          i ← 0
15      i ← i + 1
        // data subround
16      if x ≠ 0 then
17          upload to station x
18          σ_prev ← x
19          w_left ← w_c
20      else
21          w_left ← w_left − 1
```

We also simplified the context assuming that clients are static. Such assumption does not weaken the model because performance depends heavily on position, and client ID's can be assigned to clients at the beginning of the interaction relating them to positions. In other words, a client changing position can be simply assigned a new ID.

In our simulations all clients are activated simultaneously in batch, and leave the system over time as they run out of battery. Thus, we describe our environment with state space S as a tuple $\langle BS_{dist}, w, e \rangle$, where BS_{dist} is a list of distances of base stations to clients that can be obtained from GPS and beacon transmissions from stations. $w = \{w_1, ..., w_n\}$ is a finite set of clients' laxities. $e = \{e_1, ..., e_n\}$ denotes the remaining battery levels of all clients. A client only have access to its local observations, i,.e. $\langle BS_{dist,i}, w_i, e_i \rangle$. The joint action space A is such that, for each client i, the action space is the subset of stations reachable from i. The reward function R is as defined in Sect. 3.1.

To build our simulation, we used an open-source unified scalable framework called Ray [1]. The custom multi-agent environment was set up via Gymnasium, a maintained fork of OpenAI's Gym library [9]. In order to train clients' policies distributedly, each client learns its own PPO policy independently which is mapped to its ID. In addition, Ray Tune, a hyper-parameter optimizer, was used for hyper-parameter tuning and training.

For our simulations, we chose $n = 100$ clients and $n = 10$ base stations, whereas the constants in the reward function were set to $\epsilon = 1$, $\delta = 2$, $\rho = 1$, $\eta = 1$, and $\xi = 1$. Other parameter combinations were also tested, obtaining similar results. The network was initialized with all clients located at randomly chosen distances from stations, ranging from 10 to 100. The laxities are set to 2^i, where i is chosen randomly and $0 \leq i \leq 10$. Clients start with the same initial battery levels. All clients take actions simultaneously and rewards are given after. A client leaves the system, or *deactivates*, if its remaining battery level is zero, or not enough for one more transmission. After all clients deactivate, the system resets and a new learning episode begins.

We used the following PPO related parameters for training. The training iteration is 20. The training batch size is 50,000. The stochastic gradient descent (SGD) mini-batch size is 2048 and epoch sets to 30. The learning rate is 0.0001. Gamma and lambda are set to 0.99 and 0.95 respectively.

We evaluate performance of our approach by the competitive ratios defined in Sect. 2 over the last learning episode only. That is, we consider the learning period as pre-processing, whose running time becomes negligible in the limit for long enough usage of the network. The results of our simulations can be seen in Figs. 1, 2, 3 and 4. A discussion of those results follow.

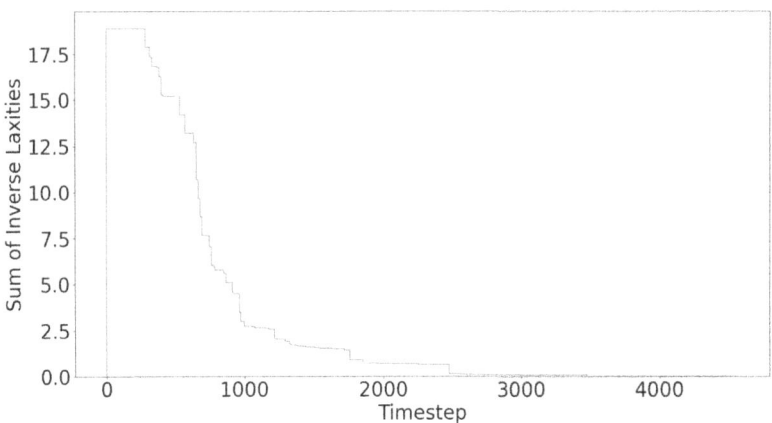

Fig. 1. Active clients aggregated weight per round.

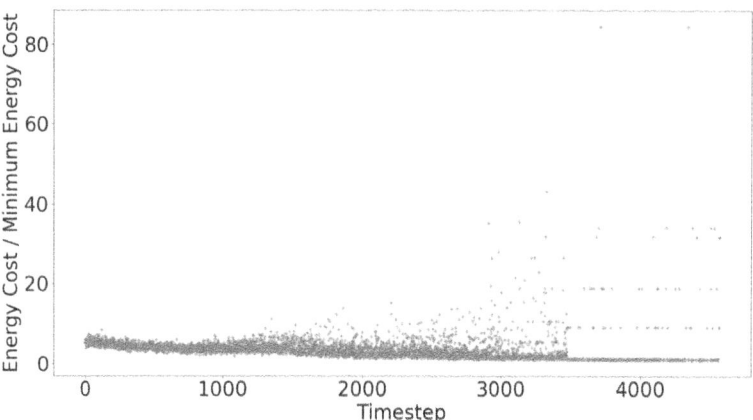

Fig. 2. Energy ratio per round.

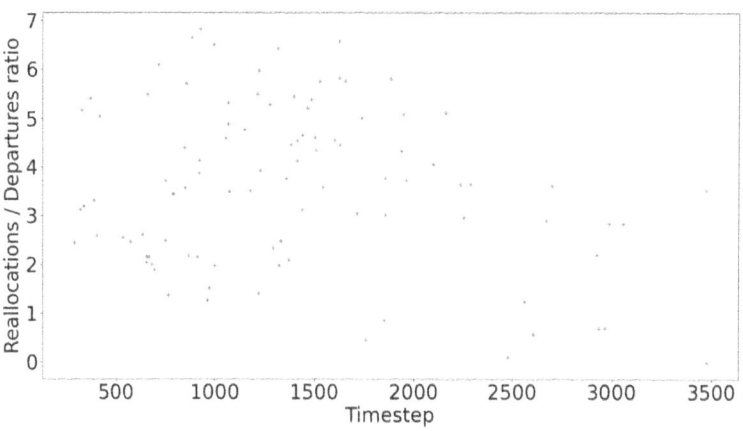

Fig. 3. Reallocation ratio per round.

5 Discussion and Open Problems

Figure 1 shows the aggregated weight of active clients per round in the last episode of our simulations. We observe that by round 2500 most clients have deactivated after running out of battery. Thus we focus on the evolution of competitive ratios up to that round. We can see in Fig. 2 that up to round 2500 the energy ratio in most rounds is well below 10, and in Fig. 3 that the reallocation ratio is well below 7. Figure 4 shows the impact of previous episodes of learning, including the same metrics during episodes 3, 100, and the last episode 147. These ratios show improvement as the learning continued.

For comparison with previous work, we can see in [11] (Figure 9, batched arrivals, uniform laxity distributions) that the reallocation ratio in that work was also in most rounds below 7, but frequently above that bound 7. Energy is

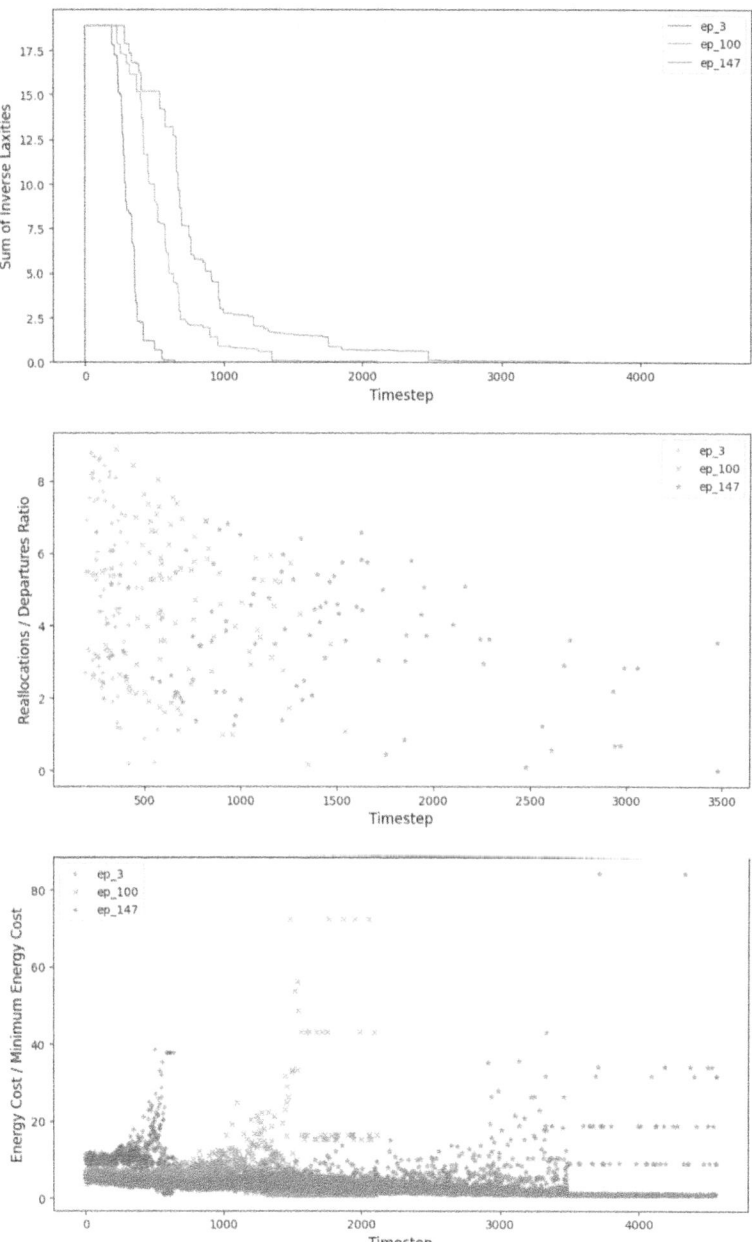

Fig. 4. Comparison of three learning episodes.

not evaluated in that work. We conclude that we achieve similar performance with a distributed algorithm that uses only local information, in contrast with the centralized scheduler in [11]. On the other hand our algorithm requires a learning phase as preprocessing, but anyway as mentioned earlier preprocessing time becomes negligible in the limit for long enough usage of the network.

The latter observations, combined with the stations providing new ID's according to client location, and informing new clients upon arrival of the policies learned previously by other clients, show the potential of our approach to SA when clients have all the same bandwidth requirement: our system computes policies for SA by distributed learning, to be used for future clients at no additional scheduling cost.

Open problems left for future work include studying the impact of different bandwidth requirements, making relevant the consideration of channel usage ratio. To encourage more cooperative actions, a centralized critic can be introduced to help improving global performance. Due to the graph nature of the network, incorporating Graph Neural Network (GNN) is also worth exploring. A theoretical analysis of convergence of MARL in the SA problem is also a fundamental open question.

Acknowledgments. This study was partially funded by Pace Univ. SRC and Kenan Award.

Disclosure of Interests. The authors have no competing interests to declare that are relevant to the content of this article.

References

1. Anyscale Inc.: Ray (2024). https://www.ray.io
2. Bar-Noy, A., Ladner, R.E.: Windows scheduling problems for broadcast systems. SIAM J. Comput. **32**(4), 1091–1113 (2003)
3. Bar-Noy, A., Ladner, R.E., Tamir, T.: Windows scheduling as a restricted version of bin packing. ACM Trans. Algorithms **3**(3), 28 (2007)
4. Bernstein, D.S., Givan, R., Immerman, N., Zilberstein, S.: The complexity of decentralized control of Markov decision processes. Math. Oper. Res. **27**(4), 819–840 (2002)
5. Chan, W.-T., Wong, P.W.H.: On-line windows scheduling of temporary items. In: Fleischer, R., Trippen, G. (eds.) ISAAC 2004. LNCS, vol. 3341, pp. 259–270. Springer, Heidelberg (2004). https://doi.org/10.1007/978-3-540-30551-4_24
6. Cominardi, L., Giust, F., Bernardos, C.J., de la Oliva, A.: Distributed mobility management solutions for next mobile network architectures. Comput. Netw. **121**, 124–136 (2017)
7. Farach-Colton, M., Leal, K., Mosteiro, M.A., Caro, C.T.: Dynamic windows scheduling with reallocation. ACM J. Exp. Algorithmics **26**, 1.11:1–1.11:19 (2021). https://doi.org/10.1145/3462208
8. Farach-Colton, M., Leal, K., Mosteiro, M.A., Thraves, C.: Dynamic windows scheduling with reallocation. In: Gudmundsson, J., Katajainen, J. (eds.) SEA 2014. LNCS, vol. 8504, pp. 99–110. Springer, Cham (2014). https://doi.org/10.1007/978-3-319-07959-2_9
9. Farama Foundation: Gymnasium (2024). https://gymnasium.farama.org

10. Fernández Anta, A., Kowalski, D.R., Mosteiro, M.A., Wong, P.W.H.: Station assignment with applications to sensing. In: Flocchini, P., Gao, J., Kranakis, E., Meyer auf der Heide, F. (eds.) ALGOSENSORS 2013. LNCS, vol. 8243, pp. 155–169. Springer, Heidelberg (2014). https://doi.org/10.1007/978-3-642-45346-5_12
11. Halper, A., Mosteiro, M.A., Rossikova, Y., Wong, P.W.H.: Station assignment with reallocation. Algorithmica **81**(3), 1096–1125 (2019). https://doi.org/10.1007/s00453-018-0459-9
12. Khan, W.Z., Xiang, Y., Aalsalem, M.Y., Arshad, Q.: Mobile phone sensing systems: a survey. IEEE Commun. Surv. Tutor. **15**(1), 402–427 (2013)
13. Metropolis, N., Ulam, S.: The Monte Carlo method. J. Am. Stat. Assoc. **44**(247), 335–341 (1949)
14. Oliehoek, F.A., Amato, C.: A Concise Introduction to Decentralized POMDPs, vol. 1. Springer, Cham (2016). https://doi.org/10.1007/978-3-319-28929-8
15. Restuccia, F., Das, S.K., Payton, J.: Incentive mechanisms for participatory sensing: survey and research challenges. TOSN **12**(2), 13:1–13:40 (2016)
16. Ruder, S.: An overview of gradient descent optimization algorithms. arXiv preprint arXiv:1609.04747 (2016)
17. Schulman, J., Moritz, P., Levine, S., Jordan, M., Abbeel, P.: High-dimensional continuous control using generalized advantage estimation. arXiv preprint arXiv:1506.02438 (2015)
18. Schulman, J., Wolski, F., Dhariwal, P., Radford, A., Klimov, O.: Proximal policy optimization algorithms. arXiv preprint arXiv:1707.06347 (2017)
19. Sutton, R.S.: Learning to predict by the methods of temporal differences. Mach. Learn. **3**, 9–44 (1988)
20. de Witt, C.S., et al.: Is independent learning all you need in the starcraft multi-agent challenge? arXiv preprint arXiv:2011.09533 (2020)

Short Paper: An Efficient Framework for Supporting Nested Transaction in STMs

Nischay Ranjan[✉], Rohit Kapoor, and Sathya Peri

Indian Institute of Technology, Hyderabad, Sangareddy, India
{cs21resch11012,cs21mtech12011,sathya_p}@iith.ac.in

Abstract. Software Transactional Memory (STM) offers a promising avenue for simplifying the intricacies associated with concurrent programming. However, for an STM system to be truly effective, it must accommodate nesting, which will achieve composability and mitigate the extended vulnerability period associated with prolonged transactions. So far, a few protocols have been proposed for the nested STM system that supports nonlinear closed nesting. Either they do not provide any experimental evaluation of their protocol or provide concrete arguments for satisfying opacity, i.e., correctness criteria for the STM system. This paper introduces NestedBTO, an STM protocol tailored for closed nested transactions. Our protocol facilitates the parallel execution of child transactions and is based on timestamp ordering for transactions. Through extensive experimental evaluations, we observe a significant performance improvement compared to flat nesting and serial scheduling in microbenchmark scenarios involving a counter and hashtable. These findings underscore the efficacy of our implementation in optimizing transactional operations within the STM framework.

Keywords: Software Transactional Memory (STM) · Nested Transactions · Conflict Preserving Closed Nested Opacity · Timestamp Ordering

1 Introduction

Whenever a transaction invokes another transaction as part of its execution, it is called a nesting of transactions [10]. A **Nested transaction** is an extension of the basic transaction structure to a multilevel structure, a set of subtransactions that can recursively invoke other subtransactions, thus forming a transactional tree. The underlying concept of nesting encompasses several forms, including closed, open, and flat nesting [15]. Within the framework of closed nesting, the termination of a child transaction, marked by an abort, does not influence the outcome of its parent transaction. Nevertheless, it is very important to note that any successful updates initiated by the child transaction solely gain visibility to other transactions after the successful commit of the parent transaction.

The desire to achieve Composability motivates the incorporation of transaction nesting in an STM system. **Composability**, the ability to assemble independent entities into a larger and more intricate structure while retaining some essential properties present in the independent entities, forms the basis of modular programming. In the context of transactions, this translates into the ability to combine two or more subtransactions into a more comprehensive transaction.

Designing an STM (Software Transactional Memory) protocol that facilitates the nesting of transactions is a non-trivial task. The process involves tussling with inherent complexities related to contention management across various levels of nesting, as well as guaranteeing the sequential execution of nested transactions at different hierarchical levels [7,9,12,16]. In the execution of concurrent transactions within transactional software memory systems, **Opacity** [8] has stood as a fundamental correctness criterion. The challenge of ensuring opacity becomes particularly sophisticated within the context of nested transactions, where an aborted parent transaction may have committed children and vice versa.

Over the years, numerous implementations of STMs, encompassing both linear [6,11,14,18] and non-linear structures [1–3,13,19], have emerged to accommodate the complexities of nested transactions. Although some claim to adhere to opacity, issues persist, as their proofs either exhibit shortcomings or need more concrete substantiation.

Peri et al. [17] made a significant contribution by expanding the concept of opacity to encompass closed nested transactions. In alignment with this progress, our research aims to introduce a novel parallel closed-nested STM system that unequivocally guarantees opacity.

Through this paper, we introduce NestedBTO, an STM protocol designed specifically for closed nested transactions. Our protocol enables parallel execution of child transactions and is underpinned by timestamp ordering [4] for transactions.

2 System Models and Preliminaries

Transactional Semantics

A transaction, in the context of code execution, encompasses a set of operations that can include both read and write operations on t-objects. Additionally, a transaction can invoke new subtransactions during its execution, and these subtransactions can recursively invoke additional transactions. This dynamic execution pattern can be visually represented as a tree known as a *transaction tree*, where each node corresponds to a transaction or an operation, and the operations of a transaction are treated as its children. The root transaction t_0 assumes the highest hierarchical level, i.e., 0. All subsequent transactions are the descendants of t_0. Operating on a global level, the t_0 manages the globally shared transactional objects. Transactions with t_0 as their parent are classified as top-level transactions. For the sake of reference, any transaction is denoted as t_x, with a transaction having k children referred to as $t_{x1}, t_{x2}, ..t_{xk}$. The transaction's simple memory operations are called $r_x(y)$ and $w_x(y)$ if they read and write on t-obj y. Each transaction is equipped with local buffers Fig. 1, namely *read_list* and *write_list*. Additionally, it is assumed that any transaction initially executes a simple memory operation, followed by subtransaction and terminal operations. A transaction, denoted as t_p, only invokes terminal operations when all its subtransactions (children) have concluded their execution. Upon successful execution and commitment, a subtransaction's *write_list* merges with its parent's. In contrast, in the case of abortion, the proposed updates of t_p are discarded.

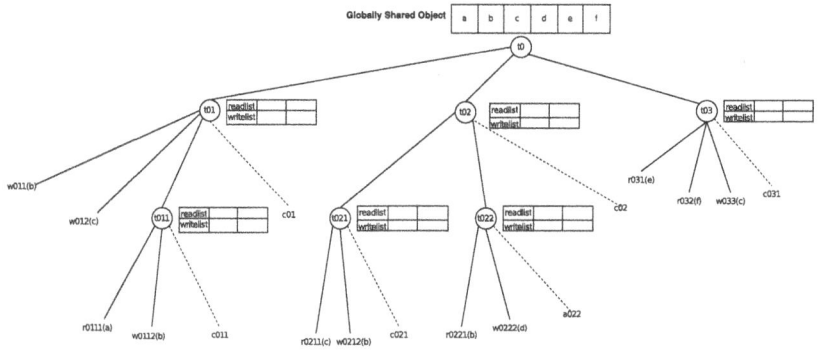

Fig. 1. Transaction flow with nesting

Computation Model

We have developed a system that allows n processes (threads), $p_1, p_2, ...p_n$, that access the collection of *t-obj* using atomic *transactions*. The processes have access to the five operations which are invoked transactionally: the *begin()* operation invokes a transaction, the *read(x)* operation returns the value v read in x, either from the transaction or one of its ancestors, the *write(x,v)* operation updates the value of *t-obj* x (local to the transaction) by v, the *assignthread(t_i)* operation invokes a *subtransaction* operation whose parent is transaction t_i, the *tryC()* operation tries to commit the transaction, updates its parent's buffer and return *commit* (in short, $\mathcal{C}$) or *abort* (in short, $\mathcal{A}$) and *tryA()* operation which aborts the transaction and returns $\mathcal{A}$.

Correctness of the Closed Nested Transactions: The **Closed Nested Opacity (CNO)** definition [17] extends, opacity to closed nested transactions. *CNO* requires a serial schedule to match the operations' sequence, maintain the partial order between transactions, and ensure lastWrite equivalence for read operations. Unlike traditional opacity, *CNO* addresses the complexities of nested transactions by providing consistent reads across all transactions, including subtransactions of aborted ones. This nuanced definition captures the intricacies of nested transactions, which are crucial for maintaining consistency in transactional systems.

3 Overview of the Algorithm

Our algorithm employs a systematic approach for assigning unique identifiers (a string), which also function as timestamps, to transactions. For instance, if a transaction holds the identifier i, it will also be its timestamp. Intuitively, the timestamp tells about the "time" the transaction began. Adding numerical suffixes to the identifiers of parent transactions results in the generation of string identifiers for their child transactions. The timestamp of the invoking transaction accompanies every read and write operation within the system. Each transaction is associated with count, term_count, and status variable. The count variable serves as an indicator of the number of children associated with a given transaction. The term_count variable stores the count of child transactions that have terminated either successfully committed or aborted. The status variable provides information about the current state of the transaction. Furthermore, each transactional object (t-obj) is coupled with two variables: $max\text{-}r$ and $max\text{-}w$. These variables store the timestamp of the most recent transaction that successfully executed a read and write operation on the respective transactional object.

Now, we will discuss the core concepts underlying the read, write, and tryC operations performed by a transaction T_i. These principles draw inspiration from the timestamp algorithms crafted by Bernstein and Goodman for databases [5].

1. **read rule:** Upon invocation of the $read_i(x)$ operation by transaction T_i, the value v retrieved is sourced either from T_i's local buffer or its ancestor transactions' local buffers. Should the $t\text{-}obj(x)$ be obtained from an ancestor's $write\_list$, T_i validates whether x has been subsequently added to its local $write\_list$ by a later transaction, denoted as T_j. If affirmed, a recursive abort function is called upon T_i, resulting in the abortion of T_i and all its descendants' transactions. Conversely, if validation fails, the maximum read timestamp $max\text{-}r$ of x present in the ancestor's local $write\_list$ is updated with T_i. If x is read from the ancestor's $read\_list$, the $max\text{-}r(x)$ in $read\_list$ is simply updated with T_i.
2. **write rule:** Transaction T_i writes data into its local buffer, precisely to its $write\_list$.
3. **commit rule:** Transaction T_i, upon invoking the tryC operation, adheres to the following procedure: Firstly, it assesses whether all its child transactions, if any, have terminated. If any child transactions remain active, T_i enters a wait state until their termination. Subsequently, for each $t\text{-}obj(x)$ within T_i's write-list, T_i evaluates whether any transaction T_k, distinct from T_i's siblings yet existing within the same transaction tree, rooted at the parent of T_i, has read from this parent transaction and committed prior to T_i (i.e., i < k). If such a transaction T_k is identified, T_i is obligated to abort. Conversely, T_i can commit if no such conflicting transaction T_k is found. Furthermore, if a

transaction T_k has written $t\text{-}obj(x)$ within the parent of T_i, and T_k and T_i are siblings with i < k, T_i must also then abort.

4 Performance Evaluation

In our performance evaluation, we analyzed our algorithm's efficiency via experiments in C++, comparing it with sequential and flat nesting approaches. Using counter and hash-table benchmarks on an AMD EPYC 7452 platform with 64 physical cores, 128 logical cores, and 256 GB RAM, we assessed performance across varying numbers of top-level transactions (#transaction). Figures 2 and 5 display our algorithm's superior average transaction commit time compared to sequential and flat nesting. Figures 3 and 6 show performance metrics with varying thread pool sizes, highlighting closed nesting's superiority as thread count increases. Figures 4 and 7 explore nesting tree width by varying subtransaction operations per transaction.

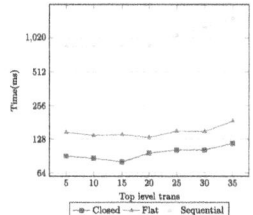
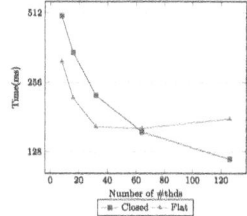
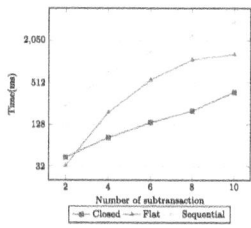

Fig. 2. #var = 1000, #thds = 126   **Fig. 3.** #var = 1000, #transactions = 20   **Fig. 4.** #transactions = 10, #thds = 126

Performance on the Counter

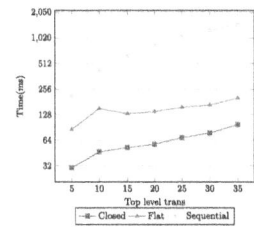
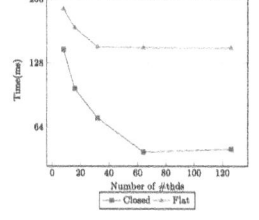
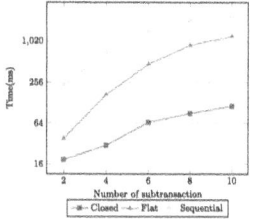

Fig. 5. #var = 1000, #thds = 126   **Fig. 6.** #var = 1000, #transactions = 20   **Fig. 7.** #transactions = 10, #thds = 126

Performance on the Hashtable

5 Conclusion and Future Work

In conclusion, this paper introduces the NestedBTO algorithm, a novel STM protocol designed for closed nested transactions. Through extensive experimental evaluations, we have demonstrated significant performance improvements compared to flat and serial nesting approaches across various applications, including counters and hash tables.

One potential direction is the extension of NestedBTO to support the multi-versioning of transactional objects. This extension would enhance concurrency by allowing multiple versions of an object to coexist, enabling more flexible and efficient transactional operations. Additionally, exploring optimizations for specific application scenarios and further benchmarking on diverse workloads could provide deeper insights into the performance characteristics of NestedBTO.

Funding Information. The work is partially funded by SERB, GoI research project: CRG/2022/009391.

References

1. Agrawal, K., Fineman, J.T., Sukha, J.: Nested parallelism in transactional memory. In: Proceedings of the 13th ACM SIGPLAN Symposium on Principles and practice of parallel programming, pp. 163–174 (2008)
2. Baek, W., Bronson, N., Kozyrakis, C., Olukotun, K.: Implementing and evaluating nested parallel transactions in software transactional memory. In: Proceedings of the Twenty-Second Annual ACM Symposium on Parallelism in Algorithms and Architectures, pp. 253–262 (2010)
3. Barreto, J., Dragojević, A., Ferreira, P., Guerraoui, R., Kapalka, M.: Leveraging parallel nesting in transactional memory. ACM Sigplan Not. **45**(5), 91–100 (2010)
4. Bernstein, P.A., Goodman, N.: Timestamp-based algorithms for concurrency control in distributed database systems. In: VLDB, pp. 285–300 (1980)
5. Bernstein, P.A., Goodman, N.: Multiversion concurrency control-theory and algorithms. ACM Trans. Database Syst. (TODS) **8**(4), 465–483 (1983)
6. Dalessandro, L., Spear, M.F., Scott, M.L.: NOrec: streamlining STM by abolishing ownership records. ACM Sigplan Not. **45**(5), 67–78 (2010)
7. Doherty, S., Groves, L., Luchangco, V., Moir, M.: Towards formally specifying and verifying transactional memory. Formal Aspects Comput. **25**, 769–799 (2013)
8. Guerraoui, R., Kapalka, M.: Opacity: A correctness condition for transactional memory. Technical report (2007)
9. Guerraoui, R., Kapalka, M.: On the correctness of transactional memory. In: Proceedings of the 13th ACM SIGPLAN Symposium on Principles and practice of parallel programming, pp. 175–184 (2008)
10. Haines, N., Kindred, D., Morrisett, J.G., Nettles, S.M., Wing, J.M.: Composing first-class transactions. ACM Trans. Program. Lang. Syst. (TOPLAS) **16**(6), 1719–1736 (1994)
11. Harris, T., Marlow, S., Peyton-Jones, S., Herlihy, M.: Composable memory transactions. In: Proceedings of the tenth ACM SIGPLAN Symposium on Principles and Practice of Parallel Programming, pp. 48–60 (2005)

12. Kobus, T., Kokocinski, M., Wojciechowski, P.T.: The correctness criterion for deferred update replication. Program TRANSACT **15** (2015)
13. Kumar, R., Vidyasankar, K.: HParSTM: a hierarchy-based STM protocol for supporting nested parallelism. In: the 6th ACM SIGPLAN Workshop on Transactional Computing (TRANSACT 2011) (2011)
14. Moravan, M.J., et al.: Supporting nested transactional memory in LogTM. ACM SIGARCH Comput. Archit. News **34**(5), 359–370 (2006)
15. Moss, J.E.B., Hosking, A.L.: Nested transactional memory: model and architecture sketches. Sci. Comput. Program. **63**(2), 186–201 (2006)
16. Peri, S., Vidyasankar, K.: Correctness of concurrent executions of closed nested transactions in transactional memory systems. Theoret. Comput. Sci. **496**, 125–153 (2013)
17. Peri, S., Vidyasankar, K.: Correctness of concurrent executions of closed nested transactions in transactional memory systems. In: Aguilera, M.K., Yu, H., Vaidya, N.H., Srinivasan, V., Choudhury, R.R. (eds.) ICDCN 2011. LNCS, vol. 6522, pp. 95–106. Springer, Heidelberg (2011). https://doi.org/10.1007/978-3-642-17679-1_9
18. Saha, B., Adl-Tabatabai, A.R., Hudson, R.L., Minh, C.C., Hertzberg, B.: McRT-STM: a high performance software transactional memory system for a multi-core runtime. In: Proceedings of the eleventh ACM SIGPLAN Symposium on Principles and Practice of Parallel Programming, pp. 187–197 (2006)
19. Volos, H., Welc, A., Adl-Tabatabai, A.R., Shpeisman, T., Tian, X., Narayanaswamy, R.: NePalTM: design and implementation of nested parallelism for transactional memory systems. In: Proceedings of the 14th ACM SIGPLAN Symposium on Principles and Practice of Parallel Programming, pp. 291–292 (2009)

Enhancing Cost and Latency Efficiency Through Service Placement in Containerized Fog-Cloud Computing Environments

Driss Riane[✉], Widad Ettazi, and Ahmed Ettalbi

IMS Team, ADMIR Laboratory, ENSIAS, Rabat IT Center, Mohammed V University in Rabat, Rabat, Morocco
riane.driss@gmail.com, {widad.ettazi, ahmed.ettalbi}@ensias.um5.ac.ma

Abstract. As the demand for resource-intensive applications grows in fog-cloud computing environments, optimizing service placement becomes paramount to achieve efficient latency and cost savings. This paper presents a novel approach for latency and cost-aware placement of services in containerized fog platforms. By leveraging dynamic resource provisioning and workload scheduling algorithms, our solution aims to minimize both latency and cost while meeting service level objectives. We evaluate the effectiveness of our method through simulations and empirical studies. The results demonstrates significant latency and cost reductions compared to traditional placement strategies. This research contributes to the advancement of efficient resource management techniques in fog-cloud environments and provides practical insights for designing latency and cost-effective service placement solutions in containerized architectures.

Keywords: Fog Computing · Cloud Computing · Cloud Native · Microservice Architecture · Containerization · Service Placement · Cost Optimization · Edge Computing · Cloud Resource Allocation

1 Introduction

With the proliferation of IoT devices, the volume of generated data increase, necessitating efficient and scalable storage and processing solutions. Cloud computing emerges to address these challenges, empowering the management of extensive generated datasets. The integration of Internet of Things and cloud introduces a perspective for internet evolution, fostering the development of intelligent services.

Despite the myriad advantages offered by cloud computing, its reliance on a centralized infrastructure poses challenges for IoT applications, necessitating the transmission of all data to the cloud for further processing. This approach increases network traffic and latency. Certain IoT applications, such as intelligent transport systems [1], industrial automation [2], online interactive gaming [3] and healthcare applications [4], demand real-time responses at millisecond scales. In situations where time is crucial, the delay caused by transferring data to the cloud becomes unacceptable, making cloud computing impractical for IoT applications that demand immediate service delivery. To overcome this constraint, fog emerges as a mediator to facilitate the communication between Internet of Things and cloud, minimizing the congestion of network and ensuring rapid response for latency-aware applications. While retaining many features of cloud computing, fog computing primarily offers storage and computational capabilities on the network periphery.

Figure 1 depicts typical fog computing architecture. Real-time IoT applications stand to gain significant advantages from this approach, given that services can be deployed closer to end-users, without transporting all data to the cloud. As a result, the fusion of cloud and fog computing architectures becomes crucial for effectively meeting the diverse demands of applications. Implementing a fog-cloud framework for Internet of Things applications shows potential for enhancing cost and latency efficiency.

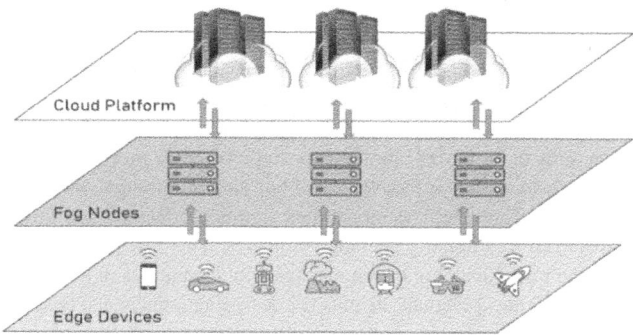

Fig. 1. Typical Fog computing architecture.

Modern applications often adopt microservices-based architecture, which decomposes complex software systems into loosely coupled components. These are deployed within containers, enhancing their maintainability. In contrast to virtual machines, containers provide resource efficiency and increased flexibility.

A principal challenge in the fog model lies in identifying the optimal resources and locations for each service. Service deployment entails finding nodes to deploy each micro-service replica from a pool of nodes fog tier or cloud computing data centers. This assignment is notably important fog environments based on containers, where the placement of services significantly heavily affects the quality of service. To achieve optimized system performance, placement approaches should take into account nodes resources constraints, variations in evolving requests, location and latency, whilst optimizing system performance.

Despite the introduction of various approaches to address the placement of services in the fog-cloud environments, current approaches present the following constraints:

- Existing methods for fog-cloud service placement problem focuses on VM-based virtualization rather than containerization.

- In such scenarios, dynamic service placement techniques become imperative, facilitating the adjustment of allocated resources for each service according to evolving demands.

This article presents a new approach to enhance cost and latency Efficiency through service placement in containerized Fog-Cloud computing environments. Leveraging Kubernetes platform, our method efficiently handles multiple replicas of services in fog computing. These replicas are strategically placed across various fog nodes, ensuring that they are closer to end-users, thus reducing the latency experienced by these users. This work employs the non-dominated sorting genetic algorithm to minimize cost and latency. Furthermore, our approach integrates a container orchestration, allowing dynamic service scaling and network data collection. Evaluation through simulation demonstrates the effectiveness of our approach.

The subsequent sections of this paper adopt a structured approach aimed at comprehensively addressing cost and latency optimization in fog computing. Section 2 provides an overview of basic concepts, while Sect. 3 discusses relevant related work. In Sect. 4, we detail the proposed approach, followed by Sect. 5, which outlines the performance evaluation of the algorithm. Finally, Sect. 6 presents a conclusive summary of findings, implications, and avenues for future work.

2 Basic Concepts

This section introduces the concept of containerization and the cloud native platform such as Kubernetes.

2.1 Containerization

Containerization is a contemporary software engineering technique that encapsulates applications and their dependencies within self-contained units known as containers. These containers encapsulate all necessary components for an application to function, including libraries, binaries, and configuration files. This methodology provides several benefits, including enhanced portability, consistency, and scalability. Containers can be deployed across diverse computing environments, ranging from individual development workstations to large-scale production servers, without encountering compatibility issues. Additionally, containerization facilitates efficient resource utilization by enabling the concurrent execution of multiple containers on the same host operating system, thereby minimizing overhead compared to traditional virtual machines. Consequently, containerization has emerged as a fundamental aspect of modern cloud-native architectures, altering software development and deployment practices.

2.2 Container Orchestration

Kubernetes [5] is one of the most popular and open-source container orchestration platform that provides a robust infrastructure for automating the deployment, scaling, and management of containerized applications across diverse environments. Through Kubernetes, developers can abstract away underlying infrastructure complexities, enabling seamless deployment and scaling of applications with high availability and fault tolerance. Its declarative configuration model and powerful scheduling capabilities optimize resource utilization, while built-in load balancing and service discovery streamline communication between application components. Kubernetes' extensibility and ecosystem of tools facilitate integration with various cloud services, enabling organizations to build and operate cloud-native applications efficiently. As a result, Kubernetes has become important for modern cloud-native platforms, empowering organizations to adopt agile development practices, and deliver resilient, scalable applications to their users.

3 Related Work

Fog computing is recognized as a new approach to tackle the challenges of the growing Internet of Things (IoT) landscape, providing a decentralized computing infrastructure closer to edge devices. As the demand for IoT applications increases, the strategic placement of services in fog computing environments becomes increasingly crucial. Several studies have explored various aspects of fog computing, revealing on its practical applications and future directions [6–8]. QoS-aware deployment of IoT applications through fog has been investigated to enhance service delivery [9–12], while techniques and methods for IoT applications in collaborative cloud-fog environments have been addressed issues related to latency [13, 14], energy consumption [15, 16], service delay [17] and cost [18–20].

Moreover, resource management in fog computing has been extensively studied, exploring various architectures [21–23] and optimization algorithms [24–27].With the increasing complexity of fog computing environments, multi-objective scheduling becomes crucial, as it enables the optimization of multiple conflicting objectives. Metaheuristic approaches, such as genetic algorithms [28–30] particle swarm algorithm [17] and simulated annealing [31] have been employed to tackle the task scheduling problem in fog computing environments, leveraging their ability to find Pareto-optimal solutions. These optimization techniques aim to address various characteristics of fog computing systems and diverse requirements of IoT applications, ultimately enhancing their performance and scalability.

While the existing body of literature on fog computing offers valuable insights and frameworks for optimizing resource management and service placement, there are notable gaps related to dynamic service scaling using containerization and latency-cost optimization techniques. Addressing these limitations can lead to more resilient, latency-efficient and cost-effective fog computing systems capable of supporting the rapidly evolving landscape of IoT applications.

4 The Proposed Approach

Our method aims to achieve a balance among multi objectives, considering factors like minimizing both cost and latency while ensuring service availability. In the following section, we will outline the formulation of the service placement problem in fog computing and then present our proposed multi-objective approach in detail.

4.1 Architecture Overview

Figure 2 shows an architectural overview of fog computing comprising client layer, fog layer and cloud layer. We suppose that the interconnection between fog devices constitutes a graph-based network. Additionally, we assume that each device is connected to one particular gateway.

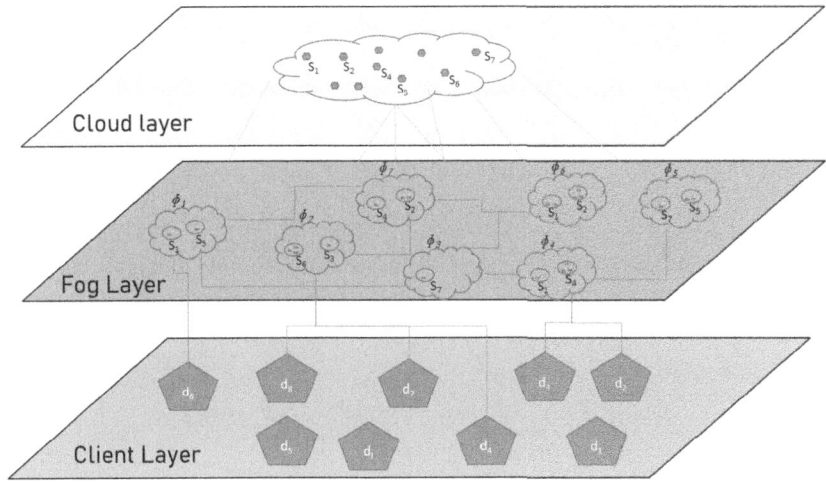

Fig. 2. Architecture overview.

In our approach, we introduce the foundational elements of our model: an undirected graph representing infrastructure, fog nodes, IoT devices, IoT gateways, application services, inter-service dependencies, fog node hosting and device identification by gateways:

- The infrastructure is represented as a graph $G = (V, E)$. V represents the set of nodes that correspond to nodes in fog model. E reflects the links between these nodes.
- $F = \{\phi_i, 1 \leq i \leq f\}$ identifies a set of fog nodes.
- $D_{i,j}$ represents the delay between two fog nodes ϕ_i and ϕ_j calculated as the sum of delays of the traversed links via the shortest path.
- IoT devices, comprising sensors and actuators, are denoted as $D = \{d_i, 1 \leq i \leq d\}$.
- IoT gateways identify devices and the services they require, denoted as:
- $G = \{g_i, 1 \leq i \leq g\}$.
- Applications services are represented as $A = \{s_i, 1 \leq i \leq s\}$ where s represents the number of services.
- $C_{i,j}$ is a binary variable that equals to 1 if service s_i calls a service s_j and equals to 0 otherwise.
- $H_{i,j}$ is a binary variable that equals to 1 if fog node ϕ_i hosts service s_j and equals to 0 otherwise.
- $R_{i,j}$ is a binary variable that equals to 1 if gateway g_i identifies the device d_j and equals to 0 otherwise.

4.2 Objectives Functions

Our optimization model consider both cost and latency in service placement decisions. By distributing replicas of each service across fog devices while considering the limited computational and storage capacities of fog nodes, our approach seeks to minimize both cost and latency, thereby enhancing the overall efficiency and performance of fog computing systems.

4.2.1 Cost Optimization

As shown in Eq. (1), the cost attributed to service placement encompasses both processing and storage costs within the fog infrastructure, denoted as $Cost_{pr}$ and $Cost_{st}$ respectively.

$$TCost = Cost_{pr} + Cost_{st} \tag{1}$$

The processing cost is related to the CPU utilization, required to handle each application service requests and the incoming request rate at the nodes, as illustrated by Eq. (2).

$$Cost_{pr} = \sum_{i=1}^{f} \sum_{j=1}^{s} cost_i^{cpu} \times N_j^{cpu} \times AR_j \times H_{i,j} \tag{2}$$

where:

- $cost_i^{cpu}$ the cpu cost of fog node ϕ_i.
- N_j^{cpu} the amount of cpu required for service s_j.
- AR_j quantifies the rate at which requests for a service s_j arrive at fog node ϕ_i.

Likewise, the storage cost is determined by the memory consumption of each service, as depicted in Eq. (3).

$$Cost_{st} = \sum_{i=1}^{f} \sum_{j=1}^{s} cost_i^{st} \times N_j^{st} \times H_{i,j} \tag{3}$$

where $cost_i^{st}$ the storage cost of fog node ϕ_i and N_j^{st} the quantity of storage required for service s_j. $H_{i,j}$ is a binary variable that equals to *1* if fog node ϕ_i hosts service s_j and equals to *0* otherwise.

4.2.2 Latency Optimization

Latency, the delay of transmitting data between devices, is a critical factor in fog computing systems. Fog platforms aim to reduce latency by decentralizing computing resources closer to the edge of the network, where data is generated and consumed. This proximity allows for faster processing and response times compared to traditional cloud-based approaches. However, managing latency in fog computing presents unique challenges due to the distributed nature of resources and the dynamic nature of network conditions.

In this context, understanding and optimizing latency is essential for ensuring efficient and responsive services in fog computing environments.

In our approach, the latency can be computed using Eq. (4) that consider different factors such as the communication between services and the interaction between devices and requested services.

$$Latency = L_{call} + L_{req} \qquad (4)$$

L_{call} represents the average latency of the communication between services, calculated using Eq. (5):

$$L_{call} = \frac{\sum_{k=1}^{f} \sum_{i=1}^{s} \sum_{j=1}^{s} C_{i,j} \times H_{i,k} \times D_{min}}{\sum_{k=1}^{f} \sum_{i=1}^{s} \sum_{j=1}^{s} C_{i,j} \times H_{i,k}} \qquad (5)$$

where D_{min} is the minimum distance between two fog nodes hosting the relevant services. This distance is computed using Dijkstra algorithm, between the two relevant nodes.

L_{call} represents the average latency of the interaction between devices and requested services by clients, calculated using Eq. (6):

$$L_{req} = \frac{\sum_{i=1}^{g} \sum_{j=1}^{s} R_{i,j} \times C_{i,j} \times D_{min}}{\sum_{i=1}^{g} \sum_{j=1}^{s} R_{i,j} \times C_{i,j}} \qquad (6)$$

4.3 Constraints

The primary constraints in our problem concern the limitations on the capacity of resources in fog nodes.

Consider CPU_i^{fog} and MEM_i^{fog} the available CPU and memory resources, respectively, in fog node ϕ_i, the used resource by services on a given node ψ_i must not exceed the node's resource capacity.

Let CPU_j^{used} and MEM_j^{used} the required CPU and memory resource, respectively, by service s_j. Equations (7) and (8) guarantee the resource capacity limitations constraints:

$$\sum_{i=1}^{f} \sum_{j=1}^{s} CPU_j^{used} \times H_{i,j} \leq CPU_i^{fog} \qquad (7)$$

$$\sum_{i=1}^{f} \sum_{j=1}^{s} MEM_j^{used} \times H_{i,j} \leq MEM_i^{fog} \qquad (8)$$

4.4 Dynamic Service Scaling Algorithm

This dynamic scaling approach ensures that the system can adapt to varying workloads while maintaining QoS and optimizing resource utilization. Adjusting the limits of resources (CPU and RAM) allows for fine-tuning the system's performance characteristics according to specific requirements and constraints.

To formulate the dynamic scaling approach mathematically, consider a set of variables:

- $U_{cpu}^{i,j}(t)$ represents the CPU utilization of replica j of a service s_i at time t.
- $U_{ram}^{i,j}(t)$ represents the RAM utilization of replica j of a service s_i at time t.
- $N^i(t)$ denotes the number of replicas of the service s_i at time t.
- $U_{avg\_cpu}^{i}(t)$ is the average CPU utilization of service's (i.e., s_i) replicas at time t.
- $U_{avg\_ram}^{i}(t)$ is the average RAM utilization of service's (s_i) replicas at time t.

For each service at time t, $U_{avg\_cpu}^{i}(t)$ and $U_{avg\_ram}^{i}(t)$ are computed using Eqs. (9) and (10) respectively:

$$U_{avg\_cpu}^{i}(t) = \frac{\sum_{i=1}^{N(t)} U_{cpu}^{i}(t)}{N(t)} \qquad (9)$$

$$U_{avg\_ram}^{i}(t) = \frac{\sum_{i=1}^{N(t)} U_{ram}^{i}(t)}{N(t)} \qquad (10)$$

As illustrated in Fig. 3, when either the average (of CPU or RAM) utilization of a replica is greater that the limits, we add a new service replica. Conversely, if both the average CPU and average RAM of a replica are below the limits, we remove a service replica.

```
Data: s_i, CPU_max, RAM_max, t
Result: N^i(t)
replicas = service.replicas_at_time(t)
CPU_list = []
RAM_list = []

for replica j in replicas:
        CPU_list.append (replica. U_{cpu}^{i,j}(t))
        RAM_list.append (replica. U_{ram}^{i,j}(t))

U_{avg_cpu}^i(t) = Σ_{i=1}^{N^i(t)} U_{cpu}^i(t) / N^i(t)
U_{avg_ram}^i(t) = Σ_{i=1}^{N^i(t)} U_{ram}^i(t) / N^i(t)

if (U_{avg_cpu}^i(t) > CPU_max or U_{avg_ram}^i(t) > RAM_max)
        N^i(t) = N^i(t) + 1
elseif (U_{avg_cpu}^i(t) ≤ CPU_max and U_{avg_ram}^i(t) ≤ RAM_max and N^i(t) > 1)
        N^i(t) = N^i(t) - 1
return N^i(t)
```

Fig. 3. Dynamic service scaling algorithm.

4.5 Cost and Latency Optimization

In this section, we try to optimize both cost and latency using an extension of the genetic algorithm called NSGA-II that addresses problems with multiple objectives. The algorithm operates by maintaining a population of candidate solutions, known as individuals, and iteratively evolving them over generations. NSGA-II introduces a fast non-dominated sorting technique to rank individuals based on their dominance relationships, ensuring a diverse set of solutions in the population.

4.5.1 Population Initialization

In order to design the structure of each chromosome, we consider a matrix $CH = M_{i,j} (1 \leq i \leq s, 1 \leq j \leq f)$, where $M_{i,j}$ equals number of replicas when of service s_i is matched to fog node ϕ_j. N^i (t) represents the number of replicas of the service s_i at time t.

Figure 4 illustrates the structure of chromosome for 6 services and 6 fog nodes. For instance, $M_{1,3} = 1$ indicates that service s_1 is hosted in fog node ϕ_3. Similarly, $M_{2,4} = 3$ signifies that fog node ϕ_4 hosts three replicas of service s_2.

i	1	2	3	4	5	6
$N^i(t)$	3	4	1	2	3	4

$$CH = \begin{pmatrix} 1 & 0 & 1 & 1 & 0 & 0 \\ 0 & 1 & 0 & 3 & 0 & 0 \\ 0 & 0 & 0 & 0 & 0 & 1 \\ 1 & 0 & 1 & 0 & 0 & 0 \\ 0 & 1 & 0 & 1 & 1 & 0 \\ 1 & 0 & 2 & 0 & 0 & 1 \end{pmatrix}$$

Fig. 4. Chromosome structure.

4.5.2 Crossover

As depicted in Fig. 5, this step uses the dynamic scaling service algorithm presented in Sect. 4.4 to streamline the generation of sub-solutions (child) for optimizing the placement of services. Operating on two solutions (parents) as two-dimensional array, it produces two offspring (child) solutions, ensuring the preservation of replica numbers for each service. By iteratively changing fog node positions between the parents at random crossover points and applying a repair mechanism to adjust replica counts

---

Data: s, f, Parent$_1$, Parent$_2$, N^i
Result: offspring$_1$, offspring$_2$

For each service s_i:
  Select randomly crossover point j where $0 \leq j \leq f - 1$
    For k in 0 to j-1
      offspring$_1$(i, k) = Parent$_1$(i, k)
      offspring$_2$(i, k) = Parent$_2$(i, k)
    For k in {1, 2}
      For each service s_i
        For each fog node
          $assigned^i = \sum_{j=1}^{f}$ offspringk(i, j)
          if $(assigned^i \geq N^i)$ then
            randomly remove excess replicas

          If $(assigned^i < N^i)$ then
            Randomly add replicas
return offspring$_1$, offspring$_2$

Fig. 5. Crossover algorithm.

within specified limits, the algorithm maintains solution diversity and quality. This process enhances the population of solutions by effectively combining genetic operators to generate offspring solutions that adhere to constraints.

4.5.3 Mutation Operator

In our approach, the mutation operators used in genetic operations are designed to expand the search space and prevent the algorithm from being converged to a solution that is locally optimal but not necessarily the best possible solution globally. The mutation operation consists of two steps:

- Randomly increasing or decreasing the number of each service instance: This involves iterating through each row of the individual's chromosome that requires mutation and randomly adjusting the number of service instances.
- Randomly selecting a subset of services in the system and instantiating them in all fog devices: Another aspect of the mutation involves randomly selecting a subset of services from the system and deploying them across all fog devices in the network.

4.5.4 Proposed Algorithm

Figure 6 outlines the proposed algorithm that uses NSGA-II. The initial population is generated using the input parameters. However, due to potential infeasible solutions within this initial population, a modified operator is applied to correct them. This operator

```
Data: ps, gn, f_i(x)
Randomly initialize population P with size ps
for each service s_i:
    call algorithm 2 for dynamic service scaling to add or remove replicas and find optimal number of replicas
End
Make initial chromosome according to replicas for each service
Use equations (1) and (4) to calculate cost and latency and evaluate the fitness f_i(x) for individuals
Assign level using non-dominated sort
Generate new population
CrossOver() and Mutation()
For k in 1 to gn
    For each parent and offspring in P
        Use equations (1) and (4) to calculate cost and latency and evaluate the fitness f_i(x) for individuals
        Assign level using non-dominated sort
        Generate solutions
    End
    Select individuals based on lower front
    Make Next generation
    CrossOver() and Mutation()
End
```

Fig. 6. The proposed algorithm.

ensures that the population adheres to constraints, enhancing its validity for subsequent optimization steps.

5 Evaluation

This section details the experiment designed to assess the performance of our approach. For this purpose, we developed our algorithm using a custom simulation environment built in the python programming language. This experiment was conducted on a PC equipped with an Intel Core i5-4300U CPU running at 2.49 GHz, 8 GB of RAM, and the Linux operating system.

5.1 Simulation Setting

Table 1 outlines the parameters and input data utilized in our experiment. To assess the advantages of deploying services within a containerized environment, we consider microservices application deployed on Kubernetes.

Our proposed approach is compared to the first fit approach that operates by initially placing services according to their requirements. This involves starting with the first fog or cloud node in the available node list and trying to allocate the service to that particular node.

Table 1. List of parameters.

	Parameter	Value
Cloud	RAM	unlimited
	CPU	unlimited
	Latency	[15 ms–40 ms]
	Cost	[$1–$6]
Fog	CPU	[2000 - 6000]
	RAM	[2 GB–8 GB]
	Latency	[5–10]
Application	#Microservices	[5–20]
	CPU	15000 MIPS
	RAM	1 GB
gateways	# gateways	15
Devices	Request incoming rate	{0.1, 0.3, 0.5}

5.2 Results

In this section, we discuss the results of the considered experiment. We try to vary the count of services from 5 to 40, the count of nodes and requests remains fixed at 40 and

1000, respectively. Experimental result shows that our proposed algorithm minimize the average latency and the cost related to the placement of services.

Figures 7 illustrate the performance of our algorithm compared to the first fit algorithm in terms of cost and latency respectively.

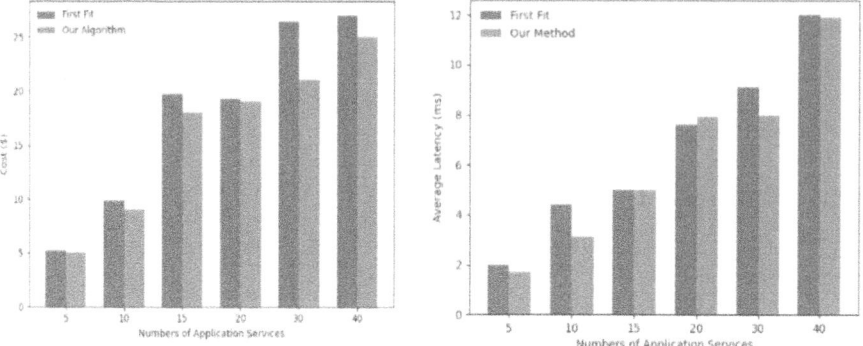

Fig. 7. The impact of numbers of services on cost and latency

6 Conclusion

This paper presents an approach for latency and cost-aware service placement in containerized fog-cloud computing platforms. As the demand for resource-intensive applications grows in fog-cloud environments, optimizing service placement becomes paramount to achieve efficient latency and cost savings. By leveraging dynamic resource provisioning and workload scheduling algorithms, our solution aims to minimize both latency and cost while meeting service level objectives. Through simulations, we evaluate the effectiveness of our method and demonstrate significant latency and cost reductions compared to traditional placement strategies. This research contributes to the advancement of efficient resource management techniques in fog-cloud environments and provides practical insights for designing latency and cost-effective service placement solutions in containerized architectures.

For future work, several promising directions emerge. Firstly, further investigation could explore the scalability and adaptability of the proposed approach to accommodate larger and more dynamic fog-cloud environments. Additionally, the integration of machine learning techniques could enhance the intelligence and automation of resource provisioning and workload scheduling processes, leading to even more efficient service placement strategies. Finally, empirical validation and deployment of the proposed solution in real-world fog-cloud platforms could provide valuable insights into its practical feasibility and effectiveness.

References

1. Mekki, T., Jmal, R., Chaari, L., Jabri, I., Rachedi, A.: Vehicular fog resource allocation scheme: A multi-objective optimization based approach. In: 2020 IEEE 17th Annual Consumer Communications Networking Conference (CCNC), pp. 1–6 (2020)
2. Wang, X., Veeravalli, B., Rana, O.F.: An optimal task-scheduling strategy for large-scale astronomical workloads using in-transit computation model. Int. J. Comput. Intell. Syst. **11**, 600–607 (2018)
3. Benamer, A.R., Ben Hadj-Alouane, N., Boussetta, K.: Online games servers placement in fog computing: An hybrid bio-inspired approach. In: 2020 IEEE 45th LCN Symposium on Emerging Topics in Networking (LCN Symposium), pp. 141–149 (2020)
4. Yan, X., Xu, X., Zheng, Y., Dai, F.: Fog Server Placement for multimodality data fusion in neuroimaging. In: Chen, X., Yan, H., Yan, Q., Zhang, X. (eds.) Machine Learning for Cyber Security, ML4CS 2020, LNCS, vol. 12486, pp. 234–248. Springer, Cham (2020). https://doi.org/10.1007/978-3-030-62223-7_20
5. Kubernetes. https://kubernetes.io/
6. Hazra, A., Rana, P., Adhikari, M., Amgoth, T.: Fog computing for next-generation internet of things: fundamental, state-of-the-art and research challenges. Comput. Sci. Rev. **48**, 100549 (2023)
7. Apat, H.K., Nayak, R., Sahoo, B.: A comprehensive review on internet of things application placement in fog computing environment. Internet Things. **23**, 100866 (2023)
8. Maddikunta, P.K.R., Pham, Q.-V., Nguyen, D.C., et al.: Incentive techniques for the internet of things: a survey. J. Netw. Comput. Appl. **206**, 103464 (2022)
9. Hashemifar, S., Rajabzadeh, A.: Optimal service provisioning in IoT fog-based environment for QoS-aware delay-sensitive application. Comput. Electr. Eng. **111**, 108984 (2023)
10. Murtaza, F., Akhunzada, A., Islam, S., Boudjadar, J., Buyya, R.: QoS-aware service provisioning in fog computing. J. Netw. Comput. Appl. **165**, 102674 (2020)
11. Mahmud, R., Srirama, S.N., Ramamohanarao, K., Buyya, R.: Quality of Experience (QoE)-aware placement of applications in Fog computing environments. J. Parallel Distrib. Comput. **132**, 190–203 (2019)
12. Haghi Kashani, M., Rahmani, A.M., Jafari Navimipour, N.: Quality of service-aware approaches in fog computing. Int. J. Commun. Syst. **33**(8), 4340 (2020)
13. Mahmud, R., Ramamohanarao, K., Buyya, R.: Latency-aware application module management for fog computing environments. ACM Trans. Internet Technol. **19**(1), 1–21 (2018)
14. Aburukba, R., AliKarrar, M., Landolsi, T., El-Fakih, K.: Scheduling internet of things requests to minimize latency in hybrid fog-cloud computing. Future Gener. Comput. Syst. **111**, 539–551 (2020)
15. Ren, X., Zhang, Z., Arefzadeh, S.M.: An energy-aware approach for resource managing in the fog-based internet of things using a hybrid algorithm. Int. J. Commun. Syst. **34**(1), e4652 (2021)
16. Reddy, K.H.K., Luhach, A.K., Pradhan, B., Dash, J.K., Roy, D.S.: A genetic algorithm for energy efficient fog layer resource management in context-aware smart cities. Sustain. Cities Soc. **63**, 102428 (2020)
17. Djemai, T., Stolf, P., Monteil, T., Pierson, J.-M.: A discrete particle swarm optimization approach for energy-efficient IoT services placement over fog infrastructures. In: 2019 18th International Symposium on Parallel and Distributed Computing, ISPDC, pp. 32–40. IEEE (2019)
18. Nikoui, T.S., Balador, A., Rahmani, A.M., Bakhshi, Z.: Cost-aware task scheduling in fog-cloud environment. In: 2020 CSI/CPSSI International Symposium on Real-Time and Embedded Systems and Technologies (RTEST), pp. 1–8 (2020)

19. Li, H., Xu, C., Wang, T., et al.: A cost-efficient and QoS-aware adaptive placement of applications in fog computing. Concurr. Comput. Pract. Exp. **35**(21), e7701 (2023)
20. Hassan, M.U., Ali, A.A., Iqbal, A., Akram, M.M., Khan, M., AbuOdeh, J.: An efficient dynamic decision-based task optimization and scheduling approach for microservice-based cost management in mobile cloud computing applications. Pervasive Mob. Comput. **92**, 101785 (2023)
21. Mijuskovic, A., Chiumento, A., Bemthuis, R., Aldea, A., Havinga, P.: Resource management techniques for cloud/fog and edge computing: an evaluation framework and classification. Sensors. **21**(5), 1832 (2021)
22. Mahmud, R., Pallewatta, S., Goudarzi, M., Buyya, R.: Ifogsim2: An extended ifogsim simulator for mobility, clustering, and microservice management in edge and fog computing environments. J. Syst. Softw. **190**, 111351 (2022)
23. Ranjan, H., Dwivedi, A.K., Prakasam, P.: An optimized architecture and algorithm for resource allocation in D2D aided fog computing. Peer-to-Peer Netw. Appl. **15**(2), 1294–1310 (2022)
24. Jana, B., Chakraborty, M., Mandal, T.: A task scheduling technique based on particle swarm optimization algorithm in cloud environment. In: Ray, K., Sharma, T., Rawat, S., Saini, R., Bandyopadhyay, A. (eds.) Soft Computing: Theories and Applications. Advances in Intelligent Systems and Computing, vol. 742, pp. 525–536. Springer, Singapore (2019). https://doi.org/10.1007/978-981-13-0589-4_49
25. Abohamama, A.S., El-Ghamry, A., Hamouda, E.: Real-time task scheduling algorithm for IoT-based applications in the cloud–fog environment. J. Netw. Syst. Manag. **30**(4), 54 (2022)
26. Hussein, M.K., Mousa, M.H.: Efficient task offloading for IoT-based applications in fog computing using ant colony optimization. IEEE Access. **8**, 37191–37201 (2020)
27. Shruthi, G., Mundada, M.R., Supreeth, S.: The resource allocation using weighted greedy knapsack based algorithm in an educational fog computing environment. Int. J. Emerg. Technol. Learn. **17**(18), 261 (2022)
28. Natesha, B., Guddeti, R.M.R.: Adopting elitism-based genetic algorithm for minimizing multi-objective problems of IoT service placement in fog computing environment. J. Netw. Comput. Appl. **178**, 102972 (2021)
29. Natesha, B.V., Guddeti, R.: Adopting elitism-based Genetic Algorithm for minimizing multi-objective problems of IoT service placement in fog computing environment. J. Network Comput. Appl. **178**, 102972 (2021)
30. Jafari, V., Rezvani, M.H.: Joint optimization of energy consumption and time delay in IoT-fog-cloud computing environments using NSGA-II Metaheuristic algorithm. J. Ambient Intell. Humanized Comput. (2021)
31. Apat, H.K., Sahoo, B., Goswami, V., Barik, R.K.: A hybrid meta-heuristic algorithm for multi-objective IoT service placement in fog computing environments. Decis. Anal. J. **10**, 100379 (2024)

Towards Generating a Dataset for Failure Prediction in Microservices Applications

Ilyass Tarhri(✉)[ID], Driss Allaki[ID], and Hamza Kamal Idrissi[ID]

Institut National des Postes et Télécommunications, Rabat, Morocco
ilyass.tarhri@doctorant.inpt.ac.ma, {d.allaki,
kamalidrissi}@inpt.ac.ma

Abstract. Microservices architecture has gained significant traction in modern software development due to its agility and scalability. However, using artificial intelligence models to effectively predict the failure of microservices workloads poses challenges, as there is a lack of comprehensive datasets that provide dedicated data to train these models. This paper presents a methodology for generating a dataset specifically designed for failure prediction tasks in microservices applications. We detail our approach for capturing relevant metrics, including the chosen workload generation method and data collection techniques. The paper then describes the characteristics of the generated dataset, including its size, granularity, and captured workload failure scenarios and patterns. Evaluation results demonstrate the utility of the obtained dataset in gaining insights into microservices performance. The aim of this work is to offer a new dataset with useful workload metrics, serving as a valuable resource for researchers and practitioners in the field.

Keywords: Microservices Architecture · Workload Metrics · Failure Prediction · Artificial Intelligence · Dataset Generation

1 Introduction

Microservices architecture fosters agility, scalability, and fault tolerance by breaking down applications into smaller, modular and independently deployable services. Although microservices provide better fault isolation than monolithic architectures, their distributed nature and dynamic interactions present challenges in accurately forecasting and anticipating system faults. Actually, existing solutions struggle to anticipate malfunctions in real-time, particularly within container orchestration ecosystems like Kubernetes. This challenge is mostly attributed to the lack of comprehensive data that accurately represents the complex characteristics of these systems under different levels of usage and operational circumstances. Such data is essential for training artificial intelligence models aimed at effectively predicting failures in microservices workloads.

Based on that, our work presents the steps we followed to generate a dataset that captures essential workload metrics that are crucial for observing complex microservices running in Kubernetes environments. We esteem that the generated dataset is a crucial asset for detecting early signs of microservices disruptions and failures, allowing for more proactive and efficient monitoring approaches.

This paper is organized as follows. Section 2 discusses related work. Section 3 presents the followed methodology to generate the dataset. Section 4 explains the characteristics of the obtained dataset. Section 5 concludes the paper and presents future work.

2 Related Work

To develop precise failure prediction models for microservice architectures, access to comprehensive and informative datasets is essential since it provides the necessary variety and volume of data to effectively train and validate the models. This section discusses existing datasets used in studies on failure prediction for microservice architectures. The aim is to highlight their unique features and main limitations in order to specify the distinctive characteristics of our work.

Several researchers used various operational metrics to enhance anomaly detection methods in microservices. [1] offers a dataset that focuses on measures such as response time percentiles and request counts. Although this dataset represents progress by providing detailed information on system performance, it may not completely encompass the typical operational complexity found in Kubernetes deployments. [2] provides useful methodologies for examining distributed tracing data. They particularly focus on metrics such as service call frequencies and response times. However, the limited scope of the current tracing dataset constrains the potential of these methodologies, highlighting a need for an extended dataset that includes a broader range of system state and metadata to enable the use of supervised learning methods. [3] examines the application of unsupervised learning methods for the purpose of detecting anomalies in microservices traces. While the researchers show that these methods are effective, the datasets utilized are not accessible to the public, which could restrict the wider verification and implementation of the suggested model in many situations. [4] provides a dataset that includes metrics, logs, and traces for fault prediction purposes. Although it provides a thorough analysis of microservice failures, its scope may be inadequate for wider Kubernetes operational situations. As shown in [5], different datasets are important when using random forest algorithms for exception scoring. Despite that, the paper does not discuss the availability of their dataset for public use. Moreover, [6] presents a comprehensive compilation of network traffic derived from Kubernetes. This dataset serves as a great basis for doing security analysis but it does not possess the comprehensive operational metrics required for predicting failures.

To fill the gap we have found in literature, we propose in this work a dataset that places greater emphasis on a wider range of Kubernetes system indicators such as CPU and memory use, problem notifications, pod status updates, and network transmission and reception issues, together with comprehensive log records. Thus, the generated dataset is intended to facilitate the training of advanced failure prediction models for microservices, which could potentially lead to more resilient systems.

3 Methodology

We selected the OpenTelemetry Demo application [7] on Kubernetes [8] for its comprehensive representation of a typical microservices workload, involving multiple services communicating over gRPC and HTTP. This selection ensures reflecting real-world microservices interactions and complexities. Furthermore, we incorporated Chaos Mesh [9], a leading chaos engineering tool, to introduce faults deliberately. This approach allows capturing a wide array of failure scenarios, significantly enhancing the dataset's utility for developing robust failure prediction models, and capturing a wide range of workload metrics under both standard and failure-induced states.

3.1 The Used Microservices Application

The *OpenTelemetry* Demo is composed of microservices written in different programming languages that communicate with each other over gRPC and HTTP. It also includes a load generator that uses *Locust* [10] to simulate user traffic.

Chaos Mesh was employed to inject various types of faults into the Kubernetes environment to test the resilience and failure recovery mechanisms of the system. The different types of the injected faults include:

- *Pod failure*: Simulating the sudden crash or unavailability of microservice pods.
- *Network latency and packet loss*: Introducing delays and packet loss to mimic network issues.
- *Resource exhaustion*: Stressing system resources like CPU and memory to test system performance under high load.

On the other hand, the telemetry data flow in the *OpenTelemetry* Demo App is configured as follows:

- Microservices emit telemetry data using OpenTelemetry Protocol (OTLP).
- An OTLP collector receives this data, which is then exported to various backend systems such as Prometheus [11] for monitoring and Jaeger [12] for tracing.
- Grafana [13] is used for data visualization, allowing to observe the effects of the Chaos Mesh-inject faults on the microservices.

3.2 Data Generation

To collect the data, we scripted a process that continuously polled the Kubernetes API and Prometheus. The script was programmed to initialize essential monitoring parameters. Fetch real-time pod statuses and metrics in a loop. Collect detailed information about CPU usage, memory utilization, network traffic, and error logs. And then fetch real-time pod statuses and metrics. The following algorithm illustrates this process.

```
Algorithm 1: Kubernetes Environment Data Collection
Result: Structured dataset of Kubernetes pod metrics
initialization: Define Prometheus URL, Namespace, Output File Path,
  Sleep Interval, and List of Pods to Exclude;
while True do
    Fetch current state of pods in the defined Namespace;
    Execute Prometheus queries for various metrics;
    for each pod in current pod states do
        if pod is not in the list of excluded pods then
            Collect and calculate metrics for the pod;
            Retrieve status, event details, and node information for the
              pod;
            Append collected data to a structured format;
        end
    end
    Write the structured data to the specified Output File;
    Sleep for the duration of the Sleep Interval;
end
```

3.3 Data Preprocessing

Data preprocessing involved multiple steps to ensure the dataset's integrity and analytical value:

- **Normalization:** We standardized numerical data to a uniform scale to facilitate comparison and pattern recognition. Workload metrics like CPU usage and memory consumption were scaled to have a uniform range, typically between 0 and 1. This scaling was crucial because it ensured that no single metric with larger values could unduly influence the predictive models. For categorical data, such as pod status indicators, we used one-hot encoding to convert these categories into a binary matrix, making them usable for machine learning algorithms.
- **Imputation:** We handled Missing values to prevent data loss and maintain the dataset's consistency.
- **Feature Selection:** We conducted a correlation analysis to identify which metrics were most strongly associated with service failures. Metrics with higher correlation were prioritized for inclusion in the predictive models.
- **Aggregation:** We aggregated metrics over suitable time windows to establish trends and patterns necessary for predictive modeling.
- **Class Imbalance Addressing:** We used techniques such as oversampling and undersampling to balance the dataset and ensure accurate model training.

4 Results

Our dataset represents a compilation of metrics that were systematically collected over a span of several hours in a Kubernetes environment. This time period allowed capturing a diverse range of scenarios. The key columns included in the dataset are described in [14].

The preprocessed data was structured systematically and saved in CSV format. The simplicity of use and wide compatibility with data analysis and machine learning tools were the driving factors in this decision.

A comprehensive examination of this dataset using a Random Forest classifier revealed helpful findings. The model underwent a thorough evaluation using KFold cross-validation, resulting in the following average metrics: an accuracy of 96.50%, precision of 53.89%, recall of 23.47%, and an F1 score of 31.88%. The categorization report for the most recent fold revealed an excellent precision rate of 97% and recall rate of 100% for the normal class (0), while exhibiting comparatively lower values for the failure class (1). These results emphasize the difficulties in accurately forecasting failures in a complicated Kubernetes environment and provide areas for further improvement of our predictive algorithms.

We are working to improve our predictive model's robustness and accuracy. The entire dataset, along with the script that generates the dataset, is accessible to the public for usage and further research via our GitHub repository [14].

The dataset shows potential for anomaly detection, resource optimization, and predictive maintenance. It is especially well-suited for adjusting the size of services in real-time to accommodate changing workloads and proactively identifying and resolving issues to improve the robustness of the system.

5 Conclusion and Future Work

Our contribution proposes a new dataset relying on different workload metrics for failure prediction in microservices applications running on Kubernetes. This work contributes in exploring the field of real-time predictive monitoring for distributed systems. This has the ability to change system observability from reactive to proactive by allowing models to interpret streaming data and provide timely insights and remedies to emergent concerns.

On the other hand, we plan to expand our dataset with data from a more diverse array of Kubernetes configurations, including variations in scale, load, and operational conditions. This expansion is anticipated to improve the dataset's representativeness and robustness, thereby enhancing the generalizability and effectiveness of the predictive models in varied real-world scenarios.

References

1. Nobre, J., Pires, E.S. and Reis, A., et al.:. Anomaly detection in microservice-based systems. Appl. Sci. **13**(13), 7891 (2023)
2. Bento, A., Correia, J., Filipe, R., et al.: Automated analysis of distributed tracing: challenges and research directions. J. Grid Comput. **19**(1), 9 (2021)
3. Xie, Z., Xu, H., Chen, W., et al.: Unsupervised anomaly detection on microservice traces through graph VAE. In: Proceedings of the ACM Web Conference 2023, pp. 2874–2884 (2023)
4. Zhao, C., Ma, M., Zhong, Z., et al.: Robust multimodal failure detection for microservice systems. In: Proceedings of the 29th ACM SIGKDD Conference on Knowledge Discovery and Data Mining, pp. 5639–5649 (2023)
5. Chen, Y.H., Chen, N.J., Xu, W.X., et al.: MFRL-CA: Microservice fault root cause location based on correlation analysis. In: 2021 8th International Conference on Dependable Systems and Their Applications (DSA), pp. 90–101. IEEE (2021)
6. Sever, Y., Dogan, A.H.: A Kubernetes dataset for misuse detection (2023)
7. OpenTelemetry. https://opentelemetry.io/docs/demo/architecture/ Accessed 17 Mar 2024
8. Kubernetes. https://kubernetes.io/. Accessed 17 Mar 2024
9. Chaos Mesh. https://chaos-mesh.org/. Accessed 17 Mar 2024

10. Locust. https://locust.io/. Accessed 17 Mar 2024
11. Prometheus. https://prometheus.io/. Accessed 17 Mar 2024
12. Jaeger. https://www.jaegertracing.io/. Accessed 17 Mar 2024
13. Grafana. https://grafana.com/. Accessed 17 Mar 2024
14. GitHub repository of our dataset generator. https://github.com/ilyasstrh/k8s-failure-dataset-generator

Dynamic Resource Allocation for 5G Device-to-Device Communication Based on Expected SARSA

Shashini Thamarasie Wanniarachchi[✉] [iD] and Volker Turau [iD]

Institute of Telematics, Hamburg University of Technology,
Am Schwarzenberg-Campus 3, Building E, 21073 Hamburg, Germany
{shashini.wanniarachchi,turau}@tuhh.de
https://www.ti5.tuhh.de/

Abstract. Device-to-device (D2D) communication is a key technology introduced with the fifth generation (5G) communication standards. D2D aids massively in catering the continuously increasing demand on the connectivity needs. Despite that, there are several challenges involved with D2D communication. Among other issues, interference management is of high importance when coexisting with the traditional cellular network. Improper interference handling in the network leads to increased system delay, low sum rate and throughput along with reduced spectral efficiency. The strategy of allocating resources such as channel, spectrum and transmission power is a fundamental component leading to interference management. In our work, we address this challenge of interference management in 5G D2D communication. We first investigate the resource allocation methods for D2D communication suggested in the literature. Then we propose a dynamic resource allocation technique for 5G D2D users based on *Expected SARSA* reinforcement learning algorithm. With simulation results, we show that the system throughput performance can be uplifted to a greater extent while maintaining a high reliability by applying the proposed dynamic resource allocation algorithm.

Keywords: 5G device-to-device communication · Resource allocation · Expected SARSA

1 Introduction

The many technological advancements and new inventions happening everyday, have changed people's needs phenomenally. Moving forward with this continous evolution has made smart devices and connectivity, everyday necessities. Moreover, there is a growing population density, specially in large cities. With these numbers growing dramatically, to ensure being connected on the go, every year the communication demand and mobile device usage keep improving drastically.

This project is funded by the BMWK - Federal Ministry for Economic Affairs and Climate Action in LuFo VI-1 under grant id 20E1911.

© The Author(s), under exclusive license to Springer Nature Switzerland AG 2024
A. Castañeda et al. (Eds.): NETYS 2024, LNCS 14783, pp. 231–246, 2024.
https://doi.org/10.1007/978-3-031-67321-4_16

Nowadays, the applications of communication go beyond simply establishing voice or data communication between two people. In many fields such as education, transportation, health, security, agriculture, production etc., data transmission between the devices has become a vital aspect for efficiently handling these services. In the traditional cellular network, each of these communication links is established through the base station. Considering the escalating demand at present, if every link goes through the base station, it is a huge amount of traffic to be handled. As a result, the base station will be overwhelmed. This incur high delays in message transmissions, reduced data throughput, reduced sum rate and degradation of the spectral efficiency [15]. To mitigate this overburdening on the base station, employing the fifth generation (5G) communication concept introduced by the third generation partnership project (3GPP) referred to as *device-to-device* (D2D) communication between the user equipment (UE) is a prominent solution. With this concept, two devices could communicate directly with each other. The technical reports TR 23803 [1] and TR 23703 [2] attached to release 12 of 3GPP specifications, detail the supported modes of direct communication. Accordingly, there are two modes: *network independent direct communication* and *network authorized direct communication*.

The first mode doesn't require any assistance from the base station network to authorize the communication. They carry out the direct communication between nearby devices based on the information locally available at the UE. Nevertheless, this mode can only be applied to proximity services (ProSe) enabled public safety UE. In the second mode, for resource allocation and nearby device detection, the base station network assistance is required by the D2D UE. This mode can be applied to any ProSe enabled user belonging in the same radio access network. Within the scope of this work, our attention is on a general D2D communication scenario. Therefore, we focus on network authorized D2D communication out of the two D2D modes.

5G D2D communication is capable of attenuating problems such as, high delay, low throughput and low sum rates in the legacy network. To this end, it is expected that the 5G D2D provides an efficient and a robust communication. However, [6] highlights several major issues associated with the D2D communication that hinder the user experience such as: peer discovery, resource allocation, resource management, interference management and power control.

Peer discovery is identifying the D2D UE in the close proximity to establish the communication link. Interference management means minimizing the interference between cellular and D2D users (see Fig. 1). The resource allocation, resource management and power control are the elements that contribute in interference management. The term *resources* signifies the channel, spectrum and power that is allocated to the D2D user. Hence, although we can address each of the above challenges individually, these can be broadly categorized into two: *interference management* and *peer discovery*. While peer discovery is an equally important research direction, here, we only focus on interference management.

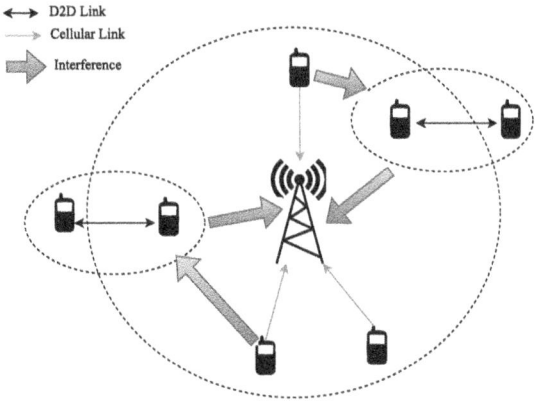

Fig. 1. Interference scenario with D2D and cellular users

In line with the two D2D modes defined by 3GPP, the spectrum utilization in D2D communication can be divided into two modes: *inband* and *outband* [13]. *Inband* is the D2D communication sector that operates over the licensed spectrum. This enables improved quality in communication with high system throughput and better spectrum utilization. This can further be categorized into two: *overlay* and *underlay*. In *overlay*, the spectrum is divided in a non-overlapping manner and allocated to D2D and cellular users [16]. This way, the D2D user always operates on a dedicated spectrum. According to results from [12], overlay spectrum sharing improves both D2D and legacy communication rates because the interference is very low. The drawback is the low spectrum utilization. In *underlay*, the D2D user shares a portion of the spectrum of the cellular user. In this mode, there is an improved spectral efficiency, high data rate and throughput. Nonetheless, the involved interference is high [16]. On the other hand, *outband* communication operates over the unlicensed spectrum. Meaning, no cellular resources are employed [13].

Our work is centered around interference management in network authorized D2D communication. Furthermore, we specifically focus on inband underlay D2D mode, as achieving a high spectrum utilization is vital. As highlighted before, resource allocation, resource management and power control are equally important for interference management. Resource allocation deals with means of allocating network resources. In the scope of resource management, the resource block scheduling is prominent. Traditional scheduling schemes such as round robin, proportional fair and best channel quality indicator (BCqi) algorithms are used for this purpose. Dynamically switching between these modes and dynamic resource block structure are also applied in resource management. In terms of power control, energy harvesting mechanisms are proposed in the literature. However, within the scope of this work we do not study resource management or power control strategies. The proposed approach thus, addresses the issue of resource allocation in order to reach our overall goal of interference management.

We first analyse the available strategies of resource allocation for D2D communication for better system performance. Many different approaches from literature in this domain are presented later in Sect. 2. Based on our findings, the majority attention can be seen currently on deep reinforcement learning (DRL) based techniques, and specifically on Q-learning and its variants. In our work, we propose a mechanism for dynamic resource allocation for D2D communication using reinforcement learning (RL). We apply, *Expected SARSA* algorithm. It is an on-policy control mechanism. This means that, it updates the policy while following it. Due to this reason, we focus on Expected SARSA rather than using Q-learning which follows an off-policy learning strategy. Therefore, we propose an Expected SARSA based dynamic resource allocation scheme for underlay D2D 5G communication system with the objective of gaining high system performance. To this end, we use throughput, signal to noise ratio (SNR), message delivery ratio and transmission delay as the performance indicators. To verify our approach, we carry out the simulations using OMNeT++ discrete event simulator [28]. 5G specific implementations are done with Simu5G [23], an OMNeT++ based 5G simulation framework.

The rest of this paper is organized as follows. Section 2 gives an overview on our findings from the previous research in the area. Section 3 elaborates our proposal and the implementation details while Sect. 4 presents the analysis of results. Finally Sect. 5 concludes the paper.

2 State of the Art

Within the research community, interference management and achieving high throughput in D2D communication is a topic that has gained a lot of interest over the years. Specifically, researchers addressing this issue have focused on different resource allocation techniques. Minimizing the interference between cellular and D2D users highly depends on how the resources such as channel, spectrum and power are being assigned to the users. In the work of Gupta *et al.* [16], they provide a taxonomy of solutions that can be applied as resource allocation schemes for D2D communications.

First category in this domain is game-theory based resource allocation schemes. Several applications of game theory can be found in the literature concerning optimal solution search for resource allocation problem in D2D communication. [26] propose *Stakelberg* game theory based algorithm for heterogeneous networks. Based on an analysis on the system performance and throughput they have validated their proposal. Another work based on the same game theory is [29]. They have also incorporated an interference alignment algorithm to serve D2D communication in underlay mode. Their proposal has achieved high sum rate and low time complexity. In the work of [21], they apply game theory with mixed strategies for D2D enabled vehicular networks. This method has been able to deliver optimized system computation capacity. The *Coalition* game theory is utilized as a strategy of resource allocation in D2D communication with co-channel and cross-channel interference in [14]. The results show that, this technique entails a maximized system sum rate and secrecy ensured resource allocation.

The second category is the graph-theory based resource allocation. Several examples can be seen among previous research which employ *coloring principle* and *centrality concept* of graph theory. Both [31,34] are examples of using coloring principle. In [31] power control and node priority calculation is utilized to optimize communication index. They have been able to achieve improved fairness with low power consumption and delay. An improved graph coloring is applied for interference graph formation in secondary clustering of D2D user in [34]. They have further applied *Hungarian algorithm* for optimal channel allocation to gain improved system throughput and access rate. Jeon et al. in [17] employ centrality concept for D2D pair selection along with a modified resource allocation scheme. With this, they've accomplished high maximum sum rate and reduction in the frequency range.

The third group of resource allocation schemes according to [16] is joint channel based mechanisms. One example is [5]. Here, they are concentrating on a Non-Orthogonal multiple access (NOMA) based D2D communication. They propose *Kuhn-Munkres* technique for sub channel allocation and *Karush-Kuhn-Tucker* conditions for power allocation. After analysing the system under different network conditions, they have accomplished improved energy efficiency and throughput. In the work of [11], their focus is on a D2D underlay multi user cellular network. They propose a matrix channel allocation algorithm where at least one cellular sub-channel is allocated for each D2D user. With simulations, they have proven that the system achieves a high spectrum utilization and efficiency.

Another subdivision in resource allocation techniques for D2D is NOMA-based methods [16]. NOMA is a multiple access scheme based on power. That is, multiple users are capable of using the same time/frequency or code resources while using different power levels. This concept is applied in order to uplift the spectral efficiency of the network in 5G [9]. One example for this category is [10] and the quality of experience is their performance indicator. Here, the sub-channel assignment and power allocation are optimized by using an iterative algorithm based on alternating optimization algorithm and constrained convex procedure technique. Two other examples in this scope are [8,9]. In the former, an interference management paradigm with uplink NOMA is proposed. In the latter, a joint channel allocation and power control mechanism for femto cell users is proposed using cognitive radio non-orthogonal multiple access.

Next category of resource allocation algorithms for D2D is Machine Learning (ML) based approaches. Out of many examples in literature, Zhu et al. [35] propose a scheme based on neural networks. Here, the D2D users in underlay mode can reuse the resources of cellular users following the proposed non-linear optimization algorithm. They conclude that high performance with a reduced computational complexity can be achieved. [19] is another work in this domain. They jointly apply heuristic equally reduced power scheme with a deep neural network based scheme for allocating transmit power for each channel. This way, they have achieved near-optimal sum rates. Moreover, in [7], they provide a framework for analyzing effective resource allocation schemes for mmWave D2D networks using ML algorithms.

As elaborated above, there exist many techniques to address resource allocation in D2D communication. Even so, one of the most popular techniques currently in use is DRL. These schemes make use of DRL techniques such as Q-learning to train the D2D user. Based on what's learnt, the D2D user can select resources for itself such as power and channels for the D2D networks. [32] propose a deep Q-network, where the D2D transmitter determines the channel resource and transmit power based on locations of mobile devices and actions taken by other D2D users. Their results depict maximization of overall effective throughput of D2D communication. In [18] double-dueling-deep Q-network is applied. Here, a centralized controller interacts with the environment to find the best resource allocation approach and deliver near-optimal performance. Double deep Q-network (DDQN) has been applied in many previous work to address resource allocation problem in D2D communication. In [30], DDQN with priority sampling (Pr-DDQN) is used by the D2D users to learn the significant features and select the channel resources and transmit power to use. High rates can be achieved through this method. [33] apply DDQN and make the D2D pairs learn the optimal strategy based on local information regarding the difference of achievable rate of D2D users and used power. The strategy has gained better convergence performance. [24] is another example of DDQN usage. They have combined DDQN with an energy harvesting model for optimization of resource allocation in D2D underlay mode to achieve high energy efficient performance.

In addition to these methods, a distance based approach to switch between the overlay and underlay is suggested in [25]. Depending on a distance threshold, the algorithm decides if to work on overlay (for short distance) or underlay (for long distance). Additionally, they alter the transmit power value to check the performance of the system in terms of system throughput. This strategy shows improved SNR values and throughput with reduced interference.

3 Methodology

3.1 Expected SARSA

RL algorithms learn to perform right actions at the right situation by observing the environment to obtain the best possible outcome. RL consists of 5 elements: state, action, reward, agent and the environment. A policy, π is the central concept of RL. An agent takes a state as the input and search for the optimal policy depending on the rewards gained by performing actions. A Markov Decision Process (MDP), is a template that can be used to define the tasks utilizing the 5 elements of RL. By modeling the task as a MDP, the agent's policy becomes a mapping from each state it may experience to a probability distribution over a set of possible actions. Computation of the optimal policy can be done using offline techniques such as *dynamic programming* or online methods that learn based on experience such as, *Monte Carlo methods* and *temporal difference methods* (TDM). Online techniques tend to converge faster as the focus is not on the entire state space as in offline methods [27].

In TDM, an agent will face the environment generating a trajectory with the visited states, taken actions and achieved rewards. This experience is then used to update the policy. TDM can be *off-policy* or *on-policy*. Q-learning is an algorithm following the off-policy learning strategy. Here, two policies: *behaviour policy* to explore the environment and *estimation policy* to engage in the optimization process are used [27]. In contrast to that, in on-policy strategies, both behaviour and estimation policies are identical. Meaning, the algorithm updates the policy while following it. SARSA is an example algorithm in this category.

SARSA name is derived from the five parameters involved in the update rule: current **S**tate (S_t) - current **A**ction (A_t) - **R**eward (R) - next **S**tate (S_{t+1}) - next **A**ction (A_{t+1}). Q-value, denoted by $Q(S_t, A_t)$ is the return expected to obtain taking a certain action in a certain state following the policy. When the environment is changing, having an on-policy exploration strategy is better as the policy also keeps changing with the environment. This is the advantage of SARSA over off-policy schemes. The additional variance imposed by the next action, A_{t+1} which slows down the convergence is the disadvantage [27].

Expected SARSA is an extension of SARSA. The strategy in Expected SARSA is taking the weighted average of the Q-values of all possible actions in the next state for Q-value estimation. This way, the variance is reduced. As a result, Expected SARSA converges faster and require less training [27]. Hence, it is beneficial to use Expected SARSA over SARSA.

Expected SARSA works as follows. First, the agent observes the current state S_t, and choose an action A_t according to the policy π. The policy is called ϵ-*greedy* policy where, $0 \leq \epsilon \leq 1$. Accordingly, with probability 1-ϵ, the agent selects an action depending on the estimated Q-values ($Q(S_t, A_t)$) for the state derived pertaining to the best reward obtained. This is called *exploitation*. Otherwise, the agent chooses a random action without prior knowledge on the reward, termed as *exploration*. Next, the agent observes the obtained reward, R for the action taken and the next state, S_{t+1}. It uses the Expected SARSA update rule:

$$Q(S_t, A_t) \leftarrow Q(S_t, A_t) + \alpha[R + \gamma(\sum_{A_t \in \delta_t} \pi(A_t|S_{t+1})Q(S_{t+1}, A_t) - Q(S_t, A_t))],$$

to estimate the Q-value of the current state-action pair where α is the learning rate. Here, δ_t is the set of all actions applicable in state S_t and γ is the discount factor, which modifies the task returns in a way that it rewards the most efficient behavior. $Q(S_t, A_t)$ is therefore, the expected cumulative reward obtained by the agent for taking a certain action on a specific state following the policy. Finally, it updates the policy π for the current state, based on the estimated Q-values.

3.2 Experimental Setup

We address the resource allocation problem of 5G D2D communication. We followed the work of [20] in Expected SARSA modeling. Our network setup is similar to Fig. 1 with a single cell. It consists of one base station (referred to as gNodeB in 5G) with one D2D pair and a variable number of interfering devices. The distance between the gNodeB and the D2D user pair is set as 50 m.

The implementation is carried out with OMNET++ using Simu5G framework. Simu5G simulates the data plane of 5G neworks and includes all the protocol layers for both UE and gNodeB. This model library contains two global entities *CarrierAggregation* and *Binder* that maintain a record of global information such as frequency resources, multicast groups etc. This way, the users are able to abstract control plane functionalities as well. Simu5G provides both infrastructure and D2D communication implementation possibilities and the ability to dynamically switch between the modes. This is facilitated via a simple BCqi check policy which evaluates the achievable bits on a single resource block in uplink direction [23]. Usage of simu5G in D2D implementations such as [4,22] can be seen in literature. In the former an evaluation between infrastructure and D2D modes is carried out. Their findings conclude that through D2D mode the spectrum utilization and the total throughput can be optimized. In latter, they apply Simu5G to analyze the quality of D2D communication in a vehicular network scenario by observing the BCqi value.

Our goal is to dynamically allocate channel resources using Expected SARSA, to achieve reduced interference in an underlay D2D scenario. At each communication cycle, the current state is observed by the agent (UE in our case), and decides which channel resources are to be used in a way that it optimizes the performance. In terms of Expected SARSA, our state and reward functions depend upon our main performance indicator, which is the system throughput. We calculate the throughput according to the *Shannon Capacity Theorem* given by (1) where, B is the bandwidth

$$Throughput = B\log_2(1 + SNR) \quad (1)$$

with SNR defined as:

$$SNR = \frac{TransmittedPower}{(N_o + \sum I)} \quad (2)$$

where N_o is the additive white Gaussian noise and $\sum I$ is the summation of total interference at D2D receiving end. The applied channel bandwidth and the transmission power thus have the most impact on this calculation. The channel bandwidth is controlled by the number of resource blocks and numerology index according to (3) including a 10% guard band, where μ is the numerology index. Numerology index defines the allocated sub carrier spacing.

$$B = 2^\mu \times \frac{NumberofResourceBlocks}{5} \quad (3)$$

To this end, we manage these resources by dynamically allocating the number of resource blocks, numerology index and transmission power. The urban macro propagation model and the path loss model according to the 3GPP 5G standardization documentation [3] form the foundation for communication establishment of this work. To bring in realistic conditions we also included Rayleigh fading and shadowing in the implementation. Nevertheless, we do not alter the other parameters that also contribute to the SNR such as: thermal noise, attenuation, fading etc. The carrier frequency is another parameter that we wanted to experiment on. The carrier frequency set up in Simu5G is done via the component carrier simple module which is inside the carrier aggregation global compound module of Simu5G. Our Expected SARSA algorithm works following the same update interval used in Simu5G. As a result, adjusting the frequency from time to time affects the entire communication paradigm. This is because, to establish D2D communication both transmitter and receiver must be on the same carrier frequency which should be a one supported by the gNodeB. This adjustment thus, require further investigation into Simu5G physical and MAC layer implementations. Hence, within the scope of this work, we did not vary the carrier frequency value or switch between the underlay and overlay modes.

We first observed the achievable throughput with default conditions from Simu5G. Accordingly, we set two threshold values for each set of experiments. Then for Expected SARSA, we chose three states pertaining to these two threshold levels. In terms of actions, we have five actions. The action consists of the number of resource blocks, numerology index and the transmission power. Table 1 depicts our action space. The values for the action space were chosen based on initial experiments without applying Expected SARSA and considering minimization of used resources. We set the carrier frequency in all the cases to be 2 GHz. The transmission power of the gNodeB is 46 dBm.

Table 1. Action space for SARSA alorithm

Action	Bandwidth (MHz) (Number of Resource Blocks, Numerology Index)	Transmission Power (dBm)
1	25 (125,0)	23
2	20 (100,0)	23
3	20 (50,1)	26
4	5 (25,0)	26
5	30 (75,1)	26

The same threshold levels of throughput are applied for the reward function and the assigned rewards are -30, 0 and 80. These vales were chosen based on experimental evaluations on fine tuning our algorithm. Additionally, we also vary the ϵ value depending on the achieved throughput to avoid any bias in the algorithm. As the state keeps changing, we also alter ϵ towards exploitation. If the throughput is better then a lower ϵ value is used and as worse the throughput gets, ϵ is closer to one. α is set to be 0.5 and γ is set to be 0.99 based on an initial experimental analysis.

The Expected SARSA algorithm runs once the the SNR measurements are recorded. After calculating the throughput with current parameters the agent receives a reward accordingly. Depending upon the current throughput, the next state is decided. Then, based on the policy the next action to be taken is chosen and the Q-value table is updated. The new action value is then read by the component carrier. This sets the number of resource blocks, numerology index and the transmission power to be used in the next communication cycle. Component carrier, then signals the binder to register the new carrier so that the channel model and other system components will be updated with the new parameters. As a result, in each communication cycle, depending on the experience gained by the UE, a new set of parameters for the resources are chosen. As the objective of the policy is to optimize the system output, the agent tends to choose actions that lead to improved performance.

As per performance evaluation criteria for our algorithm, several metrics were chosen. First, the system throughput, calculated according to (1) and the SNR based on (2) were used. Then, the message transmission delay and delivery ratio (given by (4)) were investigated.

$$DeliveryRatio = \frac{Number\,of\,Received\,Messages}{Number\,of\,Transmitted\,Messages} \qquad (4)$$

We carried out several experiments in this context to validate our algorithm. The results are discussed in detail in Sect. 4.

4 Analysis of Results

In this section, we present the results from the OMNeT++ simulations to validate our proposed concept. The results presented are obtained by averaging statistics from 30 independent repetitions done for each experiment. We considered the 95% confidence intervals. As the transmitted message, a packet size of 1000 bytes was used. The transmission protocol used was UDP. All experiments were performed for a single pair of D2D users for a simulation duration of 30 s.

In the first set of experiments, we compared the performance of the proposed algorithm with the default D2D scenario presented in Simu5G. To this end, a carrier frequency of 2 GHz, 50 resource blocks and a numerical index of 0 along with a D2D transmission power of 26 dBm were applied for the default scenario. The D2D UE s were stationary in this set of experiments.

Rather than comparing the performance between the two aforementioned scenarios in general, we evaluated the throughput performance in conjunction with two additional parameters. First parameter is the distance between the D2D pair. Three distance values between the D2D pair were taken into account: 20 m, 40 m and 60 m. The second parameter is the number of interfering devices present in the environment. We investigated the average throughput delivered under three cases: no interference, presence of 10 interfering devices and presence of 25 interfering devices. The background cell traffic generation model from Simu5G was used for this purpose. The interfering devices were also considered

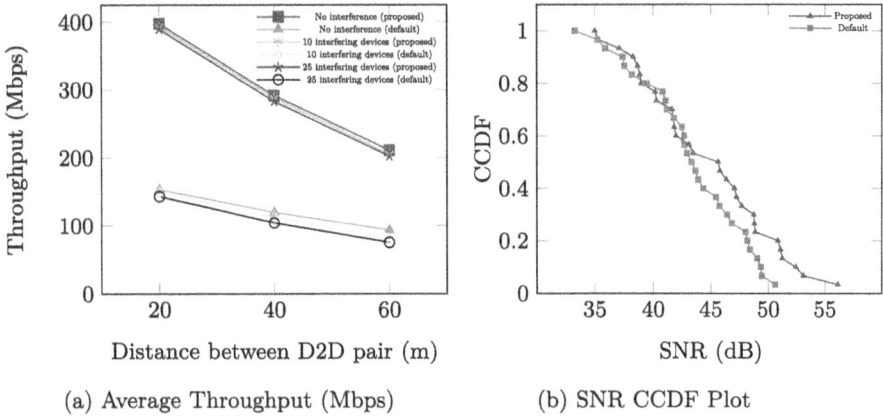

Fig. 2. (a) Average D2D throughput comparison for various distances between the D2D pair with 10 and 25 interfering devices. (b) Complimentary cumulative distributed function (CCDF) plot of measured SNR with 25 interfering devices for a 20 m D2D pair distance.

to be stationary. Moreover, we did a SNR result comparison considering the 25 interfering devices scenario for the distance of 20 m between the D2D pair. Figure 2 presents the results of these experiments.

Figure 2a depicts the average throughput comparison. The first observation is the significant improvement in the values of throughput resulted from the proposed algorithm in all considered cases. Moreover, between the no interference and interference scenarios, the difference between the obtained throughput values are lower in proposed system compared to the results of the default case. This proves that our proposed algorithm has been able to deliver improved performance even in a high interference scenario of around 25 interfering devices. The next observation is the gradual degradation of the throughput performance seen as the distance between the D2D pair is increased to 60 m. This result confirms the general norm that, the lesser the distance between the D2D pair, the higher the D2D performance. Nonetheless, even at a high distance of 60 m, the proposed algorithm has achieved a throughput higher than 200 Mbps as opposed to less than 100 Mbps delivered in the default case. Figure 2b further confirms our algorithm. We visualized the complimentary cumulative distributed function (CCDF) of the SNR values in the two situations. The CCDF obtained with the proposed scenario is shifted towards higher SNR values illustrating a better performance compared to the default case in the presence of 25 interfering devices. This result thus, establishes the fact that our concept of using Expected SARSA algorithm for the resource allocation problem of D2D communication yields improved interference management.

In addition to the throughput and SNR, we also focused on the delivery ratio and delivery delay values for reliability and delay assessment. This analysis was only for the case of 60 m distance between the D2D pair, as we wanted to test the system for a general high distance value. In terms of interfering devices, we concentrated only on the case of 25 interfering devices. We calculated the average delivery ratio and average delivery delay with the 95% confidence interval.

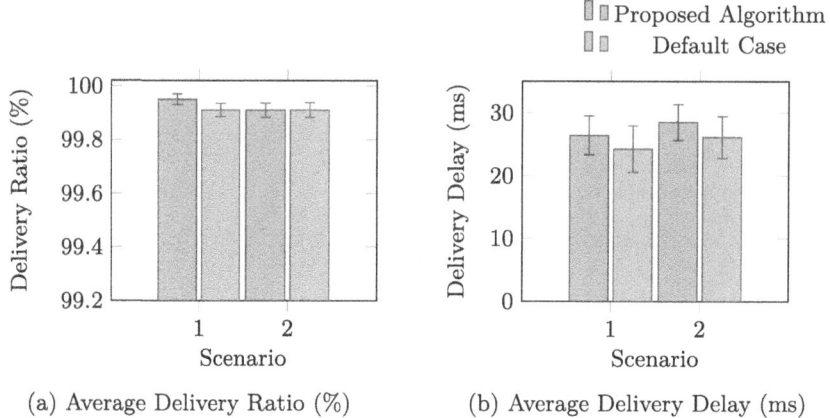

Fig. 3. Comparison of performance of (a) delivery ratio and (b) delivery delay when the distance between the D2D pair is 60 m for the two scenarios: 1 - no interference and 2 - in presence of 25 interfering devices

Figure 3a and Fig. 3b represent the results for average delivery ratio and delivery delay respectively with the 95% confidence intervals. Both the delivery ratio and delivery delay values for the proposed algorithm and the default scenario vary in similar ranges for the respective cases. The delivery ratio on the one hand, shows a slight improvement in our proposed algorithm for the no interference scenario and has remained to be the same as the default case when there is interference. In general, reaching a 99% or higher delivery ratio is the accepted behavior for a D2D communication scenario. And we should also account for the fact that these values were obtained for a D2D pair distance of 60 m. Accordingly, it is evident that applying the algorithm hasn't hindered but has enabled maintaining or further improving the system reliability even for a higher D2D pair distance.

On the other hand, the delivery delay values have slightly degraded compared to the default value. However, the difference is very low and in comparison we have reached a higher throughput without sacrificing the reliability. We accept the fact that the delivery delay in the range of 20 ms is not sufficient. Yet, the values are in the same range even for the default case which showcase the need for improvement when the D2D pair distance is high. Despite that fact, within the scope of this work, we didn't take this into our consideration.

Moreover, we also conducted an experiment to investigate the behaviour of the algorithm in a mobility scenario. We evaluated the throughput performance under three cases: D2D users are mobile and no interfering devices present, D2D users are mobile in the presence of 25 interfering devices who are stationary and both D2D users and interfering devices are mobile. For both types of devices the mobility model *MassMobility* from inet framework was applied. This mobility model describes a random mobility pattern for a mobile node that has a mass. The speed of all the UE s was set to be 20 m/s. We restricted the movement into an area of 100 m x 100 m to ensure the D2D communication is always guaranteed. Table 2 demonstrates the achieved throughput values. The mobility model incurs a random motion in all devices and the distance between the D2D users keep varying. Due to this reason, the amount of interference caused could vary and the results show that even in the case of moving interfering devices, our algorithm has been able to reach a comparatively high throughput value. This further validates the applicability of our algorithm into D2D communication scenarios for interference management and high throughput achievement.

Table 2. Throughput values in mobility scenario

Scenario	No Interference	25 Stationary Interfering Devices	25 Mobile Interfering Devices
Proposed	294.25 Mbps	292.78 Mbps	293.78 Mbps
Default	113.60 Mbps	114.23 Mbps	115.33 Mbps

One remark on our concept is regarding the computational complexity. Compared to the default system, our proposed algorithm requires around thrice as much time for simulation and incurs around 15% additional memory consumption. Nonetheless, the values were: 1 min in real time to simulate 30 s of simulation and memory consumption is around 38%. Accordingly, the values stand in a tolerable range. Hence, despite the comparatively high computational demands, the algorithm's complexity is deemed acceptable for our intended application.

5 Conclusion and Outlook

5G D2D communication is a promising solution for the increasing communication demand at present. Nonetheless, there are several challenges entailed with D2D communication. Within the scope of this work, we addressed one such issue, which is the interference management in 5G D2D communication scenario. Interference handling is prominent to avoid increased system delay, low sum rate, low throughput and reduced spectral efficiency. From different available solutions, we focused on resource allocation mechanism in this work. We investigated the available resource allocation techniques and proposed a dynamic resource allocation strategy based on Expected SARSA RL algorithm. We evaluated the system under the performance evaluation criteria of achieved throughput, SNR, delivery ratio and delivery delay. According to results from various simulations, we have validated the suitability of applying our algorithm to enhance the performance with reduced interference in 5G D2D communication. We have showed that our algorithm results in improved system throughput with high reliability. As the next steps, we want to extend the concept for an environment with multiple D2D user pairs with realistic mobility conditions. Furthermore, we want to implement and evaluate the instances of switching the carrier frequency and other parameters that can impose an effect on interference management. Additionally, it was evident from the results that the achieved delivery delay values are not sufficiently small. Therefore, we also want to study the means of degrading delivery delay alongside applying our algorithm.

References

1. 3GPP: technical specification group services and system aspects; feasibility study for proximity services. Technical Report, 23803 (2012)
2. 3GPP: technical specification group services and system aspects; study on architecture enhancements to support proximity services. Technical Report, 23703 (2013)
3. 3GPP: study on channel model for frequencies from 0.5 to 100 GHz. Technical Report, 38901 (2022)
4. Abdulqadir, M.Q., Janaby, A.O.A.: Capacity and throughput enhancement for minimum distance using D2D scheme with TCP for 5G system. In: 2022 8th International Conference on Contemporary Information Technology and Mathematics, pp. 34–38 (2022)
5. Alemaishat, S., Saraereh, O.A., Khan, I., Choi, B.J.: An efficient resource allocation algorithm for D2D communications based on NOMA. IEEE Access **7**, 120238–120247 (2019)
6. Austine, A., Pramila, R.S.: A review on recent research directions in device to device communication. In: 3rd International Conference on Inventive Computation Technologies (2018)
7. Bilal, N.M., Velmurugan, T.: A review of efficient resource allocation for mm-wave D2D communication in cellular networks using ML algorithm. In: 2023 3rd International Conference on Pervasive Computing and Social Networking, pp. 1307–1312 (2023)
8. Budhiraja, I., Kumar, N., Tyagi, S.: Ishu: Interference reduction scheme for D2D mobile groups using uplink NOMA. IEEE Trans. Mobile Comp. **21**(9), 3208–3224 (2022)
9. Budhiraja, I., Tyagi, S., Tanwar, S., Kumar, N., Guizani, M.: Cross layer NOMA interference mitigation for femtocell users in 5G environment. IEEE Trans. Veh. Techn. **68**(5), 4721–4733 (2019)
10. Chen, L., Hu, B., Chen, S., Xu, G.: QoE-driven resource allocation for D2D underlaying NOMAcellular networks. In: IEEE Wireless Communications and Networking Conference (2021)
11. Du, Y., Shao, Y., Shi, Y., Huang, W., Sun, K.: Joint power and channel allocation for D2D underlaid multi-user cellular networks. In: 2021 IEEE International Conference on Artificial Intelligence and Computer Applications, pp. 219–223 (2021)
12. Geraci, G., et al.: What will the future of UAV cellular communications be? A flight from 5G to 6G. IEEE Com. Sur./Tut. **24**(3), 1304–1335 (2022)
13. Gui, J., Zhou, K.: Cellular throughput optimization by game-based power adjustment and outband D2D communication. EURASIP J. Wirel. Commun. Networking **2018**(1), 1–25 (2018). https://doi.org/10.1186/s13638-018-1275-2

14. Gupta, R., Tanwar, S.: Interference mitigation and secrecy-ensured D2D resource allocation scheme using game theory. In: IEEE INFOCOM 2022 - IEEE Conference on Computer Communications Workshops, pp. 1–6 (2022)
15. Gupta, R., Tanwar, S., Kumar, N.: Secrecy-ensured NOMA-based cooperative D2D-aided fog computing under imperfect CSI. J. Inf. Sec. App. **59**, 102812 (2021)
16. Gupta, S., Patel, R., Gupta, R., Tanwar, S., Patel, N.: A survey on resource allocation schemes in device-to-device communication. In: 2022 12th International Conference on Cloud Computing, Data Science & Engineering (Confluence), pp. 140–145 (2022)
17. Jeon, H.B., Koo, B.H., Park, S.H., Park, J., Chae, C.B.: Graph-theory-based resource allocation and mode selection in D2D communication systems: The role of full-duplex. IEEE wireless Com. Lett. **10**(2), 236–240 (2021)
18. Kai, C., Meng, X., Mei, L., Huang, W.: Deep reinforcement learning based user association and resource allocation for D2D-enabled wireless networks. In: 2021 IEEE/CIC International Conference on Communications in China, pp. 1172–1177 (2021)
19. Lee, W., Lee, K.: Resource allocation scheme for guarantee of QoS in D2D communications using deep neural network. IEEE Com. Lett. **25**(3), 887–891 (2021)
20. Mantilla, I., Turau, V.: Comparison of WiFi interference mitigation strategies in DSME networks: leveraging reinforcement learning with expected SARSA (2023)
21. Mensah, R.N., Zhiyuan, L., Okine, A.A., Adeke, J.M.: A game-theoretic approach to computation offloading in software-defined D2D-enabled vehicular networks. In: 2021 2nd Information Communication Technologies Conference, pp. 34–38 (2021)
22. Militaru, A.V., Lazar, R.G., Caruntu, C.F., Comsa, C.R., Bogdan, I.: Analysis of message flow transmissions for an inter-vehicle communication scenario. In: 2022 14th International Conference on Electronics, Computers and Artificial Intelligence, pp. 1–6 (2022)
23. Nardini, G., Sabella, D., Stea, G., Thakkar, P., Virdis, A.: Simu5G-an OMNeT++ library for end-to-end performance evaluation of 5G networks. IEEE Access **8**, 181176–181191 (2020)
24. Qi, Y., Geng, S.: Deep-reinforcement-learning-based resource allocation for energy harvesting D2D communication. In: 2023 4th International Conference on Electronic Communication and Artificial Intelligence, pp. 85–88 (2023)
25. Randhava, K.S., Roslee, M., Nmenme, P.U., Yusoff, Z.: Radio resource allocation for interference management in device to device (D2D) 5G networks. In: 2021 International Conference on Electrical, Communication, and Computer Engineering, pp. 1–6 (2021)
26. Rathi, R., Gupta, N.: Device to device communication using stackelberg game theory approach. In: 2020 Research, Innovation, Knowledge Management and Technology Application for Business Sustainability, pp. 100–103 (2020)
27. van Seijen, H., van Hasselt, H., Whiteson, S., Wiering, M.: A theoretical and empirical analysis of expected sarsa. In: 2009 IEEE Symposium on Adaptive Dynamic Programming and Reinforcement Learning, pp. 177–184 (2009)
28. Varga, A.: The OMNET++ discrete event simulation system. In: Proceedings of the ESM, vol. 9 (2001)
29. Wang, D., Zhang, S., Cheng, Q., Zhang, X.: Joint interference alignment and power allocation based on stackelberg game in device-to-device communications underlying cellular networks. IEEE Access **9**, 81651–81659 (2021)
30. Xiang, H., Peng, J., Gao, Z., Li, L., Yang, Y.: Multi-agent power and resource allocation for D2D communications: a deep reinforcement learning approach. In: 2022 IEEE 96th Vehicular Technology Conference, pp. 1–5 (2022)

31. Xue, Y., Yang, Z., Yang, W., Yang, J.: D2D resource allocation and power control algorithms based on graph coloring in 5G IoT. In: 2019 Computing, Communications and IoT Applications, pp. 17–22 (2019)
32. Yu, S., Jeong, Y.J., Lee, J.W.: Resource allocation scheme based on deep reinforcement learning for device-to-device communications. In: 2021 International Conference on Information Networking, pp. 712–714 (2021)
33. Yuan, Y., Li, Z., Liu, Z., Yang, Y., Guan, X.: Double deep Q-network based distributed resource matching algorithm for D2D communication. IEEE Trans. Veh. Technol. **71**(1), 984–993 (2022)
34. Zhou, X., Chen, G., Hu, Y., Li, X.: D2D interference management and resource allocation scheme based on improved graph coloring. In: 2022 International Conference on Artificial Intelligence, Information Processing and Cloud Computing, pp. 184–187 (2022)
35. Zhu, L., Liu, C., Yuan, J., Yu, G.: Machine learning-based resource optimization for D2D communication underlaying networks. In: 2020 IEEE 92nd Vehicular Technology Conference, pp. 1–6 (2020)

BeRGeR: Byzantine-Robust Geometric Routing

Brown Zaz, Mikhail Nesterenko[✉], and Gokarna Sharma

Department of Computer Science, Kent State University, Kent 44242, USA
{zbrown,mikhail,sharma}@cs.kent.edu

Abstract. We present BeRGeR: the first asynchronous geometric routing algorithm that guarantees delivery of a message despite a Byzantine fault without relying on cryptographic primitives or randomization. The communication graph is a planar embedding that remains three-connected if all edges intersecting the source-target line segment are removed. We prove the algorithm correct and estimate its message complexity.

1 Introduction

Geometric routing, also called geographic routing, routing uses node locations to transmit a message from the source to the target node. Nodes may either obtain their coordinates from GPS devices or compute virtual coordinates [1–4]. Geometric routing has several attractive features. Nodes do not need to store network topology information beyond their immediate neighbors. Moreover, such routing may be stateless as nodes do not have to retain information after forwarding a packet. Compared to flooding-based ad hoc routing algorithms [5,6], geometric routing is more resource-efficient.

Geometric routing may therefore be used in cases where maintaining more extensive routing information is not practicable. It may operate in environments with high topological volatility such as vehicular networks [7] or large collections of resource-poor devices such as wireless sensor networks [8].

Despite the claim of hostile environment applicability, little research has been done on fortifying geometric routing against faults using geometric routing techniques themselves. In this paper, we address this issue.

Geometric Routing. The elementary form of geometric routing is greedy. It can be used on either a planar or a non-planar graph embedding.

In greedy routing, the packet is forwarded to the neighbor with the closest Euclidean distance to the target. However, greedy routing fails if it reaches a local minimum. A local minimum is a node that does not have an immediate neighbor closer to the target. To recover from a local minimum and guarantee message delivery, packets are sent to traverse faces of a planarized subgraph [9]. Finding a maximum planar subgraph of a general graph is NP-hard [10]. However, for certain graphs, the task may be solved efficiently. A graph is unit-disk if a pair of its nodes u and v are neighbors if and only if the Euclidean distance between them is no more than 1. Such a graph approximates a wireless network. In a unit-disk graph, a connected planar subgraph may be found by local computation at every node using Relative Neighborhood or Gabriel Graph [11–14].

A sequential geometric routing algorithm, such as the classic GFG/GPSR [11, 13], routes a single packet in the greedy mode until a local minimum is encountered. The algorithm then switches to recovery mode, which involves traversing the faces of a planar subgraph of the original communication graph. Specifically, the algorithm traverses the faces that intersect the line segment that connects the source and the target.

Algorithms such as GFG/GPSR have a problem of face traversal direction choice. A face may potentially be traversed in two directions: clockwise and counter-clockwise. Face traversal may be inefficient if its traversal direction is selected inappropriately: the traversal distance may be long in one direction and short in the other. GOAFR+ [15] finds the shorter traversal direction by reversing it once the packet reaches a pre-determined ellipse containing source and target nodes.

A concurrent geometric routing algorithm CFR [16] sends multiple packets to traverse the faces intersecting the source-target line in both directions in parallel. This naturally selects the shortest face traversal direction.

Byzantine Fault Tolerance. A Byzantine node [17,18] may behave arbitrarily. This is the strongest fault that can affect a node in a distributed system. A reputation-based approach [19,20] is considered to deal with Byzantine faults. In such an approach, a node deviating from the algorithm may be marked as faulty and avoided by its neighbors. However, a faulty node may actively resist reputation compromise, for example by accusing other nodes of faults or waiting until its malicious influence causes maximum damage. Hence, in general, such approaches may only alleviate rather than eliminate the problem.

The power of the faults may also be mitigated with cryptography [17,21,22] or randomization [23,24]. Synchrony assumptions may help with fault handling as well [25]: if packet transmission may be delayed only for a finite amount of time, then fault information may be obtained from lack of packet receipt. In a completely asynchronous system, such information is not available.

Cryptography may be too expensive for resource poor nodes, the source of true randomness may not be achievable and synchrony may be impossible to guarantee. If none of these primitives are available, the solution requires that the number of correct processes be large enough to overwhelm the faulty ones.

The complexity of Byzantine fault handling increases if the network is not completely connected. In this case, nodes may not communicate directly; they have to rely on intermediate nodes to forward the packets. Faulty nodes may tamper with such forwarding. To counter such faulty behavior, packets are sent along alternative routes. To enable this, the network should be sufficiently connected. In general topology, message transmission is possible only if the network is $2x+1$-connected [17,26,27], where x is the maximum number of Byzantine faults.

In this paper, we study Byzantine-robust geometric routing in asynchronous networks. We do not use cryptography, randomization or reputation. Instead, we use distributed geometric routing to bypass the faults.

Related Work. Sanchez et al. [19] and Pathak et al. [20] use both cryptographic and reputation-based approaches to secure geometric routing. Adnan et al. [28] propose to secure geometric routing through pairwise key distribution. Boulaiche and Bouallouche [29] use message authentication codes to prevent message tampering. Maurer and Tixeuil [30] consider containing faulty Byzantine nodes in control zones such that messages will be sent there only with the authentication form border nodes. Zahariadis et al. [31] propose a reputation-based approach to geometric routing security. Several papers discuss counteracting spurious locations reported by faulty nodes to secure geometric routing [32–34]. Recently, the problem of consensus has been explored in the geometric setting [35]. Zaz and Nesterenko [36] consider Byzantine-robust geometric routing but offer no solution to the problem. To the best of our knowledge, no Byzantine-robust asynchronous geometric routing algorithm without cryptography, randomization or reputation has been proposed.

Several related problems have been addressed with concurrent geometric routing. In this paper, we consider unicasting: sending a message from a single source to a single target. Alternatively, in multicasting, the same message is delivered to a set of nodes in the network [37]. Sequential geometric multicasting algorithms [38–40] optimize message transmission routes by forwarding the same packet to multiple targets for a part of the route. MCFR [41] concurrently sends packets along all the appropriate faces achieving faster delivery at the expense of a greater number of transmitted packets. Another related problem is geocasting; in this problem, the source needs to deliver messages to every node in a particular target area. There are several sequential geocasting algorithms [11,37,42]. Adamek et al. [43] present a concurrent geocasting solution. None of these algorithms consider Byzantine tolerance.

Our Contribution. We present BeRGeR, an asynchronous unicast concurrent geometric routing algorithm that handles a single Byzantine fault. We assume the source and target nodes are connected by three internally node-disjoint paths that do not intersect the source-target line, formally prove BeRGeR correct under this assumption, and analyze its message complexity.

2 Preliminaries

Communication Model. A finite connected graph G is embedded in a geometric plane. Two nodes may not share the same coordinates. We, therefore, use node coordinates for both navigation and node identification. Two nodes adjacent to the same edge are *neighbors*. Each node knows its own coordinates and the coordinates of its neighbors. Neighbors communicate by passing packets. The communication is bi-directional, so the graph G, is undirected. The packet transmission is FIFO, reliable and asynchronous. We assume Lamport's "oral messages" model [17] where the message is not signed but the packet recipient always correctly identifies the sending neighbor.

Nodes are either correct or faulty. A *correct* node operates according to the specified algorithm. A *faulty* node is Byzantine: it may behave arbitrarily including sending packets, dropping received packets or not communicating at all.

If a node sends a packet without receiving it first, the node *originates* the packet. A node *forwards* a packet if it receives it and then sends it to another node. If a node forwards a packet to more than one neighbor, the node *splits* the packet. If a node receives but does not forward the packet, it *drops* the packet. We assume that a faulty node drops all packets that it receives and originates all packets that it sends. The case of a faulty node forwarding a packet correctly is equivalent to dropping the packet and originating an identical packet.

Message Transmission, Source, Target. A *message* is the gainful content to be transmitted by a sequence of forwarded packets. An arbitrary *source* node $s \in G$ is to transmit a message m_s to another arbitrary *target* node $t \in G$. Besides the message, a packet may carry the source and target coordinates as well as other auxiliary information.

To simplify the presentation, we assume that s and t are not neighbors. For our purposes, the message content is immaterial provided that two messages can be compared for equality. The target may receive the message from multiple neighbors, the target *delivers* the message once it passes correctness checks. Forwarding a packet with the same message creates a message path. Consider two message paths from node u to node v. These paths are *internally node-disjoint* if the only nodes the paths share are u and v.

Planarity, Faces, Traversal. An embedding of a graph is *planar* if its edges intersect only at nodes. For short, we call such a planar embedding a *planar graph*. In a planar graph G, a *face* is a region on the plane such that any pair of its points can be connected by a continuous curve inside the face. If the graph is finite, then the area of all but one face is finite. The finite area faces are *internal* faces and the infinite area face is the *external* face.

To traverse a face of a planar graph, the packets are routed using right- or left-hand-rule. Consider a node $v \in G$ that receives a packet from its neighbor u. In the *right-hand-rule*, v forwards the packet to the next clockwise neighbor after u. In the *left-hand-rule*, v forwards the packet to the next counter-clockwise neighbor after u. We call the obtained traversal paths respectively *right* and *left* and denote them R and L. The right path traverses an internal face counter-clockwise and the external face clockwise. The left path traverses the internal and external faces in the opposite direction to the right path.

Let $G - \overline{st}$ be the graph G, without the edges intersecting the source-target line segment $\overline{st}$. The *green face* is the union of faces that intersect $\overline{st}$. In other words, the green face is the unique face that contains segment $\overline{st}$ in $G - \overline{st}$. This green face in $G - \overline{st}$ may be either internal or external. A *green node* is a node adjacent to the green face. The source and target are thus green nodes. Given a green node k, the *k-blue face* is a union of non-green faces adjacent to k. A *k-blue* node is a non-green node adjacent to the k-blue face.

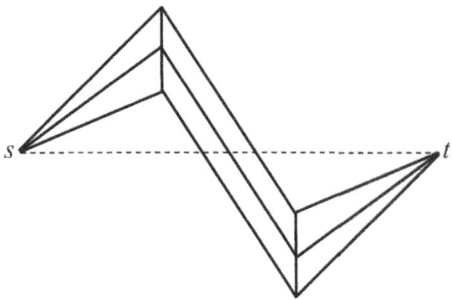

Fig. 1. A graph G, violating the Triconnectivity Assumption. Even though the graph itself is three-connected, $G - \overline{st}$ is disconnected.

The Byzantine-Robust Geometric Routing Problem. An algorithm that solves the Byzantine-Robust Geometric Routing Problem delivers the message m_s sent by the source to the target subject to the following three properties:

Validity: if the target delivers message m_t, then $m_t = m_s$;
Liveness: the target eventually delivers m_t;
Termination: every packet is forwarded a finite number of times.

Fault and Connectivity Assumptions. We consider a solution to the problem with at most one faulty node $f \in G$. We assume that s and t are correct.

The Byzantine node may originate a spurious message or stop the correct message from propagating. Thus, there need to be at least 3 node-disjoint paths to bypass the faulty node [26]. Hence, we consider 3-connected graphs.

Finding internally node-disjoint paths is difficult even if the graph is 3-connected. Our idea is to spatially separate them: one path uses the left-hand-rule traversal of the green face $G - \overline{st}$ the other—right-hand-rule. To achieve this, when forwarding the message, each green node ignores the edges that intersect $\overline{st}$. However, in general, this may eliminate potential paths to the target or leave the graph entirely disconnected. See Fig. 1 for an example. To prevent such disconnect, we posit the following graph connectivity assumption:

Assumption 1 (the Triconnectivity Assumption). $G - \overline{st}$ *is 3-connected.*

3 BeRGeR Description

In this section we present BeRGeR: a Byzantine-Robust Geometric Routing algorithm that solves the Reliable Message Delivery Problem with a single faulty node in a connected planar graph subject to the Triconnectivity Assumption.

Algorithm Outline. The algorithm operates as follows. The source concurrently sends two packets, called *cores*, to traverse the green face in the opposite traversal directions. That is, the source sends a left core and a right core.

A green node, i.e. a node adjacent to the green face, may be faulty. The faulty node may send a core with a spurious message. To prevent this, the target waits to receive both cores with matching messages before delivering their message. In this case, however, a faulty green node may drop the packet altogether and prevent message delivery at the target. To counteract this, BeRGeR has a mechanism of bypassing, or skipping, every green node. As the green nodes forward the core along the border of the green face, they add the nodes that the core visited to the packet. In addition, each green node splits the core by sending a *thread* packet that skips the next green node k. This thread packet traverses the union of k-blue and green faces.

A *braid* is a set of threads that carry matching messages in the same direction (L or R). A braid *matches* a core if it contains threads that skip each node that the core has visited and every such thread carries the same message as the core. This way, if there is a faulty green node, at least one thread skips it. Therefore, if a faulty node attempts to drop a packet or originate a forged packet, the target does not collect a matching braid and core. Since the faulty node may be only on the left or right side of the green face, a matching braid and core arrive on the opposite side regardless of the faulty node's actions.

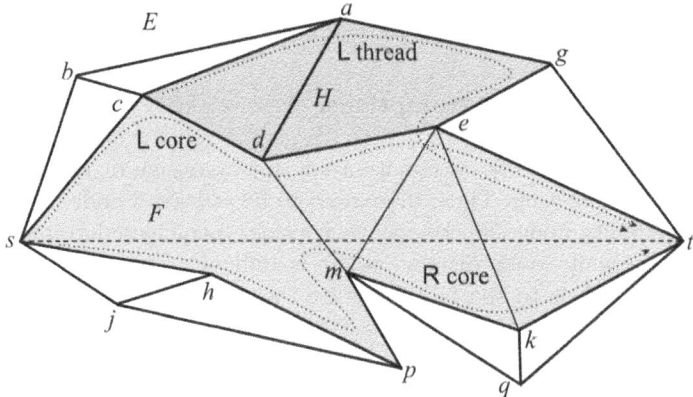

Fig. 2. BeRGeR example operation. L core and R core traverse the green face F. The second L thread, the d-thread, skips node d and traverses the union of the d-blue face H, and the green face F.

Refer to Fig. 2 for an illustration of the algorithm operation. The planar graph shown in the picture complies with the Triconnectivity Assumption. Note that greedy routing fails on this graph if the packet reaches node p since p is a local minimum. Face F is green. Nodes s, c, d, e, t, k, m, p and h are adjacent to F. These nodes are, therefore, green. Face H is the d-blue face adjacent to F. Nodes c, a, g, e are d-blue since they are not green but adjacent to the d-blue face H. Face E is the external face of the graph. The source sends two core packets that traverse F: left core L and right core R. The source also sends a left and a right thread that are not shown. The figure illustrates a single L thread that is generated by c when c receives a core. That is, c splits this core and sends thread that skips the next green node d. This thread traverses part of H and then F to reach t.

Algorithm 1: BeRGeR variables and functions

```
1  constants
2     n                                  // node coordinates
3     N                                  // set of neighbor coordinates
4     {L, R}                             // left and right packet direction

5  variables
6     T                                  // set of packets received by target

7  functions
8  nextNode(p, s, t, c, k)
9     M := {i ∈ N : i ≠ k and onThisSide(s, t, n, i)}
10    return i ∈ M : i is nearest to p in direction c ∈ {L, R}
      // node selection direction L: counter-clockwise, R: clockwise

11 onThisSide(s, t, n, i)
      // return true if the n-i and s-t line segments do not intersect
12    return n̄ī ∩ s̄t̄ = ∅

13 invalid(p, m, s, t, k, ℓ)
14    if k = p                           // sender is skipping itself
15    or (n = s and k = ⊥)               // a core arrives at s
16    or n ∈ ℓ then                      // traveled in a cycle
17       return true
18    else
19       return false
```

Algorithm Details. BeRGeR pseudocode is shown in Algorithms 1 and 2. Algorithm 1 shows constants, variables and functions used in BeRGeR. Specifically, each node maintains its own geometric coordinates n and the set of coordinates

Algorithm 2: BeRGeR Actions

```
20  source node, input:
21     t                                                      // target
22     m                                                      // message
23  source node, initial action:
24     send(m, s, t, R, ⊥, ⟨⟩) → nextNode(t, s, t, R, ⊥)       // new R core
25     send(m, s, t, L, ⊥, ⟨⟩) → nextNode(t, s, t, L, ⊥)       // new L core

26  k := nextNode(t, s, t, R, ⊥)
27     send(m, s, t, R, k, ⟨s⟩) → nextNode(t, s, t, R, k)      // new R thread

28  k := nextNode(t, s, t, L, ⊥)
29     send(m, s, t, L, k, ⟨s⟩) → nextNode(t, s, t, L, k)      // new L thread

30  every node:
31  receive (m, s, t, c, k, ℓ) from p →
32     if invalid(p, m, s, t, k, ℓ) then
33        return                                               // drop invalid packets
34     if k = ⊥ then                                           // if this is a core
35        ℓ.append(p)                        // append sender to list of visited nodes
36     if n ≠ t then                                           // packet is not at target
37        send(m, s, t, c, k, ℓ) → nextNode(p, s, t, c, k)     // forward packet
38        if k = ⊥ then                              // if received packet is core
39           k := nextNode(p, s, t, c, ⊥)              // find next green node
40           if k ∉ ℓ then                               // if k is unvisited
41              send(m, s, t, c, k, ⟨n⟩) → nextNode(p, s, t, c, k)   // new thread

42     else                                                    // packet is at target
          // green nodes neighboring t
43        coreR := nextNode(s, s, t, L, ⊥)
44        coreL := nextNode(s, s, t, R, ⊥)
          // node(s) neighboring t next to green nodes; may be
             identical
45        threadR := nextNode(s, s, t, L, coreR)
46        threadL := nextNode(s, s, t, R, coreL)
47        if     k = ⊥ and c = R and p = coreR then
48           T.add(m, s, R, ⊥, ℓ)                              // record R core
49        else if k ≠ ⊥ and c = R and p ∈ {coreR, threadR} then
50           T.add(m, s, R, k, ⟨⟩)                             // record R thread
51        else if k = ⊥ and c = L and p = coreL then
52           T.add(m, s, L, ⊥, ℓ)                              // record L core
53        else if k ≠ ⊥ and c = L and p ∈ {coreL, threadL} then
54           T.add(m, s, L, k, ⟨⟩)                             // record L thread
55        if ∃ℓ₁, ℓ₂ : {(m, s, L, ⊥, ℓ₁), (m, s, R, ⊥, ℓ₂)} ⊂ T and ℓ₁ ∩ ℓ₂ = {s} then
56           deliver m                                         // matching cores
57        else if ∃(m, s, c, ⊥, ℓ) ∈ T : ∀i ∈ ℓ, (m, s, c, i, ⟨⟩) ∈ T then
58           deliver m                    // matching core and braid of threads
```

of its neighbors N. Constants L and R denote packet traversal direction. The target node t maintains a set of packets T that it received. The target checks T to see if the received packets satisfy message delivery conditions. Function $\texttt{nextNode}(p, s, t, c, k)$ uses the neighbor p of n to select the node according to traversal direction c, either L or R. This selection excludes node k if it is skipped by a thread, and it considers only the neighbors on the same side of $\overline{st}$. This includes s and t themselves. This check is done in function $\texttt{onThisSide}(s, t, n, i)$. This function ensures that algorithm packets do not use the edges that cross the green face.

Algorithm 2 shows BeRGeR actions. There are two: the source node initial action that originates the packets (see line 23), and the receipt action taken by every node when it receives a packet (see line 31). As input, the source node s takes target coordinates t and the message m to be delivered to it. In the initial action, the source sends four packets: two cores and two threads. The cores go in left and right directions along the green face. The threads skip the first green nodes in the two directions.

The packet format is as follows: the message m; the source s, and target t; traversal direction L or R; the node k to be skipped or $\perp$ if it is a core packet; and the list of visited nodes. A core packet starts with an empty list. This list is only updated for cores. A thread carries its originator in the visited list.

Let us describe the packet receive action. First, the packet is checked for validity (see line 13). The packet is dropped if it has traveled in a cycle, a core is passing through s, or the sender p, is sending a thread that skips p. Otherwise, if the received packet is a core, p is appended to the visited node list ℓ and further processing depends on whether the packet has arrived at the target.

If the packet recipient is not the target (see line 36), then the node forwards the packet and, if it is a core packet, then the node also sends a thread skipping the next green node, provided that green node is not in the visited list ℓ.

If the packet recipient node is the target (see line 42), the recipient checks that the packet comes from an expected node and then records the receipt of the core or thread packet in T. Then, the target determines if message delivery conditions are met. Specifically, if T has a record of two matching cores or a matching core and a braid. *Matching cores* carry the same message in the opposite traversal directions. *Matching core and braid* are a core and a set of threads such that they are in the same traversal direction, carry the same message and, for every node that the core visited, there is a thread that skips it. If the target receives matching cores or a matching core and a braid, the target delivers the message that they carry.

4 BeRGeR Correctness Proof

Lemma 1. *A core packet traverses a single face of $G - \overline{st}$ and a thread skipping node k traverses a single face of $G - \overline{st} - \{k\}$.*

Proof. By the design of the algorithm, a packet traverses a single face. In forwarding a core packet, each node ignores the edges that intersect $\overline{st}$. If the source originates a core packet, this packet traverses the green face of $G - \overline{st}$. Similarly, thread skipping k originated by the source traverses the union of the green and the k-blue face of $G - \overline{st} - \{k\}$. A faulty node may send a packet in some other face, in which case it traverses that face. □

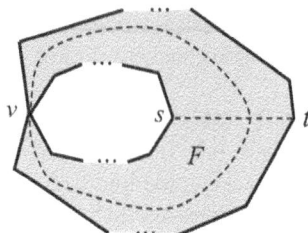

Fig. 3. Illustration for the proof of lemma 2. If left and right core paths share node v, then v can be connected by a continuous curve that separates s from t. Hence, every path from s to t contains v.

Let *left core path* be the left-hand-rule traversal path on the green face from the source to the target. Similarly, *right core path* be the right-hand-rule traversal path on the green face from s to t.

Lemma 2. *Left and right core paths are internally node-disjoint.*

Proof. We prove the lemma by contradiction. Suppose the opposite: the left and right core paths share an internal node v. See Fig. 3 for illustration. In this case, we can draw a closed curve that starts and ends in v and whose interior is inside the green face. This curve separates the plane into two areas: one of them contains s and the other t. This means that every path from s to t contains v. However, the Triconnectivity Assumption states that $G - \overline{st}$ is three-connected. This means that there must be at least three internally node-disjoint paths between s and t. Hence, our initial supposition is not correct. Therefore, left and right core paths must be internally node-disjoint. □

Let *left core* and *right core* are packets following left and right core paths respectively.

Lemma 3 (Core validity). *If the target receives a left core and a right core carrying messages m_{lc} and m_{rc} respectively and $m_{lc} = m_{rc}$, then $m_{lc} = m_s$.*

Proof The target receives a core packet from a node adjacent to the green face. According to Lemma 1, such packet traverses the green face only. According to Lemma 2, left and right core paths are disjoint. Since there is at most one fault in the network, at least one of these paths is fault-free. Therefore, either left or right core packets are forwarded by correct nodes only. In this case, it carries the message sent by the source. Hence, if the target receives two identical messages from both left and right core paths, this message is sent by the source. □

Lemma 4 (Thread validity). *If a thread skips a green node k and reaches a correct node, it is not originated by k.*

Proof. Only the source and the faulty node may originate threads. We assume that the source is correct. Therefore, we only have to consider the case of k being faulty. Note that k may potentially originate a thread that skips k, or may originate a core that splits into a thread that skips k. If k originates a thread that skips itself, then, by the design of the algorithm (see line 14), the recipient does not forward it.

Consider now the case where k originates a core. In this case, this core contains k in the list of visited nodes ℓ. Therefore, no correct node that receives this core sends a thread that skips k (see line 40). In either case, the thread that skips k is not originated by k. □

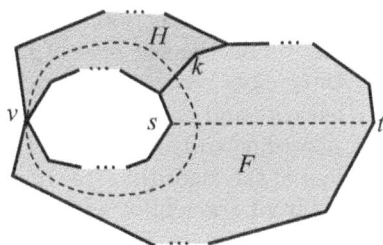

Fig. 4. Illustration for the proof of Lemma 5. If a blue face H, bypassing green node k contains a green node v, that lies on the right core path, then v can be connected by a continuous curve inside $F \cup H$ that separates s from t and, hence, every path from s to t either contains k or v.

Lemma 5. *The path traversed by a left thread does not contain any node of the right core path. Similarly, the path traversed by the right thread does not contain nodes of the left core path.*

Proof. We prove the lemma for the left thread. The argument for the right thread is similar.

Let us consider a left thread that skips some node k. According to Lemma 1, the thread either traverses the left core path or the k-blue face. Due to Lemma 2, the right and left core paths are internally node-disjoint. Hence, the left core path does not contain right core path nodes.

Let us now consider the nodes adjacent to the k-blue face. We prove this part by contradiction. Suppose the opposite: there is a node v that is adjacent to the k-blue face but lies on the right core path. We show that in this case all paths from s to t contain either v or k. Specifically, we show that the path that does not contain k, goes through v.

Indeed, removing node k and adjacent edges merges the green face and the k-blue face. See Fig. 4 for illustration. In this figure, F is the green face and H

is the k-blue face. In this case, inside this joint face, we can draw a closed curve that starts and ends in v. Therefore, any path from s to t that does not contain k, has to go through v. That is, all paths from s to t contain either v or k.

However, the Triconnectivity Assumption requires that there are three internally node-disjoint paths from s to t. Hence, our supposition is incorrect and the path traversed by the left thread, either along the left core path or along the k-blue face, does not contain a node on the right core path. □

Recall, that a *braid* is a set of threads with the same direction, left or right, and carrying the same message. A braid *matches* a core packet c if (i) c and the braid carry the same message and (ii) for every node i that c carries in its visited list ℓ there is a thread in the braid that skips i.

Lemma 6 (Braid validity). *If the fault is adjacent to the green face and the target receives a core and a matching braid carrying m_b, then $m_b = m_s$.*

Proof. We prove the lemma for the left direction. The argument for right direction is similar. The fault may be on the left side of the green face or on the opposite side. We consider these cases separately.

Let the target receive a left core and matching left braid while the fault is on the right side. In this case, according to Lemma 2, all the nodes of the left core path are correct. By the design of the algorithm (see line 47), the target accepts a core packet only if it comes from a neighbor adjacent to the green face. Due to Lemma 1, this core traverses the green face only. Since the fault is on the right core path, this left core was forwarded by correct nodes only. Therefore it carries m_s.

Let us now consider the case where the target receives a left core and a matching left braid while the fault is also on the left core path. Let f be the faulty node; that is, the faulty node is on the received core path. A correct recipient that forwards the packet records the packet sender in the visited list ℓ of the packet. Therefore, f is present in ℓ of the core packet that the target receives. Since the target receives a braid that matches this core packet, it also receives a thread that skips f. According to Lemma 4, f may not originate such a thread. Hence, the thread that skips f is originated by the source so it carries m_s. Since this thread is in the braid that carries the same message and matches the core message, they all carry m_s. □

Lemma 7. *(Liveness) The target eventually receives either (i) matching left and right core packets or (ii) a matching core and a braid.*

Proof. If the faulty node is not adjacent to the green face, then both matching left and right core packet reach the target.

Let us examine the case of a faulty node is adjacent to the green face. This means that it lies on a core path. Assume, without loss of generality, that the node is on the right core path. Then, according to Lemma 2, the left core path is fault-free. Moreover, due to Lemma 5 the paths of all the left threads are also fault-free. That is, in case the faulty node is on the right core path, the left core and a matching left braid reach the target. □

Lemma 8 (Termination). *Every packet is forwarded a finite number of times.*

Proof According to Lemma 1, every packet traverses a single face in either $G - \overline{st}$ or $G - \overline{st} - \{k\}$. The originator of the packet is recorded in the visited list ℓ of the packet. When received, the originating node drops such a packet. That is, if the packet is not dropped by the source, target or the faulty node, it is dropped by the originating node once the packet traverses the entire face.

The faulty node may record a spurious packet originator in ℓ. However, according to Lemma 1, this packet traverses some face, arrives back to the faulty node, where it is assumed to be dropped.

In a finite graph, this means that every packet is forwarded a finite number of times. □

Theorem 1. *BeRGeR: Byzantine Robust Geometric Routing algorithm solves the Reliable Message Delivery Problem with a single Byzantine node in a planar graph subject to the Triconnectivity Assumption.*

Proof. In BeRGeR, the target delivers message m_t in two cases: either it receives two matching core packets or it receives a matching core packet and a braid. According to Lemma 3, if the target receives matching core packets, the packets carry the message sent by the source. According to Lemma 6, if the target receives a matching core and a braid, they carry the source message also. That is, the target delivers only the message sent by the source. Hence, BeRGeR satisfies the Validity Property of the Reliable Message Delivery Problem.

Moreover, Lemma 7 guarantees that the target eventually receives matching cores or a matching core and a braid. That is, BeRGeR guarantees that a message is delivered by the target, which means that the algorithm also satisfies the Liveness Property.

Lemma 8 shows that BeRGeR satisfies the Termination Property as well. □

5 Constant Packet Size Extension and Complexity Estimate

Constant Packet Size Extension. In BeRGeR, a core packet carries the path that it travels, making the packet size potentially linear with respect to the network size. However, the modification to constant size cores is relatively straightforward. This modification is achieved at the expense of stateless packet forwarding. For that, the sender transmits the message in numbered fixed-size packets to the neighbor. The neighbor receives the packets and reassembles the message. If any of the packets are missing, the whole message is discarded. Since we assume no packet loss, a correct node transmits all packets. The faulty node either transmits the packets or fails to do so. The latter is equivalent to no packet transmission of the original algorithm. The correctness of the original BeRGeR is preserved.

Algorithm Message Complexity. Let us analyze the message complexity of BeRGeR during its fault-free operation. Let N and E be the respective number of nodes and edges in graph G. In the core path, each node may appear at most once. Hence, the length of the core path is in $O(N)$. Each core message transmission may be separated into $O(N)$ constant-size packets. Since the path of the core message is in $O(N)$, the total number of packets for a single core is in $O(N^2)$.

For each node on the core path, the algorithm generates a thread. Each thread travels at most E edges and the threads are constant size. Therefore, the number of thread packet transmissions generated by a single core is in $O(EN)$. There are left core and right core. Hence, the total number of sent packets is in $O(2N^2 + 2EN)$. In a planar graph, $E \in O(N)$ by Euler's formula. Thus, the overall BeRGeR message complexity is in $O(N^2)$.

6 Future Work

As described in this paper, BeRGeR is a unicast algorithm. To achieve Byzantine fault tolerance, it employs the same message concurrency techniques that are used to solve geocasting [43] and multicasting [41]. We expect BeRGeR can be adapted in a straightforward manner to produce Byzantine-robust solutions to these two problems.

BeRGeR requires the Triconnectivity Assumption to operate correctly. It states that the subgraph $G - \overline{st}$ needs to be 3-connected. In general, to enable fault tolerant transmission, any graph G needs to be $(2x+1)$-connected, where x is the maximum number of faults. However, we are unsure whether this needs to hold for the subgraph $G - \overline{st}$. Trying to relax this assumption would be an interesting research pursuit.

Byzantine-robust routing needs the communication graph to be three-connected. The maximum planar graph connectivity is 5. Thus, potentially, such a graph may enable a geometric routing algorithm that can tolerate up to 2 Byzantine faults. Finding such an algorithm is another research challenge.

BeRGeR assumes planar subgraph for its operation. There are several articles that extend geometric routing to non-planar graphs [44–46]. It would be interesting to investigate whether these techniques are applicable to BeRGeR.

It is notoriously difficult to do performance evaluation of Byzantine tolerant algorithms as Byzantine behavior is difficult to simulate. Indeed, rather than erratically dropping messages or skipping steps, the faulty nodes may collude to cause maximum damage at the weakest point of the algorithm [47]. However, it would be interesting to compare the performance of BeRGeR to non-tolerant algorithms to evaluate the expense of adding fault-tolerance to geometric routing algorithms.

Acknowledgments. We would like to thank Sam Kosco for many helpful discussions leading to the algorithm in its present form.

References

1. Imieliński, T., Navas, J.C.: Gps-based geographic addressing, routing, and resource discovery. Commun. ACM. **42**(4), 86–92 (1999)
2. Ko, Y.B., Vaidya, N.H.: Geocasting in mobile ad hoc networks: Location-based multicast algorithms. In: Proceedings WMCSA 1999 Second IEEE Workshop on Mobile Computing Systems and Applications, pp. 101–110. IEEE (1999)
3. Ko, Y.B., Vaidya, N.H.: Location-aided routing (lar) in mobile ad hoc networks. Wirel. Networks **6**(4), 307–321 (2000)
4. Kranakis, E., Singh, H., Urrutia, J.: Compass routing on geometric networks. In: Proceedings of 11th Canadian Conference on Computational Geometry, Citeseer (1999)
5. Johnson, D.B., Maltz, D.A.: Dynamic source routing in Ad Hoc wireless networks. In: Imielinski, T., Korth, H.F. (eds.) Mobile Computing. The Kluwer International Series in Engineering and Computer Science, vol. 353, pp. 153–181. Springer, Boston, MA (1996). https://doi.org/10.1007/978-0-585-29603-6_5
6. Perkins, C., Royer, E.: Ad-hoc on-demand distance vector routing. In: Proceedings WMCSA'99. Second IEEE Workshop on Mobile Computing Systems and Applications, pp. 90–100 (1999)
7. Karagiannis, G., et al.: Vehicular networking: a survey and tutorial on requirements, architectures, challenges, standards and solutions. IEEE Commun. Surv. Tutorials **13**(4), 584–616 (2011)
8. Arora, A., et al.: A line in the sand: a wireless sensor networking for target detection, classification, and tracking. Comput. Netw. Special Issue Future Adv. Mil. Commun. Technol. **46**(5), 605–634 (2004)
9. Bose, P., Morin, P., Stojmenović, I., Urrutia, J.: Routing with guaranteed delivery in ad hoc wireless networks. Wireless Netw. **7**(6), 609–616 (2001)
10. Liu, P.C., Geldmacher, R.C.: On the deletion of nonplanar edges of a graph. In: Proceedings of the 10th Southeastern Conference on Combinatorics, Graph Theory, and Computing, pp. 727–738 (1979)
11. Bose, P., Morin, P., Stojmenovic, I., Urrutia, J.: Routing with guaranteed delivery in ad hoc wireless networks. J. Mobile Commun. Comput. Inf. **7**(6), 48–55 (2001)
12. Ruben Gabriel, K., Sokal, R.R.: A new statistical approach to geographic variation analysis. Syst. Biol. **18**(3), 259–278 (1969)
13. Karp, B., Kung, H.T.: GPSR: greedy perimeter stateless routing for wireless networks. In: Proceedings of the Sixth Annual ACM/IEEE International Conference on Mobille Computing and Networking (MobiCom), pp. 243–254. ACM Press, August 2000
14. Toussaint, G.T.: The relative neighbourhood graph of a finite planar set. Pattern Recogn. **12**(4), 261–268 (1980)
15. Kuhn, F., Wattenhofer, R., Zhang, Y., Zollinger, A.: Geometric ad-hoc routing: of theory and practice. In: Proceedings of the Twenty-Second Annual Symposium on Principles of Distributed Computing, pp. 63–72 (2003)
16. Clouser, T., Miyashita, M., Nesterenko, M.: Concurrent face traversal for efficient geometric routing. J. Parall. Distrib. Comput. **72**(5), 627–636 (2012)
17. Lamport, L., Shostak, R., Pease, M.: The byzantine generals problem. ACM Trans. Program. Lang. Syst. **4**(3), 382–401 (1982)
18. Pease, M., Shostak, R., Lamport, L.: Reaching agreement in the presence of faults. J. ACM (JACM) **27**(2), 228–234 (1980)

19. Sánchez-Carmona, A., Robles, S., Borrego, C.: Privhab+: a secure geographic routing protocol for DTN. Comput. Commun. **78**, 56–73 (2016)
20. Pathak, V., Yao, D., Iftode, L.: Securing location aware services over VANET using geographical secure path routing. In: 2008 IEEE International Conference on Vehicular Electronics and Safety, pp. 346–353. IEEE (2008)
21. Dolev, D., Raymond Strong, H.: Authenticated algorithms for byzantine agreement. SIAM J. Comput. **12**(4), 656–666 (1983)
22. Katz, J., Koo, C.-Y.: On expected constant-round protocols for byzantine agreement. J. Comput. Syst. Sci. **75**(2), 91–112 (2009)
23. Ben-Or, M.: Another advantage of free choice (extended abstract) completely asynchronous agreement protocols. In: Proceedings of the Second Annual ACM Symposium on Principles of Distributed Computing, pp. 27–30 (1983)
24. Feldman, P., Micali, S.: An optimal probabilistic protocol for synchronous byzantine agreement. SIAM J. Comput. **26**(4), 873–933 (1997)
25. Castro, M., Liskov, B.: Practical byzantine fault tolerance. In: Proceedings of the Third Symposium on Operating Systems Design and Implementation, OSDI 1999, pp. 173–186. USENIX Association, USA (1999)
26. Dolev, D.: The byzantine generals strike again. J. Algorithms **3**(1), 14–30 (1982)
27. Fischer, M.J., Lynch, N.A., Merritt, M.: Easy impossibility proofs for distributed consensus problems. Distrib. Comput. **1**, 26–39 (1986)
28. Adnan, A.I., Hanapi, Z.M., Othman, M., Zukarnain, Z.A.: A secure region-based geographic routing protocol (SRBGR) for wireless sensor networks. PloS ONE **12**(1), e0170273 (2017)
29. Boulaiche, M., Bouallouche-Medjkoune, L.: HSecGR: highly secure geographic routing. J. Netw. Comput. Appl. **80**, 189–199 (2017)
30. Maurer, A., Tixeuil, S.: Containing byzantine failures with control zones. IEEE Trans. Parallel Distrib. Syst. **26**(2), 362–370 (2014)
31. Zahariadis, T., Trakadas, P., Leligou, H.C., Maniatis, S., Karkazis, P.: A novel trust-aware geographical routing scheme for wireless sensor networks. Wirel. Personal Commun. **69**, 805–826 (2013)
32. García-Otero, M., et al.: Secure geographic routing in ad hoc and wireless sensor networks. EURASIP J. Wirel. Commun. Networking **2010**, 1–12 (2010)
33. Leinmüller, T., Maihöfer, C., Schoch, E., Kargl, F.: Improved security in geographic ad hoc routing through autonomous position verification. In: Proceedings of the 3rd International workshop on Vehicular Ad Hoc Networks, pp. 57–66 (2006)
34. Vora, A., Nesterenko, M.: Secure location verification using radio broadcast. IEEE Trans. Dependable Secure Comput. **3**(4), 377–385 (2006)
35. Oglio, J., Hood, K., Sharma, G., Nesterenko, M.: Byzantine heoconsensus. In: Echihabi, K., Meyer, R. (eds.) Networked Systems, NETYS 2021, LNCS, vol. 12754, pp 19–35. Springer, Cham (2021). https://doi.org/10.1007/978-3-030-91014-3_2
36. Zaz, B., Nesterenko, M.: Using Braids for Byzantine Resistant Geographic Routing on Polyhedral Networks. In Joint Mathematics Meet, San Francisco, USA (2024)
37. Sanchez, J.A., Ruiz, P.M., Stojmenovic, I.: GMR: geographic multicast routing for wireless sensor networks. In: 3d IEEE Communication Society Conference on Sensors and Ad Hoc Communications and Networks (SeCon), pp. 20–29. IEEE, September 2006
38. Mauve, M., Füßler, H., Widmer, J., Lang, T.: Position-based multicast routing for mobile ad-hoc networks. Mobile Comput. Commun. Rev. **7**(3), 53–55 (2003)

39. Wu, S., Candan, K.S.: GMP: distributed geographic multicast routing in wireless sensor networks. In: 26th IEEE International Conference on Distributed Computing Systems (26th ICDCS'06), p. 49, Lisboa, Portugal, IEEE Computer Society, July 2006
40. Chen, K., Nahrstedt, K.: Effective location-guided tree construction algorithms for small group multicast in MANET. In: Proceedings of the 21st Annual Joint Conference of the IEEE Computer and Communications Society (INFOCOM-02), volume 3 of Proceedings IEEE INFOCOM 2002, pp. 1180–1189, Piscataway, NJ, USA, IEEE Computer Society, 23–27 June 2002
41. Adamek, J., Nesterenko, M., Robinson, J.S., Tixeuil, S.: Concurrent geometric multicasting. In: Proceedings of the 19th International Conference on Distributed Computing and Networking, pp. 1–10 (2018)
42. Lian, J., Naik, K., Liu, Y., Chen, L.: Virtual surrounding face geocasting with guaranteed message delivery for ad hoc and sensor networks. In: Proceedings of the 2006 14th IEEE International Conference on Network Protocols, ICNP 2006, pp. 198–207. IEEE (2006)
43. Adamek, J., Nesterenko, M., Robinson, J.S., Tixeuil, S.: Stateless reliable geocasting. In: 2017 IEEE 36th Symposium on Reliable Distributed Systems (SRDS), pp. 44–53. IEEE (2017)
44. Clouser, T., Vora, A., Fox, T., Nesterenko, M.: Void traversal for efficient non-planar geometric routing. Ad Hoc Netw. **11**(8), 2345–2355 (2013)
45. Kuhn, F., Wattenhofer, R., Zollinger, A.: Ad-hoc networks beyond unit disk graphs. In: Proceedings of the 2003 Joint Workshop on Foundations of Mobile Computing, pp. 69–78 (2003)
46. Kim, Y.J., Govindan, R., Karp, B., Shenker, S.: Geographic routing made practical. In: Proceedings of the 2nd Conference on Symposium on Networked Systems Design and Implementation, vol. 2, pp. 217–230 (2005)
47. Driscoll, K., Hall, B., Sivencrona, H., Zumsteg, P.: Byzantine fault tolerance, from theory to reality. In: Anderson, S., Felici, M., Littlewood, B. (eds.) SAFECOMP 2003. LNCS, vol. 2788, pp. 235–248. Springer, Heidelberg (2003). https://doi.org/10.1007/978-3-540-39878-3_19

Author Index

A
Ahmed, Ayaz 32
Allaki, Driss 225
Anceaume, Emmanuelle 1

B
Bah, Slimane 157
Bhardwaj, Gaurav 32

C
Chan Yip Hon, Boris 50
Chand, Prabhat Kumar 67

D
Delporte-Gallet, Carole 83
Dong, Lu 188
Dragoi, Cezara 100

E
Erradi, Mohammed 118
Essabri, Mohammed Ali 118
Ettalbi, Ahmed 211
Ettazi, Widad 211

F
Fauconnier, Hugues 83
Fdida, Serge 50
Fischer, Bernd 124
Frey, Davide 1

G
Garbi, Giulio 124

K
Kamal Idrissi, Hamza 225
Kapoor, Rohit 204

Kowalski, Dariusz R. 142
Kshemkalyani, Ajay D. 171
Kumar, Manish 67

L
La Torre, Salvatore 124
Lakrouni, Sanaa 157

M
Misra, Anshuman 171
Molla, Anisur Rahaman 67
Mosteiro, Miguel A. 142, 188

N
Nagendra, Srinidhi 100
Nesterenko, Mikhail 247

P
Parlato, Gennaro 124
Peri, Sathya 32, 204
Potop-Butucaru, Maria 50
Powlette, Austin 142

R
Ranjan, Nischay 204
Rauch, Arthur 1
Rebii, Jamal 118
Riane, Driss 211

S
Safir, Mouna 83
Schrammel, Peter 124
Sebgui, Marouane 157

Sharma, Gokarna   247
Srivas, Mandayam   100

T
Tarhri, Ilyass   225
Tixeuil, Sébastien   50
Turau, Volker   231

W
Wang, Michelle   188
Wanniarachchi, Shashini Thamarasie   231

Z
Zaghdoudi, Bilel   50
Zaz, Brown   247

SPRINGER NATURE

GPSR Compliance

The European Union's (EU) General Product Safety Regulation (GPSR) is a set of rules that requires consumer products to be safe and our obligations to ensure this.

If you have any concerns about our products, you can contact us on ProductSafety@springernature.com

In case Publisher is established outside the EU, the EU authorized representative is:

Springer Nature Customer Service Center GmbH
Europaplatz 3
69115 Heidelberg, Germany

The manufacturer's authorised representative in the EU is Springer Nature Customer Service Centre GmbH, Europaplatz 3, 69115 Heidelberg, Germany. If you have any concerns regarding our products, please contact ProductSafety@springernature.com

Printed and bound by CPI Group (UK) Ltd, Croydon, CR0 4YY

25/03/2026

02078187-0012